Indians of the Upper Texas Coast

NEW WORLD ARCHAEOLOGICAL RECORD

Under the Editorship of

James Bennett Griffin

Museum of Anthropology
University of Michigan
Ann Arbor, Michigan

In preparation:

James L. Phillips and James A. Brown (Eds.), Archaic Hunters
and Gatherers in the American Midwest
Dan F. Morse and Phyllis A. Morse, Archaeology of the Central
Mississippi Valley

Published:

Lawrence E. Aten, Indians of the Upper Texas Coast
Ronald J. Mason, Great Lakes Archaeology
Dean R. Snow, The Archaeology of New England
Jerald T. Milanich and Charles H. Fairbanks, Florida Archaeology
George C. Frison, Prehistoric Hunters of the High Plains

Indians of the Upper Texas Coast

Lawrence E. Aten

National Park Service
United States Department of the Interior
Washington, D.C.

1983

ACADEMIC PRESS
A Subsidiary of Harcourt Brace Jovanovich, Publishers
New York   London
Paris   San Diego   San Francisco   São Paulo   Sydney   Tokyo   Toronto

ACADEMIC PRESS, INC.
111 Fifth Avenue, New York, New York 10003

United Kingdom Edition published by
ACADEMIC PRESS, INC. (LONDON) LTD.
24/28 Oval Road, London NW1 7DX

Library of Congress Cataloging in Publication Data

Main entry under title:

Indians of the upper Texas coast.

   (New World archaeological record)
   Includes index.
   1. Indians of North America--Texas--Antiquities.
2. Indians of North America--Southern States--Antiquities.
3. Texas--Antiquities. 4. Southern States--Antiquities.
I. Aten, Lawrence E. II. Series.
E78.T4147 1982   976.4'01   82-13828
ISBN 0-12-065740-6

PRINTED IN THE UNITED STATES OF AMERICA

83 84 85 86   9 8 7 6 5 4 3 2 1

To Jerome Milton Newman
and
to the memories of
William Elliott Hyer,
Stanley Wesley Aten,
and Ripley Pierce Bullen

Contents

Illustrations

Tables

Preface

The political boundaries of Texas circumscribe an area in which several major physiographic and environmental regions converge—the southeastern woodlands, the southern plains, the western desert, and the Gulf coastal plain. In this strategic area, diverse native cultural traditions met and interacted, as is the case today with modern cultural traditions. Native cultures inhabiting the Texas coast during recent millennia broadly reflected adaptation to a desert littoral on the lower coast, and to a humid littoral on the upper coast. This book focuses on the latter region. It provides the first detailed synthesis of the region's culture history, insofar as this is currently known, and offers models at several scales of organization and evolution for testing through future investigations. The results are pertinent to scholars interested in the archaeology of Texas, of the southeastern United States, and of coastal zones in general.

The research around which this synthesis is organized began in the mid-1960s with a strong interest in the relationship between archaeological material remains and the framework of the natural environment. This approach follows closely the tradition pioneered in southern Louisiana by Fred Kniffen, William G. McIntire, and others. The initial phases of the research were largely an outgrowth of my undergraduate work in geology and independent research into the Quaternary geology of the lower Trinity River and its estuary.

By 1969, it was obvious that the greatest obstacle to research in the region was the absence of a reliable chronological framework. Consequently, my major field objective in the second (1969) season of salvage archaeology in Wallisville Reservoir was to remedy this by conducting limited stratigraphic testing in a number of selected sites. We also expected to be able to reconstruct the paleogeography of the Trinity River delta and to have a nearly complete site survey for which chronological shifts in site distributions would be documented using the newly completed culture chronology. These goals were reached, but immediately before the 1969 Wallisville season began, it was necessary to conduct a short salvage excavation at an endangered mortuary site at Harris County Boys School.

The Boys School work initiated studies leading to a more direct consideration of the social dimension of the region's extinct native societies. The analysis of mortuary practices at the Boys School and related sites (Aten *et al.* 1976) caused me to begin confronting established generalizations about upper coast native societies when interpreting the archaeological record and planning future research. Modest exploration of the social anthropology of upper coast societies continues as an important element of this book.

The second dimension realized as a result of the Boys School project was the recognition of substantial quantities of small faunal remains in the midden refuse. These were of a size that ordinarily would pass through the ¼- and ½-inch-mesh (6- and 13-mm mesh) screen sizes commonly used for excavations in the region. We experimented with methods for sifting midden refuse with 1/16-inch-mesh (1.6 mm) screen. This quickly led to an understanding that archaeological faunas based on small-mesh screen recovery were not just larger, but were qualitatively different to a very significant degree. Stratigraphic tests at Wallisville in 1969 were modified so that all midden refuse was water-sifted through a 1/16-inch-mesh (1.6 mm) window screen. This data collection was in advance of any specific problem formulation. However, the opportunity to obtain such improved subsistence data over a wide range of habitats and time periods could not be ignored. It soon became clear that entirely new concepts of coastal animal resource use would emerge from these data.

Analysis of culture chronology in the Galveston Bay Area proceeded quickly, although opportunities for similar work in the Sabine Lake and Brazos delta areas have been more limited and a great deal of work remains to be done there. In the Galveston Bay Area, it was possible, by late summer of 1969, to shift to examination of small sites to disclose the composition and structure of individual occupation episodes. This work continued through subsequent field periods at Harris County Boys School and also constituted the prime focus of the third (1971) season at Wallisville.

The initiation of water washing and fine screening as a standard procedure was opening several other basic investigative avenues. These included the expansion of studies of shellfish so they could be used as data to an even greater extent than vertebrates, the discovery of preserved vegetal materials under certain midden conditions, and the recovery of rare but important artifact categories. For example, most of our data on the coastal lithic tool industry and of glass trade beads comes from the fine-screening residues.

Obtaining improved quantitative estimates of vertebrate use made obvious the need also to pay greater attention to the shellfish components of sites. Initially, this was solely for the purpose of estimating dietary shellfish use. However, this intensive association of the native populations with the *Rangia cuneata* clam led to recognition of several other analytical uses that could be made of this ubiquitous species. Some of these concerned the following:

1. Ecological relationships between the shellfish populations and the human predator population;
2. *Rangia* shell as a radiocarbon dating medium, although the basic approach was recognized and applied earlier by J. R. Ambler and S. J. Valastro (Valastro and Davis, 1970b);

3. Individual occupation episodes in a midden;
4. Characteristic patterns of site frequency associated with different types of aquatic habitats.

One of the most important new uses being made of *Rangia cuneata* by late 1969 was the determination of shellfish mortality season and, by inference, collection and site habitation season, using principles of shellfish growth (Aten, 1981). This made it feasible to approach questions of occupation season and duration at a level of precision far exceeding that possible through more conventional means such as the assemblage of vertebrate taxa. Again, although this was in advance of full development of the method, it was clear what types of samples would be needed for this purpose and that their collection should begin.

Presentation and analysis of all unpublished data produced by this fieldwork between 1969 and 1972 would require a manuscript very much longer than the present one. Also, there is a necessary sequence to the analysis and presentation of some of this upper coast information. Documentation and construction of a chronological framework should precede attempts to deal with other diachronic data; generation of a hypothetical sociocultural framework should precede functional reconstructions; and documentation of the seasonal relationships of habitation sites should precede a consideration of the significance of subsistence and other data on energetics. Consequently, the scope of this book has been reduced to manageable size by restricting it to two of the basic frameworks needed for support of future research:

1. Reconstruction of demographic and sociological characteristics for the historic and protohistoric periods. This is needed for its own sake, but also as the best framework for generating sociocultural hypotheses for the prehistory of the area; and
2. Reconstruction of the history of material culture and the culture chronological framework.

These two frameworks are then integrated into a comprehensive model of culture change for the upper Texas coast. With its subsidiary components, this model constitutes a structure for analysis of the substantial body of data available on settlement and subsistence for the area. An earlier version of this manuscript was my doctoral dissertation. That text has been updated and edited significantly; in addition, all of Part II, The Early Prehistoric Framework, is newly written.

Acknowledgments

The completion of this phase of Texas coast research has been significantly aided by many friends and colleagues, whom I am pleased to acknowledge here. My initial exposure to the Indians of the Texas coast began in 1961 with many of my comrades in the Houston Archeological Society: Wayne Neyland, Bill and Louise Caskey, Alan Duke, Harry Hartman, and Don Lewis, among others. They willingly and patiently introduced me to the region and its archaeology as it was then known, and, in the process, stimulated an enduring interest on my part.

I also wish to give special recognition to the long and committed assistance rendered by Robert Cole, Billy M. Davidson, Glen Fredlund, and James McMichael. These men formed the backbone of my field and laboratory staff both as volunteers and as employees. There is no question that the level of effort would have been substantially less had it not been for their continuing interest and hard work.

J. Richard Ambler employed me as his field assistant during the 1966 field season at Wallisville Reservoir and significantly aided my professional development. Ambler's willingness to allow me access to his specimens, notes, and unpublished manuscript is greatly appreciated. Much of what I have been able to accomplish is based on his pioneering work at Wallisville and at Cedar Bayou.

Aura Aten spent many hours away from her school and business activities to retype portions of earlier drafts of this manuscript as well as to prepare most of the line drawings. The late R. King Harris kindly examined the four European glass trade beads and advised me on their identity. My good friend and colleague, Charles N. Bollich, has spent many hours "eyeball to eyeball" with me discussing ceramic classification issues. I also am very appreciative of the interesting discussions and background information patiently provided by William G. Haag when I visited Louisiana State University to examine Lower Mississippi Valley ceramic type collections. Charles K. Chandler kindly gave permission to use the results of stratigraphic testing performed under his direction at 41 MQ 14 by the Houston Archeological Society.

Permission to conduct test excavations was granted by Brazoria County Sheriff Robert R. Gladney (41 BO 4), L. C. Morrison (41 BO 12 and 41 BO 21), Walter Grover and the Timewealth Corporation (41 GV 5), and the late G. V. Mayes (41

CH 137). Mr. Mayes, then a Chambers County commissioner, was especially helpful to me when I was an undergraduate student and in ensuing years by repeatedly granting ready access to his family's property in the Trinity River bottomlands. His forthright cooperation was essential to the mapping of the geology and geomorphology of the lower Trinity River, a key phase of this present work.

The 1969 test excavations in the Wallisville Reservoir were supported by a National Park Service contract with the University of Texas at Austin. In carrying out this work at Wallisville and at other construction projects on the Texas coast, D. T. Graham and Ernest Wittig of the Galveston District U.S. Army Corps of Engineers were always helpful. The Shy Pond and Lake Jackson test excavations were partially supported by a Sigma Xi grant.

Comparative archaeological specimens and records from the extensive repository at the Texas Archeological Research Laboratory (TARL) of The University of Texas at Austin were frequently used. Data from my unpublished analysis of ceramics from the Singing Sands Site (41 GV 6), which were loaned to TARL by Kiki Cullum and Elaine Roberson, and from 41 HR 161, which were loaned by Calvin Howard have also been used. Sam J. Valastro, Jr., and E. Mott Davis of the Radiocarbon Laboratory, The University of Texas at Austin, were of great assistance in preparing additional radiocarbon assays to complement the series begun by Ambler.

Dee Ann Story, Thomas N. Campbell, Richard P. Schaedel, and S. C. Oliver of The University of Texas at Austin, and Anthony E. Marks of Southern Methodist University, in Dallas, provided me with very helpful professional advice and encouragement on the ethnohistory and late prehistory of the area. I am additionally grateful to Story for granting me permission to use several photographs from the TARL archives and for reviewing drafts of chapters in Part II. Sherwood M. Gagliano has been very helpful in discussing the fragmentary data on late Quaternary environments of the northern coast of the Gulf of Mexico; Gagliano also provided the drawing for Figure 8.5. Jerald T. Milanich and James B. Griffin encouraged and assisted me in bringing this manuscript into book form.

Rather than stay in the mission where the padre *provides them everything needed to eat and wear, they prefer to suffer hunger, nakedness, and other necessities, in order to be at liberty and idle in the woods or on the beach, giving themselves up to all kinds of vice, especially lust, theft, and dancing.*

The Karankawa at Mission Rosario as described by Fray Gaspar Jose de Solis [Bolton 1960: 139]

PART I

The Ethnohistoric Framework

CHAPTER 1

Introduction

The primary aim of this study is to establish a basis for advanced investigation of the cultural history and processes of native societies inhabiting the upper Texas coast (Figure 1.1) from approximately 12,000 years ago until their extermination in the wake of the European invasion. I begin by examining aspects of the historic period ethnic framework—group identities and territories, population sizes and densities, social organization and levels of integration, ritual, and cognition. Next addressed are the early cultures and their environmental setting, which was radically different from that of the present. Then, the time dimension of the later cultures and several ways it may be controlled in this area are considered, as well as certain aspects of the region's technological history. Finally, the sociological and culture-historical information are integrated into a synthesis of the systemic changes occurring during the evolution of the Native American cultures of the upper Texas coast.

Aside from the usual inadequacies of data, it has been necessary to make some selections about which lines of investigation are significant to an integrated perspective. Within the resulting frameworks, however, it should be possible to formulate useful new research problems as well as to identify the means of solving them across a broad range of anthropological issues. These issues are important to gaining understanding about the lives, history, and cultural processes of Native Americans who once lived on the upper Texas coast.

REVIEW OF PREVIOUS WORK

It is most appropriate to begin this review with the historical syntheses of Spanish scholars in the colonial period, proceeding on to discuss activities in the period of intensive Anglo settlement of Texas, and ending with the period of contemporary historical and archaeological investigations. In this discussion, hard and fast distinctions are not drawn between the data of history, ethnohistory, ethnography, and archaeology; these all overlap considerably while jointly contributing to facets of understanding of the subject. Also, chronological

3

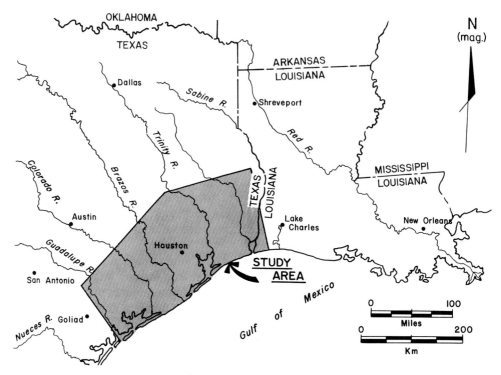

FIGURE 1.1   Index map to upper Texas coast and vicinity.

boundaries for the history of these studies should not be taken too literally; this account simply describes developments in a very general way.

Exploration and Colonization Period, circa 1528–1820

A great body of historical and ethnohistorical information exists for the period of Spanish, French, and English exploration and colonization in the coastal region of the northwestern Gulf of Mexico. Most, if not all, of the material from this period was acquired incidentally to the various administrative or political assignments of the narrators. Men such as Cabeza de Vaca, Dorantes, Joutel, La Harpe, de Bellisle, de Solis, Casañas, Rubi, de Mézières, Sibley, and many others all described places and narrated events related to their own problems and experiences in dealing with the native groups of Texas within the larger framework of Euro-American power politics.

Three synthesizers were active in this period and must be mentioned. The first was Gonzalo Fernandez Oviedo y Valdez who published *Historia General y Natural de las Indias* in 1547 (Oviedo y Valdez 1923). This review came before much was known to Europeans about the Texas area. It is significant, however, as the source of the narrative of Andres Dorantes along with yet another version of Cabeza de Vaca's experiences.

More than 200 years passed before the second synthesis, Fray Juan Agustín Morfi's *Memorias* for the history of the Province of Texas, was written sometime shortly before 1778 (Morfi 1932). Although not analytical, Morfi's *Memorias* and the subsequent *Historias* (Morfi 1935) were thorough narrative descriptions of the geography, environment, and native inhabitants of Texas as revealed in the sundry reports, journals, and chronicles of Spanish officialdom of the preceding century.

The third and by far the greatest synthesizer of this early period of discovery in Texas was José Antonio Pichardo (Hackett 1931). Prepared between the years of 1808 and 1812, Pichardo's *Treatise on the Limits of Louisiana and Texas* was much more in the modern tradition of problem-oriented scholarship than was Morfi's in that he had a specific and immediate objective—to demonstrate that Spain's claim to eastern Texas was substantive as well as formal. To do this, Pichardo had to reconstruct native group identities, their locations, and the nature of Spanish interaction with them to build a basis for Spain's assertions of having actually exercised sovereignty over, as well as merely having claimed, eastern Texas. Pichardo's *Treatise* stands as a landmark compendium of detail and critical analysis, not just of Spanish sources, but also of French, English, and American (United States) sources as well—a feat not to be approached again in quality and scope for at least another hundred years. In these intervening years, however, the native populations of the Texas coast were exterminated.

It is significant to realize, insofar as the coastal zone of Texas is concerned, that by the end of the colonial period and with the completion of Pichardo's *Treatise*, knowledge of colonial history of the area was nearly as complete as it is today. This information was, however, largely in Spanish and substantially unknown to the English-speaking world, excepting accounts of French explorations and such items as the 1714 English translation of Joutel and the reports of Sibley (both published in obscure places), as well as the mid-nineteenth-century Smith translation of Cabeza de Vaca's narrative (Joutel 1714/1966; Sibley 1807; Hodge 1907b). Most of these early studies would not begin to reemerge until around the beginning of the twentieth century.

Intensive Settlement Period, circa 1820–1890

As mentioned previously, the great work of Spanish historians at the end of the colonial period was largely unavailable to those taking part in and otherwise concerned about the primarily Anglo settlement of Texas under the Mexican government. The literature of this period is heavily laden with personal accounts of experiences and reminiscences. Through these, substantial detail was added to the body of observations of coastal Native American groups during their final period of existence (for instance, see Bollaert 1850; Bonnell 1840; Bradford and Campbell 1949; Helm 1884; Holley 1833/1973; Hunter 1966; Kennedy 1841; Kuykendall 1903). Typically, these were strongly opinionated accounts of travelers, entrepreneurs, or settlers depicting the Indians in either a clearly sympathetic or a clearly unsympathetic light (cf. Pearce 1957). None could really be said to take an objective approach to the subject, with the result that this literature must be used with care.

Initial Historic Studies Period, circa 1890–1930

By the end of the nineteenth century, the frontier receded as authority of the central government was asserted. In this period, institutions of higher learning arose and there appeared a concomitant, more formal interest in the history of the state, especially as the number of survivors from the intensive settlement period decreased. Insofar as the coastal zone was concerned, we note at the beginning of this period the appearance of Gatschet's study of the Karankawa (Gatschet 1891) and initial publication of the *Journal of the Texas State Historical Association* (1897).

Although the ensuing four decades were dominated by the extensive output of Herbert E. Bolton and his students, many other professional and amateur historians of the day published a variety of source materials, including the gradual rediscovery and translation of most of the colonial period Spanish historians (Beers 1979:103–196). These publications included Bandelier (1905), Baskett (1907), Bolton (1906, 1908, 1913, 1914, 1915, 1924), Davenport and Wells (1918), Hackett (1931), Hatcher (1927), Henderson (1928), Muckleroy (1922), Oviedo y Valdez (1923), Padilla (1919), and many others. Much of the focus of these workers was not on documentation of indigenous Indian groups per se, but on the activities of Europeans in a setting that included Indians as a component.

The paths of history and ethnohistory–archaeology began to diverge in this period. That is to say, a distinctive literature oriented toward Native Americans began to emerge parallel to that oriented toward activities of Europeans in Texas. Gatschet's Karankawa study was a precocious development in this respect. Had his informant, Alice Oliver, spent her final years in Texas rather than in Massachusetts, where she was accessible to Gatschet, the chances are that her recollections would have been much less systematic or would have gone entirely unrecorded. In any event, by 1916, J. O. Dyer, a Galveston physician, began to report data he had acquired over a period of many years' residence in Galveston. In the 10 years remaining before his death, he produced a prodigious number of pamphlets and newspaper articles for the *Galveston Daily News*.

Dyer is a fascinating source of information about the 1815–1820 period on the upper Texas coast and vicinity. Although frustrating to read because of the flowery language to which he seemingly was addicted (awkward even for that time), he nevertheless had access to valuable eyewitness sources for the end of the colonial period. At times, he displayed great insight into themes that will be discussed again later in the present study. For example, he understood much about the nature of what ultimately came to be known as the "composite band," and he had some idea of the impact of this on the kinds of conclusions to be drawn from Alice Oliver's account of Chief Antonio's band of Karankawa (Dyer 1916). He also intuitively appreciated the concept of reciprocity and that one could not simply dismiss the Karankawa as "thieves" (Dyer 1920).

Throughout this period, the developing literature about Indian groups in coastal Texas depended on the historical record because no archaeological data of any consequence were available (cf. Roessler 1883; Simmons 1903). The work of Dyer notwithstanding, the main concern of this Texas Indian literature was to discover more about the "Mound Builders" and their antecedents (e.g., Roberts 1898). By comparison, the Karankawa were considered among the rudest and lowest forms of humanity (e.g., Kenney 1897). The Atakapa–Akokisa were viewed as being somewhere betweeen these extremes and never were accorded much attention.

In the first three decades of the twentieth century, J. R. Swanton and Herbert Bolton stand above all others as synthesizers of historical and ethnographic information pertinent to Native Americans of the Texas coast (as well as elsewhere). On the negative side of an otherwise productive effort, however, Swanton crystallized certain ideas about inhabitants of the coastal zone into the vague concept of the "cultural sink" (Swanton 1924). Essentially, this concept formalized ideas of the sort attributed previously to Kenney (1897) and extended them to all Native American tribes in a very large area of northeastern Mexico, in all of coastal Texas and southwestern Louisiana, including all of the area under examination in the present study. Some 30 years were to pass before Newcomb (1956) was to definitively challenge and lay to rest the "cultural sink," although its biases informally live on; also see Willey (1968:338).

In any event, by the end of the 1920s, the greatest portion of what we know today about the history and ethnohistory of the Texas coast had been produced. This is not to say that nothing remains to be done; to the contrary, the ethnohistory of the upper Texas coast remains a fruitful field for the patient laborer (cf. Campbell 1972). On the other hand, in 1930, knowledge of the archaeology of the upper coast was almost nonexistent and it was at this time that J. E. Pearce set out in earnest to rectify the situation.

Initial Archaeological Studies Period, circa 1930–1967

Pearce began archaeological reconnaissance in the east Texas area during 1918–1920 under the sponsorship of the Bureau of American Ethnology (see

Campbell [1952:49] for citations relating to this activity). He continued this
work on his own through the 1920s, regaining late in that decade significant
financial support with which he began numerous excavations in several geographically distinct regions of Texas (Pearce 1932). Although generally interested in Texas archaeological materials wherever he found them, Pearce
seems to have been preoccupied with the role Texas may have played in the
origin and diffusion of the "high cultures," that is, agriculturally supported
chiefdoms of the American Southwest and the Mississippi Valley. In this, he
continued the traditional interest of earlier nineteenth- and twentieth-century
historians of native Texas cultures. Pearce assumed the North American occurrences of "civilization" in the Mississippi Valley and the upper Rio Grande Valley
had diffused from Mesoamerica and that Texas lay athwart routes to the former. Specifically, he believed that "at least one group of the bearers of Mound
Builder culture into the Mississippi Valley came up out of Mexico and passed
along the Texas coast [Pearce 1932:47]."

Pearce, among others (cf. Campbell 1947:40), recognized the Huastecan af-
finities of the ceramics found in the Brownsville area and consequently seemed
to have felt reinforced in his concept of the route of diffusion of civilization to
the Mississippi Valley having included the Texas coast (also see Campbell
1976:81). In his reconnoitering for evidence of this, he excavated some sites on
the upper Texas coast (Caplen and Lawrence Island—both cemetery sites in
Galveston and Chambers counties, respectively), caused surveys to be conducted
of Orange, Jefferson, and Brazoria counties (records of which are in the files of
the Texas Archeological Research Laboratory [TARL] in Austin), and personally
examined sites in the area of the Trinity River Delta (Pearce 1932:50–51). Although he seems to have thought the upper coast sites to be interesting, they
apparently did not suggest important clues relating to his main thesis. The
result was that archaeological research neither commenced in any significant
way nor were the accomplishments of his limited coastal work ever published
except those of the Caplen Site excavation (Campbell 1956).

Work performed by or under the direction of Pearce was aimed mainly at
discovery and description of objects; rarely were any attempts made at organization of this information. The earliest attempt at space–time systematics having any bearing on our knowledge of the coast was that of E. B. Sayles (1935).
Sayles relied largely on data collected by field-workers under the direction of
Pearce. Employing the same basic approaches that were proving fruitful in the
American Southwest, he subdivided the coastal shell midden remains with
respect to whether they contained ceramics or historic materials; secondarily,
he recognized physical dissimilarities within major artifact classes. On this
basis, he defined a preceramic Karankawan culture called the Oso Phase and a
ceramics-using culture called the Rockport Phase; the latter was presumed to be
the precursor of the historic Karankawa. Farther northeast along the coast, he
defined the Attacapan Phase as a ceramics-using inland group, presumed to be
very late, and associated with the historic Atakapa. Even though Sayles's de-

scriptions were vague, the space–time units he defined were not unreasonable considering the types of information that were then available. However, no research was even conducted on which to build or with which to explore the implications of this work, and Sayles's systematics fell into disuse.

The only other attempt at major synthesis in the pre-World War II period was that of Mildred Pickle Mayhall (1939) who prepared a huge compendium of ethnohistoric and archaeological information about the Atakapa, Karankawa, and Tonkawa. Despite its use of uniform culture stages, diffusion theory, and environmental determinism as integrating concepts, the fact that this work was never published is truly a shame in light of the extensive body of information it contains. In keeping with the emphasis of the time on the diffusion of food-producing cultures from Mesoamerica to North America, Mayhall provided the first discussion in Texas of the implications for this diffusion of the environmentally attractive route known as the "Gilmore Corridor" (Mayhall 1939:346). This argument was elaborately developed later by Krieger (1948), the effect of which further reinforced disinterest in the coastal prairies by virtue of their apparent lack of relevance to the leading archaeological problem of the day. The issue of the Gilmore Corridor was taken up recently by Story (1980).

Unfortunately, during this prewar period on the upper coast there were no amateur archaeologists who made and recorded site surveys and collections as Wendell Potter, George C. Martin, and A. E. Anderson did for the middle and lower coast. For this reason, major gaps are likely always to exist in our knowledge of site distribution. This is especially the case around lakes and bays that are actively eroding their shorelines and in the heavily developed agricultural and urban areas that are more common on the upper coast.

Most archaeological work in Texas ended for the duration of World War II, except that of Krieger. During this period, Krieger (1944) formulated his concepts of artifact typology, which were to have a determining effect on the course of archaeological research in Texas for at least the next 25 years. In fact, in a relatively brief period, Krieger developed his typological concepts, organized Caddoan ceramics on this basis, defined a Caddo area chronology, attempted to link this chronology with those for the Lower Mississippi Valley (LMV) and the American Southwest (Krieger 1946), and published what would remain for many years the single major report on a Caddo site (Newell and Krieger 1949).

One effect of this outpouring on coastal archaeology was the establishment of the typological and chronological frameworks of Caddo archaeology as a reference against which our meager knowledge of the upper coast could be compared in a regional context. More importantly, Krieger's work also established a conceptual and methodological pattern for archaeological research that was a substantial improvement over the approach taken by Pearce. It is difficult for us to determine, nearly 40 years later, if Krieger independently conceived these innovations or if the general intellectual setting of the times led in this particular direction. Chang (1967:5) suggests the latter. It does seem clear, however, that Alex Krieger was the earliest Texas archaeologist to bring some order out of the work of the 1930s. His work towers above all others following Pearce in the period of initial archaeological studies.

The postwar remainder of this period continued to be marked by very little fieldwork on the Texas coast. Wayne B. Neyland conducted the most extensive of several amateur archaeological surveys in the Galveston Bay region during the 1950s. These efforts documented large numbers of archaeological sites that no longer exist. The major published site investigations on the upper coast were Caplen (Campbell 1958) and Addicks (Wheat 1947, 1953). Both of these were only vaguely problem-oriented and were mainly designed to "see what was there." The most influential of these was at Addicks Reservoir, situated a short distance west of Houston. This work became the principal basis for definition of the Galveston Bay Focus (Suhm *et al.* 1954:128–130), for the extension of the concept of an Archaic LaHarpe Aspect into southeast Texas (Johnson 1962), and it figured prominently in general syntheses of culture history and culture development (Suhm *et al.* 1954:16–21; Willey 1968:477).

Wheat provided the first clear indication of the time depth of the archaeological record in the upper coast area and some of the major factors of technological development. Basically, this sequence consisted of a preceramic period marked by dart points, which was followed by ceramics-using cultures. The initial ceramics were thought to be associated with the Tchefuncte culture of Louisiana. At this point, it might have appeared as if the inland Galveston Bay Area was on the way toward receiving at least the rudiments of a chronological system, as were so many other areas of Texas at this time. However, Wheat, confronted with ceramics and projectile points from Addicks, made a fateful and, in retrospect, unfortunate choice when he concluded that temporal variation was more readily seen in the major technological categories of projectile points: expanding and contracting stem dart points, and arrow points. He viewed the ceramics as highly variable and believed that "there is no development in the native pottery diagnostic as a time marker [Wheat 1947:145]." Apparently, the reason for this view was that, at the time, paste characteristics were not considered to be significant cultural traits, although such things as vessel form and design styles were; we know now that just the reverse in emphasis is necessary to understand the development of upper Texas coast ceramics. Projectile point styles, on the other hand, have never proved to be of more than secondary assistance as a chronological tool. Moreover, because the necessary raw materials are not native to the coastal zone, such artifacts are relatively rare in their occurrence compared to ceramics.

Much of the significance of the Caplen Site studies could not be evaluated until years later with the full-scale review of Galveston Bay Area mortuary practices, in conjunction with the analysis of the prehistoric cemetery site at the Harris County Boys School (Aten *et al.* 1976). As a result, the main contribution of the Caplen work through this period of initial archaeological studies was its documentation of Caddoan ceramics and glass trade beads in an indigenous Indian context.

Other than these two major reports and numerous short notes on sites such as

Galena, Jamison, Jamaica Beach, and many others (especially in the *Houston Archeological Society Newsletter;* also see Patterson 1979), the body of systematic information on the area did not materially increase in the postwar years of this period. The emphasis, such as it was, however, was still on the definition of *phases* or *foci* of material culture. On the upper coast, the main attention in this respect went to trying to clarify the previously mentioned Galveston Bay Focus. This was a potentially long-lived period (estimated to begin about A.D. 500 and to end about A.D. 1700) during which time, little cultural change was thought to have taken place (Suhm *et al.* 1954:128–130), a view consistent with those of most earlier observers. Probably the highwater mark for elaboration of this concept came in a short note by R. B. Worthington (1961).

Worthington summarized individual culture traits, their geographic distribution on the upper coast and pointed out gaps in information. He recognized the generally late occurrence of bone-, sherd-, and "clay–grit"-tempered wares and suggested that these might prove to be useful time markers. He also was the first to suggest the need for additional foci to accommodate the temporal and spatial variety of material culture in the area.

The upper coast area continued to be listed, mapped, or classified in several culture-area and historic-developmental studies (e.g., Stephenson 1950; Kirchoff 1954; Suhm *et al.* 1954; Phelps 1964:117–123; and Willey 1968:477). Phelps's study is worth mentioning here as the most recent statement of an archaeological theory for the diffusion of Mesoamerican culture traits across the coastal plain of Texas to southeastern North America during the Archaic period. Without suggesting precise routes, Phelps postulated the existence of a "communication zone" located along the coastal plain through which projectile point styles and fiber-tempered pottery technology passed, the latter about 4000 years ago. Currently, there is no material evidence either for or against this proposal.

To some extent, the ethnohistoric literature continued to expand, as more of the important Spanish and French materials found their way into print in English (e.g., Covey 1961; Folmer 1940; Hackett 1932; Kinnaird 1958; Morfi 1935) and important ethnographic syntheses were written (Newcomb 1961; Schaedel 1949; Sjoberg 1951a, 1951b). Newcomb made the notable point that the natives of the upper coast never "became truly seafaring, [n]or gave up their ties with their inland relatives. None came close to fully exploiting the potential of marine subsistence [1961:329]." In other words, to suggest that the peoples of the upper coast were adapted to maritime life is to substantially stretch the point; a much more appropriate descriptor is *strandlooper,* as South African coastal scavenger–hunter–gatherer–collectors are commonly called.

Current Archaeological Studies Period, circa 1967–Present

By the mid-1960s, the Texas coast still was being incorporated into syntheses as an element of a regional pattern including northeast Mexico, and central and trans-Pecos Texas; recently, Jelks (1978) named essentially the same region, including the upper coast, the "Diablo Range." A marked increase in field investigations began to occur on the upper Texas coast, largely stimulated by the need for salvage archaeology and later for environmental assessment surveys.

At the beginning of the period, there was general agreement that one of the more pressing needs was a comprehensive chronological framework. This effort was begun by Ambler (1967) and Aten (1967), and continued through a series of studies culminating in Aten (1979:384–449). Ambler's research was prematurely terminated when he left the area; as a result, his formulations did not benefit from the breadth of temporal and geographic coverage he knew was needed.

Wallisville Reservoir salvage archaeology was begun by Ambler in 1967, and continued by Aten in 1969 and 1971 (Aten 1979), by Gilmore in 1972 (Gilmore 1974), and by Dillehay in 1973 (Dillehay 1975). This work progressed through several stages of major emphasis: chronology, ceramic typology, small site analysis, and subsistence analysis.

In addition to the relatively intensive work carried out at Wallisville, however, systematic work began in numerous other places on the upper Texas coast. This provided for the first time a body of data that is truly regional in character on site locations, stratigraphic testing, descriptions of technology, and on mortuary practices (Aten 1967, 1971; Aten and Bollich 1969; Aten *et al.* 1976; Dering and Ayers 1977; Fritz 1975; Hole and Wilkinson 1973; Hole 1974; McClurkan 1968; O'Brien 1971; Shafer 1968; and Story 1968). To this list should be added the profusion of environmental assessment surveys and other short descriptive reports that are now available (cf. Patterson 1979). The region lacks, however, a set of integrating models to which these data can be related.

RESEARCH OBJECTIVES

The upper Texas coast is situated at the westernmost coastal extremity of the woodlands of the southeastern United States. It is a region in which many kinds of important archaeological research are feasible. Local geologic processes are of a highly dynamic character such that much of the area's culture history must have occurred concurrently with landform development (cf. Aten 1966b; Gagliano 1977). As a result of this active geologic history the opportunities for observation of culture–environment interactions are unusually extensive and almost approach laboratory conditions. Frequently, the case will occur that occupation of a given site location will have continued while the adjacent natural habitat had changed over relatively short periods of time (cf. Ambler 1973; Aten 1971:1–4; Aten *et al.* 1976:Figure 4C).

The upper coast also is important historically by virtue of its peripheral position in relation to both the Caddo area and the Lower Mississippi Valley (LMV); that is, in terms of the relationships between the ranked-society agriculturalists of these latter regions and the cultures of their marginal hinterlands such as the Texas coast. The pursuit of research problems framed around such regional considerations is inhibited, however, because present data and models are inadequate to stage the appropriate kinds of archaeological tests. The particular line of investigation of which this book is a part has as its goal the identification of fundamental (i.e., nonsituational) elements of coastal cultural systems. The general method for pursuing this goal is (*a*) to describe the structural and quantitative relations between specific social groups and their natural and social environments and (*b*) to factor these relations out of holistic models of the societies to determine if there are significant residual elements that constitute an underlying structure. Use of this method is impeded on the coast either by an absence of descriptive models, or by models that typically are too limited in scope and are not identified as to their hierarchical relationships. The synthesis reported in this volume does not solve all of these problems; however, it does more nearly approach a holistic conceptual basis (i.e., a system of models) for assimilating descriptive information so that testing of more advanced hypotheses can be carried out.

Models, as abstract and simplified representations of reality, have three properties: scale, resolution, and degree of simplification. Most theorists recognize these attributes but describe them in rather different ways (e.g., Bateson [1979]; Koestler [1967]; Levins [1966, 1968]). In the formulation of Levins, for example, these properties correlate with "generality," "precision," and "realism," respectively. Expansion of models to reflect alternative states of scale, resolution, and simplification results in the formulation of a hierarchy of models. In such a structure, any given model constitutes description for higher levels, as well as explanation for lower levels in the hierarchy. Such a system of models serves as the *process* framework whereby either inductive or deductive methods may be employed, as needed.

Addition of the property of time provides an evolutionary trajectory to the process framework and unifies it conceptually with traditional views about the explanation of culture change in a historical framework (see White 1975:6 for discussion). Establishing an evolving, nested, hierarchical system of models is basic to historical *and* processual explanation of cultural phenomena and to progress toward identification of a nonsituational underlying structure in the cultures of coast dwellers.

In developing such a system of models, it is not meant that description is attempted for every conceivable aspect, but that at least the basic elements (i.e., the human population, a structure relating elements of the population, a material technology to articulate this structure to its environments, and means of transmitting information throughout the structure [Segraves 1974:531] are recognized, summarized, and related. This holistic approach, with an emphasis on evolution, has been crystallizing in archaeology for the past 30 years (cf. Binford 1962; Chang 1967; Clarke 1968; Plog 1974; Taylor 1948; Trigger 1968).

In the chapters that follow, major attention is given to the following three objectives.

Description of the Characteristics of Native Groups in the Study Area   To what extent can groups, their territory, population size, social organization and structure, and ritual in the historic period be defined, and do these have any meaning archaeologically and for prehistory? This study basically employs the cautiously pragmatic orientation described by Yellen (1977) in which such data are used as a guide to making better probabilistic statements or hypotheses. There is a growing awareness of the role of certain nontraditional archaeological emphases such as ritual in culture–environment interactions (e.g., Flannery 1976; Hardesty 1977; Rappaport 1968). For this reason, Part I builds upon the largely "etic" consideration of mortuary ritual in Aten *et al.* (1976) and further explores dimensions of native ritual and cognition. Through this means, a description of the inherent rationality of the life of these people is begun and an attempt is made to recognize and treat this comparatively.

Determination of How to Differentiate among the Various Archaeological Remains in the Study Area   What kinds of important technological changes occur and what are their correlates? The need to pursue cultural ecology on the basis of primary units of face-to-face interaction leads directly to focusing on human populations (i.e., on societies and not on "cultures"; see Hardesty [1977], Hawley [1973:1198], Vayda and Rappaport [1968:494], and Wobst [1974:148]).

In principle, boundaries of populations/societies are identified at the limits of a set of functional relationships (Hawley 1973:1197). Because these functional sets occur in nested hierarchies (e.g., family, band, tribe), the resulting organizational boundaries classification can also be expected to form a nested hierarchy. This is the primary reason for not attempting definition and classification of utterly abstract units such as culture phases, foci, or aspects. To do this would not improve the basis for investigation of culture–environment interactions and for establishment of a hierarchical system of models. What is done here is an attempt to align the archaeological data on technology with the primarily ethnohistorical data on social organization in order to define suitable groupings for analysis both laterally (i.e., in space) and vertically (i.e., in time).

Unification of the Ethnohistorical and Archaeological Data into a More Integrated System of Models about the Indigenous Cultures of the Study Area
Unification of the data on ethnographic, chronological, and technological issues is the major task to be addressed in this study. Nominal classifications of adaptive poses such as "maritime" or "littoral" have very narrow utility; distinguishing between such classes often is an arbitrary exercise. The data are phenomenologically diverse and the need is to transform them into more com-

parable terms. Inland hunting sites and coastal shell middens, for instance, can be distinguished easily; there are sufficient qualitative differences that a clear, nominal distinction can be made in terms of their morphology, content, and most inferred activities. However, from both a historical and a processual perspective, it is necessary to link the two together as end-members of a continuum of adaptive transformations between coast and interior, or between one coastal adaptation and another. The nominal distinctions must be recast into an interval scale of features common to the entire range for, more often than not, our target populations/societies shifted through multiple adaptive poses during an annual cycle.

This scaling will be attempted by transforming as much of the data as possible into expressions of the spatial functioning of a hierarchy of human populations: that is to say, by (a) recognition first of a social structure; (b) identification of the spatial scales at which different levels in the structure operate; (c) correlation of artifacts, artifact associations, and other behavioral phenomena (e.g., habitation seasonality) with these spatial scales; (d) postulation of organizational characteristics at each of these scale levels; and (e) description of historical vectors of change in these levels. Thus, methods are sought for converting the upper coast archaeological data, regardless of its habitat of origin, into common attributes such as chronological age, occupation season, group size, site structure, settlement pattern structure, and activities and their energy costs. The data on seasonal patterns of settlement, site structure, settlement pattern, and energy costs are not included in this volume but are now in preparation. Further details of the research design are given in conjunction with each of the major parts. An initial formulation of a system of models for the upper coast is included in Chapter 17.

ENVIRONMENTAL SETTING

A detailed description of the natural environment is not necessary for this present study. For this reason, the environmental setting will be sketched out with broad strokes and a minimum of citation. Many excellent publications are available on the natural environment of the Texas coast. *The Environmental Geologic Atlas of the Texas Coastal Zone*, published by The University of Texas at Austin Bureau of Economic Geology, provides a general overview of coastal lithology, ecology, and environmental processes as well as bibliographic coverage. McIntire (1958) includes an especially good discussion of plants and animals in southern Louisiana that also applies to a great extent to the upper coast of Texas.

The coastal zone of the northwest Gulf of Mexico strikes many visitors as a monotonous repetition of prairies (Figure 1.2) and marshes (Figures 1.3 and

FIGURE 1.2   Prairie on Beaumont Formation near Smith Point, Texas.

FIGURE 1.3   Brackish marsh and lakes in Trinity River Delta near Anahuac, Texas.

FIGURE 1.4   Fresh-brackish marsh with bordering deciduous woodlands on Beaumont Formation uplands near Baytown, Texas.

1.4) interspersed with an occasional swamp (Figure 1.5), barrier beach (Figure 1.6), or forest (Figure 1.7). In fact, it is a highly dynamic environment that has taken on much of its present form concurrent with human occupation of the area (Chapter 8, present volume; Gagliano 1977). The basic genesis of the coastal zone land surfaces is that of a series of major river deltas coalesced into an extensive and continuous deltaic plain during the Late Pleistocene. Superimposed on this massive accumulation of deltaic material, known as the Beaumont Formation, are the effects of more recent events, such as Late Pleistocene–Holocene sea level fall and rise, and the formation of the modern river deltas, estuaries, and barrier island systems. Some local evidence for the formation of these deposits is discussed in Chapter 8 and in conjunction with archaeological site descriptions in Chapter 11.

Inland of the immediate coastal zone and the Beaumont Formation are the sandier and slightly rolling terrains of the Montgomery and Bentley Formations (also known as the Upper and Lower Lissie, respectively). These formations, being better drained than the Beaumont and Holocene surfaces, commonly support pine and hardwood forests that form the western extremity of the forest belt extending eastward into Louisiana.

FIGURE 1.5   Swamp along abandoned channel of Trinity River near Liberty, Texas.

FIGURE 1.6   Barrier island topography behind storm beach on Bolivar Peninsula near High Island, Texas. Elevated woodlands in center background is the High Island salt dome.

FIGURE 1.7 Deciduous woodlands (interior forest) on Montgomery Formation uplands near Addicks, Texas.

The climate of the region is quite mild, with an average annual temperature of 21°C. Rainfall in the region averages 142 cm/year in the east and 117 cm/year in the west (Fisher *et al.* 1973:22). However, severe temperature extremes may occur (cf. Hole and Wilkinson 1973). The upper coast is crossed by several major rivers and numerous minor streams, and contains at least one natural spring area (Brune 1975:43).

River channel geometry, soils development, and geographic features indicate some considerable historical changes in temperature, precipitation and evapotranspiration during late Quaternary–Early Holocene time (Chapter 8, present volume; Graf 1966). Since about 1,000 years ago, however, significant modifications in climate have not been directly detected. This is not to conclude that none occurred—only that the sensitivity of measurement techniques has been unable to detect any. At a minimum, though, this suggests that the magnitude of any climatic fluctuations in the past 1,000 years was less than in the preceding 10,000 years.

The major natural hazard in the area is flooding, which results either from overflow in rivers or from storm tides (surges). Evaluation of the relationships between the cultural remains and the biotic environment is more pertinent for analysis of native subsistence, which is not a part of this present study. Howev-

er, the tidally influenced waters of the estuaries and streams supported enormous populations of shellfish, fish, birds, reptiles, and mammals. At present,
over 125 animal taxa have been recovered archaeologically as food remains
from the upper coast.

The lithology of the Beaumont and Recent formations is exclusively sand, silt,
and clay. No natural deposits of chert gravels are known to occur nearer than
about 100 km inland from the coast (Garner 1967:Plate I), with the result, of
course, that all lithic tool material in the coastal zone had to be imported into
the region in one way or another (cf. Appendix B).

CHAPTER 2

Background and Objectives

RESEARCH ISSUES

Several major features of prehistoric sociocultural development in the Galveston Bay Area have been identified or suggested in previous archaeological research (Aten *et al.* 1976). These features are as follows:

1. A system of mortuary practices first becomes archaeologically visible around A.D. 300 and undergoes continuous alteration in its material manifestations up to the Protohistoric period.

2. In their regional aspect, these mortuary practices are distinguishable at least from those of the Caddo cultures to the north and northeast, and from those of the inland Brazos Valley to the northwest.

3. The trend of changes in this system appears to be in the direction of greater sociocultural differentiation and complexity.

4. These developments probably were linked to other sociocultural changes less directly in evidence. Specifically, they indicate increasing energy efficiency, increasing population density, and increasing societal integration.

It is timely to state more explicit questions about these issues and to place them in a framework more useful for archaeological study. To some extent this research is possible through the archaeological record, but ethnohistorical data are an important complementary aspect. Summaries of upper Texas coast ethnography and ethnohistory are readily available (e.g., Aten 1971; Bolton 1951; Gatschet 1891; Newcomb 1961; Schaedel 1949; Tunnell and Ambler 1967; Wheat 1953) and will not be repeated here. However, the information in these summaries tends to be overgeneralized and not in a form that is useful for archaeological investigations (cf. Campbell 1972).

Indeed, little use has been made of the relationship between historical and archaeological records for the upper Texas coast. For the most part, ethnohistoric data have been used as if they were all synchronic when, in fact, some 300 years of very profound sociocultural changes are evident. The method used here has been to pose specific questions, to search the literature for pertinent data, to arrange these data with respect to their cultural and chronological

21

contexts, and then to synthesize the data into narrative and statistical accounts clarifying the questions initially posed. The following issues are examined in Part I.

What Ethnic Groups Were Present in the Area of the Upper Coast During the Protohistoric and Historic Periods? Can Their Territories Be Defined? These questions are treated in the existing literature, but in a vague way. In particular, the organizational significance or referents of group names is unclear. The issue of whether or not there was stability in the native territories throughout the period in question has rarely been addressed but is essential as a prerequisite to considering whether any linkages can be identified between the Prehistoric, Protohistoric, and Historic periods. Beyond this, if comparisons are to be carried out within the upper coast region, there need to be serious attempts to elicit more specific information about the location and nature of boundaries between native groups.

What Were the Population Sizes and Densities of Native Groups throughout the Protohistoric and Historic Periods and How Might These Have Fluctuated? Obviously native population declined to extinction in the Historic period, but can the trend be outlined with any detail and what were the contributing causes? Clearly, European settlement had an effect, but very little is known of the magnitude of native populations confronted by the nineteenth-century settlers. It is assumed that disease had its effect, but this, too, has never been analyzed for the Texas coast. Static population estimates have been presented (Mooney 1928; Swanton 1946, 1952; Aten *et al.* 1976), but the methods employed to arrive at them leave the results in significant doubt. A more reliable reconstruction of these population trends will provide a vital class of data for studying Historic period cultural processes as well as an estimate of population sizes in the latest Prehistoric and Protohistoric periods. This, in turn, may be correlated with certain archaeological data and contribute to investigation of the sociocultural developments described in the opening paragraph of this chapter.

What Evidence Exists in the Historical Record about the Social Structure and Organization of the Identified Upper Coast Native Groups? Elucidation of evidence for statuses, levels of integration, and exchange should provide a set of relationships having substantial correlates in the archaeological record. These may also provide a means for considering the impact of severe stresses that undoubtedly worked substantial modifications on the conditions of native societies in the Historic period. Most existing summaries have dealt superficially with these issues and as if the data were synchronic. The changes these institutions underwent in the Protohistoric and Historic periods must be described more specifically so that inferences for the late Prehistoric periods are not made on the basis of the much-altered societal conditions reflected in the literature dealing with Texas coastal Indians of the nineteenth century.

What Evidence Exists for Describing Cognitive Systems of Upper Texas Coast Native Societies?   The importance of this aspect of the local archaeological record is becoming increasingly clear as a result of findings reported in the general literature, and, more specifically, the recent review and analysis of Galveston Bay Area mortuary practices (Aten *et al.* 1976). In the latter study, indications were fairly strong that formal characteristics of burials (e.g., orientations, contents) and certain other features (e.g., decisions about whether and how application of the burial program should proceed with certain members of the population) would be explicable only on reference to the local cognitive system. Beyond mortuary practices lie other archaeologically visible cultural elements that may be clarified by reference to cognitive reconstruction.

METHOD AND ASSUMPTIONS

Essentially the same sources available to previous workers are used here but they have been synthesized differently. The results of this effort may be linked with the archaeological record providing an enhanced model of the structure of native cultures on the upper Texas coast. Because of the limited amount of historical material available, it has been necessary to look more widely for data than to those sources solely based on the immediate area of this study. Thus, the limited data for the Lake Charles Atakapa have been consulted to illuminate the culture of the Akokisa, as well as that of the larger Atakapa group. Also, the Karankawa group has been reviewed as a whole, since it seldom is usefully differentiated into separate local territorial groups such as the Coco with whom we are most interested.

As will be seen, seemingly inconsistent historical accounts are reconcilable, or at least plausible explanations can be given for their differences. Thus, the Bandelier (1905) translation of Cabeza de Vaca renders understandable the otherwise partially incomprehensible account of his trading activities given in the Smith translation (Hodge 1907b). And diverse accounts of ritual dances are made more usable by viewing them as reports by casual observers reacting only to those features that were of particular interest to them or as memory residue decades after the actual observations were made.

Still, there remain points in the documentation that simply do not make sense today in light of contradictory evidence, for instance, Dyer's statements of a Karankawa taboo on the consumption of oysters (Dyer 1916, 1917); Swanton's statement that the Atakapa obtained their pottery in trade from Karankawa, Avoyel, and probably the Caddo (1946:737); and the observation made both by Father Peña around 1722 (Bolton 1906:117) and later by Sibley (1807) that the Karankawa were docile and friendly towards all other Indians. Some of these inconsistencies may be errors, whereas others may be important clues; none, however, should be dismissed simply because they are not understandable at present.

The method used has been to search the literature for statements of fact and then to "seriate" these facts according to ethnic group, age, and subject matter. No historic accounts have been treated prejudicially simply because they are old or may reflect a bias, although recognizable biases are pointed out. Some of the more bizarre colonial period Spanish accounts (for example, de Solís's apparently hearsay report of the Karankawa eating alive their captured enemies) need to be treated cautiously in light of Spanish political objectives of the period. In 1833, a niece of Stephen F. Austin wrote,

> the Carancahua Indians, who inhabited the coast, were represented to be of a character, uncommonly ferocious . . . .
>
>   These representations of the character of the Carancahuas, though, in a measure true, were, greatly, exaggerated; and it is believed by many, that they were either fabricated or at least countenanced, by the Spanish authorities, to prevent intercourse with the Province, which it was not easy to guard by a military force [Holley 1833/1973:8–9].

Dyer, a major source for the early nineteenth-century Indians of the upper Texas coast, evidently was not enthusiastic about the data presented by Gatschet (1891), and characterized Chief Antonio's band, the group observed by Mrs. Oliver, as "the diseased half breed remnant of the tribe at Capano [*sic*] in 1839 [Dyer 1916:8]." Dyer was reacting to the lack of any mention of many features that his own sources reported, and in all probability, he was correct in stating that Chief Antonio's band was in a much altered state. Today we would refer to them as a *composite band* (Service 1971:47).

Newcomb, on the other hand, seems to deprecate Dyer's efforts by characterizing them as "a fragmentary ethnography of Atakapas of Lake Charles from word-of-mouth sources early in this century [1961:320]." In fact, Dyer's sources were probably every bit as good as Gatschet's, or even Swanton's for that matter; he had interviewed and recorded the recollections of individuals who had some direct experience with the coastal Indians or who had these experiences related to them at a time not far removed from the incident. The principal source of error was, as with Gatschet's data, the time lapse between an observation and the recording of it. The major difference between the reports of Gatschet and Dyer lies in the fact that they refer to separate periods of history and, therefore, to different phases in the dissolution of the Atakapa and Karankawa. Interestingly, Sjoberg (1951b) noted that Dyer's statements on the Bidai were confirmable thorough independent sources and opined that he was credible.

Another important source is the narrative of Álvar Núñez Cabeza de Vaca; the translations of Bandelier (1905), Covey (1961), Smith (Hodge 1907b), and Davenport (Oviedo y Valdez 1923), and fragments of that by Krieger (Krieger 1956) have been compared. Most of the disputation over these various translations concerns the argument about the route taken. This issue will not be joined here since I lack any special qualifications to do so and because the outcome has little impact on the present analysis. This seems justified given the level of resolution in the archaeological data and the fact that present professional judgment seems to favor the region between the Brazos River and Galveston Bay (Taylor 1961) for the initial Texas landfall of Cabeza de Vaca. There are two observations to make, however. First, the Bandelier translation by far relates most easily to all of the other information on the area and leads to the least amount of puzzlement about Cabeza de Vaca's meaning. For this reason, the Bandelier translation has been relied on more heavily than the others for ethnographic detail.

Second, and with regard to the identity of "Malhado," the island on which Cabeza de Vaca's party landed, Krieger (1956:49) is of the opinion that it was not Galveston Island but rather Oyster Bay Peninsula, by which it is presumed he means the peninsula labeled on present maps as Follets Island. This latter is an aggregation of several barrier island segments (including San Luis Island) which in modern times have gradually been consolidated by sedimentation. Krieger stresses that Galveston Island is too large to fit the estimates made by Cabeza de Vaca (i.e., roughly 0.5 × 5 leagues or about 2 × 21 km). Although a review of the geomorphology of Follets Island (actually it is a peninsula) does in fact indicate that it once was disconnected from the mainland (as suggested by Krieger) and was itself segmented, its dimensions, even if one discounts this former separation, are at present considerably smaller than those of the island described by Cabeza de Vaca.

The general trend of change in barrier islands of the Texas coast has been to larger rather than smaller size and for relatively more increase in their length than in their width. Thus, it would seem that one would seek a barrier island landform that either was as large as or somewhat larger than the historic size estimate rather than one which at present is substantially smaller as is Follets Island. Moreover, one would expect a far more accurate historical estimate of island width rather than length, and Cabeza de Vaca's estimate of width, although greater than that of Follets Island, is a reasonable approximation of the average width of Galveston Island except for its younger western portion. In any event, there may be good reasons for concluding that Galveston Island was not Malhado, but the size argument used by Krieger would not appear to be one of them. Certainly a definitive analysis of this problem should employ a holistic approach to all of the geographic information mentioned in the contemporary accounts rather than seize on bits and pieces as I have here. However, the dimensional factor seems relevant to the problem and for our present purposes, Galveston Island shall be considered the starting point for Cabeza de Vaca's travels in Texas.

Some of the accounts of La Salle's abortive attempt at colonization near Lavaca Bay (Cox 1905; Joutel 1714/1966) also have been examined. This has provided information useful for the interpretation of settlement patterns and scheduling. However, the task of identifying ethnic groups and their locations from the difficult-to-reconcile accounts of Joutel, Jean Cavelier, Father Le Clercq and Father Douay was more formidable than could be accomplished here.

Of all our sources, Sibley seems the least reliable. Whatever the reasons may have been, the fact is that many of his assertions about the native groups of the upper Texas coast either are clearly not correct, or are at such variance with other reports as to be suspect. An example is his report that the principal and "ancient" town of the Akokisa was located on the Colorado River when he is clearly referring to Orcoquisac on the Trinity (this discrepancy will be discussed further in Chapter 3). He makes other assertions that do not seem likely as generalizations, although they occasionally may have been correct with reference to individuals. For example, he placed the Bidai on the coast and on the Brazos and Colorado rivers, stated that the Karankawa used Atakapa as their language, and observed that the Karankawa were friendly and kind to all. These examples are all reviewed in subsequent Chapters in conjunction with other evidence bearing on the particular topic.

The colonial Spanish historian, José Antonio Pichardo, understood well the inaccuracies in Sibley's reports and seems to have considered him poorly informed. These errors or interpretations were generally in the direction of lessening the legitimacy of Spain's claim to the area between the Sabine and Trinity rivers. Sibley was able to use trade to win wide support among the east Texas Indians, to the consternation of Spanish authorities (Faulk 1964:68). Consequently, as an agent of the United States he may have provided biased reports because of political motivation surrounding the boundary question between the United States and Mexico rather than simply because of misinformation. In any event, it appears that Sibley's reports must be used with caution where they are not independently verifiable.

Finally, it should be noted that numerous mid-nineteenth-century sources exist that yield only a small mention of ethnographic detail, usually based on a personal experience, but in the aggregate, add a great deal to our information. Several are used in Part I, but no doubt more of these should be sought out. Indeed, it seems reasonably clear that much very useful information on ethnographic detail and ethnohistory remains to be extracted from the records of Spanish, French, and English colonial administrations (including ecclesiastical records) of Texas and southwest Louisiana and of the early period of American colonization in coastal Texas.

CHAPTER 3

Ethnic Groups
and Their Territories

In this section, we review the ethnohistoric literature for references to ethnic groups resident on the upper Texas coast. Although much of this will be familiar material to students of the region's history, a detailed effort has been made to compile and/or verify the documentary basis for interpreting the location of ethnic group territories. Moreover, many unfamiliar group names were encountered. The result of this review is that the territorial limits[1] of upper coast ethnic groups, as they existed in the Protohistoric and early Historic periods are delineated more precisely.[2] Having done this, the locations of native group enclaves in the later Historic period of the early nineteenth century are sketched out. This organization of the historic records then serves as the background for discussion of population density estimates and for boundaries to compare with the archaeological record. The most exhaustive previous effort to compile and correlate Atakapa and Karankawa group names was that of Mayhall (1939); no attempt has been made here to revise her work. The spelling of group names varies widely and particular difficulty attends any attempt to determine the identity of groups named by Joutel (1714/1966) and Casañas (Hatcher 1927). However, there were no signficant problems encountered in organizing by ethnic group the majority of the locational, population, and other data for this study.

In Chapter 5, levels of sociocultural integration are discussed at some length and preliminary conclusions about just what is meant by "ethnic group" are

[1]The concept of these limits or boundaries as used here is that they: (a) probably were zones as opposed to lines; (b) fluctuated to some extent, especially over the final 200 years or so of prehistory when populations seem to have been expanding (as inferred from increasing organizational complexity reflected in mortuary ritual [cf. Aten *et al.* 1976]); (c) were not solely determined on the basis of resource distributions; and (d) were differentially permeable depending on relations with adjacent groups. The Protohistoric period boundaries shown on Figure 3.1 are essentially first approximations of a normative reconstruction. This territorial model does not account for the whereabouts of all group members, for the evidence suggests many spontaneous, nonrepetitive journeys over considerable distances (also cf. Yellen 1977).

[2]The use of the terms protohistoric and historic follows that of Ray (1978:26) and is discussed in Part III. *Protohistoric* refers to the period from A.D. 1528 to about A.D. 1700–1725; *historic* refers to the subsequent period ending about A.D. 1850.

formulated. Although not wishing to fully anticipate that discussion here, note that most data, such as that on population size and settlement locations, for the upper Texas coast, are categorized by the names Atakapa, Akokisa, Bidai, and Karankawa. These names do not refer to equivalent levels of integration. The first three names are all *tribes*, as defined in Chapter 5, whereas the fourth name is probably a group of tribes that evidently all spoke the same basic language. The data being sought, however, often appeared in documentary sources in reference either to the collective form "Karankawa" or, alternatively, "Cujane." It is in this collective form that the information is most conveniently used. Even though the term Atakapa also is frequently used to refer to a collection of tribes all speaking the same basic language, in this case, the necessary types of data usually appear identified by tribe. The main ethnic group divisions employed, therefore, will be Atakapa, Akokisa,[3] Bidai (all three are tribes), and Karankawa (the language/tribal group).

The general question remains as to whether these groups, known in the Historic period, reflect named groups from precontact times or whether their roots lie in the disruptions of the contact period. We assume they reflect organizational distinctions from the precontact period because the dates at which group names are first recognizable (as detailed in the following) were early enough to precede any European contact at a scale that would have affected aboriginal organization. Unquestionably, these group names continued to be used until late in the Historic period, by which time the character of the groups must have been changed substantially.

KARANKAWA

This group consisted of at least five principal tribes (as the term is defined later in Part I)—the Coco, Cujane, Guapite, Karankawa, and Copane (Bolton 1915:281). Most have been known from the earliest days of historical records for the upper Texas coast. Spanish colonial officials of the eighteenth century often tended to refer to the entire group of tribes as the Cujanes (or some orthographic variant of this name) or to differentiate primarily between the Cujanes and the Cocos. The use of the name Karankawa as the principal term of reference for the tribal group seems largely to have been a nineteenth century development. At a minimum, this territorial group was distinguished by its language; other distinguishing features are suggested later in Part I. Whatever the full basis was for setting apart these local groups, apparently it was a clear

---

[3]The terms "Orcoquisa" or "Orcoquisac," which are frequently used as a term of reference for the Akokisa, will always be used here as Orcoquisac to refer to the location of the Akokisa village near the mouth of the Trinity River where the Spanish established their mission and presidio in 1755.

and unequivocal one in the view of both European and native American outsiders.

The only recent attempt at comparative analysis of the Karankawan language (the data for which are quite limited) concluded that its origin lay in a sub-group of Cariban speakers who must have made their way to the Texas coast via Central America in relatively recent centuries (Landar 1968). No independent evidence is available at present to evaluate this possibility; although Mayhall (1939:345) noted some culture trait similarities with South American Carib cultures, she drew no specific conclusions because her information was so vague.

Most of the diverse forms for spelling the Karankawa group names are readily recognizable to anyone reading the literature. There are a few exotic forms, and so that the reader will be certain of what has been included, a few notes are in order. Among the terms used by Cabeza de Vaca, most workers assume that the Capoque are identical to the Coaque, the Coke, and the Coco. Pichardo identified the Caucozi, one of the tribes listed by Casañas in 1691, as the Coco (Hackett 1932, 2:147, 176; also see Bolton 1906:116). There is, however, an exception to this view in that Gatschet (1891:35) believed the Coaques or Cokes to be different from the Coco, with the former being Karankawan groups and the latter being affiliated with the Atakapa. The Deaguanes are interpreted here to be the same as the group later identified as the Cujane; and the Guevenes (in Bandelier 1905) or Quevenes (in Covey 1961) may well be the Guapite of later authors. It should also be noted that Hodge (1907a:315) suggested the Quevenes probably were the Cujanes; this is a possibility, but these issues should be left to the appropriate specialists.

The conventional wisdom has been followed about the composition of the Karankawa group (e.g., Bolton 1915; Newcomb 1961). That is to say, there was a group of entities (of precisely what type is not yet entirely clear, although some suggestions will be made later in Part I) who apparently spoke dialects of the same language and apparently were interrelated by marriage (Bolton 1915:281). Bolton's sources indicated that "since they mingled freely with each other, it is difficult to assign definite territorial limits [1915:282]." In spite of this, he concluded (*a*) that, in general, the Coco resided on the mainland east of Matagorda Bay and about the lower Colorado River; (*b*) that the Karankawa usually resided on the immediate coastal fringe and barrier islands on and adjacent to Matagorda Bay; (*c*) that the Cujane and Guapite resided on either side of Matagorda Bay, especially to the west; and (*d*) that the Copane lived about Copano Bay. This distribution, drawn primarily from mid-eighteenth-century Spanish records, agrees reasonably well with the distribution of groups encountered by Cabeza de Vaca (assuming he landed somewhere between Galveston and the Brazos River). Unfortunately, most sources are vague on the extent to which these groups ordinarily ranged inland. Bolton (1906:115), for example, merely noted that during the hunting season and winter months, the Karankawa moved from the barrier islands to the interior.

Gatschet, however, indicated that in the early nineteenth century the Karankawa (broadly speaking) were situated within 15 miles (24 km) or so of the
mainland bay or estuary shoreline except on rare occasions (1891:46–47 [and
map]). Smithwick (1900:13) made the extremely interesting comment that
during the early years of Anglo colonization in Texas, the Mexican government
prohibited any settlement within 25 miles (40 km) of the coast so as to provide a
reserve for the Karankawa (also see Mayhall [1939:23] for mention of the "reserved land"). This zone was the subject of dispute between the colonists, who
claimed that it began at the Gulf coastline, and the government, which insisted
that it began from the indented border of the mainland. Although the colonists
evidently won the argument, perhaps due to the fact that the Mexican government was unable to enforce its policy, the governmental sensitivity to this zone
cited by Smithwick suggests, in company with Gatschet's statements, that the
inland limit of the Karankawa territory approximated a zone about 24 km
inland from the mainland coast.

An important line of circumstantial evidence supportive of this interpretation
of the significance of the Karankawa reserve concerns the early coastal missions.
In 1722, the Presidio Nuestra Señora de Loreto and Mission Espíritu Santo de
Zúñiga (i.e., Bahía) were established at the site of La Salle's Fort St. Louis on
Garcitas Creek (Bolton, 1906:116). This mission was for the Karankawa tribes of
the "Cujanes, Guapites, and Carancaguases"; by 1726, however, the mission
was relocated some 10 leagues (42 km) northwest to the Guadalupe River
"among the Jaranames and Tamiques [Bolton 1906:117]," who were more
receptive to the efforts of the missionaries. Subsequent relocations of the Bahía
presidio and mission from the Guadalupe River near Mission Valley to the San
Antonio River near Goliad in 1749 also avoided Karankawa territory (Bolton
1906). These locations, at Mission Valley and Goliad, are not a great distance
farther inland than the 40 km-wide zone known later as the Karankawa reserve.
It is the following facts of group identity and location then that were used to
compile Figure 3.1 for the Karankawa group: (a) the locations and names given
by Bolton for the early eighteenth century; (b) the same as given by Cabeza de
Vaca for the early sixteenth century; (c) mission–presidio locations; and (d) an
inland limit of roughly 40 km from the mainland shore. This territory is taken
to be the range of the various subgroups of the Karankawa tribe as they existed
in the protohistoric and early historic period at least through the eighteenth
century; it is assumed that this distribution had some prehistoric validity also.

As the eighteenth century progressed, the impact of European diseases, European culture, and European territorial occupation became increasingly noticeable in the form of native population decline (to be discussed in the next
chapter), dissolution of ethnic groups, and territorial displacement. In 1778,
de Mézières noted that about 20 families of Mayeyes (possibly a Tonkawa affiliate) and Cocos (probably a Karankawa affiliate) merged together and were
living on the coast between the Colorado and Brazos rivers (Bolton 1915:283;
Morfi 1935/1967:81; Mayhall 1939:277–279).

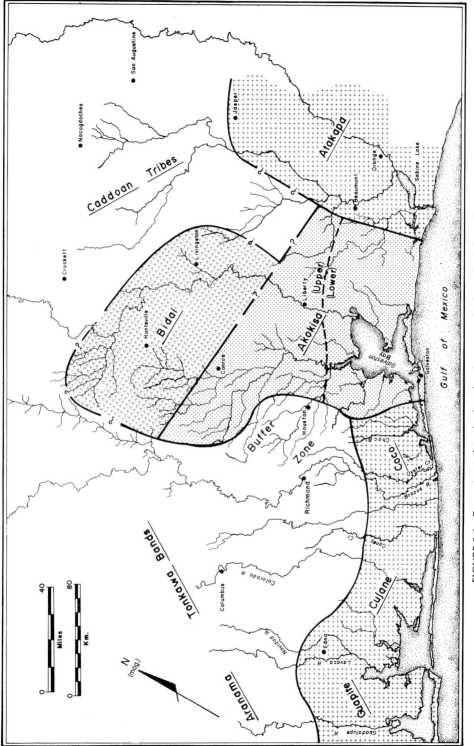

FIGURE 3.1 Reconstructed territories of native groups in the early eighteenth century.

In the latter part of this same period, evidence begins to occur of the disruption of native territorial patterns, initially through the mission system. Karankawas, Cocos, and Cujanes were present at several missions, including San Antonio de Valero, Candelaria, and Nuestra Señora del Rosario (Castañeda 1939:6, 31). In 1770, one Cujane and one Coco were baptized, and a funeral and burial for one Coco were held at Nuestra Señora de la Luz, near the mouth of the Trinity River (Castañeda 1939:97).

Progressing into the early nineteenth century, a Karankawa camp reportedly existed at the mouth of the San Jacinto River (where it meets Galveston Bay) from around 1815 until the early 1820s (Dyer 1916:2; Hunter 1966:4) and in the same general time period, a group of Cocos and Cujanes were supposed to have been located on the west side of Galveston Bay at Red Fish Bar (Dyer 1916:2). Concurrently, Dyer (1917:1) reported some Karankawa encamped at the mouth of the Sabine (presumably the river rather than Sabine Pass). Dyer's information evidently came from family records and people he queried on the matter. Independent confirmation for this dispersion of the Karankawa comes from Morse (1822) who made a survey in the summer of 1820 and found them occasionally along the western margins of Galveston Bay and the San Jacinto River; he also said that the Cocos lived in Louisiana.

Gatschet (1891:35) asserted, on the basis of Morse and others, that the Cocos had lived in Louisiana and had been allied with the Atakapa but did not fully discuss the basis for his belief. At the same time, it seems reasonably clear that the "heartland" of the Cocos was still the Brazos Delta–Matagorda Bay area (Padilla 1919:51). According to Stephen F. Austin, this same region was the territory of the Cujane in 1829 (Berlandier 1969:Figure 13). Ostensibly, inconsistent reports such as these probably reflect movement of groups and individuals engaged in exchange activities. For example, around 1780, Spanish authorities reported that the Coco and Mayeyes were trading weapons and ammunition from Louisiana to the Lipan Apache (Faulk 1964:63).

Prior to the nineteenth century, the Tonkawa were usually at peace with the Comanche and Wichita to their north, the Hasinai to their northeast, the Bidai and Akokisa to their east, the Aranama to their south, and the Coahuiltecans to their southwest. They frequently joined the Comanche, Wichita, and Hasinai in fighting the Apache, located to the west and northwest of Tonkawa territory; however, near the beginning of the nineteenth century, the Tonkawa became friendly with the Lipan Apache and hostile toward the Comanche and Wichita. In 1790, however, an alliance was formed between the Apache and the Bidai, Akokisa, and Atakapa, generating hostilities with the Tonkawa (Hodge 1907a: 778–779).

After 1770 and as a result of the complicated power politics between relatively more powerful adjoining tribes, the Tonkawa clearly extended their range to the southwest into territory that appears formerly to have been largely that of the Karankawa (Hodge 1907a:780). By this time, the Tonkawa had relocated near the middle of the Guadalupe River drainage, somewhat south of their

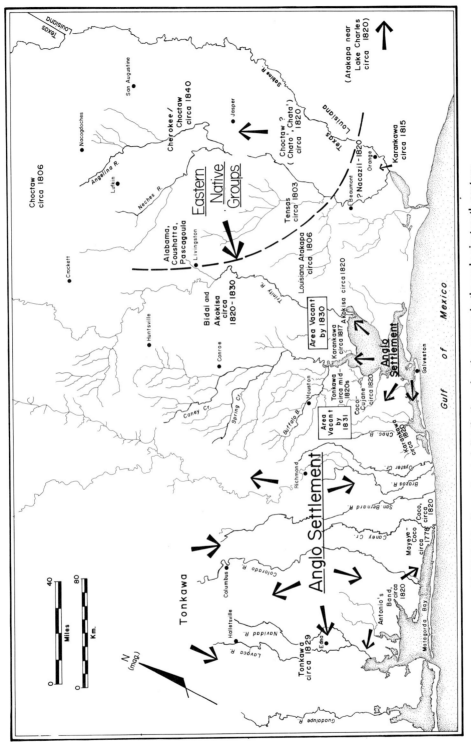

FIGURE 3.2 Reconstructed distribution of native groups in the early nineteenth century.

former territories (Berlandier 1969:Figure 13), and the hopes of the Mexican government for a "reserve" for the Karankawa in a strip 40 km wide along the mainland coast never materialized. This pressure, added to that from the Anglo colonists in the early nineteenth century, seems to have resulted in a certain amount of scattering of the Karankawa up and down the coast. As a result, we see in the map of ethnic group locations in the early nineteenth century (Figure 3.2), more a collection of enclaves than of continuous territories as was the case a century (or less) earlier. The sordid story of their remaining few years may be pieced together from several sources (Gatschet 1891; Hodge 1907a; Holley 1833/1973; Roessler 1883; also see Newcomb 1961:341–343 for additional information), most of which seem more or less to agree. It appears that by 1860, the Karankawa, long since extinct as an organizational entity, finally ceased to exist as individuals as well.

Although we are principally interested only in that portion of the Karankawa territory impinging on the archaeological study area, the population data to be described shortly are available only for the aggregate of tribes and not for individual local territorial groups. Therefore, the description of various authors (e.g., Kuykendall 1903:324; Newcomb 1961:59) has been followed for the southwestern limit of the Karankawa as being in the vicinity of Corpus Christi, and the 40-km-deep zone is extended that far down the coast for the purpose of determining the area occupied by the Karankawa. Using a polarizing planimeter, the extent of the protohistoric and early historic period territory of the Karankawa is estimated to approximate 14,200 km^2 (see Table 4.2 on page 50). This estimate includes the coastal barrier islands but excludes the coastal estuaries and associated major water bodies.

AKOKISA

The earliest mention of the Akokisa in known historical records is assumed to be the account of de Bellisle dating from 1721. De Bellisle, however, used the term "Caux," although it is not entirely clear whether he meant this to signify the native name for themselves as a group, or to the native woman with whom he lived (Folmer 1940:216). It has also been suggested that he was referring to the Cocos, although Du Pratz (who was acquainted with de Bellisle) in 1758 described the group who captured de Bellisle as "Atac-Apas" (Folmer 1940:216, Footnote 23). The weight of the evidence presented by Folmer indicates that de Bellisle's captors were a band of Akokisa, a view accepted here (also see Mayhall 1939:42), although the case is not airtight.

In the early sixteenth century, Cabeza de Vaca reported that the Island of Malhado was occupied by two groups not of the same "stock" and speaking different languages; one of these was the Capoque (previously described as

Karankawa) and the other was the Han (Bandelier 1905:72; Covey 1961; Hodge 1907a:530). Swanton (1946:85) suggests the identity of this group is with the Akokisa based on the similarity between the group's name, *Han*, and the Atakapa word for house, *an*. Such an association is not out of the question since de Mézières noted that the Akokisa occupied the lower Trinity River down to the coast where a cape (Punta de los Orcoquisas) was named after them (Bolton 1914:20). This geographic name was also reported by Pichardo (Hackett 1932, 1:350, 380). Sheridan, in 1839, identified the tip of Bolivar Peninsula as "Point Bolivar" but commented that it formerly was known as "Point Arcokisas" (Pratt 1954:44, Footnote 53), which strongly indicates that, if Galveston Island was Cabeza de Vaca's Malhado, the Han certainly did reside in or very near to a portion of the territory of the Akokisa.

As of the middle part of the eighteenth century, the Akokisa were said to reside in the area extending from the mouth of the Neches River west to midway between the Trinity and Brazos rivers (Bolton 1913:345; Morfi 1935:80). Based on his journey through the area in 1746, Orobio y Bazterra reported four Akokisa villages (Bolton 1913:344–345): (*a*) Canos's village located at the junction of the San Jacinto River and Spring Creek; (*b*) El Gordo's village on Spring Creek about 32 km above the San Jacinto; (*c*) Mateo's village "above" El Gordo's and to the northwest; and (*d*) Calzones Colorado's village located on the east side of the Trinity River about 16–24 km above the river mouth.

There seems to be some confusion in Bolton's account above the village of Calzones Colorado, which suggests there may have been two villages under his control—a possibility we are unable to reject at the present time. There does not seem to be much doubt that the first of Calzones Colorado's villages mentioned is Orcoquisac, where the French trader Blancpain was later arrested and where the Spanish mission and presidio were established (Tunnell and Ambler 1967). Moreover, Blancpain later stated that his arrest occurred at the village of Calzones Colorado (Bolton 1913:348). However, Bolton elsewhere describes the village of Calzones Colorado as being situated some 16–24 km from the mouth of the Trinity (Bolton 1913:345) and later as within a space of 6 leagues (about 25 km) above Orcoquisac and the mission–presidio complex (Bolton 1913:359; also see Kinnaird 1958). Descriptions of this latter place are sufficiently detailed and extensive that they are hard to overlook or to consider as a mistake. Padilla (1919:51), however, adds confusion to the matter by identifying Orcoquisac with Atascocito (the present day city of Liberty; Beers 1979:140) at which troops were stationed until 1812. Bolton (1913:361) also describes the location of "El Atascosito" on the Trinity some 19 leagues (about 80 km) above the presidio at Orcoquisac (also see Kinnaird 1958). Until more definitive information is available, it will be assumed there were two Akokisa villages under the headman Calzones Colorado (perhaps inhabited sequentially in the annual round) and that the more southerly of the two was Orcoquisac.

Finally, it should be noted that around 1720, the Caux (Akokisa?) went to the prairies presumably to the west of Spring Creek to hunt bison and to kill their enemies, the Toyals—a group of unknown identity (Folmer [1940] and Mayhall [1939:286] suggested Tonkawa, and Hodge [1907a:657–658] suggested Karankawa). Around 1746, the Akokisa claimed to have peaceful relations with all of their neighbors except the Karankawa proper, as opposed to the Coco or Cujane (Bolton 1915:328–332; Castañeda 1939:49). In consideration of these locational and relational factors, we have shown the territory of the Akokisa for the protohistoric and early historic periods. This has been reconstructed in Figure 3.1.

Again using planimetric methods, the land area of the Akokisa territory has been calculated to cover approximately 12,400 km^2. The Akokisa territory is obviously shaped very differently from that of the Karankawa and, to anticipate a later conclusion, the differential movement of the Akokisa population during the annual round results in their being primarily in the northern or upper part of their territory during the cold seasons and in the southern or lower part of their territory during the remainder of the year. This differentiation, although difficult to precisely locate at the present stage of investigation, can roughly be indicated by the dashed line shown on Figure 3.1. The area of the upper territory is roughly 7,200 km^2; the area of the lower territory is roughly 4,700 km (cf. Table 4.2 on page 50).

From the early nineteenth century, there is no record of the type of group dispersal that was documented for the Karankawa. The most notable example of long-distance Akokisa dispersal is undoubtedly a mistake. According to Sibley, "Their ancient town and principal place of residence is on [the] west side of Colorado [*sic*] or Rio Rouge [1807:44]" and this statement has been repeated widely (e.g., Aten 1971:7–8; Hodge 1907a:87; Newcomb 1961:319; Swanton 1946:86). Unfortunately, and aside from the fact that the cited quotation calls this their *ancient* town (which should have been clue enough that something was wrong), it ignores the remainder of what Sibley said. "Thirty or forty years ago the Spaniards had a mission here, but broke it up . . . being near the bay, [they] make use of fish, oysters, etc.[1807:44]." Sibley obviously is referring to Orcoquisac and clearly was misinformed about or misunderstood its location. Pichardo reached the same conclusion about Sibley's statement (Hackett 1932, 2:195).

The remaining sources for the period seem to indicate that the Akokisa had quietly passed into oblivion after 1830. In 1830, they were still located at the mouth of the Trinity River according to Padilla (1919:51), which is further confirmation that Sibley was wrong. Dyer (1916:5) referred to the "Bidai–Orcoquisa" around 1820 as the remnant of "two large ancient tribes" who partly occupied the territory across the Trinity River from the Coushattas. This would be located in what appears once to have been the southeastern portion of the Bidai territory. In 1828, General Teran included the Akokisa with the Bidai in a tabulation of the native population (Berlandier 1969:139, Footnote 205). It appears that the Akokisa had ceased to exist as a separate ethnic group by this time. These few data on the Akokisa in the early nineteenth century are shown on Figure 3.2.

BIDAI

The Bidai probably are important to the area of archaeological interest in this study, because they are generally acknowledged to have been closely related to the Akokisa and Atakapa (e.g., Newcomb 1961; Sjoberg 1951a, 1951b). As a result, ethnohistoric information pertaining to the Bidai are of assistance in rounding out our knowledge of the major features of the cultures of the latter groups. In addition, data on their gross population dynamics are useful for comparative purposes. Finally, at least one source has suggested that the nor-·mal territory of the Bidai extended down to the coast and it is necessary to address this point.

The earliest known mention of the Bidai is in a 1691 Spanish report about the first attempt at establishing missions in eastern Texas (Hatcher 1927). They reappear in 1718 (Celiz 1935:78) and again in 1720 (Folmer 1940:221). In this last report, de Bellisle noted that the Bidai were located about 90 leagues from where his Akokisa band was situated in their winter camp (which presumably was located on or near Spring Creek). Reckoning 2.6 miles (4.2 km) to the league (Polzer *et al.* 1977:39), a distance of 90 leagues is much too great a distance to be correct. Either de Bellisle was not correctly informed or else there is an error in transcription from the original French. Later, when rescued by the Hasinai, de Bellisle says they traveled for 4 days before reaching the Bidai (Folmer 1940:223). Assuming that they left from a camp on Spring Creek and traveled at the rate he gave earlier (i.e., 3–4 leagues/day [13–17 km/day]), they could have encountered this village anywhere along the Trinity River (above Livingston) or along Bidai Creek and vicinity. A few years later, Orobio y Bazterra traveled southwest from Nacogdoches and reached a Bidai settlement near, but still east of, the Trinity River (Bolton 1913:342). From this place, he traveled west–southwest for a distance of about 30 leagues (125 km) until they reached Akokisa villages on what Bolton interprets to have been Spring Creek. Although this estimate of the distance is a bit excessive given the beginning and ending points, as well as the directions of travel, the nature of the possibilities for error in this sort of calculation are such that Bolton's reconstruction is not troubling. Also, note that Sjoberg (1951a:53) reported the Bidai as living south of the San Antonio Road, which crossed the Trinity River at the boundary between Madison and Houston counties.

There is no other evidence from the mid-eighteenth-century period for the territory of the Bidai, although the locations of the 1810 encounters of Ker with the Bidai bear a general similarity to those described previously (Ker 1816). So, considering the possible ranges involved in these distance estimates a territory is suggested for the Protohistoric period on Figure 3.1. Measurement of the area of this territory, shown on Figure 3.1 results in an estimate of about 8900 km^2 (see Table 4.2).

In about 1820, the Bidai were reported by Morse (1822:373) to be situated on the right bank of the Trinity River about 105 km above the mouth, which location would be in the vicinity of Livingston. An identical report was also given by Dyer (1916:5), who noted that the Bidai had, by that time, been joined by Akokisa. Padilla (1919:50) also mentions a group of Bidai ("Vidaizes") but the location is ambiguous and not shown on Figure 3.2. By 1820, the Bidai territory had been intruded by other refugee Indian groups such as the Pascagoula and Alabama (Swanton 1911:31).

Finally, it should be noted that some reports state that the Bidai moved to the coast in the summers to fish (Sjoberg 1951b:397). This statement is based on Bonnell (1840:139) and Sibley (Garrett 1944:324). Bonnell, however, has been misinterpreted in that he simply noted that the Bidai fished, an activity that, of course, was done in the interior as well as on the coast. Sibley, on the other hand, said that the Bidai lived "Alternately on the Sea Shore & Back upon the Brasos & Collerado [Garrett 1944:323–324]" in a letter to the United States Secretary of War in 1809. Here again, Sibley seems to have his information mixed up, since, among all of the documentation on the Bidai, his is the only one to place their tribal territory nearly 160 km from its location as reported by others, and doing things no one else ever reported them to be doing. In the absence of independent confirming evidence, Sibley's comments will be disregarded and it will be assumed that the Bidai territory did not extend significantly below Livingston on the Trinity River. This is not inconsistent with the fact that individual Bidai ventured down to the coast from time to time, usually to enter into trade (Austin 1904:304; Hackett 1932, 1:394).

ATAKAPA

This group occupied a sizable territory, principally in southwestern Louisiana, and only extended into Texas to the approximate location of the Neches River. In the 1750s, the Atakapa were variously said to occupy the lower Neches River or to share the area with the Akokisa (Bolton 1913:345; Morfi 1935/1967:80). Some accounts indicate that the Atakapa had two villages on either side of the Neches River near Beaumont. It may even have been these two villages from which the French recruited two Atakapa headmen (Tamages and Boca Floja) and their warriors, in 1759, to go to Orcoquisac to expel the Spanish (Bolton 1913:370). In any event, the protohistoric boundary between the Atakapa and the Akokisa appears to have been located in the general lower Neches area and to have been a very open one (also see Hackett 1932, 1:395, 2:195). For this same period, Swanton (1911:Plate 1) indicated that the territory of the Atakapa in Texas reached as far north as the mouth of the Angelina River, although the authority for this is not documented.

In 1806, 300 Atakapa families were allowed to enter the province of Texas (Faulk 1964:70). Even so, the principal early nineteenth-century western Atakapa village seems to have been that located near Lake Charles (Dyer 1916, 1917; Gatshet and Swanton 1932), although isolated individuals and families were scattered widely over their former territory (Swanton 1911:362). As late as 1887, however, two dialects of Atakapa were still spoken in southwestern Louisiana (Gatschet 1887:414).

OTHER GROUPS

Several other ethnic groups have been recorded in the area of the upper Texas coast, most of these in the early to mid-nineteenth century, when native society was in its final stages of dissolution. Two exceptions to this are the Patiri, supposedly an Atakapan group, and a group of Tlascalan Indians from Mexico who were to have been relocated at the mission Nuestra Señora de la Luz at Orcoquisac.

The Patiri are known only from the fact that they were named as one of the ethnic groups present in Mission San Ildefonso (on the San Gabriel River) in 1749 (Bolton 1915:231; Morfi 1935). From this mention, virtually all conclusions have followed. Because of the Spanish practice of associating related native groups in missions whenever possible, and because members of the Akokisa, Bidai, and Deadose were also present in San Ildefonso at this time, it has been assumed that the Patiri were a distinct tribe of the Atakapan group (Swanton 1946:172; Newcomb 1961:316). Swanton even went so far as to suggest that the Patiri originally resided in the San Jacinto River Basin, possibly on Caney Creek (of which there are two in the basin), between the territories of the Bidai and the Akokisa, although the basis of his suggestion is unknown. Particularly unfathomable regarding the Patiri is why, when the region between the Bidai and the Akokisa was traversed so many times throughout the period of European exploration and colonization, there is no mention whatever of this group. As a working assumption, this has been treated as an analytical error—that there never was such a group affiliated with the Atakapa at least at a tribal level of organization. It is more likely that the Patiri were either a subgroup of the Akokisa, Bidai, or Deadose, or were an unrelated group.

The case of Tlascalan Indians appears to be one of unfulfilled expectation. In 1756, the Spanish decided to introduce a colony of 50 families into the Presidio

San Agustín de Ahumada (Bolton 1913:354) at Orcoquisac. Of these, 25 were to have been Tlascalan Indian families, in order to aid local pacification efforts. Had they been introduced, they could have had a major impact on acculturation and the archaeological record in the area. However, there is no indication in records published so far that these colonies were ever established.

Numerous tribes from the southeastern United States petitioned for and were granted permission to enter east Texas (Faulk 1964). In 1803, the Tensas were allowed by the Spanish commandant-general to settle between the Sabine and Trinity rivers near the coast (Faulk 1964:69). In 1806, 104 Choctaw families were assigned land in the northern part of the Sabine River drainage, and Coushattas also were allowed to enter (Faulk 1964:70).

Around 1820, Padilla (1919:50) reported two adjacent groups, the Chato and Chata, living on the Sabine River not very far from the sea; these groups were said to have been agricultural and to have customs like the Caddo. Although this report could have some implications for the territory of the Atakapa living around the mouth of the Sabine, by 1820 the latter were essentially eliminated as an organizational entity. Padilla's spelling of these names is very similar to that used even later for the Choctaw (e.g., Gatschet 1891; it is also similar to the form used in the *Jesuit Relations*). Significantly, this is the period in which the Choctaw, including the Houmas, Bayougoulas, Biloxi, Pascagoulas, etc. were migrating westward. Morse (1822:373) reported that some 1200 Choctaw lived along the Sabine and Neches rivers in the early 1820s. Later, Bonnell (1840:140–143) reported that the Cherokee and associated groups, including the Choctaw, had settled in the Neches–Angelina River area. These locations are shown on Figure 3.2 and are presumed to reflect the flux of the period.

Another group, noted in 1820 by Padilla about whom there is very little information, was the Nacazil who "live on the Neches River near the lagoons where it empties into the sea [1919:51]." He went on to say that they were hunters and farmers and frequented the seacoast. There is no mention in any other known source of this group although the prefix "Na" is common among Caddoan group names. Another possibility is that they may have been a composite band composed of remnants of other bands much as Chief Antonio's band of Karankawa seems to have been. The Nacazil group is shown on Figure 3.2.

Yet another displaced group in the Galveston Bay Area was the Tonkawa who were reported in the vicinity of New Washington (Figure 3.2) in the early and mid 1820s (Hunter 1966:7).

A final group to be mentioned here, since they are shown on the periphery of Figure 3.1, and since there is some useful population data about them (see Figure 4.1), is the Aranama located on either side of the lower Guadalupe River (Bolton 1914:28, 291). Gatschet (1891:163) seems to have been the first to note that the name *Xaranames* is probably identical with Aranama, and Newcomb (1961:49) made the suggestion that the group identified by Cabeza de Vaca as the Mariames also were the Aranama. This latter point is probably not correct, since both names are distinctly recorded in the records of Mission San Antonio de Valero (T. N. Campbell, personal communication 1979). Both Mayhall (1939:287) and Swanton (1952:326) identified the Mariames as the Tonkawan affiliate known as the Moruame or the Muruam. Skeels (1972:29) recently identified the Xaranames of Morfi (1935/1967) as Karankawa, but this is unlikely. The Aranama apparently were extinct by 1843 (Swanton 1952:308).

SUMMATION

Figure 3.1 represents an extrapolation of more or less definite territorial boundaries (or boundary zones) for the major ethnic groups presumed to have used the area of archaeological interest. It should be clear that these territories are identified only as normative constructs; most questions about the nature of the boundaries (e.g., their permeability and locational stability) await future studies. For the present, only first approximations are sought in order to guide the structuring of present data on ethnography, demography, and the archaeological record. These approximations should also serve to guide development of subsequent research problems. There are important temporal and spatial distinctions in the archaeological record that suggest that cultural systems differed as one crossed these boundaries. However, how they differed is a question that has not yet been confronted. For example, there are substantial differences in the ceramic chronologies for the three areas of the Brazos Delta, Galveston Bay Area, and Sabine Lake Area, as will be seen in Part III.

In addition, there are suggestions of major differences in the nature of mortuary practices between the Galveston Bay Area (Aten *et al.* 1976) and the Brazos Valley (Hall 1981) inland from the territory of the Cocos. In subsequent studies, I will report information describing the annual schedule of population movements and subsistence patterns that further supports the territorial divisions given here. For example, it will be seen that the age structure of the subsistence target population of white-tailed deer at sites in the Addicks Reservoir differed substantially from that in either the Karankawa or Akokisa sites.

It may also be suggested that the nature of these boundaries differs from place to place (and probably from time to time, although there are no data on this point). For instance, it was noted earlier that the boundary between the Atakapa and the Akokisa seemed particularly fuzzy (permeable) and that boundaries between the Akokisa and Bidai, on the one hand, and the Akokisa and the Coco, on the other, were crossed without danger by members of the adjacent groups. The northern boundary of the Karankawa group and the western boundary of the Akokisa seem to have been of a different character. The Karankawa were said not to venture too far inland because of hostile relations with the inland inhabitants. The Akokisa went to the western prairies to hunt and to kill enemies, and only warriors went on such trips. All this sounds very reminiscent of buffer zones in the northern woodlands as described by Hickerson where "the hunting bands, made up of about 15 to 20 responsible men . . . were also warrior bands [1965:43]." These different types of territorial boundaries are shown on Figure 3.1 and are discussed further both in Part III and in Chapter 14.

Figure 3.2 presents a very different and no less challenging situation, although the effect of acculturation and dissolution shall not be pursued to any extent in this study. In the early nineteenth century, territorial pressures of three basically different sorts were working on the upper Texas coast. First, there was the general southward movement of the Tonkawa, and possibly other bands, that had its most severe impact west of Galveston Bay; second, there was increasing pressure in east Texas from migrant Indian groups and individuals fleeing the eastern United States long before the United States Congress had set removal of Native Americans as policy in 1830 (Ewers in Berlandier 1969:10); and third, there was the most severe pressure of all emanating from within the area itself as a result of the establishment of Anglo settlers in the new colonies. These factors of territorial pressure working in concert with another major factor—decimation of native populations by chronic and epidemic diseases— essentially eliminated the territorial structure of the Protohistoric period shown in Figure 3.1. Left in its place were isolated native families and small enclaves of native groups, none of which (except the Alabama-Coushatta) has survived to the present day. It is the protohistoric framework of native groups and their dissolution that forms the background and further subject for Chapter 4, native population reconstruction.

CHAPTER 4

Population Reconstruction

Population size and density for given ethnic groups relate intimately to culture history, social integration, cultural ecology—indeed, to a host of historical and processual factors (cf. Dobyns 1966; Hawley 1973; Ubelaker 1975). Therefore, their reconstruction is an important fundamental parameter in the study of culture. However, with regard to the Texas coast, population size and density have never been of particular concern to anthropologists and little more than a footnote has been devoted to them in descriptive summaries of Historic period native groups.

In the analysis of Galveston Bay Area mortuary practices (Aten *et al.* 1976: Chapter 5), population estimates based on the studies of Mooney (1928) and Swanton (1911, 1946, 1952) were used for the first time as an element of analysis (as opposed to description) of this area. The estimate used (i.e., a standing population of about 300 persons in a zone about 30 km wide around Galveston Bay) was little more than a reasonable guess. In light of studies such as those of Jennings (1976) and Dobyns (1966), these estimates now seem highly suspect. Moreover, most estimates of seventeenth-century population used in the current scientific literature are traceable to Mooney and Swanton, but the data they used and their approach to these data are not always clear. In the case of Mooney (1928), the upper Texas coast sources appear to have been heavily based on information supplied by Bolton, augmented by guesses (Ubelaker 1976:278–280). As a result, and in consideration of their importance to clarifying the social context of mortuary practices, as well as investigating the man–land relationships of upper-coast cultures, a review of the original sources of population estimates for the area is undertaken here and new conclusions are drawn.[1]

[1]The direction of error in the Harris County Boys School report (Aten *et al.* 1976) was in making too conservative a population estimate. Rectification of that estimate serves to make even more likely the conclusion that archaeologically visible mortuary practices were conducted only in relatively few places and applied to relatively few people.

METHODS AND DATA

Of the basic approaches to population reconstruction—ethnohistorical, archaeological, and physical anthropological (Ubelaker 1975)—we will ultimately
need to make use of all three, if for no other reason than to develop independent
checks on the resulting estimates. The ethnohistorical approach at present is the
most practical, and is that to which nearly exclusive attention is devoted in this
study. As a result of the nature of the mortuary practices of the local native
populations on the upper coast (see Aten *et al.* 1976), the physical anthropological approach would uncover no more than a relatively small portion of their
skeletal remains. The archaeological approaches, on the other hand, probably
hold a great deal of promise: small-site studies in conjunction with habitation-
area studies (especially along the lines suggested by Weissner [1974] and Yellen
[1977]) should be fruitful, as should studies of upper coast winter encamp-
ments, winter being the season during which the maximum population aggregates apparently occurred. At present though, principal reliance must be
placed on published historical literature and documents.

The reconstruction attempted here is for the period extending from about
1700 to 1850. The standing population size (whatever it may have been) for the
seventeenth century probably can be taken as the population zenith for the
upper Texas coast, there being no apparent evidence to suggest larger populations earlier. From a reconstruction of this zenith baseline, archaeological research may work either forward or backward in time to study the population
behavior in relation to several factors, for example, technological innovations,
group fissioning and fusion, and settlement pattern changes. One may also
explore the question of functional population size for social groups in this area.
The maximum size estimates obviously have implications for adaptation, resource depletion, and other socioeconomic features. Of equal interest is the
minimum size below which the social system can no longer function. This
feature may be estimated by the population size at which groups began to
merge, as is evident in the late Historic period. It may even be asked whether the
fissioning process that presumably took place much earlier in the prehistory of
the area and the fusioning process that apparently took place at the end of the
existence of the native groups were in any way mirror images of each other.

In carrying out this review of population data, a wide range of the published
literature has been examined for estimates, although some items no doubt were
missed. These data are presented in Table 4.1 in chronological order by ethnic
group and with necessary annotations. For reasons explained in the table, not
all population estimates are used in analysis. For example, a great many Texas
guidebooks and histories of the mid-nineteenth century give population estimates, but here one needs to be cautious. These estimates were frequently
picked up without citation from earlier writers (or so it would appear); others

were written as reminiscences many decades after the observation. Principal reliance here is on eyewitness accounts, on second-hand accounts derived from the reports of an observer, or on accounts that can be supported by independent information.

Since the objective is to examine the time trends of population change through the Historic period, as well as to extrapolate back in time from this baseline, data has been included on the Atakapa, Bidai and Aranama, as well as on the Akokisa and Karankawa. Similarities or differences in their respective trends sheds light on the processes affecting gross population size. Figure 4.1 is a graphic representation of the time trends of data listed in Table 4.1.

A comment is in order at this point about how some of these data were formulated. Many records simply provide figures for numbers of families, or warriors, or men; to translate these estimates into numbers of individuals, all have been multiplied by a factor of 4. The basis for this factor is the average of several estimates of family size or ratios of men/warriors to others in the total society. These other estimates and their sources are given in Table 4.2. Although the ratios are not culturally homogeneous, they are estimates for inhabitants primarily of the upper Texas coast environment living under "primitive" conditions. Aside from the archaeological estimate derived from a much older skeletal population at Harris County Boys School (which has been excluded from the computation), the ratios are remarkably similar. The average of all estimates, except that for the Boys School cemetery, is four persons per family, which we have used to make all family/men/warrior conversions. In the process, it was assumed that there was one warrior per family and that, as used by most early writers on the study area, the terms men and warriors were used interchangeably. Of course, these assumptions may not be correct in every instance, but they reflect the best available information at present. It should be noted here, however, that Mayhall (1939:26) thought a factor of 5 was more realistic, although she did not present data to support her conclusion.

It is necessary to comment on the trends in population size for each native group. The curve in Figure 4.1a, for the Atakapa, is unfortunately very generalized, but its concave shape generally approximates the shape of population curves for the other groups for the same time period. The apparent survivorship of members of this group through the nineteenth century should be considered in light of the fact that in the early nineteenth century, many groups passed out of existence with their few remaining members becoming absorbed into some adjacent group. The recipient groups, under severe pressures themselves, were undoubtedly altered by this fusion process even though they may nominally have retained their former identity. For a brief time, the Karankawa consolidated and enlarged in this way; and the Bidai absorbed some of the Akokisa, as did the Atakapa. The Akokisa and the Karankawa disappeared at an early point in the nineteenth century. The Bidai and the Atakapa, however, seem to have retained their identity as functioning groups for a longer time. Indeed indi-

TABLE 4.1
Population Estimates for Upper Texas Coast Native Groups

Year	Reported estimate of native population	Comments	Population estimate used	Sources
		A. Akokisa		
Post-1830	Extinct(?)	—	0	No references to this group postdating 1830.
1828	40 families	Combined with estimate for Bidai.	<100(?)	Berlandier 1969:139, Footnote 205
1820	300 individuals	—	300	Padilla 1919:51
1820	200–300 individuals	Derived from Padilla (1919).	—	Berlandier 1969:139
1820	(?)	Combined Akokisa and Coco population estimate of 150 individuals; cannot separate.	—	Morse 1822
1778	50 men	—	200	Bolton 1913:347; Faulk 1964:58
1760–1770	80 men	—	320	Sibley 1807:44
Circa 1765	800 individuals	Pacheco claimed to have "reduced" two villages of 400 individuals each; this may be inflated to reflect personal accomplishment. Although not used here, it should not be dismissed altogether; it could be possible.	—	Bolton 1913:347
1764	150 individuals	All located at Orcoquisac; suggests an average of more than 100 per village.	500(?) (5 villages)	Bolton 1913:372
1756	20+ warriors	All located at Canos' village; suggests a total village population of 80 persons, confirms magnitude of 1764 estimate.	400+(?) (5 villages)	Bolton 1913:347
1747	300 families	—	1200	Bolton 1913:346
1721	200–250 individuals	Data from La Harpe and de Bellisle. If this only refers to the single band of de Bellisle, then 5 bands would total about 1000–1250.	200–250 or 1000–1250	Swanton 1946:86

Date	Estimate	Comments		Reference
1698	1750 individuals	Combined Akokisa, Bidai, Deadose estimate; basis unknown.	—	Swanton 1911:43–45
1690	500 individuals	Basis unknown; not used here.	—	Mooney 1928:13
1650	500 individuals	Basis unknown; not used here.	—	Swanton 1952:199

B. Bidai

Date	Estimate	Comments		Reference
1854	± 100 individuals	This many removed to Brazos Reserve; some were intermarried with other groups.	100	Sjoberg 1951b:395
1850	± 25 warriors	—	100	Bollaert 1850
Circa 1840	18–25 individuals	—	18–25	Bonnell 1840:139
1828	40 families	Estimate by General Teran.	160	Sanchez 1926:276
Circa 1826	± 500 individuals	Excessively out of phase with other estimates of the period.	—	Grimes cited in Gatschet 1891:39
1820	300 individuals	—	300	Padilla 1919:50
1820	120 individuals	—	120	Morse 1822:373
Circa 1805	100 men	—	400	Sibley 1807:43
1778	100 warriors	Postepidemic.	400	Morfi 1935/1967:105, Footnote 19
1777	200 warriors	Preepidemic.	800	Morfi 1935/1967:105, Footnote 19
1749	239 individuals	Combined Akokisa, Bidai, and Deadose population at San Ildefonso; cannot separate.	—	Bolton 1916:199
1690	500 individuals	Basis unknown; not used here.	—	Mooney 1928:13

C. Atakapa

Date	Estimate	Comments		Reference
1908	9 individuals	—	9	Swanton 1911:362
1907	25 individuals	Basis unknown but less likely to be a guess than other Mooney data.	25	Mooney 1928
1820	150 individuals	Combined Atakapa plus Coco; cannot separate.	—	Morse 1822:373
1805	50 men	Located near Calcasieu; may approximate a western Atakapa estimate.	200	Sibley 1807:51

(continued)

47

TABLE 4.1 (*Continued*)

Year	Reported estimate of native population	Comments	Population estimate used	Sources
1779	180 warriors	Minimum estimate; actual number probably larger.	>720	Swanton 1911:43–45
1698	1750 individuals	Apparently based on a linear extrapolation of the annual increment of decline between 1779 and 1805; not used.	—	Swanton 1911:43–45
1650	1500 individuals	Basis unknown; not used here.	—	Mooney 1928:9
		D. Karankawa		
1850	20 warriors	Probably too many but we have no basis to exclude this estimate.	80	Bollaert 1850
1843	40–50 individuals	This estimate appears in several mid-nineteenth-century Texas guidebooks; the ultimate source is unknown.	40–50	Roessler 1883:616
Circa 1840	Not more than 100 individuals	—	50–100(?)	Bonnell 1840:137
Circa 1836	200–250 warriors	Basis unknown; inconsistent with other estimates for the period.	—	Gatschet 1891:15
Circa 1836	3000 warriors	Estimate made as a very rough guess by Oliver; excessively out of phase with other estimates of the period.	—	Gatschet 1891:15
1835	± 50 warriors	In one camp near Refugio; this is an eyewitness account, but was written 50 years after the event; any total estimate from this would be huge for its period; not used.	—	Wilbarger 1889:198
1834	300 warriors	This many warriors reportedly massed at Matagorda; cannot relate this to an estimate of the Karankawa as a group.	—	Muckleroy 1922:230
Circa 1831	40–50 individuals	—	40–50	Holley 1833/1973

Date	Estimate	Comments	Estimate	Reference
Circa 1829	>100 families	Includes only Cocos and Cujanes.	>400	Berlandier 1969
1822	200–300 warriors	Karankawa, including Cokes and Cujanes.	800–1200	Kuykendall 1903:250
1822	± 1000 individuals	Basis unknown.	1000	Roessler 1883:616
1821	100 individuals	Seen at a single camp on Galveston Island; supports other estimates of high population in this period.	—	Wilbarger 1889:199
1820	± 400 individuals	For Cocos only; supports other high estimates for the period.	—	Padilla 1919:51
1820	(?)	Estimated 350 individuals for Karankawa and 150 individuals for Atakapa and Cocos; cannot adjust.	—	Morse 1822:373–374
1819	(?)	La Fitte reportedly fought 300 warriors; tends to support other high estimates.	—	Gracy 1964:41; Gatschet 1891
Circa 1805	500 men	Not clear if this is for all Karankawa groups.	2000(?)	Sibley 1807:45
Circa 1800	600 warriors	May not include Cocos; more or less consistent with previous estimate but sources unknown.	—	Bollaert 1850
Circa 1779	150 men	Unclear whether this is for the entire Karankawa tribe, or just the group of Carancaguases.	600	Morfi 1935/1967:79–80
1751	500 warriors	Excludes the Cocos; based on the 1820 Padilla estimate, we have added 500 individuals to account for the Cocos.	2500	Bolton 1906:115, 128
1690	2800 individuals	Basis unknown; not used.	—	Mooney 1928:13
1685	400 men	Margry's estimate for Bay Saint Louis Karankawa only; probably a very low estimate for the Karankawa tribal group.	>1600	Bolton 1908:274
		E. Aranama		
1843	Extinct	Contemporary estimate.	0	Swanton 1952:308
1820	120 individuals	Plus "a goodly number of women and children."	120	Morse 1822:374
1772	46 warriors		184	Bolton 1914:28, 291; cf. Faulk 1964:58
1690	200 individuals	Basis unknown; not used.	—	Mooney 1928:13

TABLE 4.2
Ratios Used on the Upper Texas Coast of the Number of Individuals to the Estimates of Men, Warriors, and Families

Ratio[a]	Basis	Source
1 warrior:4 persons	Karankawa; 100 individuals included 25 warriors.	Bonnell 1840:137
1 family:4 persons	Karankawa; circa 1840	Gatschet 1891:65
1 warrior:3.5 persons	Basis unknown	Swanton 1911:43–45
1 family:4 persons	Akokisa; basis unknown	Bolton 1913:346
1 family:3.7 persons	65 Akokisa, Bidai, and Deadose families totaled 239 individuals.	Bolton 1916:199
1 family:4.9 persons	From census of persons under Spanish control in 1775.	Morfi 1935/1967:103
1 family:3.98 persons	From Akokisa or Coco skeletal data, circa A.D. 1500	Aten *et al.* 1976:90
1 family:6.38 persons	From archaeological skeletal data, circa A.D. 900	Aten *et al.* 1976:90
1 warrior:4 persons	Used by Morfit in 1836 to estimate the native population of Texas.	Muckleroy 1922:241–242

[a] In summary, excluding the 6.38 person estimate, $N = 8$, $\bar{X} = 4.01$ persons, and $s = 0.40$ persons, and including the 6.38 person estimate, $N = 9$, $\bar{X} = 4.27$ persons, and $s = 0.87$ persons.

vidual members have been locatable into the early twentieth century, although their relationship culturally and biologically to the protohistoric Atakapa and Bidai is an arguable matter.

In Figure 4.1b are shown the data for the Bidai. This time trend is very straightforward and shows a sharp decline around A.D. 1775, a leveling off until early in the nineteenth century; further decline nearly to extinction by the 1830's; perhaps a slight recovery of population about the middle of the nineteenth century, and then total extinction.

In Figure 4.1c are the data for the Akokisa. The general form of this curve is similar to that for the Bidai. The record begins with a period of relatively slight decline in the early part of the eighteenth century followed by a sharp decline in the middle of the century; this is followed by a leveling off of the decline, and perhaps even a slight increase up to the first quarter of the nineteenth century, followed by a rapid decline to extinction by some time around 1830. A comment is in order here in the data used for the period of 1721. This was obtained from Swanton (1946) who said the data came from de Bellisle and from La Harpe. I have been unable to locate the source in which this figure is given, but it is absent from Folmer (1940). The number is used since it is represented as a factual accounting, and, presumably, Swanton obtained it from some manuscript source. Although we do show a 200–250 datum (marked with a subscript a), it clearly is out of phase with the later information. The interpretation here is that the estimate reportedly given by de Bellisle was for one village of Akokisa and not for the entire group. If one accepts Orobio's estimate of four or five Akokisa villages in the middle of the eighteenth century, this suggests a minimum population in 1721 of 1000 to 1250 persons, which figure is shown labeled with a subscript b.

In Figure 4.1d are the data for the Karankawa. Again, the general shape of the curve resembles the others just described. In this case, a period of decline in the last half of the eighteenth century is succeeded by a period of even more precipitous decline near to extinction in the first quarter of the nineteenth century. This decline is followed by what may have been a slight population recovery around 1850 followed quickly by extinction.

Several features of these data require some comment. The population estimate for 1685 (subscript c) was explicitly for those Indians living about Bay Saint Louis (Lavaca–Matagorda Bay) and is used here as an estimate only for the Karankawa proper. Points b and d are not entirely clear as to their referent; d, especially, may only refer to the Karankawa proper (see Table 4.1 for details). In any event, if these points are plotted graphically, as on Figure 4.1, a choice must be made of linking points a to b, or a to d to b, and so on. In view of the great differences between the sizes of these estimates, the latter alternative seems most unlikely. On the other hand, if one selects the former alternative and then links points c and d, the two resulting lines are more or less parallel. This solution to the problem is attractive if one assumes that depopulation processes were affecting all of the Karankawa tribal group approximately equally and that a roughly similar relationship would exist between the population of the various constituent tribes of the larger Karankawa group. This assumption could be very risky, but at the moment provides a serviceable explanation of the data.

Finally, in Figure 4.1e are presented the limited data on the Aranama. Here, too, the pattern resembles those for the other groups in that a period of relatively slow decline in the late eighteenth century and early nineteenth century is followed by precipitous decline to extinction.

The nature of the available data is such that the individual graphic displays in Figure 4.1 do not reflect organizations at similar levels of integration. The Louisiana Atakapa, Akokisa, and Bidai are all presumed to be constituents of the major linguistic grouping called Atakapa and are assumed to be at a comparable level of integration to the Coco, Cujane, Guapite, etc., of the Karankawa group. This assumption, of course, follows the interpretations of Bolton and Swanton and is mindful that these are based heavily on "guilt by association." For example, review their treatment of data on the Bidai. The population curve for the Karankawa reflects a more abstract organizational level than do the other curves. There is nothing to be done about this limitation at present other than not to lose sight of it.

Collectively these five population curves all suggest the same, or a similar, situation. That is, a period of apparent relative stability or slow decline in the early eighteenth century is followed by a major, in some cases almost in-

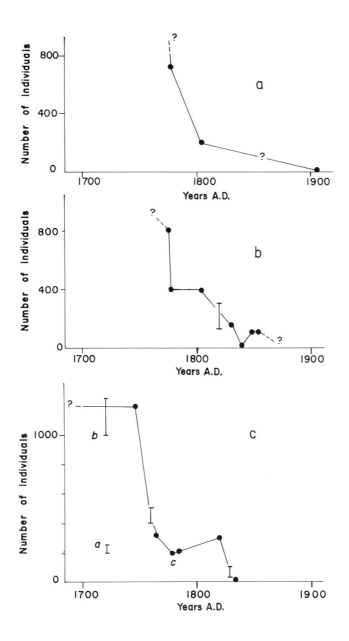

FIGURE 4.1 Population estimates—(a) Atakapa (Louisiana), (b) Bidai, (c) Akokisa, (d) Karankawa, and (e) Aranama—and (f) model of population decline—for upper Texas coast native groups in the eighteenth and nineteenth centuries.

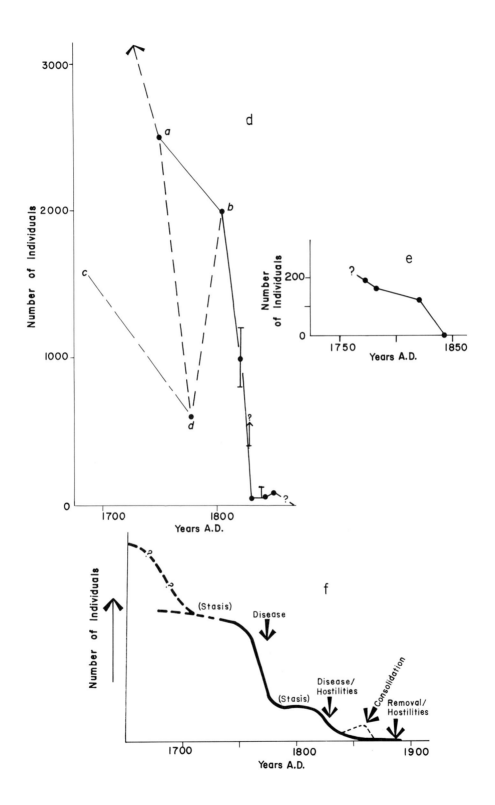

stantaneous, decline in the third quarter of the eighteenth century, followed either by another stasis or by a period of much reduced rate of decline into the early part of the nineteenth century. This decline is followed by another sharp decline in the first quarter of the century with some groups becoming extinct and others showing a slight and short-lived period of population recovery and then going into extinction, usually about the middle of the century.

These patterns do not reflect a simple model, but one that likely embodies several components (Figure 4.1). Its principal features are twofold: a "stairstep" form in which population size descends to extinction; and, frequently on the last step, a slight rise or recovery. The suggestion has already been made that this latter feature may be due to consolidation of local groups into composite bands. The former feature (i.e., the stepwise decline) has not been discussed at all up to this point and in order to know on what basis to try to reconstruct protohistoric population levels, an attempt must be made to understand the immediate operative factors in the decline.

Mooney (1928:7, 12), in reference to the Gulf states generally, considered the chief causes of population decrease to be smallpox, alcoholic dissipation and demoralization, wars, slave raids, restraints of mission and reservation conditions, and removals to reservations. It might also be presumed that some of these factors, singly or jointly, had some impact on fecundity. Of these causes, there probably are only three major possibilities affecting the upper Texas coast: change in the rate of death through armed conflict, increased death through disease and associated factors, and relocation out of the area.

In general, the period of exploration and colonization by the Spanish was *not* marked by any significant armed conflict that would have resulted in a regular, ongoing death toll as a new component of the area's mortality rate. On the other hand, such conflict did occur between native groups; but since we presume this to have been a feature reaching far back into prehistoric times (cf. Bandelier 1905:74), it is difficult to conclude that this may have introduced any new pressure for population decline into the situation. However, once Anglo colonization of concessions from the Mexican government began in the 1820s, armed conflict (i.e., raiding) became a more common feature of native–European interaction, especially for the Karankawa. It is difficult to estimate whether the resultant death toll was sufficiently large to make a major impact except that by this time the native population had been so reduced that *any* further reduction was probably a serious matter.

The Spanish also made a rather ineffective attempt at establishing a mission system in Texas as part of their program to exercise political control over the area (cf. Kinnaird 1958:172). This effort did involve the relocation of natives from time to time, but rarely seems to have been permanent so far as the coastal groups were concerned. The impact of the missionary effort on population structure is not discernible at present. Later, Indians were relocated to reserves, but only the remnant of the Bidai, among the groups we are interested in, seems to have been affected by this. The third factor, disease, is one for which enough data exist to recognize its major significance in the upper coast demographic history.

IMPACT OF DISEASE

Almost from the moment of Cabeza de Vaca's arrival on the Texas coast in 1528, natives began dying from diseases introduced by Europeans. The serious impact of epidemic diseases is often cited, but usually in a vague way, and no one has attempted to assess quantitatively the role of these diseases in the demography of the upper Texas coast native populations (however, see Ewers 1973 for a nearby example). In recent years, documentary studies have brought the magnitude of this problem more into focus. As a general matter, the population decline in the first century or so of frequent European–Indian contact has usually been in the range of 75–95% in most areas that have been studied (Cook 1973; Dobyns 1966; Jennings 1976; Stearn and Stearn 1945).

In the case of the New England colonies, a 1765 report noted that among the English settlers the mortality rate was about 12–14%. Among native groups, however, mortality rates, even into the nineteenth century, were commonly 55–90%, although this rate varied widely from ±1% to over 95% depending on such factors as type of smallpox, virulence of the virus, and type of care received (Stearn and Stearn 1945:14–15).

Typically, disease struck native populations in two forms (cf. Cook 1973): widespread and lethal epidemics of infectious diseases producing spectacular mortalities in short periods of time, and chronic diseases producing a continuous long-term impact. Cook concluded that the mean annual population decline among New England Indians referable to all types of diseases amounted to about 1.5% of the existing population with 88–100% of the population reduced in the first century of contact (1973:497). In the major study of this issue, Dobyns concluded that a depopulation ratio of 20:1 (i.e., a reduction of 95%) existed about a century or so after the initiation of regular contact (Dobyns 1966:414).

Such high mortalities were not solely a matter of the inability of the native immunity systems to cope with new viruses. More difficult to assess than actual accounts of epidemics and mortality figures are the predisposing causes "such as exposure to weather, malnutrition or outright starvation, bad sanitation, and an all-pervasive feeling of despair," which rendered populations highly vulnerable to disease (Cook 1973:505). Cook goes on to note that to the extent disease resulted in the decline of native populations, this was a medium acting "essentially as the outlet through which many other factors found expression [1973:506]." Evidence of these kinds of factors was not often recorded for the upper Texas coast, but is not totally absent. For example, Wesolowsky and

Malina (in Aten *et al.* 1976) suggested that several systemic factors relating to the settlement pattern resulted in seasonally specific mortality for the prehistoric period. This would seem to indicate the existence of some of the predisposing factors mentioned by Cook. There is also a note on the mental state of the Karankawa in the early nineteenth century: "their continued wars . . . have reduced them to a mere handful, and their spirits have met with a corresponding depression [Bonnell 1840:137]."

There is evidence to indicate that, in general, the type of health care they received contributed significantly to a reduction of the mortality rate among native groups. In an 1898 case among the Pueblo Indians, application of European medical practices reduced smallpox mortality from 74% to 10% (Stearn and Stearn 1945:15). In addition to the nature of health care, a general failure by Native Americans to appreciate the significance of quarantine (even though its use as a control measure was known) also contributed to the enlargement of local smallpox outbreaks to epidemic proportions (Stearn and Stearn 1945:16).

Specific records of epidemics among the native groups of the upper Texas coast are largely absent. There are some lines of evidence, but to place these in any kind of meaningful perspective, it is necessary to reach farther afield for records of chronic and epidemic disease. In order for these to have any significance for the problem of reconstructing upper coast native population sizes, it is necessary to establish that the conditions or the opportunities existed for infection to have occurred (cf. Cook 1973:486; Ewers 1973).

Prior to the first quarter of the eighteenth century, direct European intrusion into the area of the upper Texas coast was very slight. The only known contacts in this early period were Cabeza de Vaca and his shipmates in 1528, La Salle's attempt to establish a colony on Lavaca Bay in 1685, and Alonso de Leon's expedition to drive out La Salle in 1690. There is evidence that both Cabeza de Vaca and La Salle brought infectious diseases with them (Morfi 1935/1967:138; Nixon 1946:32). Around 1720, contacts between the European and the Indian of the upper Texas coast began with the captivity of Simars de Bellisle, the La Harpe expedition to the Texas coast, and the expedition of the Marquis de Aguayo to establish a mission and a presidio at the site of La Salle's fort, and steadily increased in frequency. Although direct records are largely absent, the previously cited 1745 expedition of Orobio y Bazterra discovered evidence of fairly intensive efforts by the French to establish influence among the Indians along the Spanish–French frontier.

Thus, French traders from the Mississippi were reported by the Akokisa to have traveled by ship and overland venturing up the Neches, Trinity, San Jacinto, and Brazos rivers since at least 1738 or 1739 (Bolton 1913:342–344; Castañeda 1939:48). Presumably this means that the Karankawa, Akokisa, Bidai, and western Atakapa, at least, were being reached along the coast by the French in this early time period. Indeed, Blancpain, the Frenchman who was arrested by the Spanish at Orcoquisac in 1754, claimed that he had traded with the Atakapa for more than 25 years (Bolton 1913:348). Blancpain further claimed that until a short time before his arrest at Orcoquisac he had been accompanied "by a considerable party [Bolton 1913:349]." If true, these contacts would have exposed some upper Texas coast Indians to sources of chronic, if not virulent, infectious diseases from Blancpain's and similar parties as early as circa 1725.

It is known, further, that Orobio y Bazterra discovered that the French came to the area annually; that they came in summer, which could mean almost any time between May and October; that the French were not in the area in March; that Blancpain was arrested at Orcoquisac in October; that he had been out trading with the Atakapa for the previous two months; and that there was an implication of trading with the Bidai, as well as the Akokisa (Bolton 1913:342–344). From this it might be concluded that the French trading in the upper Galveston–Trinity Bay area most likely took place in the August–October period to take advantage, among the Akokisa at least, of the probable annual congregation of the bands about the upper end of the bay prior to their return to winter camps (Folmer 1940:217). The significance of this is not only that the opportunities for contact with Europeans existed, but also that these conditions may have optimized the chances for transmission of infectious diseases in the coastal environment.

There also is an account of Frenchmen being lost among the Cujanes in the early 1740s and another party of French being shipwrecked while searching for the first group in 1744 or 1745. It seems to be generally acknowledged that these accounts and especially the capture of Blancpain in 1754 were only the more noticeable aspects of general French and, later, English intrusions on the coast and inland principally for the purposes of the fur trade (Morfi 1935/1967:373).

In any event, these discoveries by Orobio y Bazterra initiated a period of intense Spanish counter-activities that lasted essentially until the abandonment (in 1771) of the mission and presidio at Orcoquisac. Prior to the establishment of these in 1756, Spanish agents acting as traders regularly visited the Akokisa and the Bidai. But, evidently, throughout this period of greater Spanish attention, the French continued to penetrate the area to some extent (Bolton 1913:343–344). For example, in 1759 there were reports of French encampment among the Karankawa on the Brazos River (Bolton 1913:369). More significantly, an incident was reported in which 2 Frenchmen and 100 Louisiana Indians entered the Akokisa country, probably to the east of Orcoquisac. These groups attempted to arouse the natives into attacking and eliminating the Spanish mission and presidio complex at Orcoquisac, but they were repulsed by the Spanish (Bolton 1913:369).

In this same period of the 1750s, the Indians from Bidai and Akokisa villages visited Los Adaes and one Akokisa headman, known as Canos, even visited New Orleans (Bolton 1913:351). Also, in this period of the mid-eighteenth century, the impact of the Spanish mission system was beginning to be felt among the native groups of the upper Texas coast. Coco, Cujane, Karankawa, Bidai, Akokisa, and others entered and left missions throughout Texas and in the process received and transmitted infectious diseases.

Throughout the last half of the eighteenth century, the problem of shipwrecks continued, probably at an accelerating rate. The Karankawa and Akokisa made something of a name for themselves as a result of their habit of plundering such wrecks. In any event, in the 1760s, a band of Acadians was shipwrecked on the central Texas coast and made their way overland back to Louisiana (Bolton 1913:376–377).

By the last quarter of the eighteenth century, the English were regularly penetrating eastern Texas along the coast and inland rivers possibly in preparation for a settlement (Morfi 1935/1967:426). In 1777, an English packet boat carrying bricks and other materials to supply just such a settlement was attacked by Atakapa Indians in the mouth of the Neches River (Morfi 1935/1967:62).

Trading activities became progresssively more intense along the coast into the early nineteenth century. According to Dyer (1917:4), the members of the Lafitte commune on Galveston Island (circa 1817–1821) found it more profitable to dispose of the merchandise they captured by trading it off to the Indians than by selling it to middlemen in New Orleans or Baltimore. In this trade, Lafitte's group operated along all of the Gulf coast from the country of the Aranama on the west to the Mermenteau River of south Louisiana in the east. They entered navigable streams and harbors and included on their rounds some white settlements that were already in existence.

From this evidence it can be concluded that the period of early European–Native American contacts brought abundant opportunities for the transmission of disease. As will be seen shortly, virulent epidemics ravaged the native populations to the east and southwest of the area in the sixteenth and seventeenth centuries. The effect of these epidemics on the upper Texas coast populations would have depended to a large degree on the amount of interaction among the respective local territorial groups. As of 1720, however, there can be no doubt that the opportunity for European transmission of infectious diseases to the native populations of the upper Texas coast was frequent and grew in intensity with the passage of time.

Before reviewing the record for disease outbreaks in the general Texas area, it must be understood that an equally important aspect of the impact of diseases on native populations was the effect of endemic and chronic diseases. These went largely without notice as individual entities against the more spectacular mortalities of the periodic epidemics. Cook (1973:493 ff.) has pointed out that diseases such as tuberculosis, dysentery, pneumonia, influenza, spotted fever, measles, and syphilis (French disease) subjected the native populations of New England to "uninterrupted attrition." There is no reason to believe that the situation in Texas was any different.

There is little information on precisely which diseases were afflicting the coastal populations of Texas; smallpox and measles were certainly present in the area or very nearby (Morfi 1935/1967:307; Bolton, cited in Newcomb 1961:36; Sibley 1807:40). References are also made to yellow fever (Dyer 1917:5;

Gatschet and Swanton 1932:16; Pratt 1954); dysentery (Dyer 1917:107); malaria (Ewers 1973:107; Kinnaird 1958:177); fevers, skin diseases and venereal disease (Morfi 1932:55), and scurvy (Kinnaird 1958:177).

Mention is made of other serious illnesses but their identity remains unclear. Cabeza de Vaca, for example, said "the natives fell sick from the stomach, so that one half of them died [Bandelier 1905:64]." This was suggested to have been cholera by Nixon (1946:32). Sibley (1807:41) noted that around 1790, "a dreadful sickness" struck the Caddos.

In spite of these other records, there is no doubt that periodic smallpox epidemics were the major killer. Smallpox epidemics were recorded in Mexico every 17 or 18 years beginning in 1520 (Stearn and Stearn 1945:42).[2] Within a month of the arrival of Cabeza de Vaca's group, fully half of the population of the native village that had rescued them on the beaches of Malhado had died from a disease that apparently was viral in nature—possibly cholera. Campbell (1977) notes that the populations of the southerly Coahuiltecan groups in northeastern Mexico began to decline as a result of diseases once European settlements were established in the late sixteenth and early seventeenth centuries. Bosque's 1675 expedition through Eagle Pass and into the Edwards County area of west Texas encountered three tribes that were being affected by smallpox (Bolton, cited in Newcomb 1961:36).

When La Salle arrived at Matagorda Bay in February of 1685, he visited a native winter camp containing about 50 huts (Joutel 1962:50). The presence of such a large native village as well as the lack of any mention of disease suggest that the central coast had not yet been affected. However, not long after this, two survivors of La Salle's colony near Lavaca Bay told Alonso de Leon that during the 1688–1689 period more than 100 of the settlers had died from smallpox (Morfi 1935/1967:138). Although one can only speculate about possible effects of this outbreak, the fact that La Salle's colonists did not appear to mingle with the natives may mean that the smallpox did not necessarily spread to them at this time. On the other hand, the fact that this period is synchronous with major epidemics that raged in the eastern United States (Stearn and Stearn 1945:22) is an ominous sign. In 1691, Father Massanet reported an unidentified epidemic disease had spread throughout eastern Texas and Louisiana killing at least 3000 Caddo (Mooney 1928:12; Nixon 1946:4). And in 1698–1699, the whole lower Mississippi Valley was affected by a smallpox epidemic (Stearn and Stearn 1945:33).

In fact, Stearn and Stearn (1945:22) have shown that during the seventeenth and eighteenth centuries, the eastern North American colonies were struck by a continuous series of violent smallpox epidemics, some of which were quite widespread. The dates of these were approximately in the years 1633–1634, 1649, 1666, 1678, 1689, 1702, 1721, 1730, 1752, 1764, and 1778–1779. These

---

[2]The first definite record of smallpox north of Mexico is the 1633–1634 epidemic in the New England colonies (Cook 1973; Stearn and Stearn 1945:20–22).

epidemics became progressively more widespread, as the disease was on its way to becoming endemic to the continent. The most widespread and fatal epidemics occurred in 1747, 1763, and, especially, 1779 (Stearn and Stearn 1945:42); many of these dates coincide with the Texas reports.

Numerous records of native mortality in Texas exist as soon as extensive contact with the Spanish missions began in the period about 1750. An epidemic occurred in San Antonio around 1750 that reduced the numbers of neophytes there (Bolton 1906:122). In 1749, Fray Benito Fernández de Santa Anna went among the Coco on the coast to try to persuade them to return to La Candelaria mission on the San Gabriel River from whence they had recently left; he found them in their homeland suffering from smallpox and measles (Morfi 1935/1967:307). It appears that the Bidai at Mission San Ildefonso were heavily struck by disease in 1749 (Bolton 1915:232). In 1751, a group of 54 Cujane moved to Mission Espíritu Santo de Zuñiga on the Guadalupe River for a period of only 2 ½ months; while there, the missionaries baptized 15 of these natives on their deathbeds (Bolton 1906:126). Disease is not mentioned as the cause but would certainly seem to be indicated for such a high mortality. Finally, we note that by the 1750s, the Coahuiltecan bands on the lower coast had been severely reduced or eliminated by smallpox and measles (Bolton 1914:1, 27).

In 1764, a smallpox outbreak occurred in the Mission Espíritu Santo de Zuñiga at Goliad in which many Indian neophytes and whites died (Mayhall 1939:115, Footnote 142). In 1766, smallpox and measles were reported epidemic among the Karankawa on the Texas coastal islands (Castañeda 1939:179, 220; Nixon 1946:11). In 1767, while at Presidio Nuestra Señora de Loreto, Nicolas de Lafora noted, "There is a strong tendency toward scurvy and a great many people die of it. Few escape malaria in any year [Kinnaird 1958:177]."

In 1778–1779, smallpox raged throughout the east Texas area killing, among others, about half of the Bidai warrior population (Mooney 1928:12; Morfi 1935/1967:105, Footnote 19; Stearn and Stearn 1945:46). Finally, we have the mention by Sibley (1807:41) of "a dreadful sickness" around 1790. Another major epidemic of smallpox occurring in 1801 devastated the remaining native populations on the Plains from the Dakotas to the Gulf of Mexico (Mooney 1928:12; Sibley 1807; Stearn and Stearn 1945:75). Subsequent to this time, smallpox was endemic throughout the North American continent (Stearn and Stearn 1945:77), and Berlandier (1969:84) reported in 1828 that smallpox occurred among the Indians every 16 years.

MAXIMUM POPULATION LEVELS, CIRCA A.D. 1700

As a result of this review it is seen that severe epidemic (and, presumably, chronic) diseases surrounded the upper Texas coast area on all sides almost from the time of first contact in 1528. And while it is exceedingly difficult to evaluate the impact of disease on protohistoric population sizes in the study area, it simply cannot be doubted that Indians of the upper coast suffered severely from the 1720s onward. The inference of major impact is unavoidable and is no different from the experience of the native populations in other areas.

The only mediating factor to be considered seriously as an element working against the establishment of basic conditions for the epidemic spread of disease was the native settlement pattern, especially the scheduling and size of population aggregation. At present, little more can be done than to speculate on the quantitative impact of the more dispersed settlement pattern among the coastal groups as opposed to, say, village agriculturalists. One may confidently draw the further inference that any population level indicated by the data for the mid-eighteenth century period, will be one already depressed, perhaps substantially, from the protohistoric levels. It is difficult, though, to develop specific numbers to express this. The best that may be hoped for at this time is a qualitative model that will serve to advance the issue of estimating sizes of native populations on the upper Texas coast.

The extrapolation methods utilized by Mooney (1928) and Swanton (1911) for the upper coast native groups are not entirely clear. Mooney usually employed an additive approach, sometimes called the "dead-reckoning" method (Ubelaker 1974:2). Swanton's figures are best, although not precisely, replicated by a linear model based on the average rate of decline in the 1779–1805 period. Later, however, Swanton (1952) yielded to Mooney's figures, which were slightly lower. In any event, today we have the benefit of a number of studies of population decline, most of which demonstrate population decay trajectories of a more or less concave form. As described earlier for the Texas coast, local variations may be expected. The best hope at present for developing a model is probably to deduce some reduction factor or rate to apply to their nadir population levels for the Texas groups as was done by Dobyns (1966) and Cook (1973).

A major difficulty with this approach is in deciding on the size of the nadir in a population being steadily reduced to extinction. Practically speaking, and since Dobyns's major thesis is that disease was the main agent of decline (a view with which I agree except possibly for the very latest period when extinction was finally brought about), the nadir should be that lowest level to which population declined primarily due to disease, but from which population survival and recovery would have been possible, all other factors being equal. It is assumed this level is approximated in the Texas data by the break or stasis in the population curves that occurred sometime around 1800 (Figure 4.1). After this stage in the population decline, other factors assumed greater significance than disease and drove the populations down to extinction. Among these factors were Anglo appropriation of Indian lands, failure by the Mexican government to enforce the "Karankawa reserve," genocidal policies of some colonists, and a residual disease component.

A second assumption made for this problem is in reference to the model of population behavior (Figure 4.1f). In light of the data just reviewed on the record of diseases for the area and of the opportunities for transmission to the native populations, it will be assumed that the steplike character of the model back to about 1750 was preceded by at least one more major decrement in the period from 1720 to 1750. Beyond this assumption, each group still must be reviewed separately rather than simply applying a blanket depopulation ratio.

The nadir level for the Akokisa was about 200 individuals and the maximum known population was about 1200 persons in the mid-eighteenth century (Figure 4.1c). A 75% reduction ratio is unlikely since this would result in an original population of 800 persons—less than that observed by several reporters at the period of the 1750s. On the other hand, a 95% reduction ratio would result in an estimate of 4000 persons, which is unattractive only in that there is not a shred of other evidence in its support. For our purposes here, we have simply split the difference and suggest a reduction ratio somewhere in the range of 85–90%. The former rate approximates the highest observed population in the mid-eighteenth century; the latter is speculative but allows for pre-1750 decreases. This latter estimate (about 2000 persons) recalls the claim by Captain Pacheco to have "reduced" (i.e., to mission life) two Akokisa villages of 400 persons each (Bolton 1913:347). This claim usually has been dismissed as boastfulness in a missionary field generally devoid of accomplishment. Also, it is not in accord with the other two contemporaneous estimates (by Orobio y Bazterra and Miranda; see Table 4.1). On the other hand, it is generally agreed that there were five Akokisa villages. If Pacheco's estimate was accurate and reflected the size of all the villages, there would have been a total population estimate similar to that just deduced. Another way to look at this is that even if Pacheco overstated his accomplishment, this does not require that he overstate the actual size of the Akokisa villages. Moreover, Pacheco spent several years in the area, whereas Orobio y Bazterra and Miranda only passed through briefly; as a result there is just as much, if not more, reason to suspect the Orobio y Bazterra and Miranda estimates as to discount the Pacheco estimate.

The Bidai have been approached in a very different manner. Probably because of their less intensive contact with European traders in the mid-eighteenth century, the nadir of the Bidai appears to be about 400 individuals. As a result, to apply the same 85–90% reduction ratio as was done for the Akokisa will result in very high protohistoric population estimates—so high that they seem most unlikely. Instead, the 1749 statement of Father Ganzabal has been recalled to the effect that, if he had the means to support them, he could have added to Mission San Ildefonso *all three* bands of the Bidai and *all five* bands of the Akokisa (Bolton 1915:232). Because of the apparent great similarity between the culture of the Bidai and of the Akokisa, the possibly risky assumption is made that these bands were about equivalent in size and that the Bidai therefore should be roughly $\frac{3}{5}$ the size of the Akokisa. This may be an uncertain approach, but it seems more rational than trying to conjure up a reason to adopt a different depopulation ratio for the Bidai than for the Akokisa, es-

TABLE 4.3
Territorial Areas, Protohistoric Population Sizes, and Population Density Estimates

Territorial group	Area[a] (miles²)	Area[a] (km²)	Population estimate (proto-historic) (c. 1700)	Population density[b] (per mile²)	Population density[b] (per km²)	Other population estimates Mooney (1928)	Other population estimates Swanton (1911)	Other population estimates Swanton (1952)
Atakapa	—	—	1333–2000	—	—	1500	1750	1500
Akokisa	4600	11,900	1333–2000	0.43	0.17	500	—	500
Upper territory	(2800)	(7200)	—	0.71	0.28	—	1750[c]	—
Lower territory	(1800)	(4700)	—	1.11	0.43	—	—	—
Bidai	3500	8900	800–1200	0.34	0.13	500	—	500
Karankawa	5500	14,200	4000–6000	1.09	0.42	2800	—	2800

[a]Rounded off to nearest 100.
[b]For purpose of this table, densities were only calculated for the larger population estimate when a range is given.
[c]Also includes Deadose.

pecially in the absence of any independent verification. The results of these approximations are shown in Table 4.3.

Since it has not been possible to prepare complete maps of the Atakapa territory, making impossible the preparation of population density computations, no special attention is given to population estimates for this group. If the provisional 85–90% reduction ratio derived here is applied, estimates are obtained that are identical to those for the Akokisa. Whether or not this is reasonable cannot now be determined.

The nadir population for the Karankawa tribal group is approximately 2000 persons, but this step in the population curve is not as well defined as it is for some of the other groups. Again, to apply a reduction ratio of 85–90% would result in enormous protohistoric population estimates, which might be correct, but for which there is no independent confirmation. Again, the major factor, as with the Bidai, is probably the relatively lower level of contact intensity with the Europeans in the early eighteenth century. For example, Bolton noted,

> the Karankawan tribes of the coast proved hostile to the French and Spaniards alike, and, while their savage life and inhospitable country offered little to attract the missionary, their small influence over the other groups of natives rendered them relatively useless as a basis for extending Spanish political authority [1908:252].

Here, there are many possibilities, and for reasons solely of internal consistency in this study and as an interim strategy until better data are available, the same reduction ratios will be applied to the Karankawa as were applied to the Bidai. Both the Karankawa and the Bidai appear to have been somewhat less exposed to Europeans in the earlier part of the eighteenth century. In other words, this suggests that the Akokisa, and probably the Atakapa as well, bore the brunt of losses from the transmission of pathogenic organisms, primarily from French traders in the second quarter of the eighteenth century, and as a result were in a more advanced state of reduction at the time of the 1800 stasis that I have adopted as the local population nadir.

POPULATION DENSITIES

Given the preceding reconstructions of territories and population sizes, population density estimates also have been calculated for all native groups but the Atakapa (Table 4.3). These indicate very close similarity between the Karankawa territory, occupying a wholly coastal area, and the coastal part of the Akokisa territory. Moving to the interior, there is a population density gradient that is greatest at the coast and declines as one goes to the interior through the inland winter territory of the Akokisa and on to the territory of the Bidai. We are not interested in quibbling over the absolute magnitude of these numbers. However, as a result of applying similar assumptions to all groups, a measure of internal consistency may have been achieved in postulating population size and territorial area relationships on the upper Texas coast. The previously mentioned agreement between density estimates for the Karankawa and the coastal Akokisa is an encouraging indication of such internal consistency. However, independent verification may be sought by comparison of the upper coast data against (a) previous estimates of population densities among hunter–gatherers; (b) theoretical models of density gradients; and (c) theoretical models of the ratio of actual population density to the potential maximum population density of an area.

Kroeber (1939:171) used Mooney's population estimates, which have been argued here as being too low. Kroeber's estimates for territorial area on the upper coast are much larger than those used here (from Figure 3.1) and their source is unknown. As a result, his estimates of density are lower than those in Table 4.3 by many orders of magnitude and further comparison does not seem useful. Okada (cited in Fried 1967:55) has reported densities ranging from 1.9 persons per km^2 (Andaman Islands) to 0.002 persons per km^2 (Barren Ground of the Canadian Arctic) for egalitarian band level societies. Steward (1955:125) gave estimates of 0.1–0.01 persons per km^2, but did not consider either of the extreme situations cited by Okada. Wobst (1974:170) assembled data on population densities for hunters and gatherers around the world and determined them to range between 0.002–0.8 persons per km^2. Thus the measured population densitites for the upper Texas coast (Table 4.3) are within the middle of the ranges as given by Okada and by Wobst. Unfortunately, this is not a particularly useful comparison except at the grossest level of differentiation from food-producing societies.

A model for comparison of the density gradient going inland from the coastal zone may be constructed with data available in the ecological literature on the primary productivity of various habitats. Fortunately, much of what is needed has already been compiled (Casteel 1972). In Casteel's study, the closest approximation of the habitat transect represented by the coastal Akokisa–Karankawa, inland Akokisa, and Bidai territories are the population densities for tertiary consumers in salt marsh, temperate terrestrial herb, and temperate deciduous forest ecosystems (23.6, 15.5, and 9.3 persons per km^2 respectively). If Casteel's data and the Texas data are normalized by expressing the inland densities as a decimal fraction of the coastal density, the *structure* of the two data sets may be compared. In this comparison, both the coastal Akokisa and the salt marsh ecosystem are set arbitrarily at a value of unity. The remaining values are as follows: (a) 0.64 is the inland Akokisa and 0.66 the temperate terrestrial herbs ecosystem; (b) 0.34 is the Bidai territory and 0.39 the temperate deciduous forest ecosystem. The congruence between these two data sets is strong evidence that the Texas reconstructions express valid orders of magnitude differences between the several tribal territories.

In addition to examining the structural validity of the population density reconstructions, one also may test whether the relationship is realistic between

the magnitudes of the Texas density reconstructions and the potential maximum density levels (assuming consumption of 100% of net primary production) in the same three model habitats used above. Estimates of the amount of
net primary production actually used in supporting human food needs range
from 0.5–5% (Casteel 1972:21–22). An approximation of this proportion in the
Texas situation can be made by determining the ratio between measured densities for the Texas habitat and for the corresponding model habitat. The results
range between 2.2 and 2.9%, again confirming that the upper coast population
reconstructions are broadly consistent with theoretical expectations and may
serve as a starting point for subsistence and other studies requiring population
estimates.

CHAPTER 5

Social Organization

Having presented estimates of the territories, population sizes, and population densities of the local territorial groups of the upper Texas coast in the protohistoric and late historic periods, it now is appropriate to consider the organizational features of these societies insofar as these may influence or be reflected in the archaeological record. Although vague descriptions of the social organization of upper coast groups may be found (e.g., Newcomb 1961), the effort to use this information in the analysis of archaeological data began with the analysis of Galveston Bay area mortuary practices (Aten et al. 1976).

At that time, it was assumed, on the basis of very tenuous evidence, that male-centered egalitarian bands were the organizational concept that would link together the status, mortuary practice, technological, population, and scheduling data obtained from the archaeological record. Although this was probably a fairly safe assumption, more evidence can now be offered for further clarification. This chapter begins with a review and expansion of the status framework initially outlined in Aten et al. (1976:102–105). These statuses are then integrated into a hierarchy. This is followed by a consideration of relationships between organizational entities and individuals as evidenced through their reciprocal relations.

STATUSES

As we try to develop a sociological frame of reference for the archaeological record of the upper Texas coast, it is necessary to attempt to define the actors, or social personae, through whom cultural processes were enacted. The identity and relationships of these should be reflected in various ways in the archaeological record. An initial exposition of seven statuses as recognized in Galveston Bay area mortuary ritual was given in the Boys School study. Based on the ethnohistoric literature, it is possible now to go farther in defining statuses insofar as they are ones which have some impact or influence on the archaeological record as presented in this study. Clearly, it is possible for any given

individual to have occupied several statuses, either simultaneously or sequentially; this issue, however, does not concern us at present. The approach taken to
the question of status generally follows the treatment given by Fried (1967) and
Service (1971). The statuses recognized in this study are sociocentric in nature;
that is to say, they are categories (such as "headman") that were recognized by
the society at large rather than categories dependent on the relationships between two individuals (such as "father").

The status of "headman" or "chief" is recognized among all of the groups
discussed in previous portions of this chapter: the Atakapa (Dyer 1917:3;
Gatschet and Swanton 1932:11), the Bidai (Ker 1816; Sjoberg 1951b), the
Akokisa (Bolton 1913:345), and the Karankawa (Dyer 1917:4; Gatschet
1891:63). Among the former three groups, this status is only identified in reference to periods the groups were encamped in villages. This suggests that the
maximal social unit over which the headman exercised any authority was that
collection of bands that congregated on an annual basis into villages. There is,
of course, a single mention that, for the Atakapa, there were "many chiefs, one
being head of all the rest [Gatschet and Swanton 1932:11]." This may mean that
each of the warm season groups had a headman and the village headman
exercised authority over these during the cool season village occupation. There
are other possibilities, but at least the choices are few in number.

The situation among the Karankawa might have been somewhat different.
During the early nineteenth century both "civil" chiefs (whose succession was
hereditary in the male line) and "war" chiefs (who were designated for the
occasion) were reported by Gatschet (1891:63), although his source is unknown.
Descent as a factor in succession of the headman also is ambiguously hinted by
Helm (1884:82).[1] The war chief status was evidently intermittently used and
there is no positive indication of its existence among the other groups.[2]

The status of "civil" chief, or headman, was evidently a subdued one in that
there is no mention of it either by Cabeza de Vaca or by Simars de Bellisle for the
local groups described by them. Usually the role of headman "is to lead where
his followers choose to follow [Adams, 1975:223]." There is no direct indication
of their being in a position to dispense power and/or goods in a patron–client
relationship which would have been the case if any kind of ranking had existed
(Adams 1975:229). The utter failure of attempts by the Spanish to install a head
chief over the Bidai and Akokisa (Bolton, 1915:232) is only further indication

[1]Schaedel (1949) suggested centralized authority was beginning to be institutionalized late in the
historic period among the Karankawa. While there is no evidence to dispute Schaedel's observation
(and significant research could be directed at the question), the *protohistoric* character of Karankawa organization seems not unlike that of the Akokisa and Bidai.

[2]Gatschet more than once compares the Karankawa to the Creeks whom he had previously
studied. Since he described this war chief–peace chief dichotomy for the Creeks (Anonymous
1887:406), we probably should be very cautious in accepting his description of this for the Karankawas until some independent confirmation is available; he may well have inadvertently forced
the issue.

that consent authority was the basis for these statuses. There is equivocal evidence for the identification of this status in the mortuary practices documented at the Harris County Boys School Cemetery (Aten *et al.* 1976:102).

There are records of the status of "shaman" among the Atakapa (Dyer 1917; Gatschet and Swanton 1932), and the Karankawa (Bandelier 1905; Gatschet 1891:69) and may be implied for the Bidai (Bolton 1908:225). A brief review of the nature of shamanism as it might be expected to be manifested on the upper Texas coast was presented in Aten *et al.* (1976:103–104) along with the form of its appearance in mortuary contexts. These will not be repeated here, although it is now possible to add a few new observations. As noted in the 1976 study, shamans were accorded special rites in mortuary ritual reflecting their special status as intermediaries with the supernatural world. Beyond this, Cabeza de Vaca reported that among the Capoque the shaman may have had two or three wives whereas other men had only one (Bandelier 1905:66). Whether this was true for the other groups is unknown, although this possibility might be considered based on the folktale recounted in Gatschet and Swanton (1932) (quoted here in Table 5.1:A-15), which indicates that monogamy was the rule for the Atakapa.

In Table 5.1 are listed a number of references to the activities of shamans among the Atakapa and Karankawa, and there is no reason to believe that similar activities were not commonplace among the Akokisa and the Bidai. These activities most often had to do with leading ritual dances and curing. Among the Atakapa, the shaman was also responsible for the preparation and application of fish poisons. An important differentiation among shamans was recorded by De Solís (1931:41) who noted that to the Karankawa there were two "divinities" for whom there were shamans to direct rituals and dances (cf. Table 5.1). The association of these two "divinities" with themes common to primitive societies certainly makes the presence of this distinction among the other local groups a real possibility that should be searched for in new studies. This feature will be discussed more extensively in Chapter 6.

Other statuses are based on craft skills, sodality membership, age, sex, and slavery.[3] A review of the presently identifiable craft skill statuses is given in Aten *et al.* (1976:104) and concerns flint knapping, weaving, and bead manufacture. To some extent, these craft skills are sex-linked but other indicators of status distinctions based on sex are seen in the prohibition of participation by women in most dance rituals and in the division of labor. For example, fire making and pottery manufacture were male activities and the erection and removal of portable dwellings, cooking, and gathering of firewood were female activities (Gatschet 1891).

Age statuses are suggested but are not precisely defined by the practice of

[3]We use the term *slave* as "people who are appended to the band . . . who may have special work tasks, but who usually occupy the role of resident outsiders [Adams 1975:226]." Such persons are not slaves in the sense of property as in more complex societies.

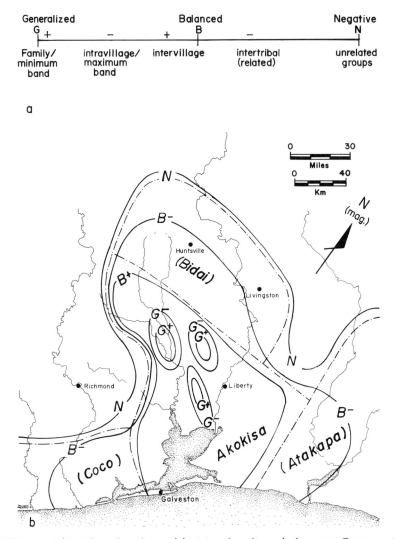

FIGURE 5.1. Schematic reciprocity models: (a) reciprocity scale for upper Texas coast; (b) reciprocity "map" for protohistoric Akokisa. (Note that the number and location of "G" units is intended only to indicate their multiple nature, not their specific geographical location.)

infanticide, differential presence of grave goods between young and old, and in the division of labor. Thus, Karankawa children reportedly spent most of their time playing in the water (Helm 1884:42; Gatschet 1891:68) and in the process collected clams for subsistence purposes (Helm 1884:42).

The status of slave is reflected in the treatment of Cabeza de Vaca and his companions (Bandelier 1905), DeBellisle (Folmer 1940) and Ker's Negro companion (Ker 1816). Another type of status reported only for the Karankawa so far were the "berdaches," men dressed as and performing the roles of women (Schaedel 1949:125).

Finally, among the last types of status observed (only in the Galveston Bay area so far) are those based on ritual distinctions in mortuary practice that probably relate to belief systems. Such religious sodality membership was reviewed in Aten *et al.* (1976:104) and is reflected in the two basic orientation groups of burials—those with heads to the east and those with heads to the west. Another type of sodality is inferred from the ethnohistoric record and concerns the several different types of dances performed (cf. Table 5.1), which, for the Karankawa at least, were associated with the two separate "divinities" (mentioned previously); on this basis we infer the likelihood of at least two dance sodalities.

Collectively, this information describes a *minimum* of 18 statuses potentially recognizable in the archaeological record.[4] Certainly many others were present, although the visibility of some (such as a hunter or food collector highly respected for consistent success) is doubtful. It probably is not useful to attempt to tabulate these statuses by local territorial groups because the existing information—documentary, as well as archaeological—is so sketchy that resulting patterns are not likely to be meaningful. Again, this is a minimum estimate of statuses present on the upper coast and aside from the possibility of an inherited Karankawa headmanship, there are no indications of ranking.

LEVEL OF INTEGRATION

In 1764, Captain Pacheco, the Spanish commander at Orcoquisac, tried to persuade residents of the several Akokisa and Bidai villages to enter the mission there. Calzones Colorado's people, who resided at or near Orcoquisac, evidently did so, while the others indicated a willingness to enter mission life provided they each had one in their own territory (Bolton 1913:372). This incident reflects a sense of identity among the groups involved that brings up the question of their nature.

In the study of Galveston Bay area mortuary practices (Aten *et al.* 1976), a picture was given of aboriginal society organized as egalitarian bands, subdividing and re-forming according to a regular seasonal schedule, probably having had shamans as the only (or principal) sociocentric status, and certainly to have been focused on a hunting and gathering subsistence. The actual situation must

---

[4]An additional status of "trader" is twice described in the upper coast literature (Bandelier 1905:74; Kelley 1955) but in neither instance was this status occupied by a resident of a local upper coast group.

TABLE 5.1
Ethnohistorical Documentation of Elements of Native Ritual and Cognition on the Upper Texas Coast.[a]

A. Atakapa

Origin Myths and the Supernatural

1. <u>Swanton 1907:286, 1911:363</u> From the 1802 Martin Duralde manuscript "The Atacapas pretend that they are come out of the sea, that a prophet or man inspired by God laid down the rules of conduct to their first ancestors (peres) which consisted in not doing any evil. They believe in an author of all things; that those who do well go above, and that those who do evil descend under the earth into the shades. They speak of a deluge which swallowed up men, animals, and the land, and it was only those who resided along a high land or mountain . . . who escaped this calamity."
   <u>Comment</u> This story bears obvious similarities to Christian theology although there may have been some conceptual compatibility with older native myths. See item 2 below. Contrary to the suggestion of Swanton (1907:287) there is not known to have been any inundation of lower Louisiana during the period of human occupation other than intermittent tidal or river flooding.

2. <u>Dyer 1917:6</u> The Lake Charles Atakapa believed they came out of the sea "being cast up in large oyster shells, from which the first men grew."
   <u>Comment</u> This passage is compatible with the origin portion of item 1 above.

3. <u>Dyer 1917:6</u> "Men that were eaten by men, and those that died from snakebite, were believed to be incapable of entering a second life, hence were eternally damned."
   <u>Comment</u> Implied afterlife or, possibly, reincarnation for humans; may imply a supernatural character resembling, or the powers possessed by, the snake.

Rituals

4. <u>Gatschet and Swanton 1932:11</u> "They danced painted with red and white paint and, when relatives had died, with black paint and with feathers on their heads, sounding a rattle at the dancing place."
   <u>Comment</u> The use of the color triad red, white and black is also found among symbols of the Bidai and Karankawa; also it is important to note the association of black with the mortuary ritual and red/white with other ritual.

5. <u>Dyer 1916:10</u> They "used the yaupon leaves as a beverage, but did not drink large quantities of the decoction, as was the case in the ceremonials of the Trinity River Indians."
   <u>Comment</u> This suggests that the ceremonials involving purging reported for the Karankawa and, by implication, for the Akokisa were not part of the Atakapa ritual framework, or may just not have been observed by Dyer's informant.

6. <u>Dyer 1916:3</u> Circa 1820, "They had no temple and no religious ceremonials, except the 'chi' dance, which was patterned after that of the Carancahuas."
   <u>Comment</u> Cannot presently evaluate this statement; we do not know the identity of the "chi" dance, but supports use of "pooled" data.

7. <u>Dyer 1916:12; 1917:2</u> "The chief as a rule did not bother with the daughters (the females of the clan) except on certain ceremonial occasions. This happened whenever the victorious warriors captured a brave, swift or strong enemy; or killed one in combat. The body stripped of certain portions of the flesh, was left on the field, but the human steaks, dried and smoked, were carried back to the camp. Before all others, the pregnant females were lined up, and the chief placed a morsel of the enemy's flesh into each mouth, expressing the sentiment that the unborn babes might acquire the particular attribute (of valor, strength, or fleetness), which of late was inherent in the body now partitioned."

8. <u>Dyer 1917:6</u> At the time of birth, the father (or at least the husband of the mother) rested for the last week of the pregnancy and was fed by friends and relatives.

TABLE 5.1 (*Continued*)

The Shaman and His Activities

9. Dyer 1917:4 In 1810, at a time of hunger, the bodies of shipwrecked sailors washed ashore near the mouth of the Calcasieu and the bodies were roasted by the Atakapa with the intention of eating them as food. They deliberated about whether to do this and finally the shaman gave his opinion "that if the Atakapa were to eat the flesh of white men, their skin would become spotty." As a result, they did not eat the bodies.

    Comment The logic may have been related to the story told by the Bidai headman about how red and white men were made (see item B-1).

10. Dyer 1917:3 Fish were drugged with fish poisons made from unknown plants sprinkled over the water by the shaman.

    Comment This suggests the possibility that one of the shaman's functions was as maker and user of drugs for whatever purpose and that this was simply an aspect of his magical powers.

11. Gatschet and Swanton 1932:18 "When anyone was sick, the Atakapa believed he had been given bad medicine. One night they assembled at his house, entered it, and danced religious dances all night, shaking gourd rattles and playing on fiddles. While they were mourning, they sang and afterwards an Indian conjurer came to see him and treated him and was paid for it. They would not let others go in. They would not let young people go in. If a sick person died, they believed that something wicked has caused it."

    Comment Although not evident from this quotation, the context here is dancing, singing, and mourning for someone sick but not yet dead. This account of the source of sickness is similar to Dyer's. It also indicates one type of ritual (i.e., for the recovery of someone sick).

12. Gatschet and Swanton 1932:14 An "Indian conjurer" cured a chief's wife of a bad cold by sucking out blood. He was paid one horse for this.

    Comment This method of treatment and the receipt of payment were documented for the Karankawa also.

13. Dyer 1917:2 The Atakapa shaman (in 1819) reported that he could cure most diseases except smallpox (called the white man's disease). He treated a case of dysentery with a hot extract of an astringent red root along with exposure of the patient for several days to smoke and steam inside the hut where the patient was located. For several days subsequent, the diet was confined to a shellfish broth.

    Comment This exposure to smoke and steam was a common technique and was reported for the Bidai as a treatment for typhoid fever. It also leaves us uninformed about what constituted a disease (cf. Ackerknecht 1971:62).

Folktales

14. Swanton 1907:287–288 "A favorite story of both Chitimacha and Attacapa tells how a person once became angry and wanted to destroy the world, so he went down into the marshes and set fire to the dry grass. A little bird perched on a tree and made fun of him. 'If you don't stop talking I will kill you,' said the evil-disposed man. By and by, as the bird would not stop, he picked up a shell and threw it at the bird, which it hit in the shoulder, making it bleed. That is how the red-winged blackbird came by its red wings. When the fire came along to where a ·giant lived, he put his sister between the valves of a shell and held her up as high as he could reach. In doing so he made the corrugations on the shells that can be seen today. 'Well!' he said, 'I have saved my sister.' The fire started up a great quantity of deer and other game, and men went down and killed them. Then they thanked the evil-minded man for benefiting them so much. I was told by an Attacapa that the story also contained an allusion to the jack-o'-lantern, which seems likely."

(*continued*)

TABLE 5.1 (*Continued*)

Comment Several items of interest; first, the explicit association of red to symbolize blood; second, the use of a bird as an antagonist; and third, the allusion to the practice of setting fire to the prairie as a means of driving game as a subsistence technique.

15. Gatschet and Swanton 1932:11 The following anecdote was recorded as part of a text taken down from two Atakapa informants, but its form is very much like a folktale. "A man had but one wife, and when a man had two it was a bad thing. Palnal's older wife beat him to death. His other wife beat him. When Palnal's older wife beat him to death, his body lay on the ground three or four days with the head mashed in. The water he had drunk ran out of his ears."

Comment This sounds as if it is the explanation or rationalization of the sanction against more than one wife. The significance of this is enhanced by the fact that shamans were permitted to have more than one wife.

16. Gatschet and Swanton 1932:12 Cakta'lko (Human-skin-desirer): "When an Atakapa was dead he turned into a being desiring skins, and they called him by this name. When one first encountered him, he appeared to lack a head but afterwards they say his head bent forward and his body all covered with hair."

Comment This tale may be related to the episode of skinning a killed enemy described by De Bellisle.

B. Bidai

1. Ker 1816:126–127 The following explanation was offered by the Bidai headman who wished to keep Ker's negro companion. "But I was informed that they thought him far superior to white men, in consequence of his being black: they supposed him to be made of a superior quality of clay, and that the red clay ranked next; but the white men they thought were made of the poorest kind of clay, and that the Great Spirit, after he had made them, had pity on them and gave them learning, but would not bestow it upon black and red men, because they were pure and spotless as they were first made. The white men, they said, had polluted themselves, and their learning had been a great evil amongst all nations and kindreds of people. They believed that the red men would yet be blessed with all the good stores of nature, and have dominion over all the country, and that the slaves would be all set at liberty. I [i.e., Ker] soon grew weary of this conversation."

Comment The association of the three colors red, black, and white in this story is a commonly employed opposition in our data on the area. The reasoning employed in differentiating between the three races of men seems similar to that employed 300 years earlier by the Capoque among whom Cabeza de Vaca resided. When the Capoque requested Cabeza de Vaca to be a healer, they claimed that the white men were more knowledgeable than the Indians.

2. Sjoberg 1951b:399 Typhoid fever victims were placed on a scaffold and smudge fires were built underneath; the dense smoke was supposed to effect a cure. Their treatment for dysentery was to take a concoction of boiled roots and sparkleberries (*Vaccinium arboreum*).

Comment Although the details of application differ, the basic techniques are similar to those applied by the Atakapa shaman.

C. Akokisa

1. Folmer 1940:219 When de Bellisle's band attacked the Toyals and killed one, they returned the body to their camp. There, they dismembered it at least to the extent of removing the head and arms and the body was skinned. It then was entirely eaten.

Comment Compare with the Atakapa folktale (item A-16); also see Ackerknecht (1971).

2. Folmer 1940:220 When ɑe Bellisle's band returned from the bison hunting expedition with news that a Toyal had been killed, they all danced for 2 days primarily celebrating the killing

TABLE 5.1 (*Continued*)

of an enemy. De Bellisle implies that this dance was done by the women and that pieces of the slain Indian's body were used as part of the celebration.

Comment This is the only instance known in which women participated in a dance, in that area; also compare with item A-7.

3. Dyer 1916:10 The Lake Charles Atakapa "used the yaupon leaves as a beverage, but did not drink large quantities of the decoction, as was the case in the ceremonials of the Trinity River Indians."

Comment This implies the existence among the Akokisa at least of the type of purging ritual described below for the Karankawa.

4. Bolton 1913:372 "Heathen idols and ornaments" were turned over to the Spanish missionaries at Orcoquisac by members of Calizones Colorado's band when they entered the mission in 1764.

Comment This indicates that the Akokisa rituals involved tangible paraphernalia, some of which should be discoverable archaeologically.

5. Folmer 1940:220 The Indians of De Bellisle's band evidently believed him to be possessed of some metaphysical capabilities since they expected him to have foreseen and warned them how many Toyals were in the group they were about to ambush. They were not afraid to punish him for his failure to warn them. They may have decided this could safely be done as a result of their experience with him during the preceding summer.

Comment This behavior toward the white man also recalls the attitude of the Capoque toward Cabeza de Vaca; see Chapter 6. The pattern of initially being more or less hospitable to the white man followed by harsher treatment occurred with Cabeza de Vaca, De Bellisle, and Ker, and suggests a pattern.

D. Karankawa

Supernatural Entities and Dance Rituals

1. *De Solis 1931:41 The Karankawa had two divinities, Pichini and Mel, for which there were separate ritual dances for funerals, victory in war, and success in food collection. These cults had separate shamans to supervise these rituals.*

Comment This is an especially significant comment. It may relate to the duality in the Galveston Bay Area mortuary practices between the east and west oriented burials. Although the significance of the name "Pichini" is not known now, the name "Mel" is very similar to the Atakapa term for black–blue and to the Karankawa term for "dead."

2. De Solis 1931:40–41 According to De Solis, there were two types of ritual dances—festive (successful hunts, etc.) and sad (funerals, etc.) and that the principal distinguishing feature was the musical or rhythm instruments used and, of course, the music that resulted. In the festive dance, turtle shell or gourd rattles, reed whistles, and the *avacasele* (an unidentified instrument) were used. In the sad dances, the *cayman* (also unidentified) was used. The dancing was done around a large bonfire and was kept up for three days and nights. Women never dance in these rituals but remain at a distance. The men paint themselves with red and at other times with black.

Comment Since there is a possibility that *Mel* can be associated with the color black, we may suggest that *Pichini* can be associated with red. The nonparticipation of women in these dances stands in sharp contrast to De Bellisle's description of the Akokisa dance (item C-2).

3. Gatschet 1891:18 Oliver described the following ritual conducted after a successful hunting or fishing expedition. It was always conducted at the full moon; the Indians assembled in one hut around a fire for boiling yaupon drink. The ceremony leader was totally covered by skins and

(*continued*)

TABLE 5.1 (*Continued*)

chanted as he moved about the fire bent over nearly double. All participants chanted with the chants growing louder as the ritual went on. It would last all night and there is no mention of exclusion of women. Instruments used were gourd rattles, whistles, and a fluted piece of wood over which a stick was drawn producing a "droning noise;" possibly this was the *avacasele* mentioned by de Solis (item D-2).

Comment Presumably this dance ritual is at least partially similar to one of those described by de Solis. It also bears some similarities to that described by De Bellisle.

4. Gatschet 1891:66 Oliver also described a dance that took place when an Indian became incensed at what was considered to be meddling by one of the Anglo settlers in the Indian's domestic affairs and they decided to attack the settler's home. In preparation for this attack, a ceremonial dance was held that night during the full moon. This evidently was a short dance for the attack was initiated the same night.

Comment This is the only record of a ceremonial dance prior to an event rather than after. There is no mention that the yaupon drink was used.

5. Bandelier 1905:61 Cabeza de Vaca wrote that upon arrival of the Spanish among the Capoques who had just rescued them from exposure on the beach that "one hour after our arrival they began to dance and to make a great celebration(which lasted the whole night)."

6. Bandelier 1905:68 According to Cabeza de Vaca, the Capoque, after going to the seashore in early May, ate blackberries for a whole month "during which time they danced and celebrated incessantly."

Comment This may possibly be a seasonal ritual, but in any event would appear to have been a celebration of the relative abundance of food after the lean winter period.

7. De Solis 1931:42–43 De Solis reported a dance in which a victim (a captured enemy) was tied to a stake in the center of the dancers who would jump up and cut pieces of flesh off of the living victim, roasting and eating them in sight of the victim until he finally expired.

Comment De Solis evidently did not view this firsthand; it may simply be an embellished version of one of the other dances of which we have record involving the consumption of human flesh in a less bizarre (from the perspective of the Indian cosmos) fashion.

8. Gatschet 1891:70–71 "They sent the smoke of tobacco through their nostrils first to the north, then to the east, west and south in an apparently unconcerned and careless manner." They also made a practice of staring at the sun when it disappeared into the sea.

Comment Cardinal directions are most evident in upper coast mortuary ritual. See Aten *et al.* (1976:104–106).

9. Gatschet 1891:58 "The boys very probably had their initiation trials like those of other Indians, but ceremonies connected with the puberty of girls have not been noticed among them by the white settlers."

10. De Solis 1931:41 De Solis described ordeals in which many young men or adolescents participated to qualify for the chieftainship. These ordeals involved fasting in the bush for days at a time and scarification rites.

Comment Newcomb (1961:72) notes that the Spanish may have mistaken puberty or some other initiation rites for a chieftainship qualification ordeal. This may have been what Gatschet referred to (item D-9). Moreover, in an egalitarian society, one might characterize male puberty rites as a chieftainship qualification ordeal.

Domestic Rituals

11. Gatschet 1891:69 An individual went by two names, at least where Europeans were concerned—an Indian name (which they would not reveal) and an English or Spanish surname. The explanation according to Gatschet was to preclude the Indian's spirit from being summoned inadvertently after he had died.

TABLE 5.1 (*Continued*)

12. Gatschet 1891:67 The couvade was not observed. (But see item A-8.)
13. Dyer 1916:6 A month or so before birth, the father (or husband of the mother) would take some steps such as fasting, care in the diet and care to prevent any injury in the expectation that any injury to the father "could be transmitted to the infant" and that "any evil spirits acquired by ingestion of flesh containing the same, would forthwith seek lodgment in the infantile corpus."
14. Dyer 1916:8, 10 The Karankawa "fasted whenever he thought that he had swallowed an evil spirit; which evil spirit should not be fed but allowed if possible to die of starvation." They "believed disease was derived by swallowing flesh of animals which contained evil spirits."

Shamans and Their Activities
15. Bandelier 1905:69 The Capoque wanted Cabeza de Vaca and his companions to act as shamans, which they at first refused to do and for which the Indians withheld their food. An Indian told Cabeza de Vaca that he could cure pain with a heated stone "so that we who were wiser men, surely had greater power and virtue."
    Comment The basis for this point of view is unclear, but it is of more than passing significance in that very similar attitudes were evident in two additional but unrelated incidents—by the Akokisa when they had De Bellisle with them in 1721 (item C-5) and by the Bidai when they detained Ker in 1810 (item B-1).
16. Dyer 1916:7 The Karankawa shaman burned fish liver on the end of a reed, the smoke from which was applied to the nostrils to drive "evil spirits" away from the body; he would also try exorcism and incantations, and transfer of the problem to an animal—frequently a dog who would be tied to the patient for a period of time.
17. Gatschet 1891:69 "One of the medical or conjuring practices of these Indians was to suck the disease from the patient's body, and welts could often be seen on their skin."

[a]Does not generally include mortuary ritual; see Aten *et al.* 1976 for recent review.

have been more complex than this. A new composite reconstruction of the more or less essential organizational features of the upper coast societies follows. It is based primarily on data from the western Atakapa and the eastern Karankawa.

To anticipate certain conclusions to be discussed in a report being prepared (Aten, unpublished data–1971) on the subject of spatial patterns and scheduling, both the Karankawa and the Akokisa (and probably the Bidai as well) had an annual pattern of aggregation in late fall and winter and dispersal in warm seasons. The latter seems to have involved band sized groups (circa 25 individuals) or smaller. The cool season aggregates are of uncertain size, but indications are they may have been between 100–400 individuals; this estimate is based on reports about the size of Akokisa and Karankawa villages (Bolton 1913; Joutel 1962:50). Consequently, there is a situation in which sets of bands were periodically aggregated into villages under a headman at which level are seen the strongest indications of group identity.

These villages, however, also had interrelationships that made them identifiable as a group as well. The nature of these interrelationships is not entirely clear but they must have existed or the villages would not have had a collective identity as Akokisa, Bidai, Coco, Cujane, etc.[5] It is not at all likely that an authority structure existed above the level of the village except on a temporary basis when engaging in hostilities. This is suggested on the assumption that the instances of gathering 200 or more warriors, usually to fight Europeans (e.g., Gracy 1964:41), would not have been possible from a single village.

Bolton's (1913:346) description of the response of Akokisa villages to competing efforts by the Spanish and French to gain influence among them during the 1750s indicates that the village headmen or "chiefs" were the highest regular form of authority and that the several Akokisa villages ordinarily did not function under a single authority figure. The same situation still existed in 1778 when the Spanish attempted to organize the Bidai–Akokisa confederacy and appointed a Bidai headman (by the name of Gorgoritos) as chief (Bolton 1915:232). This creation appears to have evaporated rapidly and is not known to have had any impact on social integration for either the Bidai or the Akokisa.

A number of classificatory systems have been put forth to describe the levels of integration of human society, only a few of which are reviewed here, in order to place upper Texas coast aboriginal society in a broader theoretical framework. Steward (1955:123) proposed the *patrilineal band* concept to refer to patrilineally related family aggregates consisting of between 25–100 persons practicing exogamy and patrilocal postmarital residence.

Service (1971) modified this concept on grounds that descent was not a prime mover in band society, at least as a general matter, and he defined the *patrilocal band*, which also was exogamous and virilocal. The next higher level of integration for Service (1971) was the *tribe*, which, in his conception, was a level of integration that could be achieved in different ways. The tribe was seen as a "large collection of bands" linked together by complex institutional features (pan-tribal sodalities) that were largely shaped by adaptation to the external constraints on the group.

Fried (1967), approaching the problem from the perspective of the political basis for society, described *egalitarian* organizations and *ranked* organizations. The former, in which all statuses for any given age–sex grade were accessible to those capable of filling them, consisted of families and bands. The latter (i.e., ranked societies) (*a*) consist of chiefdoms in which each status is not necessarily accessible to each person who is capable of filling it, (*b*) have denser populations, and (*c*) usually are established on a subsistence base of agriculture. For Fried, however, the concept of *tribe* is meaningless as an intermediate evolutionary entity between *bands* and *chiefdoms*. Tribes are seen basically as an

---

[5]It should be understood at this point that the terms *Atakapa* and *Karankawa* are used as structural equivalents primarily linguistic in nature, and *western* (or *Louisiana*) *Atakapa*, *Akokisa*, *Bidai*, *Coco*, *Cujane*, *Karankawa*, etc. as structural equivalents at an organizational level of abstraction. Unfortunately, the dual use of *Atakapa* and *Karankawa* in both senses is embedded in the literature and readers should understand from the context which sense is being used in any given instance.

evolutionary dead end consisting of an amplification of the basic characteristics of band society.

This may very well be the case from the perspective of general evolution; however, as Adams (1975:225) noted, if there were no such category as *tribe*, it would be necessary to invent one. That is to say, there is a substantial difference between dealing with a band (even though, as an exogamous unit, it implies the existence of at least one other band) and dealing with a coordinated set of bands (Adams 1975:231). The nature of this coordination is seen similarly by Service, Fried, and Adams, varying widely through some combination of such features as language, marriage alliances, consanguinity, warfare, sacred dogma, and so on (Adams 1975:218ff.; Fried 1967:154ff.; Service 1971:100ff.).

In Adams's view, the tribe develops primarily through a fissioning process acting on the basic units of social organization—the patrilocal bands. Tribes continued to exist presumably because they had some survival value. Thus, for example, a proscription on food gathering by a family (i.e., domestic unit) when a member died (Bandelier 1905:67) made aggregation of the Karankawa bands into winter villages a highly adaptive feature in view of relatively higher winter mortality rates (Aten *et al.* 1976).

The concept of the *tribe* as defined by Service (1971) and Adams (1975) is the most comfortable means of referring to the upper Texas coast local territorial groups (i.e., the Akokisa, Bidai, Coco, etc.). The character of the internal organization of these tribes appears to have been a series of maximum bands (Steward 1969; Wobst 1974:152), which formed the cold season village aggregates (about 400–500 persons), and numerous minimum bands that were the warm season transient groups of about 25 persons (cf. the microband–macroband concept of MacNeish 1964:532). It should also be noted that, although Service's modification of Steward's band concept de-emphasized the role of descent as an organizational feature, Cabeza de Vaca indicated that descent was a factor in residency among the Capoque (Bandelier 1905:71).

Late in the historic period, when the upper coast tribes were being subjected to the stress of imminent disolution in the face of European settlement, as well as encroachment by other Indian groups on their territory, new bands began to emerge, which in some cases may not have been exogamous and did not always consist of related families (cf. Ewers 1973:112). The earliest known example of this was the group of Mayeyes and Coco, who joined together and settled around the mouth of the Brazos and Colorado rivers as early as 1778 (Morfi 1935/1967: 81). Other examples are (*a*) the Bidai, who were joined by the Akokisa in the early nineteenth century, (*b*) the Lake Charles Atakapa who absorbed Akokisa, western Atakapa (i.e., from the Sabine Lake area), Houma, Tunica, and Chitimacha (Swanton 1911; 1952), and (*c*) probably Chief Antonio's band of Karankawa (Gatschet 1891). The nature of all these groups seems to be reasonably well described by the concept of the *composite band* (Steward 1955:143–144; as modified by Service 1971:47), and it is in this sense that the term is used here.

Although little more can be done than note the possibility, recall that

Gatschet (1891:63) described the existence of both a hereditary "headmanship" and a dual leadership in the form of a "peace chief" (headman) and a "war chief," designated in some way for the occasion. If Gatschet was correct, and not simply overwhelmed by the Creek model, this implies the existence of both skill authority and power authority (Adams 1975:34). This, in turn, would strongly suggest that an evolution toward a more centralized (and reliable?) authority structure than existed in the protohistoric tribes was underway late in the historic period (cf. Schaedel 1949) simultaneously with the formation of composite bands.

RECIPROCITY AND TRADE

In societies of the level being discussed here, one might safely assume the presence of generalized reciprocity, as was done in the analysis of Galveston Bay Area mortuary practices (Aten *et al.* 1976:98), albeit with very little direct evidence. Reciprocity or exchange is based on sociological transformations between the flow of materials and social relations. It is largely through this means that order is maintained in the absence of institutionalized centralized authority (cf. Fried 1967:35; Sahlins 1965; Service 1975:61ff.). Such exchanges operate at all levels within and between groups primarily to "cause peace" in Service's words (1975:71). That is to say, reciprocity minimizes inequities between individuals, creates bonds between groups and is a positive adaptive force both in the sense of these two factors and in the sense that it provides a means for the flow of raw materials, finished goods, and services where needs exist. Whereas the presence of reciprocity only was assumed previously in the earlier mortuary study, further review of the literature has revealed a number of specific examples of reciprocity in action on the upper Texas coast that help to give shape to the assumption.

There is only one indirect indicator in the known archaeological record for the presence of reciprocity: the skeleton of a "crippled" young adult male discovered at the Harris County Boys School Cemetery (Aten *et al.* 1976:81–82) who, it is assumed, would have been unable to survive to adulthood (death occurred in the mid-twenties) in such a society without considerable assistance. Beyond this, there is an implication of sharing the products of hunting among the Akokisa when De Bellisle noted he was given his portion of buffalo meat from an animal he did not kill (Folmer 1940:220). Other descriptions of food collecting given by De Bellisle are not particularly clear about its distribution, although the quantities involved (for instance, the 500 bird-eggs collected by three men [Folmer 1940:215]) certainly imply sharing. In any event, the application of generalized reciprocity to foodstuffs among hunter–gatherers is virtually a truism.

There are several statements made in reference to the Karankawa groups that are even more revealing. For example, Cabeza de Vaca said the following about the Capoque:

> [They] are very liberal towards [sic] each other with what they have [Bandelier 1905:71].

> [They] have the custom, when they know each other and meet from time to time before they speak, to weep for half an hour. After they have wept the one who receives the visit rises and gives to the other all he has. The other takes it, and in a little while goes away with everything. Even sometimes, after having given and obtained all, they part without having uttered a word [Bandelier 1905:72; also see Oviedo y Valdez 1924:232, Footnote 7].

> When a son or brother dies no food is gathered by those of his household for three months, preferring rather to starve, but the relatives and neighbors provide them with victuals [Bandelier 1905:67].

In reference to the Matagorda Bay Karankawa in the late historic period, it was noted that

> Ignorant of any rights of property in our sense of the word they showed their thievish inclination by purloining food, knives, clothing and such household articles as they could use for themselves; but were not burglars [Gatschet 1891:64].

Dyer noted

> Our Indians have been generally accused of dishonesty, when really they were often guilty, not of theft, but a lack of that appreciation of 'mine and thine' as considered and practiced by white men [1920].

And Mayhall (1939:24), in reference to the theft of domesticated animals from colonists by Indians, noted that the Indians simply did not conceive of ownership of property as whites did; when wild foods diminished, they went after domesticates instead. When viewed from any other perspective than that of reciprocity, these citations are mere curiosities or even may be interpreted as maladaptive (e.g., Krieger 1956:51–52).

Obviously, obtaining women for marriage purposes, unless by force, had to involve exchange; the only questions are about how this was structured. The institution of bride service existed among the Capoque and was implied by Cabeza de Vaca to have occurred over a large area of the upper coast (Bandelier 1905:67). This, as manifested in the study area, was a reciprocal exchange wherein a man obtained a woman and in return provided food to the family of the woman for a specified period of time, an approach common in hunting and gathering societies (cf. Williams 1974:23). This description of bride service still does not answer the question of structure, however.

The only mention of an incest prohibition is for the Lake Charles Atakapa: "Relatives were not allowed to marry, since it was as if brothers married sisters and sisters married brothers [Gatschet and Swanton 1932:11]." Although one cannot be sure if the terms *brother* and *sister* were used here as biological kin types or more figuratively, it is worth noting that in the Atakapa language, a male ego's sisters, maternal and paternal aunts, and female cousins are terminologically merged (Gatschet and Swanton 1932). They form a social identity or a group of persons who probably all behaved toward the male ego in the same way. This behavior presumably included a prohibition on marriage, or else it would be "as if brothers married sisters." By this means, there probably is effective documentation of band exogamy among the Atakapa. There is no a priori reason to assume this did not obtain for the Bidai and Akokisa and perhaps for the Coco, Cujane, and Karankawa.

Given the likely existence of exogamous virilocal (or perhaps patrilineal) bands, it remains to be considered with which groups exchange of women may have taken place. Here one can only suggest possibilities. One very real possibility would have been the existence of a moiety system within each of the tribes; this is an attractive possibility because such a dyadic character would be compatible with several other dyadic cognitive structures to be discussed in the next chapter. Aside from the logical possibility, the only actual description of a moiety system on the upper coast is given in the following quotation (unfortunately, there is no indication of the original source):

> [Take] a low tribe for an example. It was divided first into two bands, or brotherhoods. The members of each were prohibited from marrying in their own band, but had to seek husband or wife, as the case might be, in the opposite division. Thus the bands were continually changed and perpetually renewed. The Carankaways were divided into two such bands, each with a chief. The only two of whom we have any knowledge did not agree in the policy they were to pursue toward the white people. But tribal law did not admit of separation; and the advocate of peace was overruled, and all involved in common destruction [Kenney 1897:29–30].

Alternatively, there could simply have been opportunistic exchanges between villages for alliance purposes. In order to establish alliances with other villages in the tribe, there must have been mechanisms that differed in some important respect from alliances with adjacent, but culturally similar, tribes (e.g., between Akokisa and Bidai). If not, then the tribal identitiy is not likely to have been maintained through time, and identification with individual maximum bands (villages) would have been the principal concept for differentiating "us" from "them." In light of this, it seems reasonable to suggest that the individual tribes tended to define a more or less nonexogamous space. That is, women tended not to be exchanged beyond the tribal limits. There were other important relationships between the Atakapa, Akokisa, and Bidai (e.g., peace, similar language) that were lacking between the Akokisa and some of the Karankawa or the Tonkawa, for instance. These tribal and dialectical boundaries probably marked discontinuities in the intensity of exchange rather than any absolute limits beyond which exchange did not occur.

Another major area of reciprocity concerned the exchange of goods and raw materials; that is, trade, although we prefer to reserve this term instead for the more commercial form of exchange introduced by the Europeans to the area (cf. Pires-Ferriera and Flannery 1976:287). The data on material exchange–trade are not abundant, but there is more than might seem at first glance—enough, in fact, that the data must be organized into their respective functional contexts.

Temporally and functionally, distinctions are made between the exchange relations of indigenous character from those trade relations introduced by Europeans primarily after the early eighteenth century. These latter relations may be distinguished further into those principally of the eighteenth century which turned on the fur trade and those primarily of the early nineteenth century which were of a more generalized mercantile character. The upper Texas coast has been considered essentially as a unit from which materials were exported and into which other materials were imported. For prehistoric and protohistoric aboriginal exchange, these "external" relations were primarily with inland areas; for the historic period, we cannot exclude considering that precontact aboriginal patterns of exchange still persisted, but so far as the available data are concerned, the very active European trade has obscured any view of them except for the single report of Lake Charles Atakapa trade by Dyer (1917:5). "Internal" exchange relations (i.e., within the upper coast) are not discussed, since virtually no data are available. The data and relationships presented here are summarized in Table 5.2.

Aboriginal exchange probably was carried out through two mechanisms: (a) in the absence of evidence to the contrary, an individual to individual chain-like exchange structure is assumed (Rappaport 1968:107); and (b) through the activities of traders (e.g., Cabeza de Vaca and Juan Sabeata, chief of the Jumano and Cibola Indians) who actually devoted a significant portion of their annual pattern of activities to obtaining goods in one location and transporting them to another (sometimes over very great distances) to be exchanged for other goods. This latter form of exchange evidently was not especially common, judging from the encouragement given to Cabeza de Vaca to become a trader (Bandelier 1905:74). Moreover, Sabeata, in the 10 years or so for which there is information on his activities, is only known to have ventured into the territory of the Karankawa in 1689 (Kelly 1955).

Nevertheless, the eastern Texas archaeological record contains many instances of artifacts being found in one area which must have originated elsewhere. For this reason, it is assumed the chain-like exchange system described by Rappaport must have existed even if it became interrupted from time to time and place to place. It is assumed further that the types of goods reportedly traded by Cabeza de Vaca and Sabeata, and by the Lake Charles Atakapa (Dyer 1917:5) describe the types of materials that moved through the aboriginal exchange systems. The traders simply were an alternative means of facilitating this movement, perhaps only in times when kin or putative kin-based trading partnerships were not functioning across major sociological boundaries.

The various kinds of materials listed in Table 5.2 as having moved through aboriginal trade systems could have moved in very different ways because of their different functional relationships. Examples of such different types of exchanges in egalitarian society are given in Pires-Ferriera and Flannery

TABLE 5.2
Contents of Aboriginal and Historic Exchange–Trade.

Exports	Imports

Aboriginal Exchange

Subsistence

Dried, smoked fish[a]	Maize[b]

Utilitarian

Seaweed (medicinal)[a]	Lithic materials[a,c,d]
Oyster shell knife/scraper (Karankawa only)[c]	Canes[c]
	Sinews[c]
	Cement[c]
	Skins (deer, bison, bear)[c,d]
	Ceramics[a,d]
	Sandstone for abraders, net weights, and small manos and metates[d]

Symbolic or Ornamental

Olive shell tinklers?[x]	Red ochre[c,d]
Columella beads[c]	Deer hair tassels[c]
Columella pendants[c]	Ground stone beads and sinkers[d]
Shark teeth[a]	Ceramic ear spools[d]
Bird feathers (heron, crane, pelican, wild geese)[a,d]	

Historic Trade

Early

Skins (deer, bison)[e]	Trade beads, "trinkets"[d,e]
Animal fat[e]	Firearms[e]
Horses[e]	Clothing[e]
Corn (Bidai only)[e]	Tobacco[e]

Late—circa 1810

Dried, smoked fish[a]	Miscellaneous goods from captured vessels[a]
Spanish moss (bedding)[a]	Flint and chert nodules for the Karankawa "market"[a]
Flint and chert nodules from Atakapa for retrade to Karankawa[a]	

[a]Source: Dyer (1917:4–5).

[b]Source: Miranda cited in Bolton (1915:335).

[c]Source: Cabeza de Vaca (Bandelier 1905:75); also, archaeological evidence of oyster shell knives in Brazos delta, in Aten (1971, present volume).

[d]Source: Archaeological evidence (Aten 1967, 1971, present volume; Aten *et al.* 1976; Campbell 1957; Duke 1962).

[e]Source: Bolton (1913:341, 342, 346, 348); Faulk (1964:63, 83–99).

(1976:287–289); unfortunately, there are no upper coast data to deal with this question at such a level of refinement. Alternatively Rappaport's (1968:105–109) discussion of trade relations among the Maring of New Guinea presents some more generalized observations, which may be of use, on this issue.

In the Maring study, Rappaport pointed out that when the exchange system turns principally on items that are crucial for survival, a serious inconvenience may result if and when one of the trading partners either cannot or will not produce the item needed by the other side. The solution to this problem in Rappaport's view is to combine nonutilitarian valuables with the exchange of necessities and to make them interchangeable. This, of course, says nothing more than that a diversified approach is safest. There is always likely to be something one side has that is in demand by the other. As a result, the exchange chain will usually continue to operate in the absence of a managerial function.

As indicated in Table 5.2, the coast Indians primarily exported symbolic or ornamental items and imported primarily utilitarian items. Actually, there is a considerable variety in these lists, much of which should be archaeologically visible. As a result, it may ultimately be possible to map out the internal origin and distribution of many of these items within the upper Texas coast area and the passage through the area of others (e.g., olive shell tinklers from the south Texas coast).

Early in the historic period (i.e., the eighteenth century), a much more restricted set of items was exchanged by the Indians with the French, Spanish, and English. These related primarily to subsistence for the European colonists and to supplying the fur trade. Although there is direct information only for the Atakapa, it seems probable that this activity supplemented, but did not replace, the continued patterns of aboriginal trade, although these likely proceeded at a much reduced intensity due to the substantial population declines of the period.

The impact of the fur trade is worthy of special note here. In Chapter 4, the evidence was described for regular annual trading meetings between the Europeans and the Indians dating perhaps as early as the 1720s. It has also been reported (Nixon 1946:50) that, at the time of his capture in 1747 at Orcoquisac, the French trader Blancpain had in his possession some 2300 deer hides! Under such conditions, one must certainly ask what impact the fur trade had on the basic patterns of native social organization and life in the eighteenth century. Relevant to an understanding of this problem is the classic study of Murphy and Steward (1955). They concluded that:

> When the people of an unstratified native society barter wild products found in extensive distribution and obtained through individual effort, the structure of the native culture will be destroyed, and the final culmination will be a culture type characterized by individual families having delimited rights to marketable resources and linked to the larger nation through trading centers [Murphy and Steward 1955:353].

Archaeologically, increased quantities of lithic tools and refuse have been observed in historic period sites of the Galveston Bay area (see Part III). Presumably, increases in the quantities of deer and bison bones in such sites, as well as shifts in scheduling and location to those areas containing more deer and bison should be found. One has the impression that the Karankawa, however, were disinclined to participate in the fur trade to the extent undertaken by the Akokisa, Bidai and Atakapa. As a result of the largely hostile relationship between the Karankawa and the colonists, historic period Karankawa occupation in the Brazos River delta reflects a shift to exploiting the subsistence opportunities in less accessible habitats (Aten, unpublished data–1971).

There is little mention of the fur trade after the late eighteenth century, and by the early nineteenth century the emphasis in trade had shifted to items other than just furs. After intensive white settlement of the coast began in the post-1820 period, the coastal Indians had essentially nothing of value with which to enter a trading relationship. After this period, Indian society and lifeways were no longer functional in conjunction with the dominant white society of the Texas colonists. Moreover, by this time huge proportions of the native populations had been eliminated, and the native groups were largely reduced to enclaves in their former territories. By the late historic period, it seems unlikely that the patterns of aboriginal exchange remained. Elsewhere, situations have been described wherein native societies

> lacked any goods to offer in exchange and thus were forced to accept a dependent status vis-a-vis White society; they settled on reservations . . . and were compelled to subsist on White rations and whatever residual employment might be available [Gould, Fowler and Fowler 1972:278].

SUMMATION

What, in a general way, do these additional indications of reciprocity and exchange suggest about the cultures of the upper coast? Sahlins (1965) elaborated a theory of exchange relations based on a continuum ranging from "pure" gifts at one extreme to attempts "to get something for nothing with impunity" at the other. When observed ethnographically, this continuum was found to be best expressed by its end points (generalized reciprocity and negative reciprocity) and by its middle (balanced reciprocity). This approach has been used widely and seems to provide a convenient framework for summarizing upper coast exchange.

Generalized reciprocity categorizes transactions in which there is no necessary expectation of return, that is to say, the giver does not stop giving in the absence of reciprocation and customarily only transfers food items. "A good pragmatic indication of generalized reciprocity is a sustained one-way flow [Sahlins 1965:147]"; and this usually occurs in the presence of close kinship.

Balanced reciprocity is a direct exchange—value for value more or less—that, in contrast to generalized reciprocity, is a situation in which one-way flow is not functional. In other words, the absence of appropriate reciprocation within a suitable period of time leads to the disruption of relations between individuals or groups. The social relations at issue are regulated by the continuation of approximately equal exchanges (applied more to goods and marital arrangements than to subsistence items). Slight inequities in these transactions are a prime mover in maintenance of the relationship by causing subsequent exchanges.

Negative reciprocity is conducted in the presence of the most distant kin relations or when these are absent. It refers to a wide range of transactions from sociable forms such as commercial-like activities to theft and stealing by force. Reciprocation ranges from cleverness or skill in bargaining to mounting counterforce measures.

Through these various means, important economic interdependencies are insulated against fundamental social cleavages (Sahlins 1965:154). To the extent that the levels of integration and kinship coincide, the nature of reciprocal relations may also correspond to a model in which generalized reciprocity characterized the family (i.e., the domestic unit in Adams's [1975:218] terminology) and the minimum band. Balanced reciprocity characterized the intervillage relations (maximum band) and those with related tribes whereas negative reciprocity characterized relations with distantly related or unrelated tribes and with Europeans. According to this concept, exchange relations are arrayed along a continuum; the relative positions along this continuum occupied by the types of social units recognized so far in this chapter are suggested in Figure 5.1a.

A further conception may be gained of the application of these exchange relations to the upper coast area in the schematic reciprocity "map" for the Akokisa shown in Figure 5.1b. The contour values relate to the scale shown in Figure 5.1a. Such maps for the other upper coast tribal groups should structurally resemble the one shown for the Akokisa. In this schematic representation, which really is little more than an application of Sahlins' concentric model (Sahlins 1965:154), it is shown that generalized reciprocity occurs within numerous localized centers. As kinship distance (a de facto function of geographic distance in our model) increases, a gradual shift away from generalized reciprocity takes place. The rate of falloff in this is related to group social relations in the larger environment.

Situationally, intertribal symbiosis would alter this Akokisa model somewhat (Sahlins 1965:155) by expanding outward the limits of the more sociable forms of exchange. This is only dealt with on a normative basis at the present time insofar as protohistoric period relations are evident. As has been emphasized by Sahlins, there is a variety of circumstances that may occur to thwart or modify exchange behavior. For example, no matter what moral imperatives exist as the driving force behind generalized reciprocity, an "affluent" individual may decline to share resources with a kinsman in need. The impact of idiosyncratic or even systemic factors in this respect is difficult to assess. However, a major sanction available in band–tribe society was the withdrawal of reciprocity in which the dissatisfied party might leave one band and join another (Fried 1967:12).

No doubt there were limits to the groups which would or could be joined, perhaps limited most often to movement within the tribe, less often to within the linguistic group, and much less often to culturally or linguistically unrelated groups. That is to say, most realignments would take place within residential groups (minimum bands) comprising a village, next most often between villages (maximum bands), and finally between tribes within the same linguistic group. This is probably one basis for the frequent shifts referred to for the Karankawa by Bolton (1915:282; also cf. Yellen 1977).

This proposed model of exchange relationships in the protohistoric period also constitutes a baseline against which the impact of the severe stresses and hardships of the late eighteenth and early nineteenth centuries can be measured. These stresses undoubtedly worked substantial modifications on the conditions of native societies and their exchange systems. It may be suggested that the major impact of these changes was to shift the bulk of transactions away from generalized and balanced reciprocity and toward negative reciprocity as a result of the creation of composite bands, diminution of involvement of close kinsmen in day-to-day activities, increase in commercial relations with Europeans, and the rise in murderous relations with Anglo settlers (particularly for the Karankawa tribes). This is a model which should be amenable to examination and elaboration through use of a joint archaeological–ethnohistorical approach.

CHAPTER 6

Ritual and Cognition

Many features of a culture appear curious or inexplicable in the absence of a conceptual framework against which to array them so that they impart meaning. Examples of this have already been presented in this part, and more will be given shortly. Examination of cognitive structures, in our case primarily through the medium of ritual, is a means of describing the society's system of classification of "things" in its own terms. This provides an indication of features that were locally significant (Sturtevant 1968). Put another way, we seek to suggest the form of those "homemade models" designed to perpetuate a society by facilitating the flow of information between systems of matter and energy (cf. Buchler and Selby 1968; Flannery and Marcus 1976; Rappaport 1971).

Such systems or models are built upon sacred symbols that "function to synthesize a people's ethos . . . their most comprehensive ideas of order [Geertz 1966:3]." It may be assumed, based on the population decline and dissolution of native groups, that such cognitive structures began disintegrating subsequent to the 1750 period. What is done here is to pick up bits and pieces of information and to suggest some relationships among them that may have obtained in the protohistoric period prior to this dissolution. As with the data on social organization, all that is available on ritual and cognition has been pooled for the four principal groups discussed here. It certainly is well known that the referents of such symbols can vary greatly, and so to attempt pooling of such data from separate sociological entities to arrive at a more or less comprehensive account entails some risk. The only justifications are that (a) the groups involved are very similar culturally and are closely related historically and spatially, and (b) most of all a heuristic device is sought that will help stimulate and structure further research on these proposals in both archival and archaeological sources.

The most important result of this effort is that the existing data suggest certain relationships in world view that are related also to behavior and to the archaeological record. The cognitive structure suggested in this section is very generalized and presumed to be more or less basic to all of the local territorial groups. An example is given wherein this aspect of culture is seen not quite so far removed from archaeological analysis as is sometimes imagined. Furthermore, we note that there is a specific set of cognitive features to be explored in ethnohistoric research and that there are certain identifiable structural lines in the archaeological data that relate to cognition.

The bulk of what is described in this section may be ascribed to that category of cultural activity called religion. Although they also are a part of what usually is termed religion, the data on mortuary ritual will not be provided in this chapter to any significant extent because a reasonably current account of this is given in Aten *et al.* (1976, especially see 93–107), and a summary is given in Chapter 14. So that there is a clear understanding of the anthropological concept of religion being used here we note that

> Every religious system consists . . . of a cognitive system; i.e., it consists of a set of explicit and implicit propositions concerning the superhuman world and of man's relationship to it, which it claims to be true [Spiro 1966:101].

Such propositions are, in essence, what Rappaport (1971:69) calls "ultimate sacred propositions"; propositions that are not necessarily logical or necessarily susceptible to empirical confirmation. In the model to be described shortly, these will be referred to simply as "sacred propositions."

From these or from similar native world view concepts were once derived the solutions to virtually all of the social questions of the day. Because the cultural acts involved were social, public, and observable, they now are encoded to a significant extent in the archaeological record.

In Table 5.1 are assembled all of the known ethnographic and ethnohistoric data bearing on the issues of ritual (except mortuary ritual) and cognition. As Sturtevant (1968:479) has pointed out, "the main evidence for the existence of a category is the fact that it is named." By enumerating the ritual and cognitive elements and their stated or presumed relationships, it is possible to construct a schematic representation of how these relations may have been structured (Figure 6.1). This preliminary model consists of three basic domains: first, a set of initial sacred propositions; second, a set of rituals that effect a transformation of some sort upon "real" entities or conditions; and third, a set of derivative sacred propositions.

Initial sacred propositions. The first domain includes a creator responsible for establishing everything that follows. Below this are found at least two basic structural lines in world view that may be simplified into a dichotomy between "death" and "life." Then there are a series of sociocultural categories under death and life to which various sorts of rituals are addressed. The most provocative of the subdivisions here is the dichotomy between death and life.

The local recognition of this distinction begins with the observation of de Solis that the Karankawa had two "divinities," *Pichini* and *Mel* (see Table 5.1:Item D-1). While there is some question whether these really were divinities in the minds of the Karankawa (as opposed simply to the identifiers of structural subdivisions or aspects of ritual), it is significant that de Solis went on to assert that these subdivisions had separate rituals and shamans for their supervision. The translation is imprecise as to whether the separation of ritual dances was in

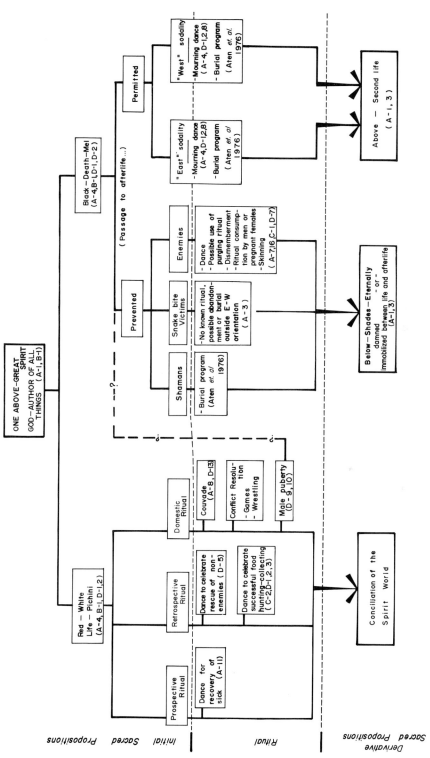

FIGURE 6.1 Preliminary model of cognitive structures for upper Texas coast native groups. (Note: A-7, A-16, C-1, D-7, etc., refer to entries in Table 5.1.)

terms of complete sets of dances for all purposes in each subdivision, or only for certain types of dances to be assigned to each subdivision; the model adopts the latter approach, but only because it intuitively seems the more likely.

In reviewing the sundry accounts compiled in Table 5.1, one is soon struck by the frequent use, in various contexts, of some or all of the color triad, red–black–white. This is a particularly interesting point because of the widespread application of these colors in the symbolism of primitive societies. Turner (1966) has reviewed this subject noting that red and white generally relate to a life context whereas black is used most often in relation to death and the cessation of activity. Moreover, while numerous colors are named in the Atakapa language (Gatschet and Swanton 1932), Karankawa only includes red, white, black, and blue (Gatschet 1891; Landar 1968). The use of the color blue, however, is frequently related closely to the color black (Turner 1966).

Recalling that de Solis identified *Mel* as one Karankawa divinity, it is further noted that in Karankawa, the word for dead is *mal*, and black is *pal*. In Atakapa, the word for black and for blue is *mel*. There is some difference in the systems of orthography used in these several sources and so we cannot be completely sure that these similarities are more than superficial. However, on the basis of these correspondences between lexical attributes, and until there are linguistic studies of this question, a relationship is assumed among *Mel*, the color black, and death. No such correlations have been discovered for the other "divinity," *Pichini*. Nor is any direct evidence known for a correspondence between the colors red and white, *Pichini*, and the life context of world view. However, such an association would be most logical and entirely similar to the situation in many other societies (cf. Turner 1966). Furthermore, it is quite possible that the color symbolism does not precisely correlate with the concepts of life–death and *Pichini–Mel*. At the moment there are multiple possibilities, but the model given in Figure 6.1 reflects the associations implied by the evidence available.

Moving to the next level of organization in the initial sacred propositions, the known kinds of "life" rituals have been classified into some basic functional categories. Although these are simply devices created for this analysis it seems clear that the "life" rituals were channeled in various directions. Three ritual classes or contexts are suggested: (*a*) *domestic* ritual operating largely within the family unit; (*b*) *prospective* ritual in which some outcome for the advantage of the entire residential group is sought; and (*c*) *retrospective* ritual in which a desired outcome was received and is celebrated.

On the "death" side, all activity seems geared to a concept of the afterlife. That is to say, ritual was used to facilitate the entry of some individuals into the afterlife, and to deny such entry to others. For this reason, "death" ritual has been subdivided according to these objectives. A further level of classification has been employed in which the categories come directly from either ethnohistoric or archaeological data. For individuals whose entry into the afterlife was sought, ritual seems to have varied depending on membership in one or the other of two sodalities marked in mortuary practices by body orientation to either the east or the west (Aten *et al.* 1976). Interestingly, among the Cherokee, the color black was associated with death *and with the west* (Mooney, cited in Turner 1966:75), further supporting the plausibility of this interpretation. For individuals whose entry into the afterlife was to be prevented, three classes have been identified: enemies, shamans, and snakebite victims.

Rituals. The second domain consists of a series of rituals designed to transform the target in some desired way. Thus, for the "life" category, rituals have been identified on Figure 6.1 that operate in some specific context for the purpose of coping with the spirit world so that a desired outcome could be achieved. It is necessary to be somewhat more vague about this category than about the "death" category. In the latter, the ethnohistoric and archaeological data define rather well the thrust of the necessary ritual activities having the objective of causing certain individuals to reach the afterlife and of preventing others from reaching this goal.

It would seem likely that a high degree of archaeological visibility should be entailed in these ceremonies. This is especially true for the death rituals, although if substantial advances are made in small site analyses and the identification and study of winter settlements, it is possible that the life rituals also will yield to investigation. In any event, archaeological evidence for cognition is inherent in mortuary ritual patterning, the occurrence and character of human skeletal remains (e.g., with respect to dismemberment; cf. Aten *et al.* 1976:78), identification of statuses and roles, discovery and interpretation of ritual paraphernalia (cf. Table 5.1:item C-4), and in identification of the material referents of the red–white–black triad and the associations of these items.

The use of red items is relatively easy to identify in that ochre or other minerals were the principal substances used (e.g., in graves, on ceramics, and on bone artifacts). White may have been symbolized through shell beads, shell pendants, and bird feathers suggested by the presence of blunt socketed bone projectile points presumably used for fowling) all of which are known to have figured in ritual contexts. Black, on the other hand, is an elusive color archaeologically in that it was probably employed most often through the application of charcoal (as in tattooing; Gatschet 1891:19, 62; Dyer 1917:3–4) and, possibly, vegetable dyes. Certain more substantial black materials also may have had significance, such as exotic black rock types that are occasionally encountered (e.g., Hartman 1963) and designs painted on ceramics with asphalt.

Derivative sacred propositions. The third and final domain suggested is one in which the desired outcome of some particular ritual transformation is specified. For the life rituals, little can be said except that this class of rituals served to conciliate the spirit world. That the spirit world was of enormous concern to members of primitive societies is clear both in the general literature on this subject, and, regarding the native inhabitants of the upper Texas coast, from the materials included in Table 5.1. Little shape can presently be given to this dimension, however.

More can be done with respect to the death rituals. Here, there was a clear objective of getting appropriate individuals into the "second life" and of preventing others from doing so. It is unclear at this point, whether the terms "below," "shades," and "eternally damned" were really equivalent and whether they reflected a concept of a place (e.g., "hell"), or if it meant an entrapment or immobilization between the conditions of "life" and "afterlife." It is reasonably clear from the literature that "spirits" of one sort or another were "known" to exist in and close to (or accessible to) the day-to-day reality of the people. Thus Cabeza de Vaca, De Bellisle, and Ker were all expected, or suspected, by the Indians, to have some degree of supernatural powers, as did the shamans. Spirit entities inhabited food (and probably other substances) and could cause sickness (cf. Table 5.1). Other spirits could be recalled from the afterlife by uttering their name (Table 5.1:item D-11).

Crude though it necessarily must be at the present stage of research, the cognitive model suggested in Figure 6.1, *or one similar to it*, is helpful for structuring research. This is because it must have been from such a model that natives derived explanations about situations that had occurred and deduced strategies for action. It is through references to such hypothetical frameworks that one is able to suggest cognitive explanations for the separate form of mortuary ritual for shamans (Aten *et al.* 1976:103), for the occurrence of dismembered human remains (Aten *et al.* 1976:78), and for a host of other situations in the ethnohistoric literature. For example, within a month or so of the arrival of Cabeza de Vaca and his companions on Malhado, the Indians began to die at an accelerated rate until within a short time one-half of them were gone (Bandelier 1905:64). The natives first concluded that the deaths were caused in some supernatural way by the Spanish and resolved to kill them. They were dissuaded from this only because they reasoned, logically, that since large numbers of the Spanish were also dying (albeit from other causes), the "malady" was not in the power of the Spanish to control.

This line of native thought probably is closely related to the fact that the three Europeans stranded in the area for whom detailed records of their experiences are available (Cabeza de Vaca, De Bellisle, and Ker) all were initially received in a relatively comradely way. But after a period of time had elapsed during which the natives apparently satisfied themselves that the Europeans were not in possession of fearsome supernatural powers (for the accounts make it clear this was on their minds), the three were suddenly subjected to all manner of inhospitable treatment.

There are other important illustrations. Cabeza de Vaca (Bandelier 1905:64) describes the incident when, shortly after reaching Malhado, several members of his group ate the bodies of their dead comrades. The Capoque were deeply upset by this cannibalism and indicated they might have killed the Europeans had they known of the practice earlier. This episode has been mentioned as a curious contradiction in behavior by the Karankawa (Krieger 1956). However, if the details on timing and significance of native rituals are reviewed in light of the cognitive model (Figure 6.1), it can be suggested that the natives were shocked at the Spanish eating the bodies of their deceased comrades not because of an abhorrence of the practice, but because the comrades were not "enemies." Rather, the dead were members of their own social group, who, by this act, were being deprived of entrance into the afterlife. Such a way of treating "kinsmen," as opposed to enemies or those possessed by or in contact with supernatural entities (e.g., shamans), would have seemed quite unthinkable to the Capoque given a cognitive model like that in Figure 6.1.

Returning now to points made in the introduction to this chapter, recall that it was proposed (following Rappaport 1971) that ritual and cognitive systems served a regulatory function in the flow of information between systems of energy and matter. The model proposed here serves such a function for some segments of the physical and social environment, especially in the area of relations with other individuals and groups. In addition to discovering new cognitive elements and clarifying this structure through additional ethnohistoric research, there is a real need to explore the relationships between such cognitive models and social organization. For example, there should be a fairly clear relationship between the band–tribe structure and how one might be treated with respect to the "death" rituals. There should be relationships between both the "life" and "death" ritual frameworks and the issue of population size regulation. There also should be locally definable relationships between reciprocity type and ritual conflict resolution, and so on.

Finally, it is necessary to point out that Figure 6.1 is only an attempt to begin construction of a model of cognition and ritual for the protohistoric period, and this is essentially a synchronic model. The analysis of mortuary practices for the Galveston Bay area (Aten *et al.* 1976) has clearly shown that major aspects of the mortuary ritual changed through time. As a result, it should be assumed that the overall cognitive model also changed. For example, there is a shift over a very long period of time in the frequency of east- versus west-oriented burials such that, by the time of the protohistoric period, the proportion of east-pointing burials had been reduced to nearly zero.

Indeed, the whole elaboration of the cognitive framework, to the extent that it was a means of defining and coping with the social environment, would be expected to have undergone its greatest development during the time when population increase and fissioning of bands into tribal entities had progressed to the point that the available landscape had become, or was becoming, filled. That is to say, vacant space between local territorial groups had become reduced to a minimum and population densities had become elevated to a level commensurate with the product of environmental resource potential and available technology efficiency. Once this occurred, a host of new forms of social interaction problems would have appeared requiring intellectual solutions rather than merely avoiding the problems by seeking refuge behind the barriers of vacant space (cf. Wobst 1974:155). At present, it cannot be said over what period of time this might have taken place, although it probably was over the period in which mortuary ritual was becoming more formalized, and especially after the establishment of cemeteries in the area (i.e., subsequent to circa A.D. 200 and circa A.D. 700, respectively [Aten *et al.* 1976]).

Based on her research, Dee Ann Story has suggested (personal communication 1979) that elaboration of mortuary and other ritual in east Texas may have been a concomitant of the rise of agriculture and of the associated uncertainties (or fluctuations) in productivity. These developments occurred more or less simultaneously with those just described for the upper coast (i.e., circa A.D. 750–800). While there is no evidence for agriculture on the coast, the possibility and implications should be considered of the east Texas ceremonialism having been assimilated, in an attenuated form, into coastal cultures for the purpose of providing a cognitive structure to cope with the local human ecological problems described above. It may also be suggested for future consideration, that native groups of the coast and east Texas were responding in alternative ways to similar ecological problems.

PART II

The Early Prehistoric Framework

CHAPTER 7

Background and Objectives

Numerous isolated finds of stylistically distinctive Paleo-Indian and Archaic projectile points and other characteristic early artifacts such as Clear Fork gouges make it reasonably clear that the Gulf coastal plain had been occupied by Native Americans since at least 12,000 years ago. An extended review of the evidence for these occupations may be found in Gagliano (1977).

Because many diverse habitats in the region have been surveyed for archaeological sites over the years, one would expect that at least some late glacial and early postglacial sites would have been discovered by now. The fact that this has not occurred, except for Late Archaic shell middens, the oldest of which are radiocarbon dated to about 3500 years ago, must point to the fact that early preceramic sites of the upper coast are unlike later sites in some fundamental respects. Either they are constituted differently, are distributed differently, or both. Because of this extremely limited archaeological visibility, conceptions of the preceramic cultures, which amount to 80% of the Native American cultural history for the area, remain largely hypothetical (Story 1976, 1980).

The best data available for preceramic cultures of the coastal plain region presently come from the inner coastal plain of central Texas (Story 1980:11), an area well beyond the region included in this book. *In situ* Paleo-Indian and Early Archaic components of stratified middens have been reported from the inland part of the upper coast (e.g., Patterson 1980) but are difficult to evaluate. The typology of their diagnostic artifacts has not been verified and the middens are so tightly stratified that discrete occupational components and technological assemblages cannot readily be distinguished. Recent reviews of Texas coast Archaic archaeology have attempted to outline problems for future research, and these constitute nearly everything in the way of conventional archaeological information (Corbin 1976; Hester 1976a; Story 1976). Thus, it seems clear that the past half century of active archaeological fieldwork on the coast has not led very far with respect to the problem of early cultures. An impasse in historiographic, much less processual, research exists and rethinking of the problem is needed rather than simply intensifying the effort.

Most archaeologists assume that late Quaternary environmental changes affected the nature and disposition of early archaeological sites along the Texas coast, even though these changes have never been analyzed in detail. Eustatic sea level movements, modifications in regional climate, rates of sedimentation, and other processes have markedly affected landscape evolution on the Texas coast during recent millennia. Such processes also have imparted distinctive time and space configurations to the distribution and internal characteristics of archaeological sites. Because these configurations are independent of endogenous cultural changes, archaeological investigations in this region generally must be accompanied by detailed geomorphic and geological analysis so that accurate explanation of site content and distribution can be made.

The coastal zone, as a major element of the terrestrial geographic configuration along the northern Gulf of Mexico, has undergone extensive relocation during the late Quaternary. Indeed, the coastal zone probably did not begin to impinge upon its present position on the upper coast until sometime around 4000 years ago. Therefore, archaeological sites possessing coastal oriented cultural adaptations should not be expected on the present coast earlier than this time period.

One key to understanding early cultures on the upper coast is to know that the geography, natural habitats, biota, climate, and human settlement around any given fixed point on the land (e.g., an archaeological site) has changed significantly. Earlier and later cultures alike were affected by this, but in different ways. Early cultures were displaced on a grand scale. However, once sea level essentially stabilized, around 3500 to 4000 years ago, there still was significant environmental impact on the later cultures from establishment of the barrier systems, shoaling and enlargement of estuaries, progradation of alluvial valleys, and relocation of stream channels on river deltas. During this time, the cultural and natural history of each coastal drainage basin became more distinctive.

Unlike the later cultures, the pre-pottery cultures lived through both the major reshaping of the coast's geography, and the major reorganization of its climate and biotic environments. What can still be observed of early cultures from archaeological sites on the *present* Texas coast is a severely truncated segment of the original record. Consequently, a review of the archaeology of the early cultures involves heavily deductive arguments based to a great extent on geological evidence. One might ask why such an effort should be devoted to archaeological remains so inaccessible as those submerged on the continental shelf and buried under estuarine fill. It seems to me there are several important reasons for doing so.

First, consideration of submerged archaeology is crucial for an adequate understanding of any early archaeological remains that may be found on the present coastal plain. As will be seen in the ensuing two chapters, the extent of environmental "truncation" that has taken place can be estimated with the result that fairly specific expectations can be stated about the remaining terrestrial record of early archaeology.

Second, consideration of late Quaternary environmental changes and their impact on the archaeological record has significant theoretical implications about the economic and social basis of early cultures in the New World. Although in recent years there has been a trend away from superficial assumptions about early man having been exclusively a big game hunter (Johnson 1977), the evolving concepts about early subsistence economies still turn around terrestrial resources. The inception of littoral and maritime oriented economies is widely assumed to be a feature of the Middle Archaic, or about 5000 to 4000 years ago. But surely it is more than coincidental that coastal zones in most unglaciated areas of North America only began to reach their present locations at that time. The frequently used explanation that the Middle Archaic marked initiation of progressive discoveries by man of an ever-widening range of coastal resources usually is based on evidence far more easily explained as the expectable consequence of coastal geographic evolution. Indeed, there is every reason to expect that early coast dwelling cultures were experienced users of littoral resources. What this meant, however, in terms of such things as technology, seasonality, organization, and economic relationships among classes of resources is not known because nearly all of the coastal environments and, as a result, the sites of cultural activity, for the periods coeval with early man are now removed from conventional observation.

Third, the time when evidence from submerged archaeological sites will be in hand is drawing closer. Exploitation of oil and gas resources on the continental shelf has provided a stimulus for considering in more detail the prospects and methods for finding and exploring submerged archaeological sites. The approach, conceptually, is simple:

1. Reconstruct submerged paleogeography based on geological data.
2. Estimate the kinds of archaeological sites which may be submerged.
3. Estimate the characteristics of submerged archaeological sites which are likely to be observable.
4. Estimate the probabilities for association of the predicted site types and reconstructed landforms.
5. Test and revise these models through geophysical and bottom sampling observations of submerged landforms predicted to be the location of anticipated site types.

Large-scale reconstruction of submerged natural environments in the northern Gulf of Mexico has been accomplished to the extent of identifying the major natural systems (Gagliano 1977). This aspect of the modeling problem is continued for the upper Texas coast portion of the continental shelf in the next chapter. As geologic research, environmental protection, and industrial surveys continue, a very large body of data is accumulating, principally in the form of subbottom profiles, which is dramatically expanding the capability for developing highly detailed submerged landform reconstructions.

Gagliano (1977) suggested the types of sites to be found submerged and their likely association with landforms. Until recently, however, it has not been possible to go the final step and test the associations. Although archaeologists have suggested and urged the use of various technologies such as coring, diving, submersible vehicles, underwater television cameras, and the like, there remain distinct economic limitations to the practicality of most such techniques for routine archaeological research. The most feasible approach is to employ a submerged site survey procedure that makes integrated use of relatively conventional remote sensing and bottom-sampling instruments which are already familiar and in common use for other purposes. An initial formulation of analytical procedures established methods and criteria for mechanical and geochemical analysis of sediments from box or tube core samples to distinguish cultural from natural sediments on the northern Gulf of Mexico coast (Gagliano *et al.* 1981). Once these methods have been applied and refined, it is likely to be only a matter of time before the first submerged habitation sites will be identified on the Texas and Louisiana continental shelf.

One might also ask what is the likelihood that archaeological sites submerged by a rising sea level will have survived to be documented. There is no reason to assume a priori that all such sites would have been destroyed by the surf zone and coastal currents. The situation, though, is a complicated one. Preservation will have depended on several factors: (*a*) the type of materials comprising the site; (*b*) the sedimentary substrate under a site; (*c*) the degree of exposure of the landform on which a site exists to destructive erosional processes; (*d*) the rate of sea level rise at the time of site submergence; (*e*) the energy level of the surf zone at the site location; (*f*) the amount of post-submergence sedimentation; and (*g*) the degree to which a submerged site continues to be impinged by the wave base and the energy of wave motion. A realistic expectation for early sites on the northern Gulf of Mexico is that some will have disappeared without a trace, others will be in relatively pristine condition, and many will be in intermediate states of preservation ranging from moderate erosion to total disaggregation into lag deposits. All reconnaissance data from such sites, whatever their degree of disturbance, are exceedingly valuable.

Because of the water depths and huge areas involved, it seems likely that no matter what kind of underwater excavation techniques have been or may be developed, most data identifying drowned terrestrial archaeological sites will be obtained from remote bottom sampling. From these samples, locational data, estimates of the age of occupation, and perhaps limited estimates of activities can be obtained, as well as an evaluation of the practicality of more extensive direct examination through underwater excavation techniques. When shell middens are encountered, the information yield easily could go much farther (Aten 1981). Estimates of habitation intensity, habitat characteristics, and shellfish collection season could be made, and mass spectrometric methods applied to mollusc shells would permit estimates of absolute age and water temperature (as a reflection of air temperature and climate).

Because there is a growing technological capability for archaeology to deal with both the landward and the submerged seaward portions of the coastal territory once inhabited by the Native Americans, more can be done than just acknowledge that there may be or probably are submerged sites. And the first step toward realizing this potential is to prepare a coherent historical framework to organize the highly fragmented data sets from the preceramic cultures. Ordinarily the approach would be based on projectile point typology, seriation, and cross dating, but as noted earlier this has not been a successful approach on the upper Texas coast for several reasons:

1. For periods prior to the Late Archaic, no archaeological sites have been found with sufficiently good stratigraphic separation of habitation zones to permit adequate definition of the "resident" upper coast artifact morphological categories, their ontogenies, and their absolute dates. Consequently, projectile points from the region are largely obtained from uncontrolled collections organized according to typologies worked out for central and northeast Texas.

2. Although there are no good alternatives to this approach for classification of archaeological specimens just now, the significant difficulties with it are that while many individual artifact types are shared, the assemblages for central and northeast Texas as a whole seem to be different from those of the coast. Moreover, the central and northeast Texas types themselves have poorly known ontogenies which are a weak basis for organizing upper coastal archaeological assemblages.

3. In addition, there is limited agreement about morphological characteristics of many of the defined projectile point types. Application of the typologies often is dominated by unacknowledged idiosyncracies that frustrate synthesis of what few collections do exist; in computer jargon, this means "garbage in, garbage out."

4. And even if the projectile point morphologies, ontogenies, and distributions were well understood, their theoretical content presently would be too limited to permit deduction of very much beyond age estimates and an historical framework.

As a result, a direct archaeological approach has not been used. Instead, it is assumed that the culture–environment linkage was more determinant for the early cultures than it was for the later cultures. Because a great deal of unsynthesized paleoenvironmental data exists for the upper Texas coast, these are documented and integrated in Chapter 8. Then, in Chapter 9, an environment-based periodization is used to state expectations about the resident early cultures of the time. Finally, the meager archaeological evidence is correlated with the environmental history. This approach has the advantage of being a chronological framework with theoretical implications for suggesting the basic elements of habitation by native cultures in the coastal zone of Texas from the final millennia of the last glacial period until the present geographic configuration of the coast became established. By investigating and elaborating these environmental and cultural hypotheses, the impasse in historiography of the early cultures of the upper Texas coast should be broken.

CHAPTER 8

Late Quaternary Environments

INTRODUCTION

The purpose of this chapter is to present sufficient information about the late Quaternary environmental history of the upper coast to support the discussion of early native cultures in Chapter 9, and to provide a context for the descriptions of archaeological stratigraphy in Chapter 11. In the following sections, information is presented on these topics:

1. Late Quaternary stratigraphic units and their spatial, superpositional, and chronological correlations.
2. An initial interpretation of continental shelf paleogeography linked with the previously described late Quaternary stratigraphic units.
3. An interpretation of fluvial–deltaic stratigraphy and chronology for the modern floodplains of the Trinity and Brazos rivers.
4. A model of late Quaternary paleoclimates for the upper coast.

With this information, it will be possible to draw preliminary conclusions about geography, climates, and habitat distribution over most of the time period that the Texas coast is known to have been inhabited by man. For a more detailed introduction to the geology of this region see Aronow (1971), Beard (1973), Bernard and Le Blanc (1965), Bernard *et al.* (1970), Fisher *et al.* (1972, 1973), Gagliano (1977), and Nelson and Bray (1970).

TERRACE STRATIGRAPHY

The Quaternary portion of the coastal plain of Texas is comprised primarily of an offlapping series of coastwise (i.e., coast parallel) terraces deposited during interglacial (high sea level) stages. These units were formed by alluvial and deltaic sedimentation and occur in a roughly 150 km wide belt subparallel to the coast. The youngest of the coastal terraces is nearest the Gulf and is known as the Beaumont Formation. It has a low relief surface and was deposited during the Sangamon and Wisconsin stages. The Beaumont is the western continuation of the Prairie Formation of Louisiana.

The coastal terraces are dissected more or less perpendicularly to the coast by streams draining the interior and are bounded at the coast by estuaries, marshes, and barrier systems. The glacial stages (lower sea levels) are represented by fluvial terraces formed during stillstands along the major streams and by erosional unconformities (Barton 1930; Bernard and Le Blanc 1965; Bernard *et al.* 1962; Doering 1956). While the coastal terraces long have been recognized as Pleistocene in age, deposits of the stream valleys, estuaries, and barrier islands generally have been viewed as very young features, postdating the establishment of sea level at its present elevation. The first clear documentation of intermediate-aged features in the coastal zone came with Bernard's (1950) description of the Deweyville "Beds" along the Sabine and Neches rivers (see Figure 1.1). This surface was described as early Recent in age and intermediate in altitude between the Beaumont Formation uplands and the Recent (Holocene in the terminology used here) floodplains.

Geomorphic mapping carried out along the lower Trinity River, the next major stream to the west of the Neches, has confirmed the existence of a series of fluvial terraces ranging from late Pleistocene to Holocene in age (Aten 1966a,b). Although similar intermediate terraces have not been found outcropping in the coastal portion of the Brazos River valley, the next major stream west of the Trinity, there is evidence they exist, but have been buried by the aggrading modern floodplain. Based on a variety of criteria, such intermediate terraces are now recognized along numerous Gulf coast streams (Gagliano and Thom 1967). Because the most comprehensive late Pleistocene–Holocene stratigraphy of the western Gulf coastal plain is preserved along the Trinity River, this shall be summarized as the basis for connecting the environmental history of the Texas coast with more general models of sea level and climatic change.

Description of the terrace stratigraphy of the lower Trinity River was based on U.S. Army Corps of Engineers topographic maps, prepared at a scale of 1:1000 and a contour interval of 1 foot, supplemented by air photo mosaics to the same scale; by U.S. Department of Agriculture aerial photography; and by field checking of lithology, topography, and soil profiles. Criteria for distinguishing terrace levels were elevation, rates of slope, and preservation characteristics of geomorphic features. The distribution of the mapped terrace remnants is shown in Figure 8.1; stratigraphic relationships between the mapped terraces are illustrated in Figure 8.2. Data for the Trinity River valley section of Figure 8.2 are from original mapping by Aten using the sources described above; the Trinity estuary slope profiles were compiled from reinterpretations of subsurface core data in Rehkemper (1969:Figures 2–14, 2–15, 2–16, and 2–18) and bathymetric data from Fisher *et al.* (1972:Topography and Bathymetry Map); the continental shelf portion of Figure 8.2 was compiled from interpretations of subsurface core data in Nelson and Bray (1970:Figures 4 and 5) and bathymetry on the Houston,

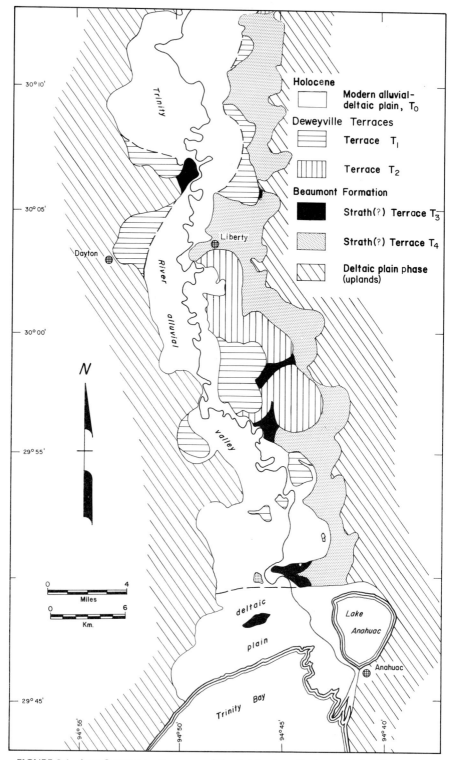

FIGURE 8.1 Late Quaternary terraces and floodplain along the lower Trinity River, Texas.

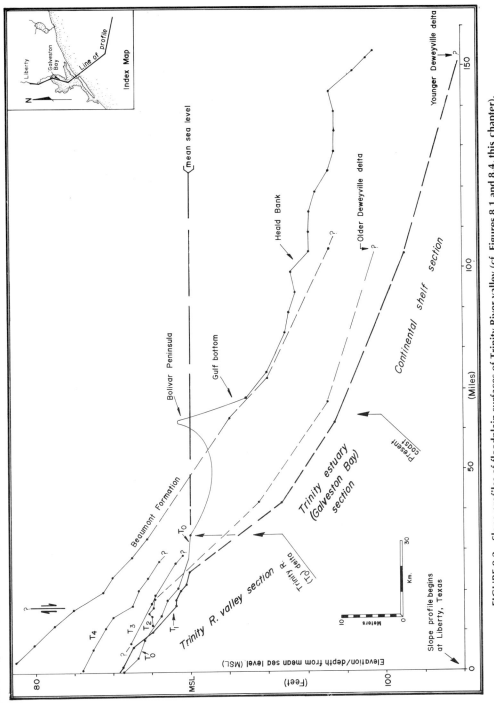

FIGURE 8.2   Slope profiles of floodplain surfaces of Trinity River valley (cf. Figures 8.1 and 8.4, this chapter).

Bay City, and Bouma Bank sheets of the National Ocean Survey Outer Continental Shelf Resource Management map series.

Beaumont Formation   This formation makes up the margins of the Trinity River valley. It is the oldest stratigraphic and highest topographic surface along the lower Trinity and is composed of a titled plain of coalesced river deltas characterized today by pimple mounds and meander belt ridges reflecting abandoned courses of the ancestral Trinity River (Aronow 1971:43–51). Except where incised by the modern drainage network, this surface has very low relief and slopes gently to the south at a rate of about 2 feet per mile (0.4 m per km) along the Trinity River–Galveston Bay estuary. Near the coast, the Beaumont is overlapped by Holocene marsh and barrier beach sediments, although it is being exhumed locally in the nearshore zone between High Island and Sabine Pass. The sediments comprising this formation are intensely oxidized to a depth of several meters.

Aronow (1971:51) reviewed attempts to date the Beaumont and concluded it was a minimum of 30,000 years old, and probably at least 37,000 years old. All Beaumont Formation deltaic plain materials dated thus far have been shells from either the Smith Point–Fannett–Houston Barrier (here referred to simply as the Smith Point Barrier) or from fossil reefs in what once were lagoons landward of the barrier. These specimens have all been "dead" to any detection of radioactive carbon. However, the Pleistocene Trinity River meander belts mapped by Aronow (1971) all breached the barrier and prograded their meander belts to terminations in apparent birdfoot deltas farther to the south and east. Consequently, these meander belts are younger to some degree than the Smith Point Barrier system.

This extension beyond the barrier system generally has been viewed as a continuous progradational development of the deltaic plain (e.g., Rehkemper 1969:16; Graf 1966:48). However, a river of such low discharge (cf. Table 8.1) as the Beaumont Formation Trinity probably was unable to prograde a birdfoot delta into the open Gulf. Even today, the relatively larger Brazos, Colorado, and Rio Grande rivers are only able to produce cuspate deltas. In these cases, the significant energy differential between coastal processes and delta processes causes the former to dominate (cf. Galloway 1975:92). Therefore, the existence of Beaumont Trinity River meander belts and birdfoot deltas seaward of the Smith Point Barrier must mean deposition during a period of lowered sea level. This could have occurred either as a lowering directly from the Smith Point Barrier level to a new coastal position, or perhaps as Farmdalian reoccupation of the earlier (perhaps Altonian) Smith Point coastline (more or less) after a regression–transgression cycle (Figure 8.3). In either event, this later coast would have been contemporaneous with the more recent Beaumont meander belts (such as Aronow's China and Big Hill ridges) and the Ingleside Barrier of the central Texas coast (cf. Otvos 1980:90; Wilkinson *et al.* 1975). S. M. Gagliano (personal communication 1982) has obtained three radiocarbon dates ranging

YEARS B.P.	STAGE	SUB-STAGE	GEOMORPHIC SURFACES (based on Trinity R.)	SEA LEVEL PHASE	EVENTS
2,500 – 4,000 – 6,000 – 10,000 –	HOLOCENE	(Undefined) post-Two Creekan	///// ///// / / Modern alluvial-deltaic plain, T_0 ° multiple delta positions still visable (Figure 8.7) /// //// ° Alluvial ////// channel "B" / / ///////// groups ///// ////////// ///// ////////// "A" //////////////	stable (±) trans-gression	° Floodplain aggradation; progradation into estuary ° Development of modern estuary; stream discharge increases ° Adjustment to slowly rising sea level (?) ° "Altithermal"; low discharge ° Transition to interglacial hydrologic conditions
11,000 –	WISCONSINAN	Two Creekan	Deweyville Terraces — Terrace T_1	regression	° Floodplain entrenchment ° Continued high discharge and erosion
13,000 –			Deweyville Terraces — Terrace T_2 ? ? ? ?	transgression	° Very high discharge; extensive lateral erosion of valleys
18,000 –		Woodfordian	////////////////// ////////////////// ////////////////// ////////////////// ////////////////// //////////////////		° Continental shelf submergence resumes;
20,000 –			Beaumont Formation	regression	° Continental shelf emergence continues to maximum exposure
			Terrace T_3 [strath]		° Continuation of T_4 conditions
25,000 –			Terrace T_4 [strath]		° Discharge increases; emergence of continental shelf begins
30,000 –		Farmdalian	Deltaic plain phase (as mapped by Aronow 1971)	stable (±)	° Interglacial hydrologic and climatic conditions; multiple meander belts

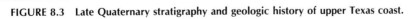

FIGURE 8.3 Late Quaternary stratigraphy and geologic history of upper Texas coast.

between 25,000 and 30,000 years ago documenting coastal features in south Louisiana which appear to be equivalent to these late (Farmdalian?) phases of the Beaumont Formation Trinity River.

Terrace T_4   Stratigraphically higher but topographically lower than the Beaumont, this terrace is characterized by very poorly preserved meander scars and abandoned channels. The T_4 surface occurs only along the east side of the valley where it can be traced nearly continuously. Because the sediments comprising this terrace, and the lower T_3, are deeply oxidized and are underlain by sediments characteristic of the Beaumont Formation (Aronow 1971:51), both may be strath terraces cut into the Beaumont Formation during stillstands of the early Woodfordian falling sea level substage (Figure 8.3). In Aronow (1971) and on the Houston and Beaumont sheets of the Geologic Atlas of Texas (Bureau of Economic Geology 1968a,b) all intermediate terrace levels between the Beaumont Formation and the modern floodplains (including the Trinity River T_3 and T_4 terraces) are mapped as the Deweyville Formation or "deposits." Although this was done partly as a mapping convenience, it has led to some confusion about the region's geologic history.

  The Trinity River intermediate terraces fall into two major groups that are important to separate for historical reasons. For example, if the intermediate terrace levels were not carefully distinguished when being sampled for radiocarbon dating material, the resulting dates should range over a period from the latest Beaumont to the earliest modern floodplain, or from about 30,000 to around 10,000 years before present. In fact, this seems to be what has occurred for estimates of the age of the Deweyville terraces (Aronow 1971:51; Bernard and LeBlanc 1965:149; Saucier 1981:12). However, in this chapter, the term *Deweyville* is used much more narrowly to apply only to the T_1 and T_2 terraces, which probably were deposited sometime during the rising sea level phase of late Woodfordian–Two Creekan–Valderan.

Terrace T_3   This terrace stratigraphically overlies but is topographically lower than Terrace T_4. It is characterized by abandoned channels, meander scars which appear to be about the same radius as those of the T_4 terrace (although none of these were preserved well enough to measure), and by point-bar ridges and swales of about 30 to 60 cm relief that are prominent as photogeologic features. Only intermittent segments of this terrace are preserved, mainly on the east side of the river valley, and their correlation is based primarily on geomorphic preservation and slope relationships (Figure 8.1). Because the sediments underlying this terrace also are oxidized (Aronow 1971:51) and resemble those of the Beaumont Formation, it too probably represents a strath terrace cut into the Beaumont during yet a lower level stillstand of the falling sea level phase of the early Woodfordian glaciation (see description above for the T_4 terrace).

Terrace T₂   In addition to the large channel geometry (Table 8.1), the T_2 terrace surface is marked by high relief (in excess of 2 meters) point-bar features. Barton (1930) noted the "wide, sweeping meanders of the ancient Trinity River." Because Beaumont Formation river meanders are similar in magnitude to those of the present (see Table 8.1), it seems likely that he was referring in a general manner to the surfaces Bernard (1950) subsequently named the Deweyville Beds. Generally known today as either the Deweyville Formation or Deweville terrace (Bureau of Economic Geology 1968a; Gagliano and Thom 1967), these extinct floodplain surfaces are distinguished from all others by extremely large wavelengths, channel widths, and radii of curvature of their meander scars. On the northern Gulf of Mexico coast, they have been described for the Pascagoula, Pearl, Ouchita, Sabine, Neches, Brazos, and Colorado rivers (Baker and Penteado-Orellana 1977; Gagliano and Thom 1967), as well as on the Trinity. The T_2 terrace also is known informally on the upper Texas coast as the Older Deweyville.

The Deweyville terraces consist of very fine to coarse sand grading in places to clayey silts and silty sands. They differ from the T_3 and T_4 terraces in lithology (i.e., much less clay), significantly less intensive weathering, constructional rather than erosional origin, better preservation of geomorphic features, and in their uniquely large channel geometry (Table 8.1). Indeed, the extreme lateral and vertical erosional capability of the Deweyville streams was the primary agent responsible for scouring and shaping the valleys of many Gulf coast river systems into their present configurations.[1]

As was implied earlier in reference to the T_4 terrace, radiocarbon dating of Deweyville surfaces is a rather muddled and somewhat circumstantial issue at present. The facts about the Deweyville terraces (i.e., the T_1 and T_2 terraces in the Trinity River valley) are that (*a*) they probably represent very large increases in stream discharge and bed load compared to hydrologic regimes either before or since; (*b*) they are aggradational features rather than erosional ones; (*c*) that they appear to be capped by the approximately 9,000-year-old peats in the subsurface under Galveston Bay (Rehkemper 1969:32,36) and Sabine Pass (Nelson and Bray 1970:Figure 7); (*d*) peat at the top of fluvial sand presumed to be Deweyville on the continental shelf is radiocarbon dated at 10,207 B.P. (Nel-

---

[1]The late Holocene deltaic plain of the Trinity River has been cored on several occasions for foundation engineering purposes: (*a*) for the Lake Anahuac reservoir (McEwen 1963); (*b*) for Interstate Highway 10 and the Trinity River Bridge; and (*c*) for Wallisville Dam. Contours drawn on the top of the Beaumont Formation as encountered in these cores indicate rather clearly that the bottom of the Trinity River valley is relatively flat. The deepest channel is that cut by the Younger Deweyville–Trinity River as it formed the Lake Anahuac (Turtle Bay) meander scar. This supports the hypothesis that lateral erosion during the relatively late Deweyville interval (Figure 8.3), instead of stream incision during the earlier, maximum low sea level period (ca.18,000 B.P.), primarily was responsible for the configuration of major river valleys on the northern Gulf coast. Saucier (1981:10) also concluded that lowered sea (base) level did not cause extensive development of entrenched stream valleys in the Gulf coast; instead he, too, concluded that late Quaternary evolution of the Mississippi Valley was primarily through lateral planation.

TABLE 8.1
Channel Geometry of Upper Texas Coast Streams.

Geomorphic surface		Channel width (ft[e])	Radius of meanders (ft[e])	Meander amplitude (ft[e])	Meander wave length (ft[e])
Trinity River					
Present channel (T₀)	N[a]	39	43	32	34
	X̄[b]	224	674	1916	3063
	SD[c]	35	329	605	799
	CV[d]	16%	49%	32%	26%
Channel group A (T₀)	N	—	41	23	25
	X̄	—	424	1267	1952
	SD	—	190	431	487
	CV	—	45%	34%	25%
Channel group B (T₀)	N	—	8	2	2
	X̄	—	713	3650	2800
	SD	—	266	—	—
	CV	—	37%	—	—
Terrace T₁ (Younger Deweyville)	N	4	4	—	—
	X̄	1498	3920	—	—
	SD	72	842	—	—
	CV	5%	21%	—	—
Terrace T₂ (Older Deweyville)	N	5	5	1	1
	X̄	1460	4330	15000	32000
	SD	277	1458	—	—
	CV	19%	34%	—	—
Terrace T₄ (Beaumont Formation)	N	12	12	—	—
	X̄	508	1950	—	—

	Col 1	Col 2	Col 3	Col 4
Beaumont Formation (China Ridge System only)				
SD	86	521	—	—
CV	17%	27%	—	—
N	10	30	14	13
$\bar{X}$	304	608	1740	2864
SD	71	155	644	538
CV	23%	25%	37%	19%
Brazos River				
Present channel (T_0)				
N	—	73	—	—
$\bar{X}$	—	894	—	—
SD	—	449	—	—
CV	—	50%	—	—
Oyster Creek channel (T_0)				
N	—	108	—	—
$\bar{X}$	—	847	—	—
SD	—	362	—	—
CV	—	43%	—	—
Bastrop Bayou channel (T_0)				
N	—	18	—	—
$\bar{X}$	—	822	—	—
SD	—	226	—	—
CV	—	27%	—	—
Big Slough channel (T_0)				
N	—	35	—	—
$\bar{X}$	—	551	—	—
SD	—	154	—	—
CV	—	28%	—	—

[a] Number of measurements, N.
[b] Mean, $\bar{X}$.
[c] Standard deviation, SD.
[d] Coefficient of variation, CV.
[e] To express channel geometry dimensions in meters, multiply feet by 0.305.

son and Bray 1970:Figure 7); and (e) other radiocarbon dates from undifferentiated intermediate terrace associations have ranged as young as circa 13,250
years ago (Aronow 1971:51).

In the original description of the Deweyville terrace, Bernard (1950:40, 70)
recognized two alluvial sequences, the older of which was Deweyville with
surface outcrop, and the younger was entrenched into the Deweyville with only
subsurface evidence. The pattern of an outcropping Deweyville surface being
cut by renewed valley entrenchment also is documented now on the Colorado
River (Baker and Penteado-Orellana 1977:413–414), with the down-cutting
there estimated to have occurred at some time in the period between 10,000 and
7,000 B. P. This is seen along the Trinity River also, except that there the surface
of the entrenched younger floodplain still can be observed as the T_1 terrace that
is described in the following subsection. The Trinity River T_2 and T_1 surfaces
both express the characteristic Deweyville channel geometry and document
most clearly that the Deweyville consists of at least two terrace levels, either one
or both of which are destroyed or buried in most other Gulf coast stream
valleys.

Taken altogether, this evidence describes deposition during a rising sea level
phase terminated by a period of renewed regression followed by further transgression and establishment of the modern fluvial conditions. Bernard (1950:40)
correlated the Deweyville surface with the Two Creekan Substage, and the
renewed valley cutting with the Mankato glaciation. This interpretation still is
the one most consistent with all the available facts, although the more recent
tendency has been to correlate the post-Two Creekan regression with the Valderan glaciation (but cf. Gagliano 1977:168). More recent findings further support this interpretation. There is strong paleontological evidence for the return
of colder waters to the Gulf of Mexico circa 11,000 to 10,000 years ago (Beard
1973:300–301; also see Ruddiman and McIntyre 1981:126). Moreover, practically all eustatic sea level curves for unglaciated coasts anywhere in the world
show the same pattern of rise, retreat, and rise in the 12,000–9,000 B.P. period
(Bloom 1977), which is inferred for the Texas coast from the Deweyville terrace
stratigraphy.

There is some evidence (Gagliano 1977:168; Nelson and Bray 1970: Figure
11), for a brief period of down-cutting around 7000 years ago. From this the
question naturally has arisen whether the Deweyville terraces might be associated with a later period of sea level rise followed by down-cutting. However, it
does not seem that a strong case can be made for such a recent age for the
Deweyville terraces because

1. The presumed Deweyville surfaces under Galveston Bay and Sabine Pass
(reported as undifferentiated, coarse-grained, fluvial–deltaic deposits) are
capped by a 9000-year-old peat horizon.

2. Evidence exists for a coastal Altithermal period at about 6000 years ago (to
be discussed later in this chapter), which would be inconsistent with simul-

taneous evidence for a coastal pluvial period so evident in Deweyville terrace channel geometry and local soil characteristics.

3. Evidence will be presented shortly that indicates that modern stream conditions were established on the Brazos River by circa 7000 B.P.

However, this argument does not preclude another period of down-cutting subsequent to the hydrologic regimen recorded in the Deweyville floodplains and which would be recorded somewhere in the stratigraphy of modern fluvial–deltaic plain complexes.

Terrace T_1   There is a second system of meander scars of similar magnitude to those forming the T_2 terrace but which occur at a significantly lower elevation. These scars are from a floodplain formed by the Trinity River under a hydrologic regimen similar to that of the Older Deweyville, but after a period of entrenchment. The T_1 terrace records a major reversal in the rising sea level phase of the late Wisconsin, probably a post-Two Creekan glaciation as was discussed previously in conjunction with the T_2 terrace. The nearly buried floodplain of T_1 is known informally on the upper Texas coast as the Younger Deweyville.

The T_1 surface is almost entirely buried by alluviation and floodplain development associated with the modern river. There is little geomorphic relief reflected on the Corps of Engineers 1 foot (30 cm) contour interval maps of the lower Trinity River, However, the point-bar deposits are distinctly shown on aerial photography by arcuate tonal bands reflecting differences in surface vegetation. This buried surface is mappable only at the margins of the modern floodplain where it has not been completely obliterated by overbank deposits and probably correlates with Bernard's (1950:40) buried alluvial sequence which was cut into the outcropping Deweyville terrace on the Sabine and Neches rivers.

Modern Floodplain, T_0   The alluvial–deltaic plain complex of the modern Trinity River consists of abundant fluvial geomorphic features in varying degrees of preservation, and channel geometry of much smaller scale than that of the Deweyville floodplains (Table 8.1). The modern deltaic plain formed by the coalescing of several delta masses (see Figures 8.1 and 8.6) is analogous to the coastwise plain (Beaumont Formation) but on a much smaller scale. The alluvial–deltaic plain is characterized by numerous remnants of abandoned main channels of the Trinity, distributary channels, inter-distributary basins now filled with lakes or marshes, and tidal channels draining these basins. The alluvial–deltaic plain of the Trinity, like those of other Texas coast rivers, formed during the final phases of rising sea level subsequent to the end of the post-Two Creekan regression–cold water period. This period began circa 9000 years ago and is termed the Holocene stage (Figure 8.3).

The total sequence of events recorded by the succession of stratigraphic units in the Trinity River valley probably applies to all of the drainages of the northern coast of the Gulf of Mexico. The succession of warm and cold water periods in the Gulf (Beard 1973), the growing evidence for a post-Smith Point Barrier Farmdalian phase of the Beaumont Formation, the wide occurrence of pluvial geomorphology (Gagliano and Thom 1967) ending after a major episode of down-cutting (Aten present volume; Baker and Penteado-Orellana 1977; Bernard 1950), and the broadly similar histories of hydrologic regimen for at least the Trinity and Brazos rivers (Table 8.1) and perhaps the Mississippi (Saucier 1981) all point at the existence of a common regional environmental history during the late Quaternary as summarized in Figure 8.3. Absolute dates for Figure 8.3 are based primarily on data from various sources summarized in Beard (1973), Gagliano (1977), and Nelson and Bray (1970).

PALEOGEOGRAPHY

Only discontinuous segments of the late Quaternary environmental history have been documented. Despite this, the overall structure of the natural environment and of its changes should be estimated and factored into analysis of Texas coast archaeological issues such as demography, settlement pattern, and subsistence. Because one of the reasons for such a complex stratigraphic evolution was response to eustatic sea level variation, a great deal of terrain that was part of the human habitat during the late Wisconsin and much of the Holocene now is either buried under estuarine sedimentation or submerged on the continental shelf. Having correlated general patterns of late Quaternary sea level changes with specific stratigraphic features on the upper Texas coast via consideration of terrace stratigraphy, it is possible to attempt an initial paleogeographic reconstruction for the region as a whole. At present, it is most convenient to approach the question of paleogeography in three separate parts:

1. The coastal record of the late Wisconsin and early Holocene (ca. 13,000–7,500 years ago), which is submerged on the continental shelf.
2. The coastal record of the middle Holocene (ca. 7,500–3,500 years ago), which primarily is documented in the nearshore continental shelf subsurface and from buried estuarine features in the present coastal zone.
3. The coastal record of the late Holocene (ca. 3,500 years ago to the present), which is found both in the presently observable coastal geography, and in the alluvial–deltaic record of the T_0 floodplain of the major stream valleys.

A first formulation of the continental shelf paleogeography for these periods is given in Figure 8.4 for the upper Texas coast. Comparable reconstructions for the adjacent Louisiana continental shelf also are available (Gagliano 1977:314–329). Developing this interpretation of submerged paleogeography involves rec-

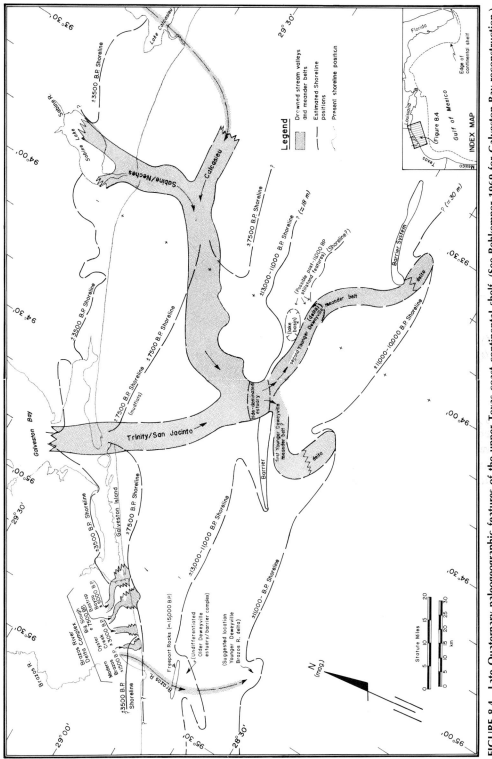

FIGURE 8.4 Late Quaternary paleogeographic features of the upper Texas coast continental shelf. (See Rehkemper 1969 for Galveston Bay reconstruction.)

onciling several kinds of data: (*a*) stratigraphic profiles (Figure 8.2); (*b*) stratigraphic history (Figure 8.3); (*c*) sea level time–depth curves (Gagliano 1977; Nelson and Bray 1970; Rehkemper 1969); (*d*) continental shelf bathymetry (National Ocean Survey Outer Continental Shelf Resource Management map series); (*e*) absolute chronological data (Bernard *et al.* 1970; Gould and McFarlan 1959; Nelson and Bray 1970; Rehkemper 1969; Winchester 1971); (*f*) sea water temperature and salinity sequences (Beard 1973; Kennett and Shackleton 1975); and (*g*) subsurface stratigraphy from cores and subbottom profile records (S. M. Gagliano, personal communication 1981; Gould and McFarlan 1959; Nelson and Bray 1970; Rehkemper 1969).

The existence and magnitude of landforms in any given instance are usually the resultants of numerous variables in the physical environment. Identifying drowned terrestrial geomorphology on the continental shelf consequently requires better assumptions than simply attempting to trace "gashes" in the shelf presumed to have been excavated by entrenched streams during glacial period low sea level. The major variables affecting development of Gulf coast stream morphology on the continental shelf during a glacial cycle probably were

1. Rate of sea level change (whether fall, rise, or stillstand);
2. Stream discharge and bedload; and
3. Position of observation along the overall longitudinal profile of the stream.

Other factors such as longshore currents, type of bedrock sediment bounding stream valleys, and so on, are assumed either to be essentially constant for this problem, or else there are no data at present (as in the case of glacial period longshore currents, although reconstruction of wind circulation patterns by projects such as CLIMAP ultimately may permit this). In any event, because the three main parameters varied significantly over the 13,000-year period being discussed here, it is desirable to specify some criteria to guide interpretation of the continental shelf data. These criteria are:

1. When sea level is rapidly rising, streams are more likely to be embayed, with tidal processes dominating delta and floodplain formation. In the period 18,000–9,000 B.P., sea level rose about 9 m per 1,000 years, while in the 9,000–3,000 B.P. period it rose only about 1 m per 1,000 years (Emery 1967:10) thereby radically reducing the embayment capability of the Gulf of Mexico for any given rate of stream discharge.

2. When sea level is lowering, progradation of meander belts and birdfoot delta formation probably will dominate the extension of stream termini.

3. Falling sea level does not automatically trigger entrenchment as the major response throughout the longitudinal profile of a river. Instead, rivers tend toward uniform distribution of work along the entire stream profile (Leopold and Langbein 1966:70) through adjustments in slope. This can be accomplished through down-cutting and/or extension of the channel's length. The latter occurs either through progradation (as described earlier for the Pleistocene Trinity where it breached the Smith Point Barrier) or by modifications in sinuosity (i.e.,

increases or decreases in the size or frequency of meandering will lengthen or shorten, respectively, the length of the stream channel).

4. Stillstands are the periods in which the greatest ramification of coastal features will occur. Specific coastal positions from periods of active regression or transgression of the strand may not be morphologically distinct in the geomorphic record.

5. No geomorphic evidence of Holocene sea levels at a higher elevation than present has been discovered in the central Gulf coast region (Henry 1956).

As a consequence of the creation of major landforms during certain geologic episodes, and also partly because of the way in which some sources have organized and presented their data, it has been convenient for this discussion of large-scale paleogeography to trace on Figure 8.4 the principal features associated with four shoreline positions in the region's late Quaternary history: 13,000–11,000 B.P.; 11,000–10,000 B.P.; 7,500 B.P.; and 3,500 B.P. These are incorporated into the subsequent discussion.

Late Wisconsin–Early Holocene

Although there is some evidence for occupation of the New World by man prior to 12,000 years ago (Haynes 1970:85–89), there is no specific indication of this along the Texas coast (Gagliano 1977:172–176). Consequently, this review begins at the end of the Woodfordian, or about 13,000 years ago. This is sufficient to include the time periods for which there can be reasonable certainty that the region was inhabited by early Indian peoples.

Defining the paleogeography of the late Wisconsin–early Holocene includes identification of the coastal termini of Deweyville streams. Information has already been presented showing that the Deweyville interval

1. Consisted of at least two floodplain surfaces, with the younger entrenched into the older;
2. Experienced substantially greater amounts of stream discharge and bedload than characterized the same streams either before or since during the late Quaternary; and
3. Probably dates to the time period between about 9,000 B.P. and 14,000 B.P.

One key to interpretation of Deweyville features on the continental shelf surely lies in the fact that in the interior, streams of this period were eroding their valleys at such a grand scale as to remake the fluvial geography. An enormous amount of sediment was removed from the interior which should be in evidence somewhere on the shelf in the form of aggradational features. Indeed, very large bathymetric features resembling a barrier island system and tide-dominated estuary are indicated southeast of Galveston Bay in the vicinity of north latitude 29°00′ and west longitude 94°30′ (Figure 8.4). The apparent barrier appears on subbottom profiles to be transgressive in origin (S. M. Gagliano, personal communication 1982). These bathymetric features can be correlated with the reconstruction of Nelson and Bray (1970) who traced the valleys of the Calcasieu and Sabine–Neches rivers to their confluence with the Trinity River.

A radiocarbon date of 10,207 ± 374 B.P. (Nelson and Bray 1970) on peat overlying the presumed Deweyville fluvial sands in the stream valley near the possible tide-dominated estuary described previously means that the Younger Deweyville stream passed through these massive depositional features which are located near 29°00′ latitude and 94°30′ longitude. Faunal and isotopic data document that the most rapid deterioration of the late Wisconsin glaciers ended about 13,000 B.P. with renewed glaciation occurring in the period of 11,000–10,000 B.P. (Kennett and Shackleton 1975; Ruddiman and McIntyre 1981:128). Presumably this 13,000–11,000 B.P. period correlates with the Two Creekan in the Midwestern glacial chronology and with the Older Deweyville streams of the northern Gulf Coast. Likewise, the subsequent 11,000–10,000 B.P. glaciation must correlate with the Younger Deweyville entrenched streams.

Nelson and Bray (1970:55) discovered that the Sabine–Neches–Calcasieu–Trinity–San Jacinto rivers, plus their coastal plain tributaries (some of which have quite large drainage basins), constituted a coordinate river system during the period that is associated here with the Deweyville interval. This means that this system must have dwarfed all others in the western Gulf of Mexico, including such large streams as the Brazos River. One effect for the region's paleogeography is immediately evident in the orientation of the 13,000–11,000 year shoreline. The Trinity–Sabine–etc. river system has augmented the central Gulf deposition from the Mississippi River in a major way. Prograding late Quaternary Trinity, etc. system sediments on the continental shelf reached far beyond the extent attained by the other major rivers of the Texas coast.

Comparison of the depth and slope of these possible Older Deweyville fluvial surfaces (Figure 8.2) with sea level curves supports the plausibility of identifying the bathymetric features, which today are at a maximum of about 20 m water depth, as the Older Deweyville shoreline of circa 13,000–11,000 years ago (Figure 8.4). Tracing this feature and water depth to the west, it is possible to circumscribe another smaller depositional center south of the present day Brazos River delta; this is shown here tentatively as the Older Deweyville Brazos delta. However, this interpretation has not been independently confirmed with subsurface data.

After 11,000 B.P., the post-Two Creekan glaciation began with an attendant shoreline regression, as has been described previously. Under the circumstances of falling sea level and large discharge–bedload, there should be a meander belt ridge trailing seaward of the Older Deweyville shoreline much as Pleistocene Trinity River meander belts trail seaward from the Smith Point Barrier. This appears to occur eastward and then southeast from the postulated Older Deweyville estuary extending out to the vicinity of the 30-m water depth (Figure 8.4).

Unfortunately, no subsurface data was available for further evaluation of this interpretation. In the early phases of this regression, the Trinity–Sabine–Calcasieu River appears to have encircled and cut off a portion of the Gulf and formed a large lagoonal feature (Figure 8.4) in the same manner that the Mississippi River has cut off Lake Ponchartrain. Another possible barrier system associated with the Younger Deweyville shoreline is in evidence north of the Trinity–Sabine–Calcasieu delta; possible other delta sites are noted to the west.

After the post-Two Creekan glaciation ended, sea level rose to the position of the 7500 B.P. shoreline (Figure 8.4), which is discussed in the description of Middle Holocene paleogeography. This sea level movement may not have been continuously transgressive since radiocarbon dates from the submerged valley of the Sabine–Neches River indicate a limited regression around 8000–6000 B.P. (Nelson and Bray 1970:Figure 11). This may correlate with the possible regression dated slightly earlier in the Trinity estuary (Rehkemper 1969:43).

Before ending discussion of the late Wisconsin–early Holocene paleogeography, there are several anomalous bathymetric features occurring in the area of the continental shelf between the 11,000–10,000 B.P. shoreline and the 7,500 B.P. shoreline, which need to be mentioned. Inspection of any reasonably detailed bathymetric chart of this area will quickly show that neither the Sabine Bank nor Heald Bank are included in the reconstruction of paleogeography on Figure 8.4. This follows the analysis of Nelson and Bray (1970:71) who concluded that they were formed as submarine sand banks during the last 3,600 years. Immediately west of Heald Bank is another large, well-defined, but unnamed bank. S. M. Gagliano (personal communication 1981) has examined subsurface profile records across this bank and believes it to be a regressive feature unlike its seaward twin which is here mapped as a barrier and part of the 13,000 B.P. shoreline (Figure 8.4). According to Gagliano, the subsurface profile records indicate this latter bank is transgressive, which is consistent with the paleogeographic interpretation adopted here. Farther to the west, but aligned with the unnamed regressive bank are the Freeport Rocks which are lithified barrier sediments. Winchester (1971) restudied the Rocks and suggested they may be on the order of 8,000 years old. It is possible (and should be investigated further) that the Freeport Rocks and the unnamed regressive banks to their east may represent the post-7,500 B.P. regression suggested by Nelson and Bray, and by Rehkemper (Figure 8.4).

Middle Holocene

This time, in some respects, is the most difficult to study in the entire late Quaternary history of the Texas coast because the submerged coastal topography has been subjected to greater modification by waves and currents, and to the most extensive burial by late Holocene deposition. On Figure 8.4 it has been possible to link together the limited paleographic reconstructions made for the

Sabine (Nelson and Bray 1970), the Trinity estuary (Rehkemper 1969), and the Brazos delta (see Figures 8.9 and 8.10) for a shoreline position dating approximately to 7500 B.P. By this time, the Trinity River had separated from the Sabine–Neches–Calcasieu River, and the Brazos River delta was nearly in the position it occupies today.

From roughly 7000 years ago to about 3500 years ago, the position of this coast retreated from seaward locations as much as 40 km offshore, to positions ranging from about 16 km inland (east of the Sabine) to about 5 km inland west of the Brazos. By the time this latter position was reached, the barrier spit and island system that today characterizes nearly the entire Texas coast probably was in incipient stages of formation (cf. Bernard *et al.* 1959; Gould and McFarlan 1959; Nelson and Bray 1970). At this time, marine waters began entering the location of present-day estuaries, and the individual histories of estuary and delta development become more interpretable.

When discussing the postglacial history of major streams of the Texas coast region, there has been a tendency to group them according to whether they are embayed and empty into an estuary (such as the Sabine, Neches, and Trinity) or drain directly into the Gulf, as do the Brazos, Colorado, and Rio Grande. A common assumption has been that all of these river valleys were drowned some significant distance inland by an estuary as sea level rose, and that the streams which today flow directly into the Gulf of Mexico have succeeded in filling their estuary (e.g., Fisher *et al.* 1972:13). It seems doubtful to me, however, that this ever was the case except that narrow coastal lagoon estuaries were established all along the Texas coast as a function of sand barrier development after formation of the circa 3500 B.P. shoreline (Figure 8.4).

Detailed geomorphic mapping of the Brazos River deltaic plain, for instance, indicates that this river was not embayed and at most only had to prograde across a narrow coastal lagoon (see Figure 8.9) during the late Holocene, much as was done in recent years by the present course of the Colorado River. These rivers, with large bedloads, apparently managed to keep their deltas essentially at the coastline during the middle and late Holocene (i.e., since about 7000 years ago) after a significant decrease in the rate of sea level rise. Consequently, Holocene paleogeographic reconstructions for streams such as these should not be based upon an embayment model. At the same time rivers such as the Brazos, even though not embayed, do take on some estuarine characteristics in their lower reaches, especially after the channel has been abandoned and the flow of fresh water has diminished. In these cases tidal processes act on the lower river channel to produce limited estuarine faunas which are reflected in archaeological sites (e.g., see the description of site 41 BO 4 in Chapter 11).

Several other of the Texas coast streams, however, clearly have been embayed. Gagliano (1977:189–192) has provided a detailed description of the evolution of such embayments and the likely association of these landforms with archaeological sites (Figure 8.5). A first approximation reconstruction of the middle Holocene development of the Galveston Bay estuary has been pre-

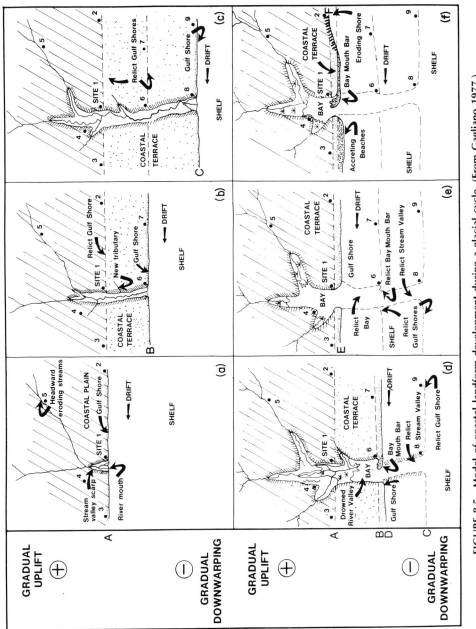

FIGURE 8.5   Model of coastal landform development during a glacial cycle. (From Gagliano 1977.)

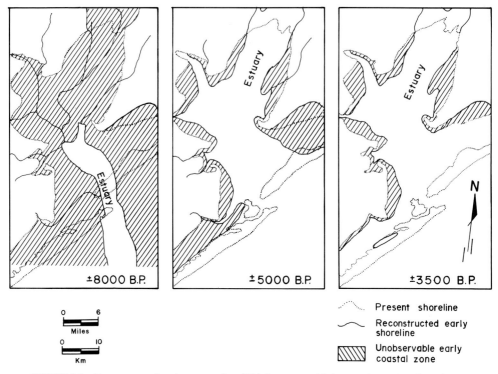

FIGURE 8.6   Reconstructed early geography of Trinity estuary (Galveston Bay). (Based partly on Rehkemper 1969: Figure 2–19.)

pared by Rehkemper (1969:44–45), which is adapted in Figure 8.6. Likewise, a very generalized model for the Sabine–Neches estuary may be found in Fisher *et al.* (1973:Figure 6).

Late Holocene

By 3500 B.P., rising sea level had stabilized and the most inland position of the postglacial shoreline transgression was reached; deposition processes then began to dominate in shaping the Texas coast. Deposits of this time period have been much more limited than for the late Wisconsin to middle Holocene times previously described. Four distinct environments of deposition should be distinguished as follows: coastal marshes, barrier spits and islands, estuaries, and floodplain–deltas. The effects of barrier development and estuarine deposition on the geographic evolution of the area were limited. The barriers forming at the mouth of the Sabine and Trinity estuaries provided limited habitats for human exploitation and occupation. Estuarine deposits mainly covered middle

Holocene deltaic and estuarine environments (cf. Nelson and Bray 1970: Figure 7; Rehkemper 1969:Figures 2–19 and 2–20). The barriers and shoaling of the estuaries also changed the character of the estuarine ecology and resources. Archaeologically, this effect is most clearly seen at the Harris County Boys School midden (41 HR 80) located near the middle of the Trinity estuary (Galveston Bay). Shellfish sequences at this site change from brackish water, to more saline assemblages, and back to brackish water assemblages (Aten *et al.* 1976:Figure 4C), an evolution consistent with expectations derived from Gagliano's model of estuary development (Figure 8.5).

The expansion of the coastal marshes (Gould and McFarlan 1959) has more directly affected much greater portions of the habitable areas of the present coast than have barriers. In particular, the marshes have filled in coastal lagoons and otherwise covered earlier deposits of the middle Holocene.

The most habitable as well as informative surfaces formed during the late Holocene are the floodplains. The modern alluvial–deltaic plain (i.e., the T_0 surfaces) constitute exceedingly complex sedimentary prisms whose history is only partly understood. To continue examining the contrast begun earlier between major rivers with an estuary and those without an estuary, the contemporary deltaic plains of the Trinity and Brazos rivers both are the loci of by far the highest density of archaeological sites in their respective regions of the coast. Understanding the middle to late Holocene channel–delta stratigraphy and habitats for these streams is essential to interpretation of these archaeological remains. The reconstructions to be given here were compiled from air photography, topographic and soil maps, field checks of landforms and lithology, as well as subsurface stratigraphy from archaeological excavations, auger borings, and engineering foundation cores.

The sequence of main channel and delta phases of the modern Trinity River is shown in Figure 8.7. Five separate positions of the main river and its delta are evident; earlier ones presumably now are buried. The ages of these channel stages on the modern deltaic plain can be estimated as a result of direct dating, and indirectly by dating associated or bracketing features (Figure 8.8). The five observable channel stages and their related facies form the environmental background against which aboriginal use of the Trinity River delta occurred. These sediments commonly are seen interfingered with archaeological deposits and are referenced on many of the site maps and stratigraphic profiles given in Chapter 11. In addition to being an important basis for subsequent habitat reconstruction and analysis of subsistence, these correlations also provide a contextual time series useful for independent verification of the chronological seriation of archaeological sites and data in Chapter 13.

Meandering channels on the Trinity were mapped and their geometry was measured in the alluvial valley above the deltaic plain because of the preponderance of straight reaches in the deltas. Unfortunately, there is a constriction in the valley width just above 29°55′ latitude (Figure 8.1) which makes alluvial valley and deltaic plain correlations difficult. In the alluvial valley between

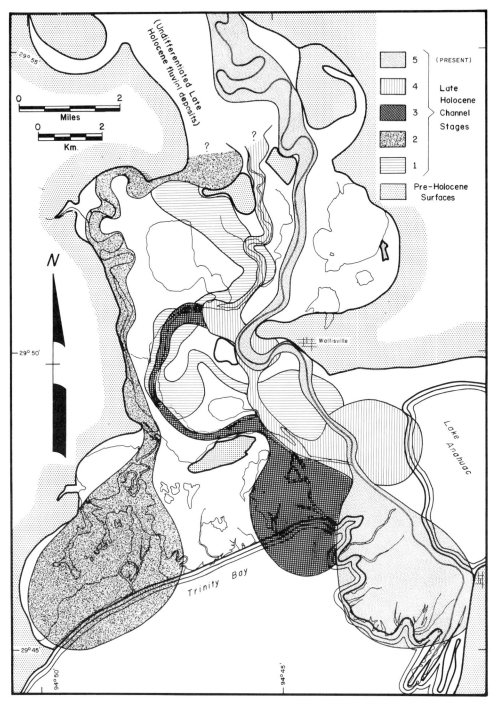

FIGURE 8.7 Late Holocene channel stages of the lower Trinity River.

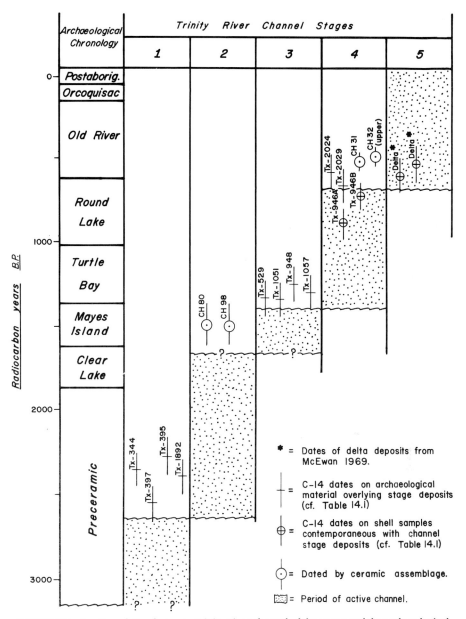

FIGURE 8.8 Age Correlation between Trinity River channel–delta stages and the archaeological chronology.

Liberty, Texas, and the valley constriction, three distinct channel stages are evident: the present channel; one west of the present channel called Channel group A; and another east of the present channel called Channel group B. Group B is nearly buried and in a greater state of geomorphic deterioration than is Group A. Because no cross-cutting relationships are evident between channels of Groups A and B, the latter tentatively is presumed to be the oldest solely on the grounds that it is more deteriorated. For reasons to be suggested later when discussing paleoclimates, it will be suggested further that Channel group A dates to the period around 6000 years ago. Consequently, if Channel group B is older than this, and the five channel stages on the deltaic plain are not much older than about 3000 years (Figure 8.8), the latter must correlate with the presently occupied meander belt in the alluvial valley. This has not yet been demonstrated with field observations, however.

Using similar kinds of data, a reconstruction also has been made for the middle to late Holocene channel stages of the Brazos River (see Figure 8.8) which differs in some details from that previously presented (Bernard *et al.* 1970:Figure 30). At least three channel stages of the adjacent San Bernard River are shown as well. Apparently the early San Bernard River channel was contemporaneous with the Early Phase of the modern Brazos River since both discharged into the same now-filled coastal lagoon (Figure 8.9).

Figure 8.10 shows very tentative chronological relationships between the Brazos River channel stages based on the relatively few radiocarbon dates available, all of which were culled from Bernard *et al.* (1970). The Big Slough channel dates were obtained from Bernard *et al.* (1970:Figure 22) where they were identified as "Recent Brazos River deposits of low or rising sea level stage" in the alluvial valley south of Richmond. A relict main channel of the probable joint Bastrop Bayou–Big Slough meander belt is located about 3¼ km to the east and is tentatively assumed to be the association for these early dates.

The Bastrop Bayou channel stage dates were obtained from Bernard *et al.* (1970:Figure 52) where they are associated with a stratigraphic unit underlying western Galveston Island identified as "prodelta silty clay, Brazos River." Because of the geographic proximity to the presumed Bastrop Bayou delta, these dates are tentatively correlated with the Bastrop Bayou channel stage of the Brazos.

The Oyster Creek channel stage dates are taken from Bernard *et al.* (1970: Figure 24) where they are identified as being associated with the Oyster Creek meander belt in the alluvial valley south of Richmond, Texas. Although it has been assumed that the modern Brazos River diverted from the Oyster Creek channel about 1000 years ago, occupation of the Dow–Cleaver Site, situated on modern Brazos River point-bar deposits probably began about 1500 years ago (Aten 1971). Because the Oyster Creek dates that are younger than about 1000 years ago were made on samples taken from locations quite close to the present Oyster Creek stream channel, the possibility is raised that there are relatively recent channel depositional loci along Oyster Creek. This is reasonable because

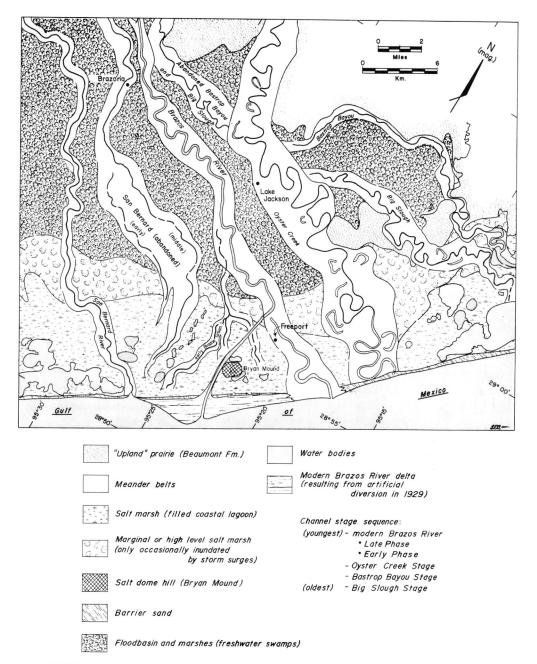

FIGURE 8.9 Geomorphology of the Brazos and San Bernard River deltas, Brazoria County, Texas. (Base map and geomorphic interpretation compiled from United States Department of Agriculture [USDA] air photo mosaics, United States Geological Survey [USGS] topographic maps, and the Geologic Atlas of Texas [Houston Sheet].)

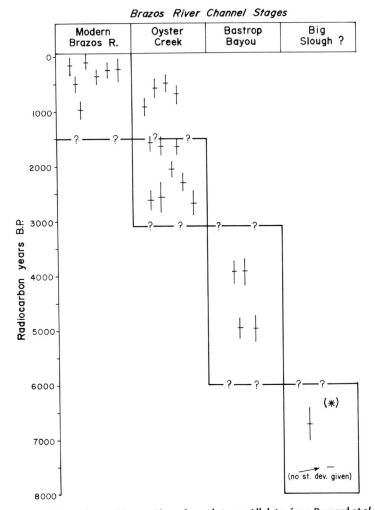

FIGURE 8.10   Estimated age of Brazos River channel stages. All dates from Bernard *et al.* (1970):
Brazos River (Figure 22), Oyster Creek (Figure 24), Bastrop Bayou (Figure 52), Big Slough (Figure
22—see text for discussion of this association).

Oyster Creek today is over 150 km long and has a sizable drainage basin and
discharge in its own right. Consequently, the interpretation used here is that the
Oyster Creek channel was abandoned by the Brazos just before 1500 years ago.
Dates for the modern Brazos River channel stage were obtained from Bernard *et*
al. (1970:Figure 22).

Finally, it is worthwhile to observe that the modern floodplain channel stages
of both the Brazos and the Trinity rivers display progressively increasing coeffi-
cients of variation around the mean radii of meanders (see Table 8.1). Because

meander radius is a basic measure of a river's attempt to distribute energy expenditure uniformly over its longitudinal profile, the progressive increase in variability in meander radius since the beginning of the Holocene may indicate that both of these rivers are still adjusting to the effects of significant shortening of their length even though sea level stabilized some 3500 years ago. In other words, given their current discharge and competence to do work through erosion and redeposition, these two rivers appear to have not yet realigned their stream gradients and channel length to significantly foreshortened postglacial longitudinal alluvial valley profiles. In this manner, effects of the last ice age may echo into the present day.

PALEOCLIMATES

There are some fairly obvious physical features on the upper Texas coast which imply past climatic conditions different from those of the present. For example, the extensive occurrence of underfit streams (i.e., streams in which the form and size of their meandering valleys far exceeds the competence of the present hydrologic regimen to shape), intensely oxidized and leached late Pleistocene sediments, and widespread caliche formation in a region that today has an average annual rainfall ranging from about 100 cm on the west to nearly 140 cm on the east. There are two types of historical data now available on climates of the upper Texas coast, although others could be developed. These are patterns of stream channel geometry and soil development.

Channel geometry

Adjustments in stream channel morphology apparently are made so as to avoid concentrating variability in any single aspect of their formative processes (Langbein and Leopold 1966:12). Consequently, channel geometry measurements, particularly the meander radius, may be used to reflect the net hydrologic regimen of the basin being drained. For this reason, measurement of channel form is a convenient initial step toward obtaining historical data on climate for this coast.

Stream channel geometry was measured along as many channel segments of the various terraces and contemporary channel stages of the Brazos and Trinity rivers as was possible (see Table 8.1) according to the definitions of channel morphology given by Leopold *et al.* (1964). In addition, channel segments were measured on the China Ridge System of the Beaumont Formation Trinity River delta because this appears to be the most recent of the several mappable meander belts of the mid-Wisconsin Trinity River (Aronow 1971:Figure 22). The age of all measured channels was estimated previously in the discussion of terrace stratigraphy except for the T_0 Channel Groups A and B on the Trinity River. For the purposes of this initial synthesis, Trinity Channel Group A can be correlated with the Big Slough channel of the Brazos River because of similarities in their channel size relationships (Figure 8.11). Trinity Channel Group B, then, would date earlier than this but not more than circa 9000 years ago, although this important correlation is greatly in need of empirical verification. Of all the geometric parameters, the meander radius will be the primary one used to describe the history of changes in stream size because these data are the most complete. It is important to note, however, that observed changes in the other geometric parameters are consistent with the patterns of change shown by the curvature measurements.

There are several points of interest in the data of Table 8.1 which also are plotted in a time series on Figure 8.11. The geometric characteristics of the present channel of the Trinity River (T_0) and of the China Ridge channel are nearly identical, indicating approximately similar hydrologic conditions during both the mid-Wisconsin and the later Holocene. Between these two end points there is documented a cycle of progressive stream enlargement to a maximum in the Deweyville interval, then reduction to a size significantly smaller than that of the present, and finally recovery to its contemporary size within the last 4,000 years, more or less. The geometry of the Holocene channels of the Brazos

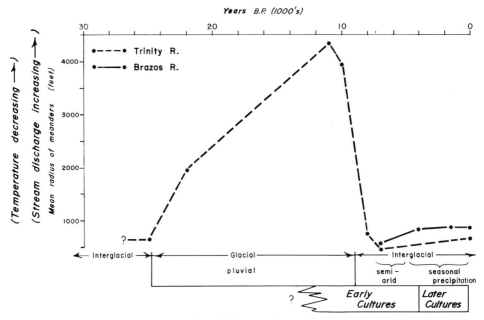

FIGURE 8.11   Initial model of paleoclimate of Texas coast.

River (where pre-Holocene stages are not observable for measurement) show an early Holocene stream significantly smaller than that of the present, progressively enlarging to its current dimensions. Evidence exists that relatively more moist late glacial and early Holocene conditions also occurred on what today are more arid sections of the coast. From the Baffin Bay region southwest of Corpus Christi, partially articulated mammoth remains dating 8,000 to 10,000 B.P. were found in alluvial deposits of the now dry Palo Blanco River, which at that time was a relatively large meandering stream (Suhm 1980:88). And this higher discharge also has been reported for earlier phases of the Nueces River and Oso Creek drainages (Hester 1980:7).

These data are important because of the known direct proportional relationship between increases and decreases in channel geometry, and similar changes in stream discharge (Leopold *et al.* 1964:295–298). Moreover, correlation of the sequence of stream geometry patterns with those of marine biostratigraphy and oxygen isotope measurements (Beard 1973; Kennett and Shackleton 1975; Ruddiman and McIntyre 1981) suggests the Texas coast experienced temperature changes which were inversely proportional to the increases and decreases in channel geometry. Two lines of evidence support the interpretation that streamflow peaked after the end of the late Wisconsin glacial maximum (Figure 8.11) rather than remaining at very high levels throughout the late Wisconsin. First, there was the previously cited period of large freshwater inflow to the Gulf basin occurring between 17,000 and 11,500 years ago (Kennett and Shackleton 1975). Also, there was the description given earlier of the deepest channel cut into the lower Trinity River valley appearing to have been the Younger Deweyville. Consequently, the thalwegs of earlier channels were at either the same or a higher elevation. Because pre-T_2 streams would have been flowing to a lower base level, the indication is that they had less erosional capability than the Deweyville streams.

This kind of geomorphology is not subtle; important changes in order of magnitude of stream regimen are rather well indicated. However, since these data are measures of *net* drainage basin behavior and because the Brazos and Trinity rivers have drainage basins extending hundreds of kilometers into the interior, the remaining question is whether these changes reflect the environment of the coastal zone as well. To examine this question, it is necessary to shift to evidence of weathering upon upper coast soils.

Weathering characteristics

Intensive oxidation and leaching of Beaumont Formation sediments of the coastal plain is almost a *sine qua non* of the formation's definition (e.g., Rehkemper 1969:13–14). Such intensive weathering probably required extended heavy rainfall at a time postdating the Beaumont's deposition around 25,000

B.P., and predating circa 9,000 B.P. after which time there is no indication of such pluvial conditions.

Another line of evidence concerns the occurrence of calcium carbonate concretions and caliche deposits in the surficial deposits of the Beaumont Formation. Caliche soils occur under cover of grasses and require semiaridity or seasonal drought conditions with not more than about 60 cm mean annual precipitation (Butzer 1964:80; Flint 1959:366). Caliche formation is widespread in the Beaumont Formation on the upper coast. Graf (1966:16–18, 74–77) noted, however, that the intensity of calichification declines from west to east along the coast with no extension east of the Sabine. It is obvious that calichification could not have occurred during the pluvial conditions producing the intense leaching and oxidation of the Beaumont Formation described above. Consequently, it must have happened since about 9000 years ago.

Carbonate concretions also were reported in Beaumont Formation sediments cored on the continental shelf within the area subaerially exposed at the time of the 7500 B.P. shoreline (Figure 8.4) (Nelson and Bray 1970:55). Because this area was submerged by 3500 B.P., thereby terminating carbonate precipitation, the time period for calichification is approximately bracketed by these dates (i.e., 7500–3500 B.P.), which also are coincident with the estimated time of reduced stream discharge (Figure 8.11).

A third line of evidence concerns formation of ferric oxide concretions in the Beaumont Formation. These too are extremely common on the upper Texas coast but have not been studied carefully. As a general matter, they are thought to form under conditions of warm temperatures and alternating wet and dry seasons (Butzer 1964:82; Graf 1966:15–18; Flint 1959:359). On the upper coast, the formation of iron concretions apparently continued into recent periods since there are relatively young (less than 2000 years old) archaeological materials that are partially encrusted from some site locations such as Pipkin Marsh (Aten and Bollich 1981). It is clear enough that the iron concretions would not form under the same conditions in which the carbonates precipitated. It is most consistent to consider, tentatively, that the iron concretions reflect the onset of seasonal conditions of precipitation that characterize the present-day climate. This would coincide with the apparent steady rise in stream discharge to current rates beginning about 4000 years ago (Figure 8.11).

The weathering characteristics described here are complicated phenomena that have not been intensively studied. Taken on their own, they might only be suggestive. In conjunction with the evidence from stream channel geometry, however, they form part of the basis for initial interpretations of the environment of the upper Texas coast's early cultures as well as a point of departure for further investigations into the paleoenvironments of the region. The apparent correlation between stream geometry and sediment weathering characteristics suggests that the patterns of change in precipitation reflected in the channel geometry were experienced directly on the upper coast and are not simply reflections of climatic episodes far in the interior.

The history of changes in the globally integrated climatic system has been shown to consist of more or less stable periods separated by relatively rapid transitions that presumably represent changes in patterns of atmospheric circulation, whatever the external forcing causes may be (Bryson *et al.* 1970:56; Wendland 1978:276). The Holocene sequence of climatic transitions has been more or less similar in Europe and North America with the result that a uniform chronology of episodes—the Blytt–Sernander sequence—has come into increasing usage (Bryson *et al.* 1970). Consequently, it seems timely to follow the lead of Story (1980) and correlate what little is known of climates on the upper Texas coast with this larger frame of reference. Sequence transition dates are from Wendland (1978:281).

Late glacial (prior to 10,030 B.P.)   This period correlates with the Deweyville terrace interval (Figure 8.3). The concensus of opinion about possible causes of the extremely high stream discharge during the late glacial period marked by the T_4 and Deweyville (T_1 and T_2) terraces is that increased precipitation or decreased evaporation, or both, were responsible (Bernard 1950:69; Gagliano and Thom 1967:36–38; Slaughter 1967:157). Soils data described above indicate these conditions occurred on the immediate coastal zone. The assemblages of fossil vertebrates for this time period in Texas include the co-occurrence of northern and southern species which today are separated by their intolerance of high and low temperatures, respectively (Lundelius 1967:315). Lundelius also described the presence of species limited by aridity whose ranges today terminate farther to the east. Thus, the Texas coastal region should have experienced milder winters, cooler summers, and higher precipitation throughout (cf. Slaughter 1967:Figure 2).

Pollen and invertebrate faunas indicate that, although the Great Plains prairie biome was drastically reduced in extent at this time, it may have existed on at least the western half of the emerged plains of the Texas continental shelf; the eastern part of this region included a much extended deciduous forest biome which probably reached southward to the now submerged continental shelf areas (Ross 1970:235–239). Such a reconstruction also is supported by vertebrate fossils. The greater proportion of mastodon in relation to mammoth on the coastal plain as well as the occurrence of certain smaller species implies forested conditions on the upper and central Texas coasts (Lundelius 1967:297, 314). Fossil localities in the coastal zone reasonably well dated to this interval are Salt Mine Valley, McFaddin Beach, Sargent Beach (Gagliano 1977:208–209, 222), and Berclair Terrace (Sellards 1940:1636). These yielded extinct mammoth, mastodon, horse, bison, sloth, giant tortoise, dire wolf, saber-toothed cat, camel, capybara, glyptodon, and armadillo. Unfortunately, data on the smaller species have been reported only for Berclair Terrace.

Pre-Boreal and Boreal (10,030 to 8,490 B.P.)   On the Texas coast, the principal direct evidence for these climatic periods comes from stream geometry. Both the Brazos and Trinity rivers appear to have undergone transition to reduced rates of flow approximating those of the present. It may be inferred that this was the interval in which precipitation reduced by several magnitudes, cloud cover dissipated, and seasonal mean temperatures became more divergent. Reduction in precipitation presumably encouraged the expansion of grasslands to the north and east along the coastal plain from their limited late glacial occurrence in south Texas. Although data on flora and fauna are very limited, the La Paloma Mammoth Site, on the lower Texas coast, has been well dated to the period principally between 9,200 and 9,800 years ago (Suhm 1980:98) and contains now-extinct species of mammoth, mastodon, horse, bison, sloth, and glyptodon. Extinction of most of the Pleistocene megafauna in Texas must have taken place by the end of this interval (Lundelius 1967:315; Slaughter 1967:161).

Atlantic (8490 to 5060 B.P.)   This is the period widely recognized as the postglacial thermal optimum (e.g., Flint 1971:432). The local hydrologic evidence indicates further reduction in rates of discharge by upper coast streams to levels roughly 40% below those of the present day.[2] Based on previously described dates bracketing the exposure of caliche-bearing sediments on the continental shelf, it also appears to have been the time of formation of caliche deposits in upper coast soils. There are indications that the intensity of caliche formation diminished rapidly to the east of the upper coast region, thus documenting that semiarid conditions spread eastward and then retreated back to the west (Graf 1966:74–77). This pattern is consistent with pollen data from central and west Texas, which indicates that a more or less continuous trend to warmer and drier climate took place there from the late glacial period on to the present (Bryant and Shafer 1977:18). Presumably this too was the period in which streams of the lower coast diminished in size—some permanently. Dillehay was unable to find any record of bison in Texas during this time period (1974:182). Presumably herds were diminished and/or relocated farther north on the Plains.

The existence of caliche in soils of the upper coast indicates the presence at this time of grasslands over the region accompanied by precipitation of less than 60 cm per year. Supporting evidence for elevated mean annual temperature at this time has been recorded in foraminiferal assemblages from the Gulf of Mexico indicating a significantly warmer climate at about 7000 B.P. (Beard 1973:300). This climatic period also has been referred to occasionally in this book and elsewhere as the Altithermal as formulated by Antevs. The presence of subepisodes of extreme intensification of these conditions (Benedict 1979; Langway *et al.* 1973:319; Story 1980) has not yet been detected on the Texas coast.

Sub-Boreal to Present (5060 B.P. to present)   This heading groups together several episodes, as climatic conditions oscillated through history to the present day.

---

[2]Although estimated to have occurred in the slightly younger 4000–5000 B.P. period, evidence has been reported from the Mississippi River Valley also indicating a decline in river discharge to about 40–60% of the present level (Saucier 1981:12).

In general, this was the time when seasonal patterns of precipitation and temperature became established. Stream discharges gradually recovered to contemporary rates, and the coastal zone reached its current position. Bison returned to the south Plains and were widespread over the coastal plain for the first 3000 years, then were displaced northward again for abut 700 years, and returned south around 700 B.P. to remain until the nineteenth century (Dillehay 1974: 182–185). Major ecotones and circulation patterns at a continental scale in North America stabilized about 4000 B.P. (Wendland 1978:281). Since that time, the upper Texas coast probably has marked the western biogeographic margin of the southeastern United States environmental area (Story 1980:Figure 2). At present, there are few specific correlations that can be made between Texas coastal data and the Blytt–Sernander climatic episodes for these last millennia. However, there is evidence for increased wetness on the northern Plains along with a major increase in dessication and grasslands on the central Plains. These changes more or less coincide with the reappearance of bison on the southern ranges circa 4000 B.P. (Wendland 1978:280) and suggest that climatic characteristics associated with grassland expansion are one of the phenomena for which evidence should be sought on the coast.

CONCLUSIONS

Examining changes in regional geography and climate throughout the late Quaternary leads to identification of the setting and important constraining factors for early human habitation of the Texas coast. Paleogeographic reconstructions of the upper coast continental shelf (Figure 8.4), of the Trinity estuary and delta (Figures 8.6 and 8.7), and of the Brazos delta (Figure 8.9) illustrate that for any location at any given time in history, the adjacent terrain may have looked quite different from either its previous or subsequent configurations. Moreover, when the history of the coast is observed from a static geographic location, such as that which is occupied by the present coast, much of the extent of earlier littoral zones has been destroyed or is covered and not directly observable. As a result, Paleo-Indian or Early Archaic archaeological data found on the present terrestrial margin of the coast generally will represent human activities conducted in an interior environment—not a coastal environment—and the observed adaptive technologies, population densities, and site types will correspond to the original environment, not to the present environment.

This situation can be perceived more easily with reference to the three parts of Figure 8.12. In part A, a schematic transect is drawn perpendicular to the coast in which the habitats of the coastal plain have been simplified into littoral, prairie, and interior forest zones. Although the dimensions of these zones varied throughout the course of the late Quaternary, they constituted the basic

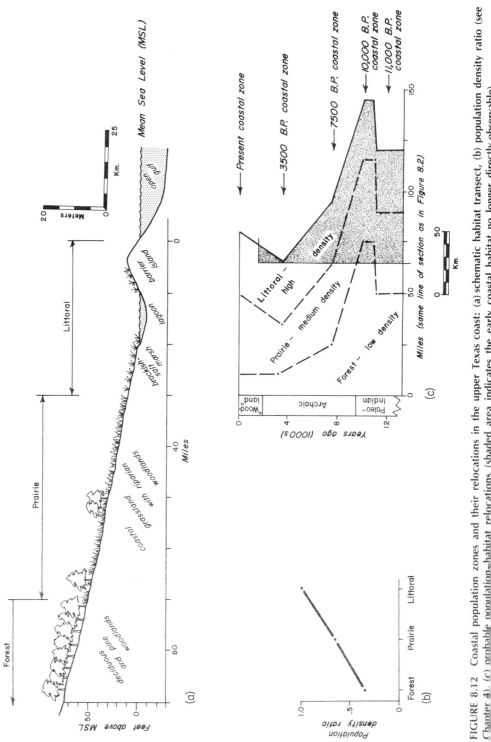

FIGURE 8.12 Coastal population zones and their relocations in the upper Texas coast: (a) schematic habitat transect, (b) population density ratio (see Chapter 4); (c) probable population-habitat relocations (shaded area indicates the early coastal habitat no longer directly observable).

environmental configuration of the coast throughout its history. The relationship of these habitats to population densities is shown in part B of Figure 8.12 using the same density ratios used in Chapter 4. Thus, the population per unit area of the prairies should be only two-thirds that of the littoral zone, and population density of the interior forests (which were much expanded in extent during the late Wisconsin and early Holocene) would be about one-third that of the littoral zone. In part C, the historical changes in the extent of these terrestrial habitats on the upper Texas coast are shown along with that portion which is removed now from direct observation. Consequently, archaeological evidence collected from the present littoral zone but dating to a period earlier than roughly 4000 years ago, will represent activities carried out in either the medium population density prairies, or low population density interior forests.

In addition to geographic and habitat evolution, it is evident that regional climate also evolved. Broadly speaking, this evolution went from an extremely humid environment with differences minimized between winter and summer mean temperatures, to a semiarid environment which possibly had more pronounced seasons of temperatures and precipitation variation, but nevertheless a much warmer mean annual temperature. Finally, climate shifted to the subhumid seasonal environments of the present day which clearly have gone through many lesser scale changes in character. These more recent changes have not yet been studied to determine their specific manifestation on the Texas coast and their impact on the native cultures. However, some exceedingly provocative possibilities exist. For example, combined use of absolute dating, morphological growth ring analysis, and oxygen isotope measurement of *Rangia cuneata* shells (Aten 1981) could lead to a very high resolution reconstruction of the temperature record for the last 3500 years through a methodology basically similar to that used in dendrochronology. In any event, investigation of the early cultures of the Texas coast and, to some extent, the later cultures as well, must take into account the evolution in geography and regional climates, and the consequential changes this evolution has caused in habitat types and their dependent biotas. This is the subject of the next chapter.

CHAPTER 9

The Early Cultures

INTRODUCTION

In Part II, the term *Early Cultures* was used to refer to the originators of archaeological materials attributable essentially to the period prior to 2000 years ago on the upper Texas coast. It was pointed out that data are sparse, are difficult to organize in terms of conventional archaeological classifications, and probably are found in an environmental setting substantially different from that in which they were formed. In this chapter, a first attempt is made to sort out a culture-historical framework for these ancient and poorly documented remains.

On the present upper Texas coast, a few preceramic shell middens can be found that date back as far as about 3700 years ago. Although these middens are rich sources of materials documenting the environment, settlement patterns, and subsistence, they contain very few preserved artifacts of any kind. Coastal habitation sites dating prior to this time are not directly visible for all the reasons of changing geography discussed in Chapter 8.

In the interior of the upper coastal plain, sites equivalent in age to the late preceramic shell middens contain a modestly higher proportion of lithic tools permitting technological and stylistic analyses not possible on the coast, but which generally lack the settlement, subsistence, and environmental data found in shell middens. The quantity of archaeological evidence representing habitation of the inland region earlier than about 3500 years ago also drops by several orders of magnitude. Despite this, meager but definite indications of Late Pleistocene and Early to Middle Holocene inhabitants are distributed widely over the area of the upper coast.

The data which now are available from the upper coast primarily are the result of coincidental finds. No sustained program of research has been undertaken to identify early coastal archaeological sites or to develop specialized techniques for determining their time–space relationships as a precursor to any structural and/or functional studies of the culture. Story (1980) attributed much of this lack of interest to a bias toward the more spectacular Woodland cultures of the east Texas area. Indeed, this bias is a continuation of the research orientation established over 60 years ago in Texas by J. E. Pearce (Chapter 1), reinforced by the apparent absence on the upper coast of the premier source of archaeological "sex appeal" in North America, Paleo-Indian sites.

As a result, explicit cultural concepts for Paleo-Indian, Archaic, and Late Prehistoric–Woodland culture-historical stages have not yet been made operational in this area. In a region like Texas, where frontiers existed between several major and different cultural patterns, it becomes particularly difficult, if not impossible to define these culture-historical stages in terms reflecting a sequence of characteristic adaptive patterns, much less be holistic. In practice, the terms Paleo-Indian, Archaic, Late Prehistoric and their synonyms are used only to denote assemblages of projectile point types. It is rare for other cultural elements to be known, and a host of traditional and very abstract assumptions about lifeways usually accompany use of the stage terminology. In other words, neither inductive nor deductive approaches can be used effectively at present because, on the one hand, archaeological data are too limited for describing distributional patterns and, on the other, the archaeological concepts are too vague for deducing hypotheses which can be field tested.

The Paleo-Indian and Archaic archaeology of the coastal plain of Texas was synthesized by Suhm *et al.* (1954) and again by others some 20 years later (Hester 1976a,b; Story 1980). Very little improvement occurred during this time and most of the recent literature has focused on describing how little more is known today than was the case 3 decades ago—much as has thus far been done here. Studies of early archaeology on the upper coast are almost exclusively exercises in the classification of diagnostic projectile points (e.g., Gagliano 1963; Jelks 1978; Patterson 1980; also see Phelps 1964). However, progress can be made toward historical understanding of the early periods if some transformations in approach are made to take advantage of the relative wealth of environmental data which are available.

The first step in this transformation is to make clear the definitions of Paleo-Indian, Archaic, and Late Prehistoric–Woodland being used here. *Paleo-Indian* is taken to refer to the cultures of the late glacial time period from roughly 9,000 B.P. to about 12,000 B.P. In the northern Gulf region, these cultures customarily have been identified by the presence of large lanceolate and, often, fluted projectile points. But, as used here, Paleo-Indian refers to all contemporaneous cultures adapted to the late full glacial period (the Deweyville terrace interval) regardless of technology. The issues of earlier glacial period Paleo-Indian cultures (MacNeish 1976) or of pre-projectile-point cultures (Gagliano 1977:198–204) are acknowledged but, with the exception of the Salt Mine Valley Site (Avery Island), will not be discussed because of a total absence of indications that such early habitation actually occurred on the Texas coast.

Archaic is used primarily to categorize cultures spanning the period of major post-Pleistocene environmental changes necessitating important shifts in adaptation. This period of environmental evolution and consequent major changes in economic adaptations seems to have been ended by approximately 3000 years ago. Unfortunately, termination of the Archaic in this region conventionally is marked by the appearance of ceramics and/or arrow points about 1500 to 2000 years ago. Even though ceramics and the bow are important energy harnessing tools, the northern Gulf coast archaeological literature contains frequent observations to the effect that the initial Late Prehistoric–Woodland cultures are only a continuation of the preceramic (i.e., Late Archaic) with the added technological features of pottery and/or arrow points. Thus, the general cultural pattern of the pottery and bow using Late Prehistoric periods actually began about 3000 years ago with the appearance of particular projectile point assemblages which are customarily designated Late Archaic. In this case, convenient typological criteria have substantially preempted the opportunity to use developmental criteria very effectively.

The Late Prehistoric–Woodland[1] cultural pattern consisted of cultures adapted to an essentially contemporary environment of sharply differentiated annual environmental cycles and a subsistence geared to this, whether through primary orientation to hunting, gathering, horticulture, or through some combination of these.

These circumstances illustrate old problems; for every organizational scheme proposed, there are important inconsistencies. If anything, it demonstrates that the level of abstraction being used is still insufficient for effective generalization. In any event, for our present needs in synthesizing information about the early cultures, it is premature and unnecessary to argue these issues to a new "conclusion" and to propose a radically different concept of familiar culture-historical terminology. It is only necessary to recognize that, in spite of the inconsistencies, there is value in viewing Paleo-Indian, Archaic, and Late Prehistoric–Woodland as broadly characterizing the three most recent stages of cultural evolution which are roughly coeval with the three most recent phases of northern Gulf coast natural history. (Similar conclusions were reached by Williams and Stoltman 1965:669).

The value in this generalization derives from the expected strong feedback relationships between the cultural and natural environments during their co-evolution. Several cultural subsystems (e.g., settlement, subsistence, technology) must be substantially dependent variables with respect to the natural environment on the upper coast. Linking the conceptual frameworks for the two environments together, especially when understanding of the cultural environment is so primitive, provides at least a preliminary basis for deriving useful and testable hypotheses about both. This strategy is made even more

[1]Operational definitions of *Woodland* culture usually make reference to ceramics, incipient agriculture, expansion of regional exchange systems, and an elaboration of ritual reflecting increasing status differentiation. The term *Woodland* is used broadly here to connote activities by populations of the upper coast which are geographically as well as culturally peripheral to the Woodland cultures of the southeastern United States. The Texas coastal cultures did share in many Woodland technological innovations, began to manifest status differentiation in material culture, and to elaborate the mortuary ritual. It is in this generalized sense that the term *Woodland* is used.

necessary because the culture chronologies thus far developed to make operational the Paleo-Indian and Archaic stages on the Texas coast are based on putative correlations with poorly dated artifact sequences elsewhere, and have almost no spatial significance at a scale facilitating regional research. At the same time, the late Quaternary geologic history of the upper coast described in Chapter 8 makes clear that many sequential sedimentary deposits and landforms are laterally offset rather than just superimposed. Because of this relationship, the geologic stratigraphy and morphostratigraphy provides both a

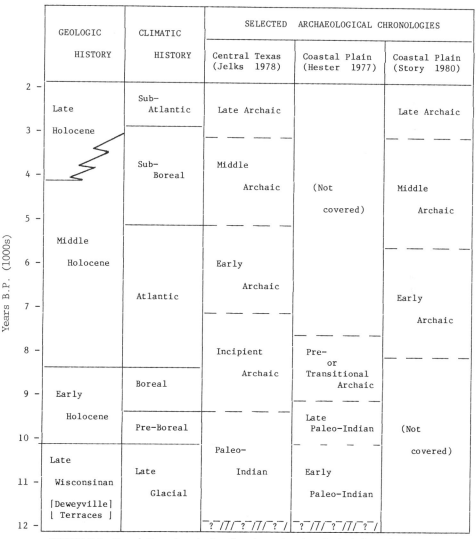

GEOLOGIC HISTORY	CLIMATIC HISTORY	SELECTED ARCHAEOLOGICAL CHRONOLOGIES		
		Central Texas (Jelks 1978)	Coastal Plain (Hester 1977)	Coastal Plain (Story 1980)
Late Holocene	Sub-Atlantic	Late Archaic		Late Archaic
	Sub-Boreal	Middle Archaic	(Not covered)	Middle Archaic
Middle Holocene	Atlantic	Early Archaic		Early Archaic
Early Holocene	Boreal	Incipient Archaic	Pre- or Transitional Archaic	
	Pre-Boreal		Late Paleo-Indian	(Not covered)
Late Wisconsinan [Deweyville] [Terraces]	Late Glacial	Paleo-Indian	Early Paleo-Indian	

(Years B.P. (1000s): 2, 3, 4, 5, 6, 7, 8, 9, 10, 11, 12)

FIGURE 9.1 Correlation of geologic, climatic, and archaeological chronologies.

chronological and a spatial organizing framework for the area based on field observations that lead directly to interpretation of ancient geography, climates, habitats, and archaeological data.

The second step, then, in transforming discussion about the early cultures is to make examination of them operational through use of the late Quaternary geology and geomorphology. One can go to a landform of particular time–space association to make observations either of that landform or of whatever may be situated upon it. For this reason, the early cultures will be reviewed under the geologic time-stratigraphic headings of Late Wisconsin–Early Holocene, Middle Holocene, and Late Holocene. Figures 8.3 and 9.1 illustrate the correlation of these three units with stratigraphy, paleoclimatic episodes and rough correlations with archaeological chronologies for adjacent regions.

LATE WISCONSIN–EARLY HOLOCENE

This period began during the final millennia of the Wisconsin glaciation and continued through the environmental changes culminating in the post-Pleistocene thermal maximum. It included all of what conventionally is known as the Paleo-Indian period and most of the transition in lithic technology from lanceolate and fluted projectile points to stemmed points during what in Texas has been termed variously as the Incipient Archaic, Transitional Archaic, or Pre-Archaic (Jelks 1978; Sollberger and Hester 1972; Weir 1976). As previously described in Chapter 8, the Late Wisconsin geography and habitat distribution was very different from that of the present day with the strand at that time being located nearly 100 km to the south of its present position. The broad outlines of this late glacial geography are summarized on Figure 9.2 for the northern Gulf coast region.

Geologic and vertebrate paleontological data indicate that the Late Wisconsin climate was cooler on the average (and had less variation from this average) during the year than is experienced in the seasonal climates of the present. The region consistently received much more precipitation (more by several orders of magnitude) than at any time since. This, combined with more persistent cloud cover, resulted in lower levels of evapotranspiration of surface water, and a cooler, very humid environment with many large perennial streams. Deciduous woodlands apparently extended over most of the upper coast and probably out onto the continental shelf. Whether a coastal prairie zone existed between the interior forests and the littoral is not known.

With very limited exceptions, the biotic (and archaeological) data now available for the northern Gulf region comes from localities which were then situated within interior habitats, primarily woodlands. Even though no unequivocal associations have been documented between man and extinct faunas on the

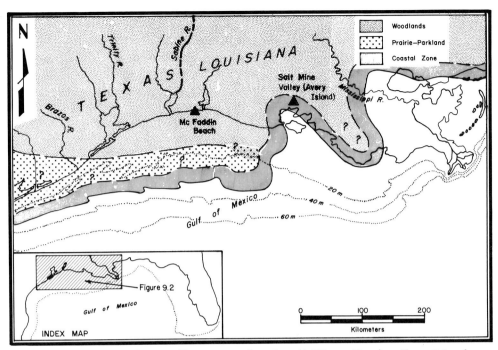

FIGURE 9.2   Regional geographic reconstruction, circa 11,000 B.P. (Based on Figure 8.4 and Gagliano 1977: Figure 7–10.)

upper coast, the Salt Mine Valley Site at Avery Island in south Louisiana (Gagliano 1977:222) and the Berclair Terrace Site on the central Texas coastal plain (Sellards 1940) both contain artifacts and bones of extinct fauna. These include mammoth, mastodon, horse, bison, sloth, giant tortoise, dire wolf, camel, sabertooth cat, armadillo, glyptodon, and capybara in stratigraphic contexts suggesting their contemporaneity. Similar fossils also have been recovered from Sargent Beach and McFaddin Beach on the upper coast. Although these fossils are less well documented, they appear to date to the same period as the Salt Mine Valley and Berclair faunas. Browsing animals would have been common in the interior forests at that time. Herds, if present at all, would have been unlikely in the vicinity of the present coastal zone but instead would have been located on prairies or parkland farther south on the continental shelf. The inclusion of the brackish water clam, *Rangia cuneata*, in the 11,000–12,000-year-old Salt Mine Valley fauna also indicates the presence of a coastal estuary near Avery Island and suggests this locality may be the only known coastal habitation site of the early periods.

The Early Holocene environments are even less adequately known probably because they mark the transition from Late Wisconsin conditions to the dessicated environments of the Atlantic climatic episode during the Middle Holocene. Consequently, it is difficult stratigraphically to separate Early Holocene evidence from either Late Wisconsin or the Middle Holocene. Two localities are known, however, which provide some direct evidence of the period. Channel Group A on the Trinity River (Chapter 8) records river hydrology at substantially reduced levels from the Deweyville regime but not as diminished as was yet to come during the Atlantic climatic episode. Also, the La Paloma Mammoth Site (Suhm 1980) is a fossil-bearing floodplain deposit well-dated to the early portion of the Early Holocene. This site contained a sizable fauna, including several now-extinct species such as mammoth, horse, bison, sloth, mastodon, and glyptodon.

Clearly the Early Holocene of the Texas coast was a time when precipitation was significantly declining and many streams became intermittent or dry. Cloud cover dissipated, increasing the region's insolation and heat loss, which resulted in increased variation about mean seasonal temperatures, a phenomenon most clearly modeled by Slaughter (1967:Figure 2). The prairie biome presumably began to expand both northward and eastward from its Late Wisconsin refuge in south and west–central Texas (Ross 1970:Figure 7). The Pleistocene megafauna became extinct by the end of the Early Holocene, and surviving species, intolerant of the increasing extremes of either winter cold or summer heat, adjusted their ranges north or southwest out of the northern Gulf coast area.

Consistent with this reconstruction of the environmental setting, archaeological data attributable to the Paleo-Indian and Transitional Archaic periods (Figure 9.1), which have been discovered in the modern coastal zone (excluding the Salt Mine Valley Site), must represent activities carried out in inland habitats, and are not related to habitation of the Late Wisconsin–Early Holocene littoral. The archaeological evidence consists almost entirely of numerous isolated finds of distinctive Paleo-Indian projectile point forms such as Clovis, Angostura, Scottsbluff, Meserve, Plainview, and Golondrina (Ambler 1967; Aten *et al.* 1976; Gagliano 1977; Hester 1980; Long 1977; Patterson 1980; Tunnell and Ambler 1967; Wheat 1953). Identification of Transitional Archaic artifacts occurs less often in collections from the upper coast, probably because fewer "diagnostic" forms have been defined. Of these, however, San Patrice points have been reported quite frequently; also reported are Bell or Early Barbed (Fritz 1975:Figure 11), and Early Stemmed (Long 1977; Shafer 1977).

Although no thorough inventory has ever been published of artifacts found on the upper coast which are presumed to date to the Late Wisconsin–Early Holocene, such artifacts are known to occur widely, if not abundantly, over the area. The reported finds vary in their context. Some were associated with midden of much younger age, as the Scottsbluff point from the Willow Lake shell midden (Gagliano 1977:209) and the Clovis specimen from the Doering Site (Wheat 1953:211). Others were discovered in secondary non-cultural contexts, such as in a stream bed or beach lag deposit (Long 1977; Wheat 1953:211). Yet other specimens have been found in contexts whose nature remains unclear, such as the Plainview point found in the sand section at Harris County Boys School (Aten *et al.* 1976:52) and the possible early projectile points found in the tightly compressed stratigraphic section at the Owen Site in northern Harris County (Patterson 1980). No convincing habitation site locations for either the Late Wisconsin or the Early Holocene have been identified on the upper coast, although several have been identified farther to the east and west. Those closest to the upper Texas coast, for example, are the Salt Mine Valley Site near Lafayette, Louisiana, and several sites along the lower Guadaloupe River—notably the Johnston–Heller Site (Birmingham and Hester 1976), which is deeply stratified in floodplain alluvium.

Although the general discovery pattern for diagnostic early artifacts on the present coastal plain has been one of isolated finds (Hester 1977:173; Story 1980), it is premature to assume this must continue to be the case. Consideration of the paleoenvironment and some reasonable assumptions about group organization can lead to a practical strategy for identification of localities visited repeatedly to perform tasks, if not actually used for residential campsite purposes. Sites like Salt Mine Valley and Johnston–Heller make clear that there is much more to be found on the coast than isolated projectile points.

The composition of artifact assemblages for this early period can be suggested by combining reports of Paleo-Indian and Early Archaic assemblages from elsewhere on the coastal plain. In addition to other projectile points that are not as diagnostic as these previously discussed, there are Clear Fork Gouges, chipped stone drills, uniface cutting and scraping tools, choppers, hammerstones and debitage, possibly grinding or milling stones, and ground stones with cigar shape and notched ends known as Waco Sinkers (Hester 1976b:8; Shafer 1977:191; Story 1980:18). An antler artifact of unknown function (Slaughter and Hoover 1965:351) and a bone projectile point (Hester 1977:171) also have been found. From the brine-impregnated sediments at the Salt Mine Valley Site in south Louisiana (Gagliano 1977:218–232) chipped stone projectile points are absent, but a highly diversified bipolar stone tool industry, a socketed bone point, cordage, and basketry all have been described from the bone bed level dated to the period 11,000–12,000 years ago.

Because this early material is sparsely distributed and strongly biased towards certain kinds of preservation and discovery situations, conclusions about distributional patterns are premature. However, some observations at least can be noted. There do appear to be regional concentrations of different diagnostic projectile points; for example, Scottsbluff points may be more common in the eastern part of the state, and Golondrina points are more common in central Texas, the lower Pecos, and south Texas (Hester 1976b:6–7). Folsom points have been found often on the lower coast, although they are not known on the upper coast. Hester (1976b) believes that by the late Paleo-Indian period, regional differentiation had occurred in projectile point styles and tool assemblages. Presumably this differentiation was to some extent due to sociological causes and to some extent an artifact of patterns of adaptation to a habitat mosaic that no longer exists. Of particular interest in this regard is the bipolar lithic tool industry at the Salt Mine Valley Site.

This industry was originally interpreted in culture-historical terms as evidence of a pre-projectile point culture stage (Gagliano 1977:232). This may be; however, simpler explanations also should be tested. For example, the bipolar tools either may represent a specialization peculiar to activities carried out at Avery Island, or they may represent the Paleo-Indian period coastal lithic technology in the region. The coast of the northern Gulf of Mexico does not contain naturally occurring deposits or outcrops of chippable stone from which large flakes can be struck and large stone tools manufactured. All such material found archaeologically on the coast had to be imported, either in unmodified, preform, or in finished tool condition.

At much later times in prehistory, the importation of stone material and artifacts from the interior was interrupted and changes in the coastal technology occurred. This caused such things as a greater emphasis in use of bone projectile points, a greater use of inferior materials like silicified wood, and widespread use of bipolar technology in some instances based on gastroliths as the only available indigenous source of lithic material (see Appendix B). In any event, the occurrence of bipolar technology at Avery Island to the exclusion of large, bifacially chipped projectile points could have been a consequence of coastal activity-specific tool needs, or by the absence or temporary interruption of an exchange system providing lithic materials and artifacts from the interior, or both.

The question of economic orientation of social groups of this period has been addressed only slightly for the eastern Texas area; Bryant and Shafer (1977:20) concluded that the woodland and parkland habitat of eastern Texas would have encouraged dispersal rather than herding of certain animal species. Consequently, they believe that big game hunting was not viable east of the South Plains and that more diversified hunting and gathering was the necessary adaptive mode. Actually, Johnson's (1977) review of Paleo-Indian use of animal food resources makes clear that known Paleo-Indian economies in south–central North America were fairly well diversified. The upper coast contained three major habitats: (*a*) the coastal zone with associated strand, estuaries, and fresh, brackish, and salt marshes; (*b*) the interior deciduous woodlands with major components in the upland forests and riparian woodlands; and (*c*) intervening parkland and possible coastal prairie forming the transition between coast and woodland (Figure 9.2). However the group territories, social organization, and annual rounds were structured, it is reasonable to expect site distributions and their artifact content to differ at least according to the two dominant habitats— coast and woodland—and perhaps for the transitional parkland–prairie zone as well. Moreover, these different adaptive assemblages should show changes through time, particularly during the Early Holocene when habitat conditions were changing to the more extensive prairie lands of the Middle Holocene.

Thus, it can be proposed that occupation of both the woodlands and the coast

initially reflected patterns of resource exploitation with less seasonal and locational emphasis because the region was covered by a more homogeneous habitat and because there was less seasonal variation in climatic conditions. Free-
roaming mastodon, mammoth, giant bison, sabertooth cat, horse, and so on,
presumably posed a very different kind of habitable environment than one
populated exclusively by smaller creatures. Consequently, early Paleo-Indian
sites should have been widely dispersed over the area, but of modest duration,
constitution, and perhaps with less frequent reoccupation than was the case
later. These conditions taken together would result in much lower archaeological visibility when compared to that created by later inhabitants of the region.

Characterizing how the coastal zone may have been used by early cultures
necessarily involves deductive considerations. Arguments for the "discovery" of
shellfish and other littoral resources as a Middle Archaic phenomenon—so-
called "esculency" and technological development theories—have little to rec-
ommend them. These are "just so" stories that ignore the overriding facts that
(a) most coastal habitat dating earlier than the Middle Archaic is either buried
or submerged and not readily available for examination; and (b) wherever such
older coast has been examined, there is evidence for use of littoral resources.
And the northern Gulf coast is no exception, for the estuarine clam *Rangia
cuneata* was collected at the 11,000–12,000-year-old bone bed level of the Salt
Mine Valley Site.

A true maritime adaptation (open sea fishing, hunting, and transport) was
never employed on the Texas coast, so far as is known, by the Late Prehistoric–Woodland cultures. Therefore, it seems unlikely that this was ever
done during the earlier periods. Coastal subsistence very likely must have meant
something akin to "strandlooping," or collection of the plant and animal resources primarily of the coast and estuary margins. It is important to note that
the extent of estuarine habitat in the early periods probably varied significantly
depending on whether the time was one of stillstand–transgression (more extensive estuaries and marsh development) or regression (reduced estuary
development).

Additionally, increased streamflow during the Deweyville terrace interval
must have significantly reduced salinity in the estuaries and nearshore open
Gulf (cf. Kennett and Shackleton 1975). Thus, the oyster, *Rangia* clam, and
estuarine fish populations normally thought of today as constituting the major
resources of Gulf coast estuaries actually may be a post-Pleistocene development. Instead, fresh and brackish water faunas may have dominated the Late
Wisconsin and Early Holocene coastal environment and would result in a different faunal configuration for early coastal middens.

The prairie–parkland habitat may have been very restricted in its extent on
the upper coast (Figure 9.2). If this was the case, it seems reasonable to assume
that it was the scene of hunting forays emanating either from the coast or from
the interior woodlands to prey on herding animals. Even if territoriality was a
feature of the band society of that day (cf. Wobst 1974), it is not known whether

these territories would most likely have been confined to coast, woodland, and prairie, or whether they would have cut across such zones.

As the Early Holocene progressed, precipitation and runoff declined and seasonal extremes in climatic conditions increased. As a result, habitats became relocated, faunas changed seasonally, and higher salinity estuary conditions developed. Archaeological settlement patterns, technology, food resources, and demographics should reflect these changes in testable fashion. First, however, surveys will have to be designed to discover sites with materials that demonstrably constitute Paleo-Indian and Transitional Archaic period assemblages. Once there is some idea of what material remains exist, hypotheses can be framed about the relationships among sites, tool assemblages, habitats, territories, and the social and natural environments of early upper coast inhabitants.

Having identified some of the potential characteristics of Paleo-Indian and Transitional Archaic archaeology that should occur on the upper Texas coast, it is possible to propose where sites of these periods should be sought within the framework of Late Wisconsin–Early Holocene geologic history. The plausible settings for archaeological campsite or task areas at that time were as follows: (a) coastal beach ridges; (b) estuary margins; (c) valley wall scarps along major floodplains; (d) natural levees; (e) upland stream margins; (f) upland and floodplain lakesides; and (g) springs, streams, rim syncline ponds, and solution ponds associated with salt domes. Depending on their location with respect to the coast, these settings would contain either shell or earth middens, or, if the site was only a task area, a particular assemblage of tools and debris related to the activity.

Most of these site settings occur submerged on the continental shelf. Those associated with barrier and estuary systems, and with salt domes are probably the most susceptible to detection given the subsea survey methods currently available (Gagliano et al. 1981). Landforms of these types that presently have been identified include the shorelines dating back 13,000–11,000 and 11,000–10,000 years, and the intervening region over which the strand transgressed and regressed (Figure 8.4). These drowned landforms can be traced farther east using Gagliano's (1977:Figure 7–10) paleogeographic reconstructions of southern Louisiana.

The riverine geography of this period may be exposed to some extent on the continental shelf (Figure 8.4), but the major exposures of this habitat are on the Deweyville terraces and adjacent valley wall of the Sabine, Neches, Trinity, and Brazos rivers (Figure 8.1) (Bernard 1950; Gibson et al. 1978:Figure 11). Although the Deweyville terraces are not known to outcrop along other major streams of the upper coast, their valley wall escarpments, under certain conditions, represent relatively unmodified Late Wisconsin geography.

It is difficult to know at what time a river valley escarpment was eroded into unconsolidated sediment unless the wall is marked in some way. For example, valley wall with adjacent Younger Deweyville terrace (even though buried by floodplain aggradation) can be assumed to have been scoured during the late Deweyville and to be unlikely to have any archaeological remains much older than about 10,000 years ago. Valley wall fronted by Older Deweyville terrace is unlikely to have archaeological remains predating circa 11,000 years ago, while valley wall fronted by early Woodfordian terraces (Trinity River T_3 and T_4 terraces) is terrain which could contain archaeology of any age back to around 20,000 years ago. These terminal relationships are particularly true for the Deweyville terraces. The erosional power of the Deweyville streams was so great that they alone were primarily responsible for determining the shape of today's coastal stream valleys, rather than, as is often thought, by entrenchment during the glacial maximum around 18,000 years ago when sea level was at its lowest elevation.

The valley wall scarp example is important because it is one of the most likely preservation settings for early archaeology. The Ernest Witte Site (41 AU 36) on the lower Brazos River near Wallis, Texas (Hall 1981), is a recently reported example of why this is so. The Witte Site and many other archaeological sites were identified along the upper scarp edge of a large radius arcuate "scallop" in the valley wall, which is readily recognized as having been cut by the meandering Deweyville Brazos River (Hall 1981:Figure 1). Many short erosional gullies ordinarily are incised from the floodplain or upland surface down to the active river channel, as can be seen along the present Brazos River. Many other topographically more subdued gullies can be seen extending down to the floodplain surface in the Deweyville meander scar near the Witte Site. These older gullies are more gentle in topographic expression because their local base level is no longer the active stream surface but the floodplain surface which is at a significantly higher elevation. As the floodplain surface has aggraded, these gullies have been filling rather than eroding, probably more or less continuously since the end of the Late Wisconsin. The Witte Site is located in the intersection of the branching arms of a y-shaped gully of Deweyville age. The site consists of archaeological strata dating back to the Middle Archaic, or about 4500 to 5000 years ago, which have been well separated by sediment accumulation on the gully floor (Hall 1981:Figure 9). In this way, major archaeological habitation and mortuary levels were preserved extremely well. These branching, valley-margin erosional gullies are one of the prime localities in which early archaeological sites should be sought because, unlike floodplains, they provide localized, identifiable, protected settings for long term accumulation of sediment and archaeological remains.

The surface of the Younger Deweyville, because of the depth of its entrenchment, usually is covered by later floodplain alluvium which obscures prospects for surveying natural levee, point-bar, and floodplain lake locations for late Paleo-Indian sites. On the other hand, excellent exposures of these geomorphic features, which may have associated archaeology, exist on the Older Deweyville terraces.

In addition to the major floodplains, there are vestiges of the hydrologically more competent Late Wisconsin drainage network that are extensively preserved throughout the uplands of the upper coast as part of the contemporary drainage pattern. Also, the surface of the Beaumont Formation, which constitutes the interfluvial uplands on the outer coastal plain, is traversed by numerous abandoned Pleistocene river channels left from the origin of the formation as a series of coalesced river deltas. These channels have been undergoing erosional deterioration and infilling, but many still trap water forming intermittent lakes. It is reasonable to assume that during the Late Wisconsin–Early Holocene these channels formed more extensive lake networks in the woodlands and parklands of the upper coast. Only one archaeological reconnaissance of such channel lakes or ponds has been reported (Neyland 1970), without identification of archaeological remains, but further systematic examination of these landforms should be carried out.

Finally, there is a possibility of early sites being associated with salt domes. On the present upper coast, there are four salt domes with major surface expression: Big Hill, High Island, Damon Mound, and Bryan Mound. These all present very individualistic problems, but early archaeological deposits could exist in association with solution ponds, springs, streams and rim synclines. The comprehensive research at Avery Island salt dome in southern Louisiana (Gagliano 1967, 1970) provides a model for investigation of salt dome mounds in Texas.

The one "site" that probably is the best known Paleo-Indian locality on the upper coast—McFaddin Beach—is not situated in any of the settings just described. McFaddin Beach is a section of Gulf beach several kilometers long near Sabine Pass (Figure 9.2). Numerous Paleo-Indian and Transitional Archaic projectile points, bones of extinct late Quaternary fauna, and numerous aritfacts of later Archaic age have been washed up and collected (Long 1977). The geology of the Gulf beach here consists of transgressive barrier beach sand overriding a 3 m thick section of Middle Holocene marsh sediment which, in turn, overlies the Pleistocene Beaumont Formation at a depth of about 1½ m below mean Gulf level. The Beaumont Formation and the Middle Holocene marsh are being exhumed all along the shoreface which extends downward to more than 6 m below mean Gulf level and is about 1 km wide (Fisher *et al.* 1973:47, Figure 15; Kwon 1969:16–17, Figure 10). No underwater examination of the locality has been reported to determine the provenience of the fossils and the artifacts, although they are most likely to be coming from either the Holocene marsh sediment or from the Beaumont Formation–Holocene marsh contact. In any event, McFaddin Beach is a locality of considerable potential which probably is associated with a Late Wisconsin–Early Holocene valley wall scarp setting and related drainage formed by extension of the Sabine–Neches river system out onto the continental shelf (Figure 8.4).

MIDDLE HOLOCENE

This period began with the onset of the post-Pleistocene thermal maximum and continued until the end, more or less, of the post-Pleistocene eustatic sea level transgression some 3000 to 4000 years ago (see Figure 8.3). In terms of the region's stratigraphy and geomorphology, this means all landforms and depositional units between the 7500 year old and the 3500 year old shorelines (Figure 8.4) and associated river channel stages. These begin with channels showing the post-Deweyville minimum stream geometry and initial enlargement before the attainment of a fully modern hydrologic regime as recorded in the latest channel stages (Figure 8.11; Table 8.1). The broad outlines of upper coast geography at this time are illustrated in Figure 9.3.

Data from this period, whether environmental or archaeological, are exceedingly sparse. Channel geometry and caliche soils are tangible evidence that the thermal maximum was experienced directly on the upper coast. At the same time, it is difficult to translate this into a very precise statement about the degree of stress in this environment for subsistence by hunter–gatherers. Perhaps the most eloquent evidence available is the fact that there are almost no archaeological data known from the upper coast which definitely are referable to this period.

The Atlantic climatic episode, the period of the thermal maximum, persisted for quite a long time and evidently included variably intensive episodes of hot, dry conditions. Streamflow declined to levels below those of the present day and many smaller streams probably became intermittent or dried up entirely.

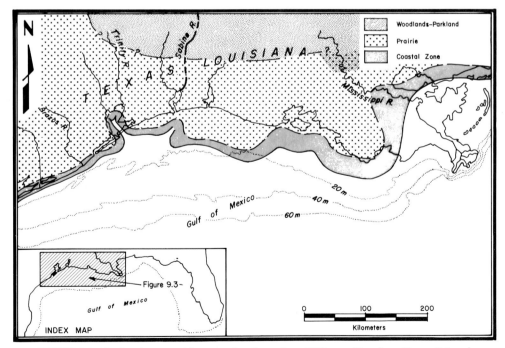

FIGURE 9.3 Regional geographic reconstruction, circa 7500 B.P. (Based on Figure 8.4 and Gagliano 1977: Figure 7–12.)

Riparian habitats must have become refuge for significantly diminished animal populations, and perhaps for human populations as well. The Pleistocene megafauna apparently was extinct in this area by the onset of the Middle Holocene. Around 5000 B.P., the size of this climatic cell diminished and its boundary retreated westward again to its present position in southern Texas. As this retreat occurred, mean annual precipitation began to increase and mean annual temperature began to decrease, leading to the present-day seasonally differentiated upper coast climate. This time of ameliorating drought conditions and of transition to seasonal, subhumid, and cooler temperatures was the Sub-Boreal climatic episode and ended circa 3000 years ago (Figure 9.1).

During the Atlantic episode (i.e., early Middle Holocene), human use of the upper coast must have been significantly more restricted than during the Late Wisconsin and Early Holocene. Although the littoral (Figure 9.3) may not have been greatly different than was suggested for the Early Holocene (e.g., no fossil eolian landforms so characteristic of the arid lower Texas coast have been identified), diminished freshwater inflow to the coast probably caused estuaries to attain salinities more on the order of the open Gulf. At the same time, the hinterland of the upper coast surely was a very different place. The prairie habitat expanded significantly, as indicated by the extent of caliche formation over the upper coast, and on the continental shelf. How far inland the prairies extended and deciduous woodlands retreated is only conjectured in Figure 9.3. The principal habitable zones would have been riparian, with the extensive upland prairies constituting a limited resource area. Whether or not band territories would have been confined primarily to the coast, the floodplains, or the deciduous woodlands located far to the interior is not deducible at this time. Given such a reduction in natural resources, the human population during the early Middle Holocene must have been significantly reduced from that of the Early Holocene and Late Wisconsin.

The Middle Holocene included all of what conventionally is recognized in the archaeological literature as the Early Archaic and a portion of the Middle Archaic (Figure 9.1). The density of Early Archaic archaeological sites everywhere on the coastal plain appears low when compared to those of the Paleo-Indian or Middle Archaic periods (Story 1980:13). Indeed, the major Early Archaic site concentrations are situated along the inner margin of the central coastal plain, an area well inland and away from the upper coast (Story 1980:14). These sites have been described as fewer, smaller, and less functionally variable than later sites.

Virtually the only Early Archaic diagnostic artifacts which have been reported *in situ* from the upper coast are projectile points such as Tortugas and possibly Abasolo from Addicks Reservoir (Wheat 1953), located in the interior (Figure 11.1). Middle Archaic forms such as Bulverde and Pedernales also were recovered by Wheat at Addicks. Unfortunately, many dart point styles known to be distributed over the eastern Texas area have not been identified very well from stratigraphic contexts nor adequately dated. Consequently, while there appears to be almost no evidence of habitation of the upper coast during the earlier part of the Middle Holocene, this must largely result from unrecognizable diagnostic artifacts for the period. Such a problem surely is compounded by the fact that much of the Middle Holocene population would have been more closely tethered to the floodplains and estuaries, habitats for which there is limited archaeological visibility.

Toward the end of the Middle Holocene, apparent Middle Archaic sites appear more or less coincident with the onset of Sub-Boreal climatic conditions (Figure 9.1). Regionally, Story (1980:22) sees more numerous sites, changes in settlement patterns, increase in population, and distinct patterns in distribution of artifacts coinciding with the major environmental zones of east Texas (woodlands), central Texas (hilly scrub), and south Texas (savanna). Demarcation of territorial boundaries probably continued to emerge on the central coastal plain and became more visibly signified by cemeteries with increasingly elaborate mortuary practices. Several such cemeteries have been discovered in the central and lower Brazos River valley (Aten *et al.* 1976:105–107; Hall 1981; Walley 1955). However, no mortuary practices of any kind are known on the upper coast until the Late Prehistoric–Woodland (Aten *et al.* 1976).

The known Middle Archaic archaeological record for the upper coast is more consequential than the Early Archaic; at least some sites have been identified. At present, the most informative Middle Archaic upper coastal site is shell midden 41 HR 80/85 at Harris County Boys School (Aten *et al.* 1976), located on the west side of Galveston Bay estuary, south of Houston (Figure 9.3). Occupation at the site began about 3700 years ago (Table 14.1) and is associated with the final phases of establishing the Galveston Bay estuary (Figure 8.6). Estuarine development is reflected in the succession of shellfish assemblages in the midden refuse. The species assemblages initially indicated brackish habitats near the site; these became increasingly more saline through the late Middle Holocene. Once the Middle Holocene transgression ended, estuarine habitats (and midden shellfish assemblages) returned to a less saline condition with the inception of Late Holocene sedimentation.[2]

The late Middle Holocene (Middle Archaic) refuse at Boys School consists of dense shell midden composed primarily of *Rangia cuneata* (brackish water clam), but with minor portions of *Crassostrea virginica* (oyster) and *Rangia flexuosa* (higher salinity clam) increasing through time. The season of *R. cuneata* collection, and presumably occupation at the site, was the month of August. The artifacts consisted of a few straight-stemmed dart points, and some flake and biface stone tools; bone or shell tools were not present at all. Examination of the chipping debris indicates that the focus of stone tool-working was on the production or reworking of bifacial tools from preforms or

---

[2]This cycle of increasing and then decreasing salinity has been recorded in many other coastal sites (e.g., Braun 1974; Gagliano 1977:Figure 5–10; Ritchie 1969:Figure 16) and usually is a function of the development of coastal geography in the post-Pleistocene period.

"spent" tools. The stone material used was predominantly chert with a small proportion of silicified wood.

Site 41 CH 57 is a shell midden located near Wallisville on the valley wall scarp of the lower Trinity River (Figure 9.3). This site also has been radiocarbon dated to about 3700 years ago (Table 14.1) and contains significant quantities of oyster shell as well as the *R. cuneata* (Valastro *et al.* 1975). No additional information on this site has been reported, but it seems certain to be associated with the higher salinity environment of the final stages of embayment of the Trinity estuary (Figure 8.6). Because of the absence of data on artifacts, it is not possible to evaluate this site culturally as Middle or Late Archaic. In terms of absolute dating and the geologic time–stratigraphy used to organize discussion of the early cultures, site 41 CH 57 clearly is associated with the final phases of the Middle Holocene; that is, effects of sea level transgression still were dominant in the upper reaches of the Trinity estuary even though progradation had resumed elsewhere. Moreover, the site's age is similar to that of the Boys School midden.

Numerous other shell middens have been inventoried on the upper coast of which some probably are unrecognized Middle Archaic sites. In the interior, however, no unequivocal documentation exists of Middle Archaic sites largely because of uncertainties over the chronological significance of many projectile point styles. Nevertheless, sites such as Addicks (Wheat 1953) and the Owen Site (Patterson 1980), in western and northern Harris County, respectively, probably have occupations attributable to this period. Unfortunately, these upland stream margin sites have such tightly compressed stratification that effective chronological separation of depositional units has not been excavated yet.

The principal Middle Holocene site settings probably are the same as those previously described for the Late Wisconsin–Early Holocene: strand, estuaries, river valleys, uplands (locally), and salt dome mounds. The 7500-year-old shoreline is in a location that now is submerged on the continental shelf, but the 3500-year-old shoreline is partially exposed on the present coast (Figure 8.4). Although much of the riverine geography of this period remains covered by water or sediment, the Big Slough and Bastrop Bayou channels of the Brazos River delta are partly exposed (Figure 8.9), as is Channel Group B on the lower Trinity River. Valley wall scarp localities figure prominently as high probablility settings for sites of this period. The important new features pertaining to site discovery in this period, however, are the establishment of the present Galveston Bay and Sabine Lake estuaries, and the earliest appearance of shell middens on the present coastal configuration.

The embayment of the Trinity River valley had proceeded to such an extent by circa 5000 years ago that the Trinity estuary occupied nearly its present configuration as Galveston Bay (Figure 8.6). Unfortunately, most of the subsequent enlargement of the estuary to its present dimension came as a result of lateral erosion of the shoreline that destroyed nearly all bay margin archaeology. The principal exception to this generalization occurred where the present location of the lower Trinity River floodplain was embayed and subsequently filled by fluvial and deltaic sediments, thereby minimizing erosion of the valley wall. Because of this, the valley wall scarp along both sides of approximately the lower 7 km of the Trinity valley may contain Early to Middle Archaic estuarine archaeology possibly buried in gully fill as described earlier in the Witte Site example. This also is the area in which the previously described site 41 CH 57 is located.

LATE HOLOCENE

Once the post-Pleistocene sea level transgression ended, about 3000–4000 years ago, a new sequence of depositional units was initiated which were associated with diversification of coastal habitats, shoaling of the estuaries, seaward progradation of the strand, and floodplain–delta evolution that has continued to the present day. This includes the area from the 3500-year-old shoreline southward to the present coast (Figure 8.4), the Oyster Creek and present channels of the Brazos River (Figure 8.9), all the exposed delta positions of the Trinity River (Figure 8.7), and Trinity Channel Group B.

Although there have been numerous short-term variations in regional climate over the last 3500 years, such as the Little Ice Age and the abnormal warm trend of recent decades, the climate of the Late Holocene essentially has been that of the contemporary Gulf coast—strong cycles in seasonal precipitation and temperature. Presumably the deciduous woodlands habitat began modest expansion again at the expense of a diminishing prairie–parkland habitat (Figure 9.4).

Because there is no comprehensive formulation about the development of the early cultures, there is little theoretical basis for deducing the nature of change from the Middle to Late Archaic, except perhaps from cultural ecology. Looking at the matter empirically, important cultural changes apparently did take place on the Texas coastal plain at the beginning of the Late Archaic, beyond the adoption of some different projectile point styles. Regionally, Story (1980:42–43) has recognized two broad adaptive patterns—the "eastern" and the "western" strategies—which may have existed earlier but which finally became distinct in the archaeological record of the Late Archaic. The eastern strategy was designed for the humid woodlands and prairies of the upper coast and involved territoriality, resource rights, limited group mobility, higher population densities, and more complex social organization. The western strategy was designed for the semiarid savannas of the southwestern coastal plain and involved defined, but often shared, rights to seasonally abundant resources, relatively higher group mobility, lower population densities, and social organization not integrated beyond the exogamous band level.

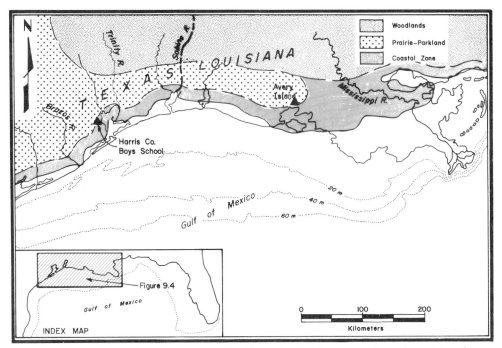

FIGURE 9.4 **Regional geographic reconstruction, circa 3500 B.P. (Based on Figure 8.4 and Gagliano 1977: Figure 7–13.)**

A great many preceramic archaeological sites are known for the upper coast area, but most of those for which absolute dates have been determined appear to postdate about 2500 years ago. It is very possible that significant expansion of the upper coast population did not occur until the onset of the fully modern climate in the Sub-Atlantic episode (Figure 9.1). The most important of the earlier Late Holocene sites, from the standpoint of regional synthesis, is still the Harris County Boys School shell midden (Aten *et al.* 1976). At this site alone, excavation has documented more than projectile points from before and after the Middle–Late Holocene transition. Specifically, the Late Holocene–Late Archaic zone at Boys School, when compared to the Middle Holocene–Middle Archaic zone, consisted of significantly higher midden refuse density (e.g., flake density doubled). Additionally, chipped stone tool fabrication shifted to focus on "cruder" biface tools (i.e., there was a significant increase in single-faceted, interior, lipped flakes), on greater diversity and quantity in projectile point styles, addition of a small but persistent proportion of quartzite to the lithic material inventory, and addition of bone artifacts (especially awls, projectile points, and beads) to the technology.

There also was a shift in season of occupation from August to May–June as determined from *Rangia cuneata* growth patterns. This might reflect restructuring of the annual round, or it may also be a function of the evolving estuarine geography. This is because during the Middle Archaic, the Boys School locality was associated with the upper or inland end of the Galveston Bay estuary. By the Late Archaic, the locality was associated with the middle estuary and somewhat different associations of estuarine resources. If the annual round were structured so that bands would be on the middle estuary in early summer and on the upper estuary in late summer, there need not have been any change in scheduling between Middle and Late Archaic to explain the change in Boys School seasonality data. Once shell samples are obtained from sites representing other habitats exploited during the Middle and Late Archaic annual round, the nature of the scheduling will be readily determinable.

The artifact inventory for the Late Archaic period is essentially the same as will be described in Part III for the Clear Lake ceramic period except that ceramics are not part of the assemblage. Although not found at the Boys School site, there also have been several finds of ground stone boatstones, plummet pendants, and bar gorgets from the upper coast area (Hartman 1963; Long 1977:Figure 15; Walley 1955). Hall (1981:289–309) recently reviewed the distributon of ground stone in Texas and concluded that virtually all was of Late Archaic to early Late Prehistoric age. The igneous rocks and minerals used to fashion ground stone artifacts apparently originated in southwestern Arkansas and indicate that eastern Texas, including the upper coast, participated in a far-reaching exchange network that also included the Poverty Point and, possibly, later cultures of the lower Mississippi valley.

Late Archaic archaeological sites, especially for the post-2500 B.P. period, occur in large numbers on the upper coast and in virtually all habitats in which subsequent natives of the area lived.

CONCLUSIONS

The history of the "Early Cultures" essentially is a three-part succession extending from the late glacial Pleistocene environments through the post-Pleistocene transitions to arid climate and finally evolving to the contemporary humid climates. Concurrently with the climatic changes, there also were major alterations taking place in the geographic configuration of the upper coast. Assuming that human populations adapt to limiting conditions in their environment, the extensive geographic and climatic modifications of the period from roughly 12,000–2,000 years ago brought significant stresses to bear on the cultural systems. The cultural mechanisms available to meet these stresses are assumed to have been social reorganization, technological innovations, alternative ways of transmitting information, and demographic changes to alter a group's energy budget. By altering one or more of these basic dimensions, it is possible to "redefine" or to manage an environmental constraint and its dependent cultural thresholds.

It has been obvious from the preceeding discussion that direct evidence for the early cultures is very limited. Present observations about the four dimensions, (a) organization; (b) technology; (c) information; and (d) energy, are largely impressionistic, but can constitute a basis for organizing future research.

Social Organization   It is not obvious at this time that any particular changes of social organization took place, or need to have taken place during the Paleo-Indian and Archaic to respond to environmental stresses. Presumably individuals, family–task groups, and minimum bands constituted the main organizational levels throughout the Paleo-Indian and Archaic periods. At least there are no data to the contrary except in Late Archaic mortuary practices of the lower Brazos valley where status differentiation seemed to be underway which may have had organizational corollaries. These three levels of organization would have been sufficiently generalized to deal with most contingencies the populations faced. Presumably, aggregation and disaggregation of the organizational levels varied at least according to the resource–habitat–climate patterns of the region at any given time.

Technology   Although some changes in artifact assemblages can be shown, their relationships to the larger characterization of social and natural environmental changes is not apparent. The technology of the early cultures was generalized and could be applied to a wide range of resource conditions and applications. If functionally important adaptive changes in technology occurred, they were more likely in the realm of methodologies (i.e., in the manner of tool use or individual deployment to obtain resources).

Information Transfer   The radically different character of habitat and resource types during the three periods of Late Wisconsin–Early Holocene, Middle Holocene, and Late Holocene suggests that there had to be significant modifications in how the early cultures transmitted information. As suggested above for organizational implications, the early Texas coastal populations (individuals, family–task groups, minimum bands) must have been arrayed very differently in response to the conditions of resource distribution in successive pluvial, arid, and humid seasonal environments. As a result, intergroup relationships to pass information about resources, themselves, and the supernatural, to enhance their perceived chances for survival, must have undergone important changes. The development of more formal patterns of mortuary ritual beginning in the Middle Archaic on the lower Brazos also may have been associated with this dimension of adaptation.

Energy The principal dimension of adaptive change which currently seems evident and expectable in the early cultures was in adjustment of net group energy budgets through change in the size or composition of populations. The apparent relative differences in frequency of artifact and site occurrences in the inland habitats over the period from 12,000 to 2,000 years ago described in this chapter may be crude indicators of population change. According to this, it would seem that population increased to a significant level by the late Paleo-Indian period (Early Holocene) and then "crashed" either to zero or to a low level through the Early Archaic (Middle Holocene) and then began to increase again through the Middle Archaic. On purely impressionistic grounds, based on the degree of visibility of archaeological evidence, the maximum population of the Late Paleo-Indian period seems most comparable to that of either the late Middle Archaic or early Late Archaic (Figure 9.1). Population in the Late Archaic appears to have exceeded that of previous periods and to have been on a trajectory of increase which extended unaffected into the Late Pre-historic–Woodland (Figure 17.1). Although the Late Archaic is rooted in the early cultures, its cultural character seems to have been primarily part of the history of the Late Prehistoric–Woodland cultures, which are the subject of Part III.

It is reasonably evident that the geological framework of sedimentary history provides a practical way to structure and examine both the early environments and early cultures of the upper coast. Until much better culture-historical data are available, the geologic framework probably is the best entrée into the early periods. The paleogeographic reconstruction undertaken in Chapter 8, along with discussion of landform–archaeological site associations in Chapter 9, provide a practical basis for stratifying the upper coast natural environment into geographic strata having cultural significance. Survey based on random sampling of these habitat strata (principally the littoral, prairie–parkland, upland, and riverine zones) can be carried out for the terrestrial portions as well as for many of the areas submerged on the continental shelf.

The practical difficulties for investigating the submerged prehistoric archaeology in the ocean environment are formidable. It is likely that most data to be acquired in the foreseeable future will come as a consequence of environmental protection activities by the offshore oil and gas industry. Because of this, it is efficient to align the survey goals and strategies used on land with those which could be employed at sea. For example, the principal coordinate system used on the continental shelf for oil and gas leasing purposes is based on a one mile (about 2.6 km²) grid.[3] It would be desirable to extend this grid landward to identify survey sample units rather than to use 7½ minute quadrangles or some

[3]In State of Texas waters, a one mile² grid is used; beyond the 3 league limit, the federal government has jurisdiction and uses a 9 mile² unit (a square 3 miles or 4.8 km on a side) which is readily divisible into one square mile units.

other grid system. By this means, it will be possible to extrapolate more readily the results about site type, density, and association from the present terrestrial zone (e.g., on the Deweyville terraces or valley wall scarps) to the extensions of these former land areas out onto the continental shelf. The 1 mile^2 grid already has been used to describe selected coastal site settings for development of subsea site identification techniques and criteria (Gagliano *et al.* 1982). Unifying the terrestrial and offshore sampling methodology should be an advantage both to science and industry.

PART III

The Late Prehistoric Framework

CHAPTER 10

Background and Objectives

The ability to assign archaeological observations to their proper chronological relationships is central to the establishment of a regional basis for inquiry into the extinct cultures of the Texas coast. In this part I develop such a chronological framework and describe the structure of the region's technological history for roughly the past 2000 years of prehistory. Unlike the environment of the early cultures, the major dimensions of geography, habitat, and climate appear to have been relatively stable during this later period. As a result, extensive problems of environmental reconstruction are not encountered, at least not on the scale dealt with in Part II.

Formulating a chronological framework for the upper coast and linking this to adjacent areas requires multiple approaches; no single chronology-building technique, at least among those presently known, can be used feasibly over the entire area. In the coastal zone, the abundance and diversity of ceramics and the relative paucity of lithic materials indicate that for the time range in which ceramics were used, the best approach is that of a ceramic pattern seriation, as verified by radiocarbon dating and geomorphic sequences. For the preceramic shell middens, a combination of several approaches is needed. These include radiocarbon dating, projectile point style occurrences, lithic material frequencies (Aten 1967), shellfish utilization frequencies (cf. Aten *et al.* 1976:Figure 4), and seasonality patterns (Aten 1981). Ultimately, it may be possible to use certain climatic events for site correlation purposes (Aten 1972:13).

In the interior of the coastal plain, beyond the region in which shell middens occur, shell usually is not available for radiocarbon dating, and ceramic diversity declines. Projectile point diversity and abundance increase substantially, and these may be seriated along with the ceramics. Occasionally these techniques can be augmented with radiocarbon dating. Supplemental approaches usable over the entire upper coast region are lithic material frequencies, the diachronic distribution of bison in archaeological faunas (Dillehay 1974), and, to some extent, mortuary patterns (Aten *et al.* 1976).

In Part I, traditional concepts of the geographic territories of native groups on the upper Texas coast during the early eighteenth century were reexamined. Largely as a coincidental result of the placement of water control and other construction projects requiring salvage archaeology,[1] the major part of the available upper coast archaeological data comes from locations centrally placed within the ethnohistorically reconstructed group territories (see Figure 11.1).

In addition to this, there long have appeared to be gross differences in prehistoric ceramic assemblages between the three main upper coast drainage systems: the Sabine–Neches, the Trinity–San Jacinto, and the Brazos. Artifact collections from the Sabine frequently contain sherds of Lower Mississippi Valley ceramics that are largely absent in the other drainages (Aten and Bollich 1969). The Trinity–San Jacinto (i.e., the Galveston Bay area) ceramics exhibit much greater abundance and variety in design styles, color, and texture than do those of the Brazos (Aten 1971) or inland in the area of Conroe and Livingston (McClurkan 1968; Shafer 1968).

Although no a priori assumption is made that prehistoric social or population boundaries necessarily will follow either synchronic or diachronic changes in ceramics, it seems appropriate at the present stage of research to treat these three drainage basin areas separately. This approach maximizes temporal variation and minimizes spatial variation in the development of local chronologies. In some respects, this is contrary to the methods used in Part I for handling data on social organization, ritual, and cognition, and previously, in the study of mortuary practices (Aten et al. 1976). However, more extensive archaeological data exist for domestic utilitarian artifacts. Consequently, they are used as the major basis for approaching local chronologies rather than the more rare artifacts whose prime referents would be social organization–structure, ritual, and cognition. Neither does this approach interfere with use of populations instead of cultures as a basis for organizing research.

In addition to the coastal geographic areas described above, a fourth area will be examined as a means for drawing some contrast to the north with the region historically occupied by the Bidai. Archaeologically, this region is best known in data from Lake Conroe and from Lake Livingston (see Figure 11.1). As a result of developing and comparing local chronologies from these four geographic areas, the prehistoric data may be compared with the ethnohistoric data on the Atakapa, Akokisa, Bidai, and Karankawa.

Because most research on the upper coast has been in conjunction with a multitude of local environmental assessment or salvage archaeology needs, a formal sampling program has not been employed at a regional level. Inspection of site survey records at the Texas Archeological Research Laboratory leads, however, to the conclusion that most terrain on the upper coast where shell middens are likely to be found has now been examined systematically. Probably 80% of the sites that remain exposed at the surface have at least been located. In freshwater terrains where shell middens do not occur, including many areas

---

[1]That is, Addicks Basin (Wheat 1953); Wallisville Reservoir (Ambler 1970, 1973; Aten 1979; Dillehay 1975; Fox et al. 1980; Gilmore 1974; Shafer 1966); Lake Conroe (Shafer 1968); Lake Livingston (McClurkan 1968); Cedar Bayou (Ambler 1967); Brazosport (Aten 1971).

remarkably close to the Gulf (Aten and Bollich 1981), the status of survey is just the reverse; probably not more than 10% of the extant sites have been identified. Nearly all of the data presented in Part III are from shell middens.

When performing test excavations for the purpose of developing historical frameworks, the priorities for data collection were to obtain

1. A stratigraphic sequence of ceramics.
2. Sequences of faunal remains, using fine screening, representing as wide a time and space range as would be possible.
3. Samples of *Rangia cuneata* shells and charcoal (paired from the same context if possible) for radiocarbon dating of cultural and environmental features.
4. Samples of *Rangia cuneata* for determining the season of site occupation.
5. Evidence (sedimentological, geomorphic, or biotic) for reconstruction of the environmental setting.

These priorities led to collection of a great deal of information, not included in this volume, concerning paleoenvironments, paleogeography, settlement patterns, subsistence, and discrete habitation episodes.

Previous coastal fieldwork tended to focus primarily upon large excavations in a few sites. However, given that a very large number of sites exist on the upper coast, and that the coast, estuaries, and riverine geography has been changing steadily, it seemed clear that to gain any comprehensive grasp on the local history of cultural adaptations, alternative field strategies would be needed that did not absorb such huge portions of time and dollar resources in so few locations. The general approach was adopted of eschewing interest in sites per se; only enough was excavated at any given location to provide stable estimates of the relative proportions of artifacts and faunal subsistence. The other items previously listed as priorities were collected as available within these constraints. Sample (i.e., site) locations usually were selected on the basis of chronological and habitat differentiation of landforms in the areas where fieldwork was to be performed.

Validation of excavated sequences of artifacts depended upon two criteria:

1. Consistency with independent sequences (e.g., those derived from artifact cross dating or from radiocarbon dating);
2. Similarity with other artifact successions occurring in independently deposited stratigraphic sequences.

Beyond this, cumulative curves were compiled for numbers of species and individuals, and for meat weight per unit of excavation in the archaeological faunas being collected. The point at which these curves flattened showed when the data were becoming redundant. This analysis indicated that for dense, stratified shell midden deposits, a sample consisting of 0.4 m^3 (i.e., four units 1 m^2 by 10 cm thick) from the same cultural component tended to yield a stable result. For discrete habitation episodes, an area of about 4 m^2 was required for sample stability, and for sparse, stratified shell midden, about 1.5 m³ was needed. With these excavation sizes as a guide, it usually proved possible to obtain samples of ceramic sequences that satisfied the two validation criteria listed above.

This approach made it logistically possible to excavate small areas in many different sites so as to sample midden deposits of diverse ages and environmental settings. By this means, an array of synchronic and diachronic data was quickly assembled for the upper Galveston Bay area and the approach was applied to a more limited extent in the Brazos Delta–West Bay area as well.

Ceramic seriation was the principal tool used for the establishment of local chronologies. The basic technique employed was the graphic seriation approach of Ford (1962). Despite the fact that this technique has received criticism, it remains a useful approach when properly applied (Cowgill 1972:382–383; Dunnell 1970). In addition to providing a measure of the degree of similarity of one archaeological assemblage to another, it provides information about the form and source of this similarity (Dunnell 1970:306). The major problematic feature of the technique is in achieving agreement on the best-fitting chronological pattern.

In the case of the upper coast, sequence patterns have been verified through independent techniques (i.e., radiocarbon and cross dating both with archaeological and geological data). Given the assurances derived from independent verification, these patterns lead to other important ideas about upper coast culture history. For example, it is evident that a frequency seriation may be used in different ways: (a) as documentation of a continuous sequence of change; and (b) as an ordinal scale after partitioning into assemblages (i.e., what Dunnell (1970) calls "occurrence seriation"). With this technique, the relative and absolute ages of artifact assemblages from sites, or portions of sites, can be estimated. One then also has the ability to examine technological trends and patterns of evolution through measurement of rates and directions of change in many aspects of culture. Documenting the initial results of this research is the subject of Part III.

CHAPTER 11

The Sites

In this chapter, archaeological sites are described from which previously unpublished data were obtained to synthesize the chronological and technological history of the later periods. All site numbers are those assigned by the Texas Archeological Research Laboratory of the University of Texas at Austin, or by the Department of Geography and Anthropology, Louisiana State University, Baton Rouge. All site locations are shown on Figures 11.1, 11.2, 11.3, 11.27, and 11.30. Unless otherwise noted, all specimens and records are curated at the Texas Archeological Research Laboratory.

Some variation occurs in the nature or precision of the documentation which follows. This is due partially to the different sources of information and partially to the fact that field procedures evolved during the years this fieldwork was being performed. Except for the use of fine (1½ mm mesh) screens and water screening, the excavation techniques employed were fairly standard. In all cases except at 41 CH 31, 41 CH 170, 41 HR 80, 41 HR 85 and 41 HR 86, the work done at a site amounted only to limited stratigraphic testing or to collecting specimens from the surface. Consequently, detailed topographic mapping was not usually performed. At Wallisville Reservoir, however, mapping prepared by the U.S. Army Corps of Engineers was at a sufficiently large scale to permit use of these maps for recording the location of archaeological test pits.

In the case of the Brazos Delta area sites, sketch maps and photography showing relationships to prominent landmarks have had to suffice. At Jamaica Beach (41 GV 5), it was possible to relocate landmarks shown on a detailed topographic map made by E. Raymond Ring in 1962–1963; this enabled accurate location of the testing in relation to earlier work.

Because of the regional reconnaissance character of this research, no special attempts were made to document the internal spatial characteristics or differentiation of sites per se. When excavating, samples were sought that would serve as stable estimators of material culture at the specific location being tested. Only when using the small grid technique on unstratified single habitation episode sites (to be reported elsewhere) was lateral, intrasite variability a research issue.

Stratigraphic tests were multiples of 1-m² units excavated in 10-cm levels unless otherwise noted. Excavated refuse was screened successively through ¼-

169

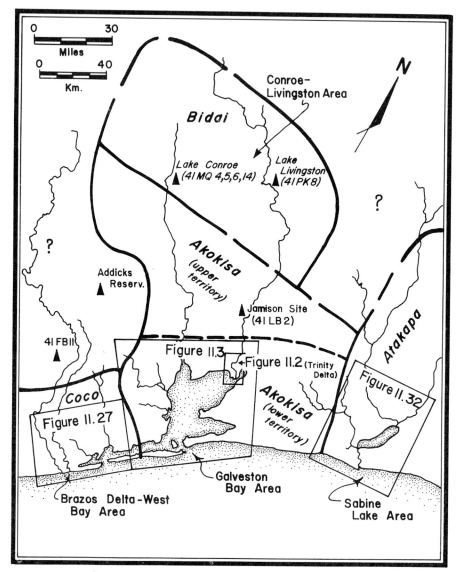

FIGURE 11.1   Relationship between ethnohistoric group territories and archaeological sites and areas.

inch (6.4 mm) screen and then 1/16-inch (1½ mm) screen to recover the very small animal bones and lithic flakes that occur so abundantly in shell middens of the upper coast.

All specimens were kept in separate bags labeled with site, grid, and level numbers, as appropriate, and were catalogued according to these proveniences.

Proveniences of all samples and specimens are given in tables in the pertinent section of Part III. References in the site descriptions to artifact types, ceramic periods, and absolute ages anticipate the analytical approaches taken and findings made in later chapters of Part III. The description of sites along the lower Trinity and Brazos rivers frequently refer to the various stages of floodplain and delta development as described in Figures 8.7 through 8.10.

GALVESTON BAY AREA

The inception of salvage archaeology in the proposed Wallisville Reservoir near the mouth of the Trinity River provided the opportunity to develop a detailed chronological framework for the Galveston Bay area. The sites reported by Ambler (1973) from his 1966 season at Wallisville only provided chronological data from late preceramic and early ceramic periods. Building on the analysis of Trinity River geomorphic history (Chapter 8; Aten 1966a,b) and employing assumptions about site–landform associations similar to those used by McIntire,[1] sites were selected for testing if they could be expected to extend artifact stratigraphy into more recent periods from the time Ambler's data ended. Once the known sites were differentiated according to landform association, final selection was made on the basis of the amount of midden accumulation and on their microenvironment associations. The latter criterion was to ensure that the faunal remains would reflect as wide a subsistence spectrum as possible. All other sites and data used from the Galveston Bay area are from other projects undertaken in the area. Whenever possible, criteria about expected data yields were used which were similar to those described for the Trinity River delta. Figures 11.2 and 11.3 are shown here to illustrate the sites selected.

Chambers County

41 CH 16 This site is located 0.4 km west of the Trinity River, south of Interstate Highway 10 (Figure 11.2). This *Rangia* midden was excavated and reported by J. R. Ambler (1973) and produced one of the earliest radiocarbon-

---

[1]Building on the earlier work of Fred Kniffen, McIntire (1958) showed that in the dynamic landscape of southern Louisiana, the creation or elimination of habitable area is directly reflected in the archaeological record. Knowledge of the history of the geological record permitted certain predictions to be made about the history of the archaeological record, and vice versa. Having an interpretation of evolution of the Trinity River delta made it possible to anitcipate the earliest time at which a site might have been occupied. Thus, it was possible to select a series of sites for stratigraphic testing that would virtually guarantee recovery of overlapping archaeological sequences for the entire time period of interest.

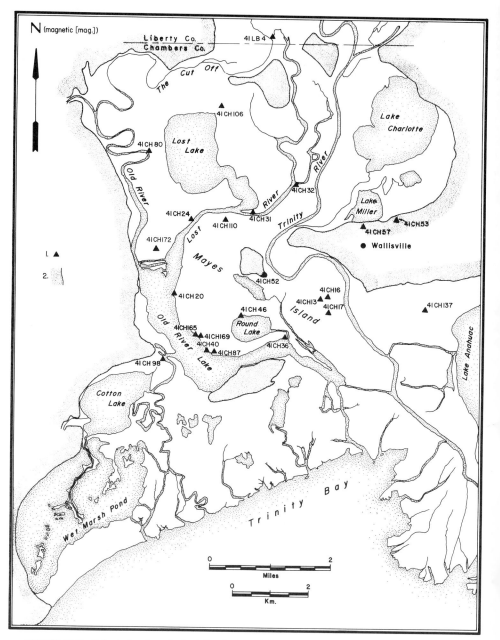

FIGURE 11.2 Selected archaeological sites in the Trinity River delta: (1) archaeological sites; (2) margin of pre-Holocene land surfaces.

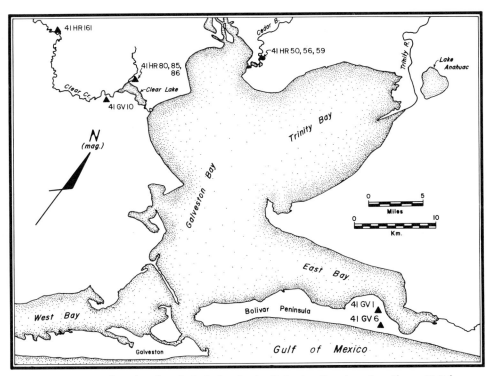

FIGURE 11.3 Selected archaeological sites in the Galveston Bay Area (see Figure 11.2 for Trinity delta site locations).

dated ceramic sequences known from the Galveston Bay area. For this reason, the ceramics were reexamined according to the typological system used in this study. The stratigraphic analysis units of "top," "middle," and "bottom" used here for the ceramics are the same as were originally presented by Ambler (1973:Figures 12 and 21).

41 CH 20   The site location is on the east shore of Old River Lake in the Trinity River delta (Figure 11.2). Two 1-m² stratigraphic test pits were excavated in 1966 (Figure 11.4) and a large collection was made of ceramics eroded from this *Rangia* shell midden. This material is of interest because three radiocarbon dates were obtained on samples from Test Pit A (Figure 11.5; see also Table 14.1). In an effort to incorporate these into the other chronological data, the ceramics from Test Pit A and the surface collection have been classified to determine the ceramic assemblages present at the site (see Table 12.2).

The excavated sherd sample is very small, but when interpreted in conjunction with the surface collection, the upper two-thirds of the midden is probably characterized by a ceramic assemblage of the Round Lake Period (see Table 14.2). Because of the poor definition of the direction of ceramic assemblage-

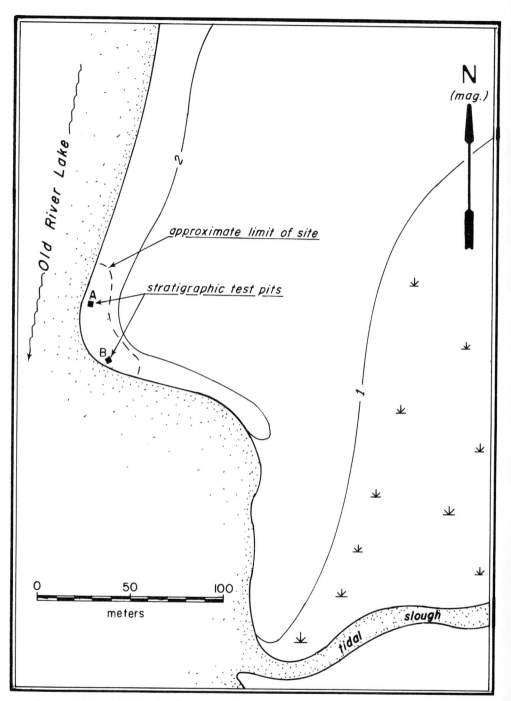

FIGURE 11.4   41 CH 20, site plan. Contour interval equals 1 ft. (30.5 cm). (Adapted from United States Army Corps of Engineers [USACE] topographic map.)

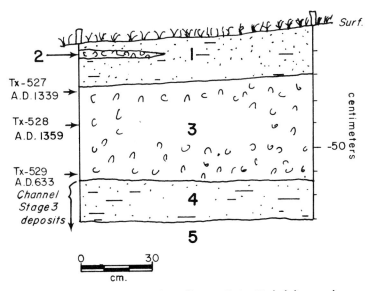

FIGURE 11.5 41 CH 20, profile of South Wall, Test Pit A: (1) dark brown clayey sand; (2) broken, wave-washed shell and sand; (3) primarily whole shell in dark brown to black clay; (4) sterile light brown sandy clay; (5) unexcavated.

change in the stratigraphic test, the possibility cannot be excluded that this is an Old River Period assemblage. The two stratigraphically higher radiocarbon dates are more consistent with the former interpretation, but do not conclusively rule out the latter.

The lower third of the midden may represent a significantly earlier occupation as is suggested by the earlier radiocarbon date. The ceramics sample is not clear evidence either for or against this possibility. The major support for the existence of such an occupation much earlier than the Round Lake Period is that nearly identical radiocarbon dates have been obtained from the earliest level of three nearby sites (41 CH 24, 36, and 165) which also are situated on top of Trinity River Channel Stage 3 deposits (Figures 8.7 and 8.8) or their equivalent. These early occupations would have been during the Mayes Island Period which is difficult to distinguish on the basis of ceramics alone.

41 CH 24   The site is located on the west bank of Lost River in the Trinity delta (Figure 11.2); this *Rangia* shell midden was tested with a 1-m² (Figures 11.6 and 11.7). The ceramics from the test indicate an early Round Lake assemblage (see Table 12.2). A radiocarbon date from the site's base is similar to those from the bottoms of the other three dated sites (41 CH 20, 36, and 165) to be found above Channel Stage 3 deposits. Evidently, there was a thin deposit of much earlier midden at the base of this site which is not recognizable in the ceramic assemblage obtained through this method of testing.

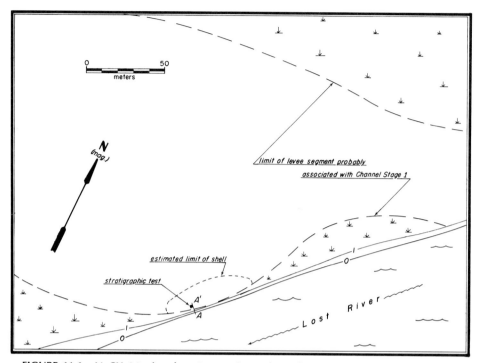

FIGURE 11.6   41 CH 24, site plan. Contour interval equals 1 ft. (30.5 cm). (Adapted from U.S.A.C.E. topographic map.)

41 CH 31   This *Rangia* midden is located on the north bank of Lost River (Figure 11.2) and was occupied during the Old River Period. It was intensively excavated (Aten 1982); only the data on culture stratigraphy are reported here (see Tables 12.2 and 13.1).

41 CH 32   This site location is the intersection of the west bank of Lost River and the south bank of John Wiggins Bayou in the Trinity delta (Figure 11.2). It was initially tested by J. R. Ambler in 1966 using volunteer assistance from the Houston Archeological Society. Additional testing was performed in 1973 (Dillehay 1975). This site has the interesting characteristic of being located at the intersection of Trinity River channel stages 1, 3, and 4 (Figure 8.7). From excavation notes in the files of the Texas Archeological Research Laboratory, it is evident that the site consisted of at least two major depositional episodes: a lower preceramic *Rangia* shell midden, and an upper ceramic-bearing *Rangia* midden. The two zones were separated in places by a thick black clay. The lower preceramic midden should have postdated Channel Stage 1 and predated Stage 3. The upper ceramic-bearing midden was most likely to have postdated Channel Stage 4. If this was the case, the ceramics from the upper zone could be expected to provide a sequence from the latest prehistoric and perhaps even the protohistoric periods of the area's history. For this reason, ceramics from grid units M-3 and M-5 from the 1966 test were classified (Table 12.2) and used in establishing the local chronology. These ceramics indicate assemblages spanning the time from the Old River Period to the Orcoquisac Period.

41 CH 36   This site is located at the intersection of the north shore of Old River Lake and the west bank of Round Lake Bayou in the Trinity delta (Figure 11.2). The site is a prominent mounded feature with a stratified shell midden accumulation. A 1 × 2 m test pit was excavated at this site (Figures 11.8 and 11.9) for several reasons: (*a*) it appeared to be stratified to a considerable depth; (*b*) a large quantity of ceramics, including incised and red-filmed wares, littered the eroded midden deposits along the beach; (*c*) the site was located in proximity to brackish and salt marshes considerably removed from the uplands; and (*d*) the site evidently was placed on top of Channel Stage 3 deposits and adjacent to Channel Stage 4 presenting an opportunity to obtain information on the age of these two geologic features.

The site proved to be stratified to a depth of 2 m with about one-third of this section permanently below the water table. A large collection of ceramics was recovered (see Table 12.2) that represent assemblages of the Turtle Bay Period and the Round Lake Period. Also obtained were lithic, faunal, *Rangia* seasonality, radiocarbon, and sediment samples.

At the time excavation of this site was carried out, it was not considered a likely possibility that plant and other perishable materials (other than bone) would be preserved. However, when removing bone and lithic chips from the

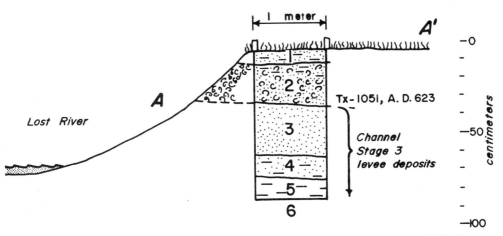

FIGURE 11.7   41 CH 24, stratigraphic profile: (1) sandy clay floodbasin deposit; (2) shell midden; (3) dark grayish brown medium-grained sand; (4) dark gray sandy clay; (5) gray clay with calcium carbonate concretions; (6) unexcavated.

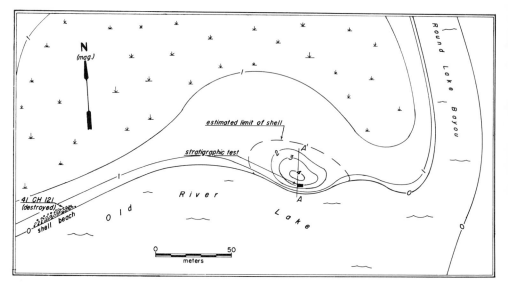

FIGURE 11.8   41 CH 36 and vicinity. Contour interval equals 1 ft. (30.5 cm). (Adapted from U.S.A.C.E. topographic map.)

fine screen residue in the laboratory, a number of seeds and other materials were noticed. The dried fine screen residue was subjected to water flotation. Although the washing treatment these residues had already received in the field had destroyed their integrity as samples of perishable materials, they could give a rough idea of what might be recovered should a similar opportunity be encountered again at a partially submerged midden. As it turned out, the flotation revealed (*a*) a large quantity of rootlets and very small charcoal fragments; (*b*) numerous very tiny snail shells from several different species, all common to marsh areas, which hardly could be economic but which are useful microenvironmental indicators; (*c*) fish scale fragments; (*d*) chitinous exoskeletons of insects; (*e*) noncarbonized seeds of various plants, including mustard, clover, hackberry, ragweed, and goosefoot; and (*f*) significant quantities of variously shaped, matted clumps of plant fibers that are presumed to be rodent scats.

41 CH 40   This is stiuated on the east shore of Old River Lake southwest of Round Lake in the Trinity River delta (Figure 11.1). Erosion and shoreline retreat have badly damaged this shell midden, and surface collecting is the only data recovery activity that has taken place (Ambler 1970; Shafer 1966). The site is mentioned here as the find spot of a unique ceramic turtle effigy that will be described in Chapter 13. Based on the proportions of ceramic types reported by Ambler (1970), the habitation of this site could date to either the Round Lake Period or the Old River Period. Based on the known age of the major occupation

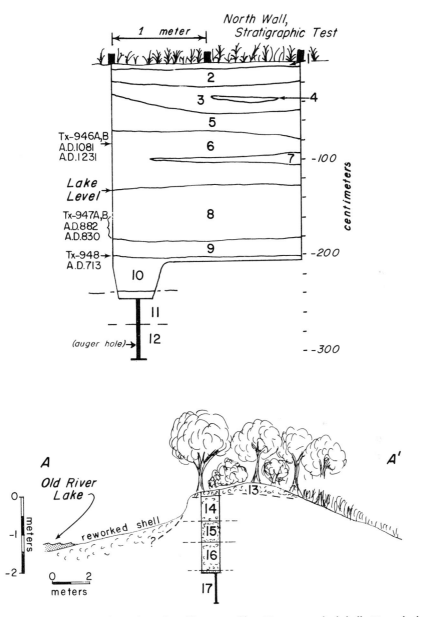

FIGURE 11.9 41 CH 36, site and stratigraphic test profiles: (1) wave-washed shell; (2) crushed and whole shell in dark grayish brown silt; (3) whole shell in dark grayish brown clayey silt; (4) crushed shell; (5) crushed and whole shell in dark grayish brown silt; (6) whole shell in light brownish gray sand; (7) whole and crushed shell in brownish gray silty clay; (8) whole shell in grayish brown sandy clay; (9) whole shell in light brownish gray sand; (10) dark grayish brown sandy clay; (11) brown sandy clay; (12) light gray sandy clay; (13) wave-washed shell; (14) midden; (15) Channel Stage 4 levee? and midden; (16) midden; (17) Channel Stage 3 levee.

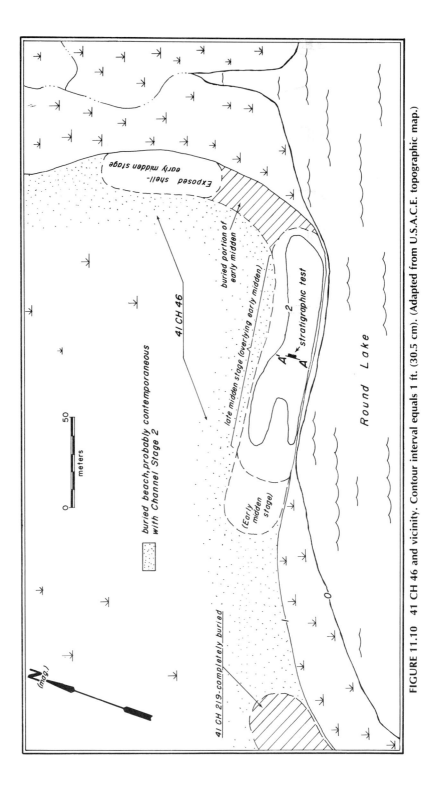

FIGURE 11.10   41 CH 46 and vicinity. Contour interval equals 1 ft. (30.5 cm). (Adapted from U.S.A.C.E. topographic map.)

of other sites (e.g., 41 CH 20, 24, 36, 165) similarly situated adjacent to the course of Channel Stage 3, the Round Lake Period is a more reasonable estimate.

41 CH 46   This site location is on the north shore of Round Lake in the Trinity River delta (Figure 11.2). It was tested in 1969 by excavation of a 1 × 2 m test pit. This test was terminated at a depth of 1.1 m because the *Rangia* midden deposits forming the test pit walls were so unstable that minimum excavation controls could not be maintained. A second attempt at testing this site was made in the 1973 season (Dillehay 1975) but this excavation was terminated at a depth of 1.7 m for the same reason.

In addition to its evident deep stratification, this site was selected for testing because its location appeared to have undergone substantial environmental change. The site appears to have been settled initially as one of a series of sites distributed along the bay-front during the time Channel Stage 2 was active (Figure 11.10). Subsequent to the formation of Round Lake and the associated brackish marshes, probably during the period Channel Stage 4 was active, the site was reoccupied (Figure 11.11). Although neither test reached the base of the

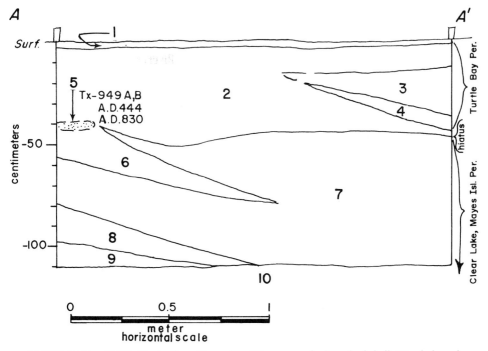

FIGURE 11.11   41 CH 46, stratigraphic profile: (1) wave-washed crushed shell; (2) whole and some crushed shell in dark gray sandy clay; (3) whole and crushed shell; (4) whole shell; (5) small hearth; (6) whole and crushed shell; (7) loose whole shell with some dark gray silty clay; (8) whole and crushed shell; (9) loose whole shell; (10) unexcavated. Total thickness of midden is estimated to be about 2 m.

midden, both appear to have spanned the transition from one natural setting to the other. Recovered ceramic assemblages (see Table 12.2) confirm that the site was occupied at least during the Clear Lake Period, the Mayes Island Period, and the Turtle Bay Period. Also obtained were faunal, lithic, seasonality, radiocarbon, and sediment samples.

41 CH 52   This site is located immediately west of the Trinity River and about 0.8 km south of Interstate Highway 10 (Figure 11.2). The site is a *Rangia* midden tested in 1966 and reported by Ambler (1973) as an early ceramic site. These ceramics were reanalyzed according to the ceramic typology used in this study (see Table 12.2) and were used as a single collection representing the Clear Lake Period.

41 CH 80   This location is on the east bank of Old River, a short distance west of Lost Lake in the Trinity River delta (Figure 11.2). The site is a *Rangia* midden

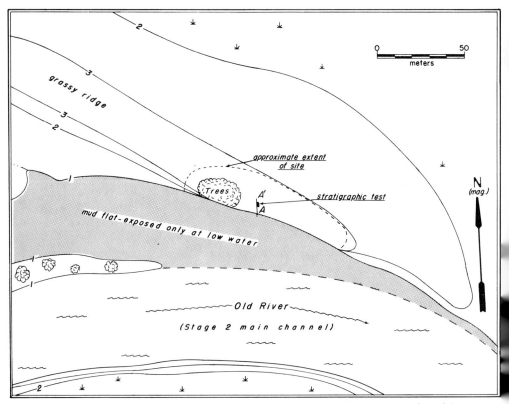

FIGURE 11.12   41 CH 80 and vicinity. Contour interval equals 1 ft. (30.5 cm). (Adapted from U.S.A.C.E. topographic map.)

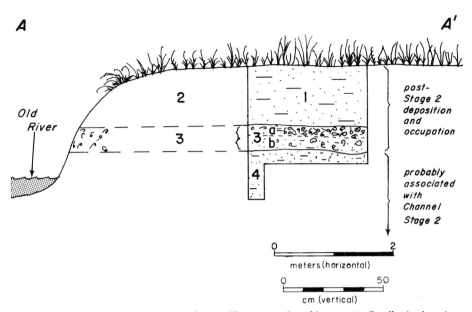

FIGURE 11.13   41 CH 80, stratigraphic profile: (1) stratigraphic test; (2) floodbasin deposits (dense grayish brown silty clay); (3) shell midden, (a) dense upper shell zone, (b) sparse lower shell zone; (4) mottled yellowish-brown sandy clay.

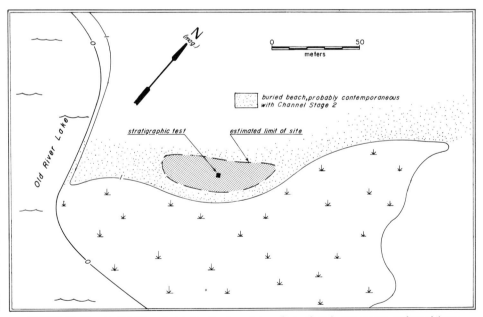

FIGURE 11.14   41 CH 87 and vicinity. Contour interval equals 1 ft. (30.5 cm). (Adapted from U.S.A.C.E. topographic map.)

located on top of Channel Stage 2 deposits in an area of predominantly freshwater marshes (Figures 11.12 and 11.13). Shell middens are exceedingly rare above
Old River Lake along Old River and along "the Cut-Off." A 1 × 2 test pit was
excavated primarily to obtain data on seasonality and faunal subsistence. The
ceramic assemblage (see Table 12.2) indicates occupation during the Mayes
Island Period.

41 CH 87 This site is located on the east bank of Old River Lake and southwest
of Round Lake in the Trinity River delta (Figure 11.2). It is a prominent
mounded feature which was selected for testing because of its anticipated depth
and because it was situated on top of a buried bay-front beach which is interpreted as contemporaneous with Channel Stage 2 (Figure 11.14). Only half of
a planned 1 × 2 m² test was excavated to a depth of 1.1 m when the work at this
site was terminated. It had become clear that the *Rangia* midden material was
extremely unstable. A deep stratigraphic test would not have been possible
without a very large excavation; this we were not prepared to do. The ceramics

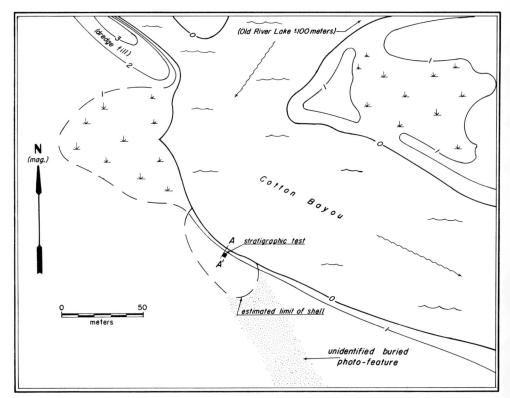

**FIGURE 11.15   41 CH 98 and vicinity. Contour interval equals 1 ft. (30.5 cm). (Adapted from
U.S.A.C.E. topographic map.)**

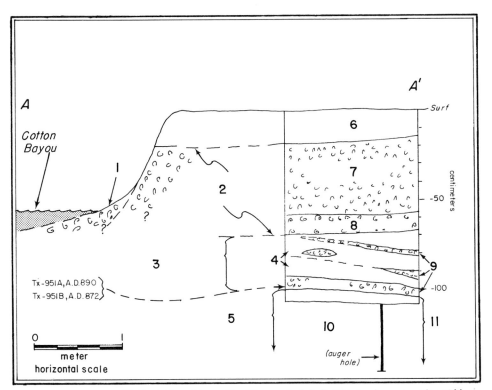

FIGURE 11.16   41 CH 98 stratigraphic profile: (1) reworked shell; (2) intensive occupation (Old River Period); (3) intermittent occupation (Mayes Island through Round Lake Period); (4) dark gray-brown silty clay; (5) post-channel Stage 2 marsh deposit; (6) dark grayish brown clay with recent debris (manure, horse bones); (7) whole and crushed shell in dark gray clay; (8) whole shell in dark brown clay; (9) whole shell; (10) unexcavated; (11) mottled dark gray clay (sterile).

from the portion of the site that was tested indicate that the latest occupations were contemporaneous with the Turtle Bay Period (see Table 12.2).

41 CH 98 This *Rangia* shell midden is located on the west bank of Cotton Bayou about 100 m west of Old River Lake in the Trinity River delta (Figure 11.2). This site was selected for testing because of the large quantity of ceramics littering the eroded midden along the beach, and because it is situated on top of landforms associated with Channel Stage 2 in an area of brackish marshes adjacent to the upland prairie. The site has no surface expression but proved to be a meter deep and to have sherds reflecting occupation spanning the period from the Mayes Island Period to the Old River Period (Figures 11.15 and 11.16; see also Table 12.2). Lithic, seasonality, faunal, radiocarbon, and sediment samples also were obtained.

41 CH 106 This *Rangia* midden is situated northeast of Lost Lake on a small Pleistocene terrace remnant in the Trinity River delta (Figure 11.2). A 1 × 2 m stratigraphic test (Figures 11.17 and 11.18) was excavated at this *Rangia* midden site because of its proximity to fluvial woodlands, freshwater marsh, and swamps. Analysis of ceramics (see Table 12.2) showed assemblages characteristic of the Turtle Bay Period and the Round Lake Period. Samples of lithics, faunal remains, shell for seasonality, and sediment also were obtained.

41 CH 110 This site is located on the east end of a prominent point-bar ridge about 0.4 km south of Lost River in the Trinity River delta (Figure 11.2). This *Rangia* midden site is situated on top of Channel Stage 3 deposits, but is adjacent to the main river channel of Stage 4. Because the main channels generally were too deep and the current too swift for native shellfish collecting to be practical, site establishment on channels usually took place after their abandonment as the main stream. This suggested that 41 CH 110 was occupied contemporaneously with Channel Stage 5, or very late in the aboriginal history

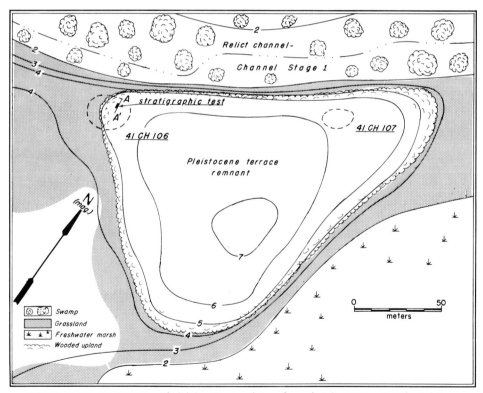

FIGURE 11.17 41 CH 106 and vicinity. Contour interval equals 1 ft. (30.5 cm). (Adapted from U.S.A.C.E. topographic map.)

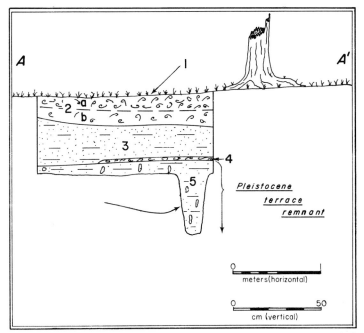

FIGURE 11.18   41 CH 106, stratigraphic profile: (1) stratigraphic test; (2) upper shell zone, (a) dense, (b) sparse; (3) floodbasin deposits (brown sandy clay); (4) lower shell zone; (5) yellowish-brown sandy clay with calcareous nodules.

of the area. A 1 × 2 m stratigraphic test was excavated (Figures 11.19 and 11.20). Ceramics from this site represented assemblages of the Old River and Orcoquisac Periods (Table 12.2), thus confirming our expectation of relatively recent habitation. Because historic artifacts were recovered in the 1969 testing, and because of the site's ready accessibility, the entire 1972 season was devoted to more extensive sampling of this site to explore questions about the cultural dynamics of the historic period (Gilmore 1974). This later work corroborated the 1969 data on ceramic chronology.

41 CH 137   This deeply stratified *Rangia* shell midden is located in the beach ridge area northwest of Lake Anahuac in the Trinity River delta (Figure 11.2). The site was tested because it appeared to have been occupied as a bay-front site during Channel Stage 3 time. Ceramic assemblages (see Table 12.2) recovered confirm that this was the case. Although the access provided by the borrow pit enabled the test excavation to reach the bottom of the midden, the deposit was so unstable that excavation controls were very difficult to maintain below 1.2 m. For this reason, and because almost no change in the ceramic assemblage (see Table 12.2) occurred throughout the midden, this test was terminated after

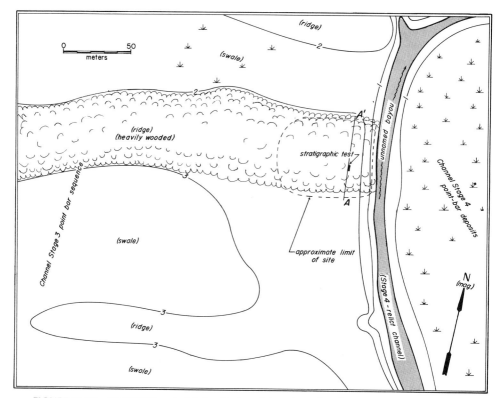

FIGURE 11.19   41 CH 110 and vicinity. Contour interval equals 1 ft. (30.5 cm). (Adapted from U.S.A.C.E. topographic map.)

excavating a 1-m² (Figure 11.21). The site appears to have been occupied in the late Mayes Island–early Turtle Bay time period.

41 CH 165   This location is on the east bank of Old River Lake due west of Round Lake in the Trinity delta (Figure 11.2). Nearly the entire site has been reduced to a lag deposit on the beach, although a small area of midden remains intact (Figure 11.22). A large collection of small water-worn sherds was made but has not been analyzed because of its poor condition. The stratigraphic section at and under the intact midden was recorded (Figure 11.23) in conjunction with the geomorphic studies. The radiocarbon date (see Table 14.1) confirms the age of early occupation along Old River Lake documented to late Mayes Island or early Turtle Bay periods at 41 CH 20, 24, and 36.

41 CH 169   This buried *Rangia* shell midden is located on the east side of Old River Lake west of Round Lake in the Trinity River delta (Figure 11.2). It is on top of Channel Stage 1 deposits in a configuration indicating the midden resulted from shellfish collection at a tidal pond now filled with marsh rather than from nearby Old River Lake (Figure 11.22). A 1-m^2 test pit was dug to obtain a small sample of midden refuse and to gain access to the base of the site for documentation of the stratigraphic relationships between the site and the underlying geomorphic features (Figure 11.24). Analysis of the ceramic assemblage (Table 12.2) indicates the site was occupied during the Round Lake Period.

Galveston County

41 GV 6 (Singing Sands Site)   This site is located in the Singing Sands subdivision on Bolivar Peninsula about 20 km east of the Galveston–Bolivar ferry

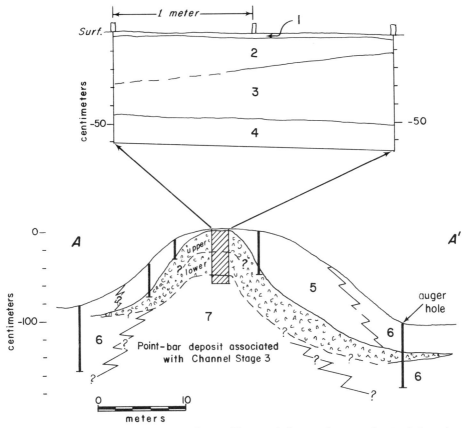

FIGURE 11.20   41 CH 110, stratigraphic profiles: (1) dark gray clayey sand; (2) whole and crushed shell in dark gray sand; (3) whole and crushed shell in dark grayish brown sand; (4) grayish brown sand (sterile); (5) dark brown clayey sand; (6) dense black clay; (7) yellowish-brown fine to medium sand. Vertical exaggeration is 10×.

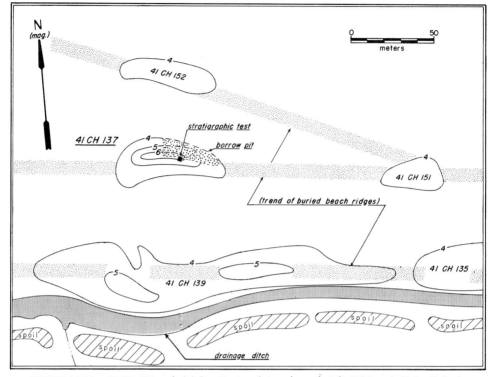

FIGURE 11.21   41 CH 137 and vicinity. Contour interval equals 1 ft. (30.5 cm). *Note:* (1.2 m) contour lines outline surface limits of sites; subsurface limits are undetermined. (Adopted from U.S.A.C.E. topographic map.)

landing and 2.4 km west of the Caplen Site (Figure 11.3). A large artifact collection was made in 1966 by Elaine Roberson and Kiki Cullum of Houston after the site was destroyed by canal dredging. This collection was loaned to the Texas Archeological Research Laboratory for study and is the only one currently available from a habitation site on Bolivar Peninsula.[2] The ceramics (Table 12.2) have been included in the analysis of the Galveston Bay local chronology for this reason.

41 GV 10   This site is located on the south bank of Clear Creek north of League City (Figure 11.3). Documented presence of grog-tempered ceramics and a radiocarbon date (see Table 14.1) suggest occupation of the upper part of the midden in the Old River Period.

[2]The sherd collection reported from the Caplen Site (Campbell 1956) is small and of uncertain provenience within the site.

Harris County

41 HR 50 (the Wright Site)   This shell midden is situated on the west bank of
Cedar Bayou about 2.4 km north of Galveston Bay (Figure 9). Testing (Ambler
1967) produced a large, stratigraphically controlled sample of ceramics, two
radiocarbon dates and matrix samples from which small seasonality samples
could be obtained. For these reasons, Ambler's original ceramic attribute sorting has been consolidated into the typological categories used in the present
study (see Table 12.2). For purposes of seriation, the four excavation levels were
consolidated into two zones since 96% of the sherds occurred in the middle two
levels of the excavation. Habitation at this *Rangia* midden occurred during the
Turtle Bay Period and the Round Lake Period.

41 HR 56   This site is located on the west bank of Cedar Bayou about 0.8 km
south of 41 HR 50 (Figure 11.3). It too was tested by Ambler (1967) and

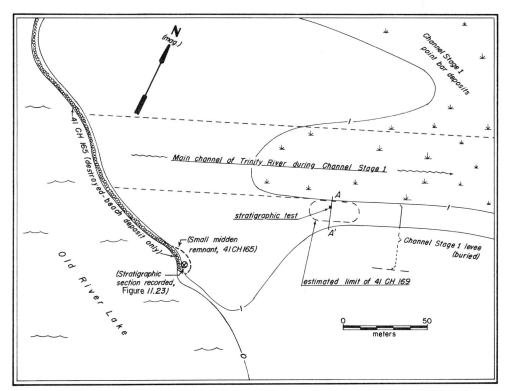

**FIGURE 11.22   41 CH 165 and 41 CH 169. Contour interval equals 1 ft. (30.5 cm). (Adapted
from U.S.A.C.E. topographic map.)**

produced stratigraphically controlled samples of ceramics, radiocarbon samples and matrix samples. The artifacts from both of Ambler's test pits were
combined on the basis of depth from the surface (see Table 12.2); otherwise the
procedure was identical to that used at 41 HR 50. Habitation at this site occurred during the Mayes Island Period and the Round Lake Period.

41 HR 59   This site is located on the west bank of Cedar Bayou about 180 m
south of 41 HR 56 (Figure 11.3). It was tested by Ambler (1967) and, although
only ceramics were available, these were regrouped and used for the present
project (see Table 12.2) because they help give definition to the trends of change
in the late Round Lake Period.

41 HR 61   This site is located near the mouth of Hunting Bayou in Galena Park
(Figure 11.3). It was excavated in 1958–1959 by E. Raymond Ring and the notes
and specimens are now on file at the Texas Archeological Research Laboratory.
The site was a 0.3-m-thick layer of *Rangia* shell midden from which a large
quantity of ceramics was recovered which now are recognizable as a characteristic Clear Lake Period assemblage. Although quantitative data are not available, the collection contains such distinctive types as Tchefuncte Plain, Mandeville Plain, and Goose Creek Stamped. Radiocarbon samples were taken from
the top and bottom of the midden, which, in the past, proved to be difficult to
interpret (Ring 1961). A reevaluation of these samples is presented in Appendix
A, from which it appears that the upper sample, once corrected, is usable and

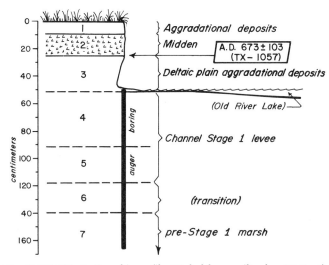

FIGURE 11.23   41 CH 165, stratigraphic profile: (1) dark brown silty clay; (2) *Rangia* **midden; (3)
mottled gray-brown silty clay with caliche; (4) gray-brown medium-grained sand; (5) reddish-
brown medium-grained sand; (6) light gray clayey silt; (7) gray clay.**

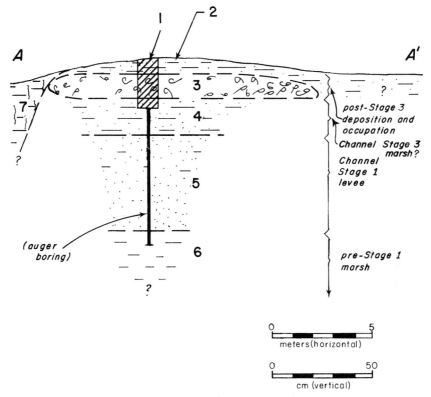

FIGURE 11.24 41 CH 169, stratigraphic profile: (1) stratigraphic test; (2) floodbasin deposits (very dense silty clay); (3) shell midden; (4) yellowish-brown dense silty clay; (5) light tan clayey fine to medium–grained sand; (6) dense dark gray clay; (7) channel fill.

the lower sample is contaminated through exchange with nonradioactive carbon from the Beaumont Formation.

41 HR 80, 85 (Harris County Boys School)   This site is located on the east side of Mud Lake, just north of Clear Lake (Figure 11.3) and was reported in Aten *et al.* 1976.

41 HR 161   This site is located on the north side of Clear Creek about 0.5 km west of the intersection of Clear Creek with the Galveston–Brazoria County line (Figure 11.3). The artifact collection used here for ceramic seriation purposes was excavated by Calvin D. Howard of Houston and was donated to the Texas Archeological Research Laboratory. This site is an earth midden and was excavated on a 5-foot² (1½ m²) grid and by (15 cm) levels, and represents habitation during the Clear Lake Period.

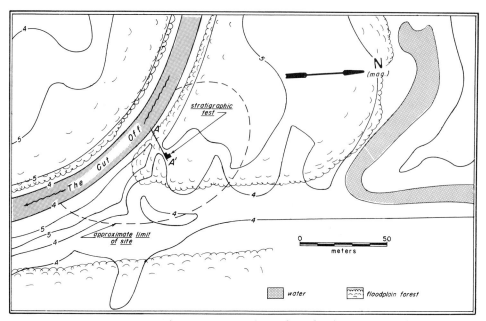

FIGURE 11.25   Contour map of 41 LB 4. Contour interval equals 1 ft. (30.5 cm). (Adapted from U.S.A.C.E. topographic map.)

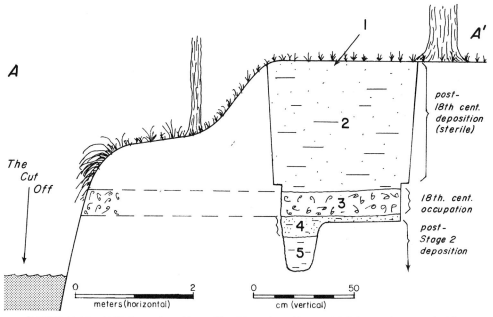

FIGURE 11.26   41 LB 4, stratigraphic profile: (1) stratigraphic test; (2) light tan clayey sand with irregular laminations (flood deposits); (3) shell midden; (4) mottled olive brown sandy clay; (5) dark gray clay.

Liberty County

41 LB 4   This *Rangia* midden is situated on the east bank of the "Cut Off" (the relict main river channel during Channel Stage 2) about 0.5 km north of the Liberty County line (Figure 11.2). Situated on top of Channel Stage 2 deposits and in the downstream end of the Trinity River valley fluvial woodlands, this site also is the farthest inland *Rangia cuneata* shell midden known in the lower Trinity valley. Because of the site's potential to provide at least subsistence data from a portion of the Trinity delta not previously tested, a 3-m^2 test pit was excavated (Figures 11.25 and 11.26).

   The site was only 15 cm thick and was removed as a single stratigraphic level. The ceramic assemblage is datable to very late in the protohistoric Old River Period (see Table 12.2). In addition to the aboriginal artifacts, the test produced European glass trade beads, and faunal and seasonality samples.

BRAZOS DELTA–WEST BAY AREA

The opportunity to begin investigation of the Brazos delta area began in 1971 with salvage archaeology at the Dow–Cleaver Site near Lake Jackson (Aten 1971). This site consisted of a series of thin habitation refuse zones which bracket the period from late preceramic to historic. Additional sites were selected for testing on the basis of diversity in biotic habitat associations. Although a geomorphic reconstruction of the Brazos River delta was prepared (Figure 8.9), site–landform changes were not as frequent as those mapped in the Trinity delta.

Brazoria County

41 BO 4   This site is situated next to Hudgins Bend, a cutoff meander of Oyster Creek, about 5½ km from the Gulf of Mexico (Figure 11.27). The site is stratified within floodplain aggradational deposits consisting of a very dense reddish brown silty clay. Although the full extent of the site was never determined, the occupation zone exposure around the edge of a borrow pit appeared to be very thin and not very dense. Of particular interest here, unlike most other shell middens tested on the upper coast, was the great variety of shellfish species evident, even though the total quantity of material was very small. These all appeared to be food remains and included the following: *Rangia cuneata*, *Crassostrea virginica*, *Polinices duplicatus*, *Thais* sp., *Dosinia* sp., *Dinocardium* sp., *Mercenaria mercenaria*, and possibly *Modiolus demissus granosissimus*.

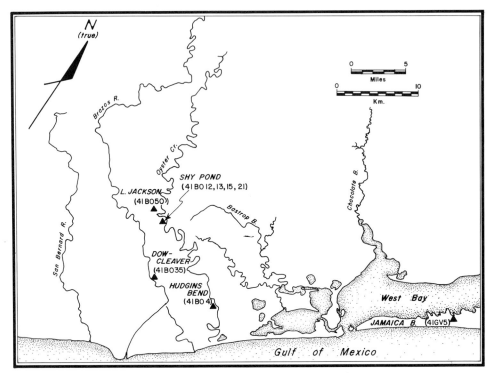

FIGURE 11.27   Selected archaeological sites in the Brazos Delta–West Bay area.

An attempt was made to strip off a sizable area using the small-grid technique employed at 41 CH 31 and 41 HR 86 because (*a*) the location of the site was so near the coast, (*b*) *Rangia cuneata* was present, permitting determination of seasonality, and (*c*) the unstratified cultural layer lay near the surface (i.e., at a depth of about 10 cm). Unfortunately, the clay content of the matrix was much higher than anticipated, drastically slowing progress in both the ¼-inch (6mm) mesh and 1/16-inch (1½ mm) mesh screens. This, combined with the onset of very severe electrical storms, forced abandonment of the site after only 2 m² had been excavated.

The excavated material was supplemented with a very careful collection of all cultural material visible along the eroding bank of the borrow pit for about 5 m in either direction from the excavation (Figure 11.28). Because the midden material from the two excavated grid units, washed through window screen, produced no significantly different artifactual or faunal specimens, it is assumed that the borrow pit collection is useful as an extension of the excavated collection. For purposes of analysis of gross technology, chronological and seasonality estimates, and faunal analysis, all of this material was lumped together into a single, small, but very interesting collection (see Tables 12.2 and 13.1). Especially noteworthy are the whole and broken oystershell-cutting tools. Because of the impermeable silty clay matrix, the preservation of all cultural materials was unusually good. This occupation appears to date early in the post-main grog-tempered period or equivalent to the Old River Period of the Galveston Bay area chronology.

41 BO 12 This site is east of the Brazos River at the town of Lake Jackson (Figure 11.27). 41 BO 12 was one of at least 20 small *Rangia* middens scattered on point-bar ridges (formed by Oyster Creek), primarily to the north of a large water-filled point-bar depression known as Shy Pond (Figure 11.29). The Shy Pond locality was examined carefully for either stratified or single occupation layer sites. This was for the purpose of continuing the work begun at the Dow–Cleaver Site (41 BO 35) in the previous year (Aten 1971). Location of reasonably intact sites might reflect a temporal progression from one point-bar ridge to the next. However, the area had been so intensively vandalized that this was impossible. The Shy Pond vicinity resembled a battlefield, with trenches and holes and back-dirt piles everywhere. Finally two small areas of *in situ* midden were selected for testing, one of which was 41 BO 12.

An area 2 by 3 meters in size was located on the crest of a point-bar ridge. One of the corner squares was excavated in an abortive attempt to maintain control by individual occupation lenses, as was done at 41 BO 35 and other sites in the area. Unfortunately, the site consisted of a large number of closely stratified individual occupation lenses which could not be observed well enough to

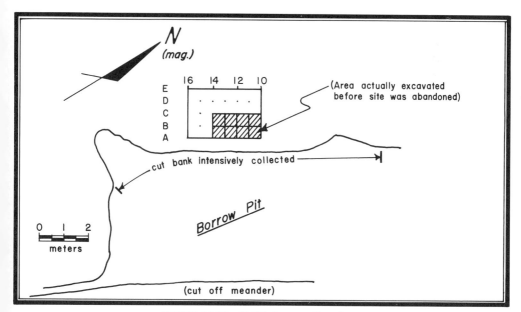

FIGURE 11.28   41 BO 4 excavation plan.

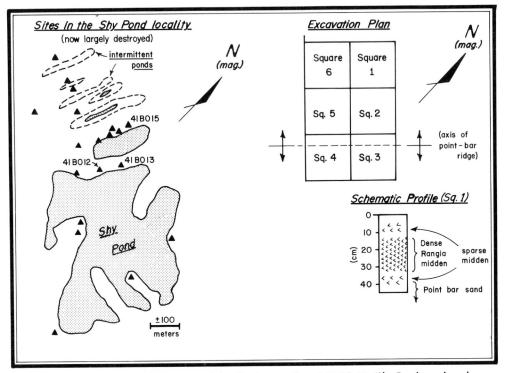

FIGURE 11.29   Shy Pond site map and details of excavation at 41 BO 12. (Shy Pond map based on drawing prepared by Robert L. Cole.)

excavate separately. Consequently, the remaining 5 squares were excavated in 10-cm levels to a depth of 40 cm, which penetrated the deposit (Figure 11.29). The midden material was all screened through both 6 mm mesh and 1½ mm mesh screens. Artifact, faunal, and seasonality samples were collected from this site. Habitation spanned the period from prior to the introduction of grog-tempered ceramics to the main grog-tempered period.

41 BO 13   This site is located near 41 BO 12 (Figure 11.29). The ceramics reported by Hamilton (n.d.) were sufficiently numerous that they could be reclassified and used for seriation purposes (Table 12.2). Habitation at this site dates to the main grog-tempered period.

41 BO 15   This site is located very near 41 BO 12 and 13 (Figure 11.29); two radiocarbon dates were obtained from this site on shell and charcoal samples (Hamilton n.d.). The results, however, are equivocal and are not used except for discussion purposes in Appendix A. The ceramic collection was small and unsuitable for seriation purposes. Qualitatively, the presence of sandy paste and bone-tempered sherds, as well as the absence of grog-tempered sherds, would support interpretation of a late, protohistoric period occupation.

41 BO 35 (Dow–Cleaver Site)   This site is located on the east side of the Brazos River near Lake Jackson (Figure 11.27). Excavations here were reported in Aten (1971).

41 BO 50   This location is situated on the eastern shore of Lake Jackson, formed in a cutoff meander of Oyster Creek (Figure 11.27). A small hole dug about 10 m from the shore of the lake indicated that at this place, the site consisted of two thin *Rangia cuneata* shell lenses separated by about 5 cm of sterile silty clay. A narrow trench 4 m long was dug to maintain stratigraphic control and 6 1-m grid units were excavated by first stripping off the upper shell zone, and then the lower zone. Proveniences were recorded by grid and shell zone (see Figure 11.30). When excavating grid square 5, zones 1 and 2 were inadvertently

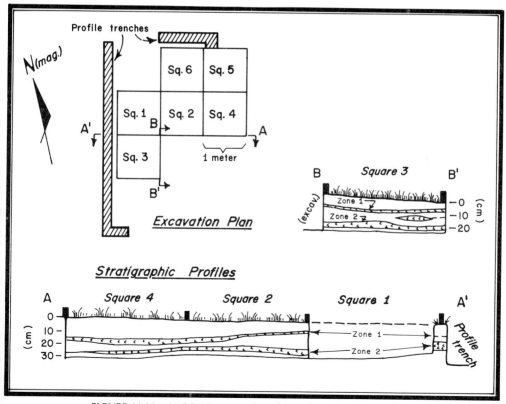

FIGURE 11.30   41 BO 50, excavation plan and stratigraphic profiles.

mixed together and the material from this unit is therefore not included in the analysis of the site.

Both zones contained ceramics, arrow points, seasonality samples, and a large quantity of faunal remains. A single pair of radiocarbon samples was taken from the lower zone (Zone 2) in Square 1 (see Table 14.1). These indicate the lower zone may have been deposited as early as A.D. 300. Although both zones contained grog-tempered ceramics (6 sherds and 14 sherds, or 4% and 12% in the lower and upper zones, respectively), the close vertical proximity of the two zones may mean that the sherds in the lower zone are intrusive. Because of the firmness with which this pottery is dated to the post-A.D 1000 period in the Galveston Bay Area, I am skeptical that it could date so early in the Brazos Delta Area. Although something could be wrong with either the 41 BO 50 radiocarbon samples or with assumptions about the local ceramic history, the most likely problem source is the close vertical stratification of the two zones. The upper zone is undoubtedly habitation refuse from the main grog-tempered ceramic period, equivalent to the Round Lake Period of the Galveston Bay Area.

Galveston County

41 GV 5 (Jamaica Beach Site   This midden and cemetery site is located adjacent to Lufkin and Ostermayer bayous approximately midway along the length of Galveston Island on its West Bay side (Figure 11.27). It was originally excavated in 1962–1963 (Aten 1965; Ring 1963) and an analysis of the cemetery was presented in Aten *et al.* (1976:72–75). In 1971, the site was retested for the purpose of obtaining a controlled sample of artifacts and faunal remains from a barrier island settlement, one possibly occupied during the winter season.[3] Using detailed topographic maps of the site prepared by E. Raymond Ring at the time of the original excavation, it was possible to isolate an area of the midden that appeared not to have been disturbed. At this location, a grid of 6 1-m square units was used (Figure 11.31). These were excavated in 10 cm arbitrary levels to a depth of 50 cm, which penetrated the cultural deposit. In an effort to verify the absence of cultural zones at greater depths, Test Pit 1 was excavated an additional 80 cm, terminating once sterile beach deposits were reached.

The stratigraphic profile (Figure 11.31) shows a succession of beach deposits overlaid by a 1-m thick zone of eolian deposits. The midden zone is incorporated in the upper half of the eolian deposits.

Several radiocarbon dates were obtained at the time of the 1962–1963 excavation (see Table 14.1) on oyster, *Littorina*, and *Dosinia*. Whether, or how much,

---

[3]Ethnohistoric data (Bandelier 1905) document that some late prehistoric and protohistoric habitation of the upper coast barrier islands took place during the winter.

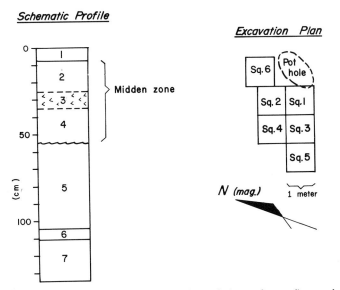

FIGURE 11.31   41 GV 5 (1971 test): (1) eolian sand; (2) dark gray brown fine sand; (3) major midden and shell density; (4) pale brown fine sand; (5) very pale brown fine sand, eolian; (6) yellow-brown fine sand, weak ferric cement; (7) very pale brown fine sand beach deposit.

correction might be needed for these samples has not been determined. It is possible they are too old by 1 or 2 centuries; however, this does not materially affect the chronological interpretation developed later in Chapter 14. This site evidently was occupied in later prehistoric and protohistoric times.

CONROE–LIVINGSTON AREA

The Conroe–Livingston Area is situated immediately north of the Galveston Bay Area and was the location of reservoir salvage archaeology at Lake Conroe and Lake Livingston (McClurkan 1968; Shafer 1968; the 41 MQ 14 data are used through the courtesy of Charles K. Chandler). These data have never been synthesized. However, because they are located on the northern frontier of the upper coast, a culture-historical framework for Conroe–Livingston would have considerable relevance to both the archaeology of the Galveston Bay Area and to understanding better the region's ethnohistory. For these reasons, ceramic and radiocarbon data for selected sites have been compiled into an initial seriation in Chapter 14. All five sites used for this purpose are middens in sand which were repeatedly occupied over long periods of time. Extensive burrowing by gophers and poor soil preservation conditions have destroyed or heavily damaged most structural features and most organic materials including bones. Consequently, the stratigraphic relationships at these sites are not as sharply recognizable as at shell middens. In spite of this, a useful seriation has been compiled.

SABINE LAKE AREA

The Sabine Lake Area is the least studied of the three major upper Texas coast estuary–river delta systems. The region has been extensively surveyed for shell middens and a large number of artifact collections (principally ceramics) have been made. However, the only controlled excavations have been at the Gaulding Site *Rangia* midden (41 JF 27) by the Texas Archeological Society, and at pimple mound earth middens 41 JF 26 and 31 by Charles N. Bollich and Lawrence E. Aten (cf. Aten and Bollich 1981). These excavations and the three radiocarbon dates available for the area (see Table 14.1) provide information primarily for the very late ceramic and very early ceramic periods; the remainder of the area's prehistory is still known only from survey collections. These data are the subject of a study now underway by Bollich and Aten and will not be introduced here. In the interim, the chronological formulation published in Aten and Bollich (1969) will be used as the basis for organizing data needed for comparison with the Galveston Bay Area.

OTHER SITES

Data from sites in adjacent areas are used at various points in the description and analysis to provide comparative materials. Most are published and need not be redescribed here. However, one site which has not been mentioned in the literature is 41 FB 11.

Fort Bend County

41 FB 11   This earth midden site overlooks Big Creek and its floodplain west of the Brazos River and southwest of Richmond, Texas (Figure 11.1). The site consists of a sizable midden area and an associated cemetery. It has been subjected to pot-hunting for many years principally because of the cemetery. Three 1-m square stratigraphic tests were excavated in 10-cm levels in 1971 by

FIGURE 11.32 Subsiding *Rangia cuneata* shell mound (41 CH 36) in marshlands of the Trinity River delta.

FIGURE 11.33 *Rangia cuneata* shell midden (41 CH 98) incorporated in subsiding stream levee, Trinity River delta.

Robert L. Cole of Lake Jackson. Summary data on ceramics and lithics from two of these test pits are used in this report. The artifacts are now in the possession of Cole who is analyzing them further. The faunal remains are curated at the Texas Archeological Research Laboratory, Austin. It has been included here primarily to provide an interior site to contrast with the Brazos Delta Area sites.

As noted earlier, the major source of archaeological data from the upper coast until now has been from shell middens. Most of these are composed of the brackish water clam, *Rangia cuneata*, although a few oyster (*Crassostrea virginica*) middens exist. Generally, however, other freshwater, estuarine, and Gulf shellfish occur only as minor constituents in *Rangia cuneata* middens. The most common shell midden types are described below.

1. Large shell mound (Figure 11.32) having significant topographic expression, vegetation unlike that in surrounding marsh, and depth usually extending significantly below the water table. These sites are usually found only in
river deltas and are actively subsiding.

2. Small stream levee middens which have not topographic expression and
are incorporated wholly within the levee deposit. These sites may be thickly
stratified accumulations (as in Figure 11.33) or may be a stratified sequence of

**FIGURE 11.34   Single occupation episode shell midden zones separated by floodplain sediments
(41 HR 33) near mouth of the San Jacinto River.**

FIGURE 11.35 Nearly destroyed *Rangia cuneata* midden (41 HR 56) on retreating valley wall scarp near mouth of Cedar Bayou.

thin, single occupation episodes (Figure 11.34) which are extremely useful for intrasite documentation. Levee sites usually are discovered only where erosion has exposed them in the stratigraphic section. Occasionally, they are located by probing along buried landforms as at 41 CH 219 (Figure 11.10). The few midden sites known from the coastal barriers are physically similar to the small levee sites in that they are rapidly buried by sediment—in this case, beach sand carried by wind or storm surges.

3. Shell middens perched on low bluffs overlooking the estuaries and adjacent drowned stream mouths; these are being rapidly destroyed as erosion undercuts the bluffs around the bay margins (Figure 11.35).

Sites of the first two types are being incorporated, intact, into the geological record to a significant extent. Sites of the last type are in a very advanced state of destruction throughout the upper coast region.

CHAPTER 12

Ceramic Artifacts

Spaulding's (1973:149) observation that discussion of artifact types and typology in the archaeological literature has become bogged down in a "semantic quagmire" may be concurred with readily. The objective here is not to enter the competition, but only to be clear about what has been done in this study.

The essential first step in developing a classification is to identify its purpose. Is the purpose to generate inference about artifact function and behavioral patterns, or to produce a seriation (Spaulding 1973:149)? Alternative classifications of the same material usually are possible. They may even be necessary to serve various purposes, depending upon the criteria needed to solve the problem at hand (cf. Read 1974:220).

Determination of taxonomic objectives has been a judgment made as a result of the goals of this study and of the known information potential of the artifact classes. Indeed, our objectives vary according to the class of artifacts in question. The primary use made of ceramics, by far the largest aritfact class present on the upper coast, is to develop a chronological seriation; secondarily, there is interest in describing any synchronic spatial variation in the resultant classes. The primary objective for classification of lithic artifacts, however, is for recognition of functional and behavioral classes; secondarily, certain attributes may convey some chronological data. The principal objectives for the other artifact classes (bone, shell, and a host of miscellaneous materials) are for reconginition of functional and behavioral classes. If organization of artifacts around these primary objectives additionally conveys other useful information, that is a bonus for which we will be grateful but do not necessarily expect to occur.

In the artifact classification to follow in this chapter and the next, a formal typological framework is employed only for the ceramics and for certain of the projectile points. For all other classes only informal descriptive categories are used. The differences between the approach to typology used here and that discussed at length by Phillips (1970) are so negligible as to not be worth raising; they would only be nit picking. Phillips's exposition is a clear, common-sense and practical approach to the definition of specific taxonomic tools to solve specific problems.

It also should be noted that the scale of artifact description changes between the ceramics and the nonceramics. *Classes* of ceramics are described and the occurrence of these classes at individual sites is reported. For the nonceramics, however, actual specimens in hand are described from the sites. Ceramics are used as the primary basis for Late Prehistoric–Woodland culture chronology. This is because ceramics are abundant and nonceramics are so scarce. Because of this difference in mode of treatment, the nonceramics are dealt with separately in the next chapter.

INTRODUCTION

The ceramic typology used here involves (*a*) a minimum of subjective judgments in assigning specimens to a cateogy, thereby maximizing replicability; (*b*) criteria of regional significance to facilitate broad correlations; and (*c*) a sufficient number of categories to allow the approximate dating (i.e., probably within a range of 200 years in most cases) of archaeological components. This precision has been achieved only for the Galveston Bay Area but can be available for the Sabine Lake and the Brazos Delta–West Bay areas once supplementary stratigraphic test data are obtained. It is not suggested that this approach will serve all purposes, that at some later time a different approach to the question of organizing archaeological data in a time framework should not be possible, or even that this formulation is the only one possible at present.

In addition to primary dependence on the new data collected for this study, reliance has been placed on much of the data previously reported by Ambler (1967, 1970, 1973). Although Ambler treats his data somewhat differently than I have, it is reliable, well documented, and relatively easy to use in alternative formats. If undue attention in the following discussion seems to be devoted to Ambler's work, it is because of its utility. Differences between his formulation of cultural space–time systematics and this one have been developing over the years and received their most extended comparison in his 1973 report.

In the present study, I will comment further on these different approaches, although not for the purpose of trying to demonstrate that my approach is necessarily more acceptable. The fact is that both approaches may work, depending on the problem at hand. Our differences presently seem to be reducible to Ambler's interest in defining "culturally" significant artifact types and cultural "phases." On the other hand, this study attempts to recognize artifact types on the basis of unequivocal physical attributes and to measure their chronological and spatial behavior through use of a series of temporal assemblages called "periods" without employing untested assumptions or inferences about cultural or sociological reality at the outset.

Ambler's approach leads to analysis in terms of archaeological cultures, but this can be an unstable or, at the opposite extreme, an excessively rigid structure for conducting analysis. The approach employed here leads to establishment of a stable time–space system of reference that can be used to provide a temporal context for any aspect of ancient human behavior that is archaeologically visible. Being unconfined by an organizing framework of "cultures" or "phases," analysis may be approached more on a populational basis, thereby leaving the necessary flexibility for pursuing such issues as (a) linkage of the archaeological and ethnohistoric records and (b) cultural ecological studies. Phrasing our approaches in this manner, it is no longer fruitful to ask whether Aten or Ambler is "right"; the only answer that can be given is that we appear to have different epistemological orientations. In the following pages we only wish to discuss why Ambler's formulations of types and phases have not been retained as tools for the populational approaches that are of current interest.

This is begun by noting that Ambler (1973:76) is in agreement with me about the contention that Phillips's (1970) approach to type–variety classification is the best taxonomic device available for the upper coast (Aten 1971:20). However, the present study is the first to substantively implement this approach in the area.[1]

The type–variety system is a device for organizing the physical and distributional attributes of a set of artifacts. It is not predicated on historical or social relationships. The latter are inferences to be drawn from "mapping" the distribution of physical properties, preferably according to hypotheses which have been posed. Decisions made in developing a typological framework must be directed at enhancing the logic, clarity, and replicability of the resulting system. This cannot be done by simultaneously trying to maximize the physical and historical logic, as well as the social logic of the system (cf. Phillips 1970:24). The latter usually is uncontrollable at this stage of analysis; if one includes it in taxonomic decisions, there will be no practical basis (i.e., replicabilty) for achieving consensus among users of the system.

Many of the problems in dealing with early ceramics at Wallisville described by Ambler (1970, 1973) are paralleled in Phillips's (1970) discussion of type–variety classification. In my judgment, Ambler has understated the difficulties in distinguishing among groups of sandy paste sherds (cf. Ambler 1970:22). Likewise, it has been difficult to replicate Ambler's classification of Wallisville Plain after reexamination of the specimens.

These circumstances reflect some of the range of interests to which the artifacts in question may be subjected. They also reflect some of the variation in professional approach that normally occurs.. But the typological framework employed at a regional scale should be sufficiently robust to remain relatively unaffected by such circumstances. This is the sort of within-type (i.e., "type" as

---

[1]In the report on the Dow–Cleaver Site (Aten 1971) the type–variety terminology was used but no varieties actually were proposed.

an unequivocally sortable class) and within-technique variation for which the type–variety approach is most needed.

Given the separate properties of types and varieties, one is not compelled to resolve alternative views about varieties on an "either–or" basis; *varieties*, unlike types, need not entirely partition space or matter on a mutually exclusive basis. The same sherds simultaneously may be classed in more than one variety to answer different questions or, possibly, to better answer the same questions. It is not necessary for there to be wide acceptance of the validity of a variety. It is necessary, however, for there to be substantial agreement on the nature and replicability of the type, within which varieties may be proposed or disposed with relative ease.[2] For instance, Goose Creek Plain, as it is used here, will always be a class similarly recognizable by most workers, whereas Wallisville Plain already has proved a very difficult class on which to obtain reproducible results. If Wallisville Plain, as a class, answers useful questions, it should be designated a variety of Goose Creek Plain.

To summarize, the issue of ceramic classification can be reduced to the following simple proposition. Classification addresses two objectives: (*a*) identification of unequivocal, reproducible artifact classes (types); and (*b*) identification of less reproducible classes (varieties). Both kinds of classes aid in "mapping" time–space distributions of artifacts and of associated phenomena; however, the first kind is the basis for more stable and expansive organizing frameworks than is the latter.[3]

HISTORY OF CLASSIFICATION

The identification of attributes and attribute combinations of importance to the solution of particular problems takes time to emerge from analysis (cf. Phillips 1970:25). This evolution for the ceramics of the upper Texas coast is described in the following (also see Figure 12.1).

1. The earliest formalization of ceramic taxonomy for the upper coast was presented by Wheat (1953:184 ff.) in describing sherds excavated in the Addicks Basin Reservoir. He described the local ceramics as consisting of "a single, highly variable ware divided into two subtypes, decoration serving as the primary criterion for the separation." By way of intratype variation, Wheat recognized

[2]Quite apart from the preceding matters, analysis of ceramics on the upper Texas coast often has lacked clear focus on what information was being sought. Also, reports frequently employ careless or uncritical use of technical terms and display unfamiliarity with the literature. These are worse than useless conditions because they mislead the unwary.

[3]A judgment still must be rendered about whether the resulting classes also convey useful information, for the converse is quite possible, that is, valid classes conveying useless or trivial information.

Ceramic Categories		Wheat 1953; Suhm et al. 1954	Worthington 1959	Shafer 1966	Aten 1967; Aten & Bollich 1969	Ambler 1970	Aten 1970; Aten & Chandler 1971	Ambler 1973	Aten et al. 1976	Aten 1979
		SOURCES								
Tempered	bone	Goose Creek Plain	San Jacinto Plain		"bone-temp. plain"	Orcoquisac Plain	"bone-temp. plain"	Orcoquisac Plain	"bone-temp. plain"	"bone-tempered" —plain —incised
	grog		S. J. Incised	Goose Creek "grog-tempered"	San Jacinto Plain; S. J. Incised	San Jacinto Plain; S. J. Incised	San Jacinto Plain; S. J. Incised	San Jacinto Plain; S. J. Incised	San Jacinto Plain; S. J. Incised	Baytown Plain —var. San Jacinto —var. Phoenix Lake; San Jacinto Incised —var. Jamison —var. Spindletop
	sand	G. C. Incised	Goose Creek Plain; G. C. Incised	Goose Creek "sand-tempered"	Goose Creek Plain; G. C. Incised; G. C. Red-filmed	Goose Creek Plain; G. C. Incised; G. C. "Red"	Goose Creek —Plain —Incised —Red-filmed	Goose Creek —Plain —Incised	Conway Plain	O'Neal Plain, var. Conway
Untempered	sandy paste	Tchefuncte Stamped		Tchefuncte Stamped		"Wallisville Plain" (informal)	"early sandy paste" (Wallisville Pl.)	Wallisville Plain	Goose Creek —Plain —Incised —Red-filmed —Stamped; Mandeville Plain	Goose Creek Plain —var. unspecified —var. Anahuac; G. C., —Incised, —Red-filmed, —Stamped; Mandeville Plain
	clayey or silty paste					"Lost River Plain" (informal); Tchefuncte Stamped	"Lost River Plain" (informal); Tchefuncte Plain; Tchef. Stamped	Lost River Plain; Tchefuncte —Plain —Incised —Stamped	Tchefuncte —Plain —Incised —Stamped	Tchefuncte —Plain —Incised —Stamped

FIGURE 12.1 Evolution of ceramic classification system for upper Texas coast chronology. Alternative synonymous terms for grog tempered are "clay" tempered, sherd tempered, and "clay-grit" tempered. Conway Plain was recognized and named by C. N. Bollich. Ambler (1967) and Tunnell and Ambler (1967) employed informal descriptive categories and did not contribute directly to the development of the region's ceramic classification.

that while most sherds were sandy,[4] some in the upper levels of the sites were bone- and sherd-tempered. The only other typological category recognized at Addicks was Tchefuncte Stamped[5] as represented by several sand-tempered sherds with a rocker-stamped design.

2. At the Houston Archeological Society Pottery Symposium in 1959, R. B. Worthington presented a paper noting that results of stratigraphic testing near the mouth of the San Jacinto River indicated a disjunct time distribution of "sand-tempered" ceramics versus clay-tempered (i.e., sherd-tempered) and bone-tempered ceramics. He went on to suggest that the latter two paste categories be separated from "sand-tempered" ceramics and that this new group be called San Jacinto Plain and San Jacinto Incised, with the name Goose Creek left to the "sand-tempered" ceramics. The paper was never published and the idea remained informal for several years.

3. Reporting on his survey of Wallisville Reservoir, Shafer (1966) essentially followed the approach taken by Wheat. He did, however, employ paste categories as a basis for separation rather than using arbitrary groupings of paste categories into types.

4. The likelihood that paste categories would be a technological feature highly sensitive to chronological variation[6] was indicated strongly by the results of a study that included comparison of the rank orderings of Trinity delta surface collection paste category proportions with the chronological sequence of river channel stages associated with the site locations from which the collections

[4]Until probable sand-tempering in the Conway variety of O'Neal Plain was recognized by C. N. Bollich in the early 1970s, thereby providing a counterpoint of physical characteristics to those of the untempered sandy paste wares, the latter occupied a limbo position in terms of assumptions about their basic paste technology. Beginning with Krieger's (Newell and Krieger 1949:133) expression of doubt about these being tempered pastes, and continuing to the present day, these sherds are variously described as tempered, untempered, or "Does it really matter how the sand got there since it obviously functioned as tempering?" In addition to Newell and Krieger, see Nunley (1963:33), Aten (1967:10–11), and Aten and Bollich (1969) for further discussion of this issue. Following the arguments stated in the latter two sources, the existence is assumed of five basic paste categories, two of which are natural sediment assemblages and are assumed to be untempered; the remainder are pastes which had to be created by a potter. These assumptions are reflected in the organization of Figure 12.1.

[5]G. I. Quimby concurred with this classification and J. B. Griffin did not (Wheat 1953:190). The rocker-stamped design is distinctive and identical to that found on Tchefuncte Stamped. Given Wheat's use of decoration as the primary criterion for separation, it is understandable that he and Quimby identified this as Tchefuncte Stamped. On the other hand, a ceramic vessel is a complex structure in which the whole is more than the sum of its parts. The type–variety system affords an opportunity to be more structurally holistic at the level of the type and still to be able to focus more narrowly when dealing with one or a few attributes. Indeed, single attributes can be most efficiently traced through many types merely by their recognition as design modes (e.g., interior incising as discussed in Neyland and Aten 1971) or technological modes (cf. Phillips 1970:28–30). The wisdom of Griffin's more holistic approach has been borne out by the recent recognition of these sherds (Goose Creek Stamped) as part of the Goose Creek ceramic series indigenous to the upper Texas coast.

[6]Spatial variation of paste categories within the coastal zone was not recognized until later.

TABLE 12.1
Correlation of Sandy Paste Ceramic Frequencies with Trinity River Channel Stages.

Sandy paste sherds (%)	Trinity River Channel Stage[a]	Site Number (41 CH __)[b]	Number of Sherds
25	3(?)	41	84
25	2(?)	29	12
41	3	37	116
42	2 or 3	19	38
43	3	36	76
44	3	38	41
46	3	40	54
46	2(?)	28	115
60	4(?)	45	15
62	pre-3(?)	35	39
62	3	31	8
64	3 or 4	7	33
75	1(?)	33	12
75	1	26	105
76	1, 3 and/or 4	32	33
82	1	25	33
82	1	24	97
84	1	20	151
95	1	51	19
100	2(?)	30	6
100	1	17	55
100	1	14	21
100	1(?)	46	6
100	1(?)	21	17
100	1	16	5
100	1	15	49
100	1	8	8
100	1	1	6

[a]From Figure 8.7.
[b]All inventory data for these sites is on file at Texas Archeological Research Laboratory, The University of Texas at Austin.

were made (Aten 1966b; also see Table 12.1). Reinforcing this were previous observations on the relatively late time occurrence of sherd and bone tempering. As a result, paste categories were used as a major basis for ceramic analysis at the Jamison Site (Aten 1967). My first review of the sand "tempering" problem was presented there, concluding that it would be best to adopt Nunley's (1963) suggestion that the term "sandy paste" be substituted unless tempering could actually be demonstrated. Supported by results of the Jamison excavation, the description of San Jacinto Plain and Incised was formalized (and was confined exclusively to grog or sherd tempering).[7] By this time also, sufficient data had been collected on the occurrence of a fugitive red wash on the sandy paste

[7]The terms *temper* and *grog* are used in their strict sense throughout this study. *Temper* is aplastic material added to pottery clay by the potter; *grog* is substantially aplastic material, such as fired clay

ceramics to permit definition of the type Goose Creek Red-Filmed, primarily a plainware, but occasionally incised. Bone-tempered ceramics were rare and handled as an interim descriptive category.

5. This same basic approach to typology was carried through in the first attempt at an upper Galveston Bay Area ceramic seriation (Aten and Bollich 1969). In the portion of this study reporting initial work on ceramics of the Sabine Lake Area, major problems with classification of grog-tempered sherds were described. It was relatively easy to recognize that the types finally described as San Jacinto Plain and Incised were heavily represented, as was the distinctly different Lower Mississippi Valley (LMV) grog-tempered plainware. San Jacinto is relatively thin and contains moderate amounts of grog-temper in sandy clays; LMV plainwares are thicker and have abundant grog fragments in a fine clay matrix. The problem was an enormous group intermediate in appearance between San Jacinto and the LMV material. We temporarily coped with this problem by not attempting to subdivide the grog-tempered ceramics. However, dissatisfaction at this inability to adequately measure a potentially revealing relationship between indigenous and LMV ceramic technologies predisposed Bollich and I to receive Phillips's (1970) exposition of the type–variety taxonomy. Also of significance to the present narrative is that it was the 1969 paper that first documented the great extent of LMV technological impact in the eastern portion of the upper Texas coast. In time, this led to understanding something about the occurrence of small amounts of similar material in Wallisville Reservoir (first reported by Shafer 1966:24).

6. When reporting on the second archaeological site survey at Wallisville Reservoir (i.e., the Trinity delta) undertaken in conjunction with the salvage archaeology program there, Ambler (1970) began to synthesize preliminary views on ceramic taxonomy and cultural systematics. These were developed from data obtained in the analysis, then incomplete, of late preceramic and early ceramic sites at Wallisville, as well as from work along lower Cedar Bayou (Ambler 1967) and at the Spanish colonial site of Presidio San Agustin de Ahumada (Tunnell and Ambler 1967).

Ambler began, evidently with some reluctance, to move away from the attribute analysis employed in the Cedar Bayou and Presidio reports, and to state his findings in an incipient typological framework. In making this shift, the concept was accepted of San Jacinto Plain and Incised as the grog-tempered ceramics of the area. He went on to name Orcoquizac Plain as the bone-tempered type, although it remains something of an enigma.[8]

---

or finely crushed sherds, which is used as a pottery temper (Shepard 1963:25). The objection of Phillips (1970:34) that the term *grog* has no specific meaning is not correct.

[8]This pottery was manufactured in an aboriginal technological tradition but constitutes about 30% of the sherds from the site of the Spanish Presidio at Wallisville. At no known aboriginal site in the Galveston Bay Area, historic or prehistoric, does bone tempering constitute more than about 5% of the total assemblage, and overall, it is exceeded in its rarity in native ceramic culture only by Goose Creek Stamped and Tchefuncte Stamped.

Excavations at Wallisville had produced the first Tchefuncte and Tchefuncte-like ceramics from a controlled excavation. The former were physically identical to LMV Tchefuncte Plain; the latter consisted of sandy paste sherds bearing rocker-stamping and a sizable number of undecorated sherds showing mixtures of Tchefuncte and Goose Creek paste characteristics. Ambler (1970) chose to group this latter material (called Lost River Plain) without direct consideration of similar sherd categories from Louisiana that were essentially identical to Wallisville materials. This is not necessarily unwise but requires a clear development of purpose; this will be discussed further in the following section. Also, at this time, Ambler began to consider differentiation of the sandy paste ceramics into an early form (Wallisville Plain) and a later form (Goose Creek Plain).

7. In 1969 I began excavating the Harris County Boys School site as well as much of the stratigraphic testing in the Trinity delta. The Wallisville work was designed to involve sites younger than those tested by Ambler so the character of the material would not significantly overlap. The Boys School testing, however, produced a sizable collection of Tchefuncte and Tchefuncte-like sherds. In a preliminary review paper prepared before intensive analysis had been carried out (Aten 1970), the major thrusts of Ambler's (1970) formulation were accepted with the exception of Orcoquizac Plain. Later this acceptance was modified after (a) direct comparison of early Galveston Bay ceramics with those from the Sabine Lake Area and the LMV, coupled with (b) the realization that early sandy paste ceramics comparable to Wallisville Plain did not occur at Boys School in company with the Tchefuncte material there.

8. In 1973, Ambler reported on the 1966 season of excavations at Wallisville. The definition of Orcoquizac Plain was left standing and Wallisville Plain and Lost River Plain were formally proposed. He went on to define the Lost River Phase for the early ceramic period but let the 1970 proposals for other phases drop. At this time, the more extensive descriptions of the proposed two early pottery types made clear to me the difficulty in distinguishing Wallisville Plain from Goose Creek Plain, and Lost River Plain from Mandeville Plain and Tchefuncte Plain.

9. In the final analysis of artifacts from excavations at Harris County Boys School (Aten et al. 1976), nearly all of the components of the local ceramic assemblages were described within a typological framework in which the principal bases for separation were temper (or the lack of it), paste category, decoration, and paste texture. Bone-tempered ceramics were still referred to by ad hoc descriptive terminology. San Jacinto Plain and Incised continued to be recognized as the local versions of grog-tempered ceramics. However, this concept essentially ignored the problems described earlier in classifying grog-tempered ceramics of the Sabine Lake Area.

By this time, also, Bollich had developed the concept of a locally produced sand-tempered pottery on the basis of extensive surface collections and from our joint excavations in the Sabine Lake Area. This pottery, informally referred to as "Conway Plain" after the bayou along which it was first recognized, was subsequently recognized in the Galveston Bay Area collections of Ambler, as well as others. The relevance of this category at the present time is in tracing alternative forms of tempered versus untempered ceramics across the southern United States.[9] Conway Plain sherds previously had been classified with sandy paste ceramics.

The main departure from Ambler's formulations occurred when dealing with the untempered ceramics. Part of the reason given by Ambler (1973) for grouping all Tchefuncte-like sherds together as Lost River Plain was the observation that the Tchefuncte assemblage in Texas was much attenuated in the variety of vessel forms and design styles when compared to that in southern Louisiana (Aten and Chandler 1971:15; also see Aten *et al.* 1976:18). However, we excavate sherds, not abstractions such as "assemblage," "phase," or the like. If two sherds are morphologically identical in terms of the chosen criteria, and have contiguous distributions, there is no practical basis for saying they are different.[10] In this case, direct comparison of the Galveston Bay specimens with specimens from the Sabine Lake Area and the LMV (including hundreds of sherds from the Tchefuncte Site) made clear the morphological identity of Texas sherds with the types Tchefuncte Plain, Tchefuncte Incised, Tchefuncte Stamped, and Mandeville Plain. Since we are dealing with artifacts that are morphologically identical, which occur in similar chronological positions, and which are from geographically adjacent areas, what is the basis for creating different taxonomies for the two areas? The issue is not whether it can be done, but whether it should be done. We cannot create uncorrelated analytical structures in every locality and expect to advance scientific analysis. Lost River Plain is unsuitable as either a type or a variety because it violates the integrity of an existing taxonomy that is based upon paste categories as one of the most sensitive distinctions defining important temporal and spatial variation. As such, retention of the proposed Lost River Plain type would lead to obscuring the measurement of important technological and historical relationships between the upper Texas coast and southern Louisiana.

Wallisville Plain, on the other hand, is clear enough as to its defining characteristics and does describe variation within the sandy paste ceramics. However, identification of many sherds has proven to be exceedingly difficult and the limits of the class's distribution are hard to define. Indistinguishable sherds also occur with some frequency at other times than with early ceramics. For example, many sandy paste sherds from late Old River Period and Orcoquisac Period sites in the Trinity delta cannot be distinguished from early examples of Wallisville Plain. Wallisville Plain appears to be a variation in sandy paste ceramics

---

[9]Tempering was a major innovation in ceramic technology; in the central Gulf coast, sand tempering (reflected in the Alexander and O'Neal types of southern Louisiana and on the upper Texas coast by Conway Plain) appears to have briefly preceded the introduction of sherd-tempering.

[10]Locational context occasionally has been used as a criterion, but only when not making such a separation seemed inherently absurd (cf. Phillips 1970:48).

which is primarily confined to the Trinity delta area and is most effectively handled by means of definition of a variety within a larger type.

With the completion of preliminary versions of the Galveston Bay Area ceramic seriation and a review of the local distribution of sandy paste rocker-stamped pottery (previously identified as "Tchefuncte Stamped"), the distinctive physical and temporal characteristics of this pottery became apparent. Therefore, these sherds were classified as the new type, Goose Creek Stamped (Aten *et al.* 1976:27).

In the present volume, an initial formulation is attempted of the previously recognized classes with respect to the type–variety taxonomic framework that has been mentioned so often on the preceding pages. As a practical matter, variety nomenclature will be used within those types for which subtype divisions are presently needed. The full-blown type–variety jargon will not be thrust upon the reader for named types not previously subdivided. For these, the type name will be used, as before, with the understanding that all are to be considered "variety unspecified."

I still am unwilling to refer to bone-tempered ceramics in anything other than descriptive terminology for the reasons previously discussed (also see Aten 1971); no new information has developed concerning this question.

Terminological treatment of the grog-tempered wares has had to undergo significant modification. Analysis of the fourteenth-century ceramics from Trinity delta sites has now produced strong stratigraphic evidence (at sites 41 CH 31 and 41 CH 98) for a very short period of time in which the grog-tempered ceramics of the area consisted almost exclusively of sherds indistinguishable from those grog-tempered plainwares of the LMV. This is an extension into the Galveston Bay Area of the grog-tempered plainware classification problem previously described for the Sabine Lake Area. The matter could no longer be ignored as one of local variation in source material or technology. The problem now is a regional historical one that needs to be coped with so that analysis can proceed in an orderly way in both the Sabine Lake Area and in the limited time of its effect in the Galveston Bay Area.

Phillips (1970:47–48) has thoroughly discussed the problem of classifying LMV grog-tempered plainwares. These ceramics appear with the Marksville Period and remain in the LMV throughout the remainder of the region's aboriginal culture history. Many regional and chronological variations occur in these wares and they have proved very difficult to subdivide. Criteria have ranged from paste, color, texture, sound when dropped, vessel form, and so on, all with limited success. As we begin to try to integrate data among regions, however, it must be recognized that the major and overwhelming feature of grog-tempered plainware throughout the central and western Gulf coast (and inland) is its essential continuity rather than its discontinuities. This is a matter unlikely to be satisfactorily handled other than on the basis of what Phillips (1970:48) has called a "super type"—Baytown Plain—and a host of local or regional varieties of which the class, San Jacinto Plain, is one. As a result of these considerations, upper coast grog-tempered ceramics have been reorganized into two types: Baytown Plain, and San Jacinto Incised. Baytown Plain is further divided into two varieties: San Jacinto (formerly the type of San Jacinto Plain) and the Phoenix Lake variety more characteristic of LMV plainwares. San Jacinto Incised likewise has been divided into the Jamison variety (the sandy paste grog-tempered sherds) and the Spindletop variety for the LMV grog-tempered pastes. The recognition of a vague sequence of incised design assemblages within the type San Jacinto Incised (Figure 12.2) may be pointing further in the direction of incipient varieties.

To complete classification of the tempered ceramics, Conway Plain, the sand-tempered pottery, is here referred to as O'Neal Plain, variety Conway, because of the occasional presence of noded rims which are characteristic of O'Neal Plain. This appears to be a sufficient category to organize the Galveston Bay Area sand-tempered ceramics which likewise occur on an early time level. In the Sabine Lake Area, it may be necessary to define a later variety because of its longer duration and paste modifications which take place there.

Among the untempered ceramics, the fine clay paste Tchefuncte Plain, Tchefuncte Incised, and Tchefuncte Stamped occur in very small quantities for which there presently is no necessity to attempt definition of varieties. Similarly, for the sandy paste wares, there currently is no need to define varieties for Goose Creek Incised, Goose Creek Stamped, and Goose Creek Red-Filmed. We note, however, that the recognition of several Goose Creek Incised design assemblages (Figure 12.2) may lead to definition of varieties for this type.

For the sandy paste plainwares, some attention must be given to the recognition of varieties. Before doing this, two points made earlier are reiterated. First, at a type level, there must be sorting criteria applicable to sherds, not to abstractions about assemblages, for such a procedure then becomes tautological; that is, the assemblage defines the sherds, while the sherds define the assemblage. Second, definition of types or varieties should be as a tool directed at a problem.

These observations are pertinent to the sandy paste plainware problem in the following way. I have examined tens of thousands of these sherds from all chronological periods in sites from the Brazos to the Sabine and from the coast inland to Conroe, Livingston, and McGee Bend. Throughout this area, the sandy paste plainwares are extraordinarily homogeneous. Sherds taken from virtually any time or place within this area could be exchanged and not be very conspicuous. That is to say, replicable typological sorting criteria could not be defined to subdivide this regionally distributed plainware that would have recognisable cultural significance. This suggests that all of the sandy paste plainwares of southeastern Texas (and, perhaps, southwestern Louisiana) should be arrayed under the single type, Goose Creek Plain, with local varieties defined as the occasion warrants.

For the level of precision needed in the development of ceramic seriations and local chronologies in this study, equivocal categories in any major degree are not

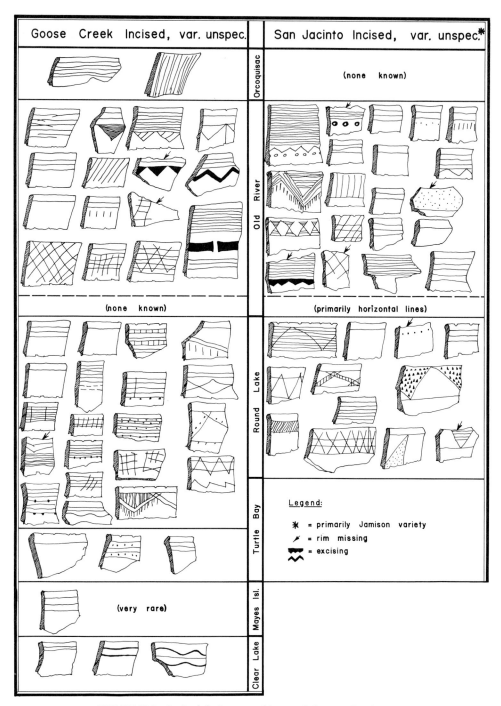

FIGURE 12.2 Incised design assemblages, Galveston Bay Area.

helpful. As a result, only the type Goose Creek Plain has been employed, rather than to use sandy paste plainware varieties such as would be described by Wallisville Plain or any of several other possibilities. A single exception to this approach was made when trying to trace the earliest ceramics in the Galveston Bay Area. Two sandy paste classes were useful in measuring relationships between the ceramic technology of the LMV Tchefuncte wares and the ceramics usually thought of as Goose Creek. These were Mandeville Plain and a second class of sherds that shared attributes of both Mandeville and classic Goose Creek Plain, thus far recognized only at the earliest Trinity delta sites. On the assumption that the latter class would be helpful in describing the relationships among Tchefuncte, Mandeville, and Goose Creek, it was set apart as the Anahuac variety of Goose Creek. As used here, Goose Creek Plain, variety unspecified, means all Goose Creek plainware other than the Anahuac variety.

Mandeville Plain has had an uneasy history ever since it was introduced more than 30 years ago. Should it be associated with the Tchefuncte or with the Alexander ceramics? It appeared to be neither one nor the other, and various solutions have been offered over the years. Phillips (1970:109–110), in the most recent comprehensive review of the matter, was unable to place Mandeville in his classification scheme, and suggested that if the concept was to be retained, it probably should be included as a variety of Tchefuncte Plain.

Despite this, the view from Texas indicates that Mandeville Plain needs to be kept available as an essential tool for documentation of the relationships between Tchefuncte ceramic technology and the sandy paste ceramics as these occur on the upper Texas coast and in southwestern Louisiana. Very little archaeological work has been done in the latter area. However, the research of Bollich and Aten on the east side of the Sabine, Springer's excavation at Little Chenier on the Mermentau River (Springer 1973), and informal reports all indicate that southwestern Louisiana is a region with a major presence of both sandy paste and sand-tempered pottery. It is entirely possible that the reason Mandeville Plain has been difficult to use systematically is because its region of greatest occurrence is not the LMV but southwestern Louisiana, an area which still remains something of an archaeological *terra incognita*. As presumptuous as this may sound, it may ultimately prove to be most logical to classify Mandeville Plain as a variety of Goose Creek Plain. Indeed, close inspection of the taxonomic decision tree (Figure 12.3) illustrates the inconsistency of retaining Mandeville Plain as either a separate type or as a variety of Tchefuncte Plain.

In my judgment, the key to an integrated taxonomy for Gulf Coast ceramics is to recognize the evolutionary succession which has occurred there in basic ceramic paste technologies. Possibly beginning with fiber–tempered wares (which may or may not be tempered), but certainly beginning with postfiber-tempered ceramics, we first have temperless wares (such as Tchefuncte, Goose Creek, and Mandeville) succeeded by tempered wares. Among the latter the earliest are sand-tempered (such as Alexander, O'Neal, and Conway), followed by grog-tempered (such as Baytown, San Jacinto, and Marksville), followed in

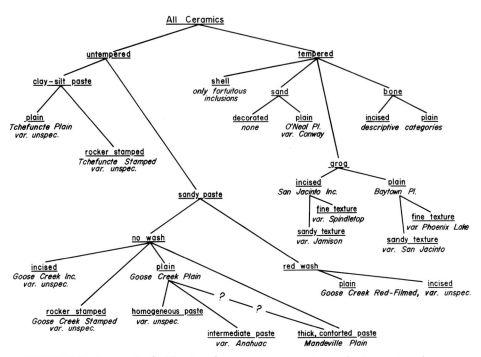

FIGURE 12.3 Taxonomic decision tree for upper Texas coast ceramics (rare categories not included).

the western Gulf by bone-tempering (such as Leon Plain and Orcoquizac Plain) and shell-tempering (such as various Caddoan and Mississippian plainwares). The principal taxonomic difficulties that occur have been in the practical discrimination of types among the plainwares within each of these major ceramic technologies.

Certainly no one would (or should) have difficulty distinguishing between Goose Creek Plain and Tchefuncte Plain; an absolute separation is always possible between these two ceramic taxa even though both are temperless. However, they are the end-members of a technological continuum of materials and techniques. Points in sequence along this continuum can be identified, beginning at the clayey end and progresssing to the sandy end, as the following plainware taxa: Tchefuncte; Mandeville; Anahuac variety of Goose Creek; the Goose Creek sherds identified by Ambler as Wallisville Plain; the Goose Creek characteristic of the Brazos delta and of the Conroe–Livingston Area; and the hard, dark-colored sandy paste variety sometimes referred to as "classic" Goose Creek.

Thus, whereas distinguishing Tchefuncte from the hard, dark Goose Creek sherds presents no difficulty, there simply is no end to the arbitrariness and nonreplicability associated with distinguishing attribute combinations that are adjacent to each other along this physical continuum. Similar problems can easily be described for each of the other basic ceramic technologies listed above. Phillips (1970) solved this problem for the LMV grog-tempered plainwares by designating them all as varieties of the single type Baytown Plain. Judging from his discussion, Phillips must not have been too satisfied with this "supertype," but it seems to me that such a supertype for each of the major technology plainwares is the appropriate solution to this problem. It solves most of the outstanding problems with the use of plainwares for chronological purposes, and would permit a refined mapping and measurement of the dispersal of basic ceramic technologies throughout the central Gulf Coast, and probably the eastern Gulf as well.

DESCRIPTIONS

A decision tree summarizing the hierarchy of decisions currently used to arrive at a taxonomic designation for upper coast ceramics is given in Figure 12.3. The distribution of sherds used for this study is given in Table 12.2. In identifying these ceramics, freshly broken sections on all sherds were examined with a binocular microscope at low power ($10\times$ to $20\times$). This procedure is not merely a methodological ritual, but is essential for accurate analysis of upper coast ceramics. Moreover, the need for this form of examination does not diminish with experience. For example, fugitive red-filming often is detectable only through identifying microscopic traces of ochre film on the sherd surface. Distinguishing between sand-tempered pastes and sandy pastes, the latter representing naturally occurring sediment assemblages, requires careful examination of grain sizes and frequencies. And, more often than not, magnification is required to recognize grog-temper in the pastes of the San Jacinto varieties either because of smudging (cf. Ambler 1967:40), small grog size, low grog frequency and/or lack of color differentiation. Although a microscope will not guarantee competent typological analysis, competence is not possible without using one.

The approach to ceramic description taken below is a modification of the approach employed in my earlier reports on upper coast ceramics. Physical descriptions and photographic illustrations of most of the classes now have been published. The new collections reported here appear to be represented adequately by these earlier descriptions insofar as paste, texture, and surface treatment are concerned. Instead of repeating this descriptive material, the following are provided for each category: (*a*) a list of references to the most useful sources of description; (*b*) a summary of the principal distinguishing characters which lead to identification of the class, along with observations on methodological problems when appropriate; and (*c*) a summary of the time and space distribution of the class on the upper coast.

TABLE 12.2
Ceramic Frequency Distribution

Provenience (site; level or stratigraphic zone)[a]	Ceramic types[b]													Total sherds[d]	Remarks
	Goose Creek						Bone-tempered plain		Baytown Plain		San Jacinto Incised		Miscellaneous types			
	Plain		Incised		Red-filmed											
	(no.)	(%)	(no.)	(%)	(no.)	(%)	(no.)	(%)	(no.)	(%)	(no.)	(%)	(no.)	(%)		
									Brazoria County							
41 BO 4																
single lens[c]	27	35.5					3	3.9	46	60.5					76	
41 BO 12																
0–10	29	90.6							3	9.4					32	
10–20	78	91.8							7	8.2					85	
20–30	106	100.0													106	
30–40	47	100.0													47	
41 BO 13 (Reexamined in TARL coll. by Aten; originally reported by Hamilton 1970)																
all units	271	92.2	1	0.3					22	7.5					294	
41 BO 35 (Stratigraphic test data reorganized from Aten 1971: Table 2)																
Zone 1	114	84.4	4	3.0			1	0.7	14	10.4	1	0.7			135	
Zone 2B	100	94.3							6	5.7					106	
Zone 3B	15	100.0													15	
41 BO 50																
Zone 1	107	88.4							14	11.6					121	
Zone 2	146	96.1							6	3.9					152	

					(Anahuac variety)		(Mandeville Plain)		(Tchefuncte Plain)		(Conway variety)					Specimens reclassified by Aten; originally reported by Ambler (1973).
41 CH 16																
top	33	54.1	1	1.8	3	4.9	17	27.9	2	3.3	6	9.8			61	
middle	14	25.5	1	1.8	8	14.5	28	50.9	2	3.6	2	3.6			55	
bottom	7	20.6			8	23.5	13	38.2	3	8.8	3	8.8			34	
41 CH 20																
Surface collection	247	51.0	6	1.2	1	0.2	1	0.2	220	45.5	8	1.7	1*	0.2	484	*Shell-tempered plain
"Test Pit A"																
0–20	14 }	73.3	2 }	6.7					2 }	20.0					16	
20–40	8 }								4 }						14	
40–65	7	87.5	1	12.5											8	
41 CH 24																
0–10	95	85.6	6	5.4	6	5.4			4	3.6					111	
10–20	127	84.6	10	6.7	4	2.7	3	2.0	5	3.3	1	0.7			150	
41 CH 32 (Grid units M-3, 4, & 5)																
0–10	48	94.1	1	2.0					2	3.9					51	
10–20	216	94.3	5	2.2					6	2.6	2	0.9			229	
20–30	51	52.0	2	2.0			1	1.0	45	45.9					98	
30–40	14 }	38.5							18 }	53.8	3 }	7.7			35	
40–50	1 }								3 }						4	

(continued)

223

TABLE 12.2 (Continued)

Provenience (site; level or stratigraphic zone)a	Ceramic typesb														Total sherdsd	Remarks
	Goose Creek						Bone-tempered plain		Baytown Plain		San Jacinto Incised		Miscellaneous types			
	Plain		Incised		Red-filmed											
	(no.)	(%)	(no.)	(%)	(no.)	(%)	(no.)	(%)	(no.)	(%)	(no.)	(%)	(no.)	(%)		
41 CH 36																
0–10	15	18.5	2	1.5					73	74.5	5	4.0	2*	1.5	95	*Shell-tempered
10–20	11								32		1				46	
20–30	11	24.7	2	3.5					22	62.4	3	8.2	1*	1.2	38	*Shell-tempered
30–40	10		1						31		4				47	
40–50	51	50.6	5	5.8	3	1.7			33	34.9	5	6.4	1*	0.6	95	*Shell-tempered
50–60	36		5						27		6				77	*Shell-tempered
60–70	9	56.3	2	12.5	1	1.6			9	29.7					21	
70–80	27		6						10						43	
80–90	43	77.5	5	7.5	4	9.7			2	5.4					54	
90–100	29		2		5				3						39	
100–110	47	80.6	7	9.7	2	4.5			1	0.7	2	1.5	2*	3.0	61	*Shell-tempered
110–120	61		6		4								2*		73	*Shell-tempered
120–130	69	91.0	4	3.0	6	5.5			1	0.8					80	
130–140	50				1										51	
140–150	91	90.2	4	4.1	9	5.6									104	
150–160	149		7		6										162	
160–170	146	93.5	4	2.8	4	2.5									157	
170–180	120		4		3		1	0.4							127	
180–190	130	91.5	6	7.1	1	1.6									137	
190–200	102		12		3										117	

41 CH 46

Provenience	Plain (n %)	Stamped (n %)	(G. C.[g] Stamped) (n %)	(Anahuac[g] Variety) (n %)	(Mandeville[g] Plain) (n %)	(Conway[g] Variety) (n %)	Tchefuncte Plain* (n %)	Goose Creek Stamped* (n %)	Total
0–10	37 94.9	1 2.6						1 2.6	39
10–20	57 96.6	2 3.4							59
20–40	88 96.7	3 3.3							91
40–50	67 100.0								67
50–60	55 98.2	1 1.8							56
60–70	59 100.0								59
70–80	41 93.2	3 6.8							44
80–90	43 93.5	1 2.2					1* 2.2	1 2.2	46
90–100	24 }96.1								24
100–110	25 }	1 2.0						1* 2.0	27
(Base of midden not reached)									

41 CH 52

Provenience	Plain (n %)	Stamped (n %)	(G. C.[g] Stamped) (n %)	(Anahuac[g] Variety) (n %)	(Mandeville[g] Plain) (n %)	(Conway[g] Variety) (n %)	Total
All units	75 81.5	1 1.1	1 1.1	6 6.5	6 6.5	3 3.3	92

41 CH 80

Provenience	Plain (n %)	Stamped (n %)	Total
Single level	88 98.9	1 1.1	89

41 CH 87

Provenience	Plain (n %)	Stamped (n %)	Total
"B" 0–10	12		12
10–20	15		15
20–30	11 }98.6		11
30–40	12 }		12
40–50	12 }		12
50–60	9	1 1.4	10

*Tchefuncte Plain

*Goose Creek Stamped

Reclassified by Aten; originally reported by Ambler (1973)

(continued)

225

TABLE 12.2 (Continued)

Provenience (site; level or stratigraphic zone)[a]	Ceramic types[b]														Total sherds[d]	Remarks
	Goose Creek				Red-filmed		Bone-tempered plain		Baytown Plain		San Jacinto Incised		Miscellaneous types			
	Plain		Incised													
	(no.)	(%)	(no.)	(%)	(no.)	(%)	(no.)	(%)	(no.)	(%)	(no.)	(%)	(no.)	(%)		
"A" 60–70	9														9	
70–80	13														13	
80–90	13	95.9		4.1											13	
90–110	27		1												28	
110–120	8		2												10	
(Base of midden not reached)																
41 CH 98 0–10	47	29.0	6	3.7			2*	1.2	107	66.0					162	*Including 1 incised and 1 grog and bone-temper
10–20	2	2.2	1	1.1			2*	2.2	85	92.4	2	2.2			92	
20–30	1	2.6							37	94.9	1	2.6			39	
30–40	17	14.7							96	82.8	3	2.6			116	
40–50									47	95.9	2	4.1			49	
50–60	51	77.3	2	3.0	1	1.5			12	18.2					66	
60–80	94	92.2	5	4.9					3	2.9					102	
80–90	115	100.0													115	
41 CH 106 "B" Surface	47	79.3	4	2.0					26	17.2	1	1.5			74	
0–10	114								9		2				129	

Table (continued) — ceramic sherd counts and percentages by provenience

Provenience	n	%	n	%	n	%	n	%	n	%	Total	Remarks
"A" 10–20	58	96.0	1	1.3	1*	2.6					60	*Incised
"A" 20–30	8										8	
"A" 30–40	6		1								7	
41 CH 110												
(1969 test)												
"B" 0–10	6										6	
"B" 10–20	24	93.8			1*	3.1					26	*Incised and punctated.
20–30	23		2	1.7			10	26.1			39	*Goliad (?) riveted handle
"A" 30–40	14	64.7					16		1	0.8	31	
"A" 40–50	40				2*	2.5	5				49	*incl. 1 grog and bone
(1972 test; Unit N116/W102—data consolidated from Gilmore 1974: Table 17)												
Zone 1	359	96.8	2	0.5	4*	1.1	4	1.1			371	*incl. 1 incised
Zone 2	59	90.8	3	4.6	2*	3.1			1**	1.5	65	*Incised; **Rockport (?)
Zone 3	100	85.5	4	3.4			13	11.1			117	
Zone 4	35	51.5	4	5.9			15	22.1	13	19.0	68	
41 CH 137												
0–10	5										5	
10–20	47										47	
20–30	26		3	6.0	1	0.8					30	
30–40	13										13	
"B" 40–50	7	93.2									8	
50–60	12										12	
60–70	8		1								9	
70–80	1										1	
80–90	5		3								8	

(continued)

TABLE 12.2 (Continued)

Provenience (site; level or stratigraphic zone)[a]	Ceramic types[b]														Total sherds[d]	Remarks
	Goose Creek						Bone-tempered plain		Baytown Plain		San Jacinto Incised		Miscellaneous types			
	Plain		Incised		Red-filmed											
	(no.)	(%)	(no.)	(%)	(no.)	(%)	(no.)	(%)	(no.)	(%)	(no.)	(%)	(no.)	(%)		
90–100	1														1	
100–110	2														2	
110–120	9														9	
"A" 120–130	12	100.0													12	
130–140	6														6	
140–160	15														15	
160–208	5														5	
41 CH 169																
Surface	22								18		1				41	
0–10	1	52.9							7	41.2	2	5.9			10	
10–20	13								3		1				17	
Fort Bend County																
41 FB 11																
0–10	69	57.9	1*	0.8			49	41.1							119	*Punctated only
10–20	323	94.2	2*	0.6			15	4.4	3	0.9					343	*Punctated only
20–30	60	100.0													60	
30–40	14	93.3					1	6.7							15	
Galveston County																
41 GV 5																
0–10	35	66.1	2	3.8			1	1.9	15	28.3					53	
10–20	96	53.3					20*	11.2	60	33.3	4	2.2			180	*Includes 1 incised

Level	n	%	n	%	n	%	n	%	n	%	n	%	Total
20–30	160	66.7					13*	5.4	55	22.9	12	5.0	240
30–40	47	88.9					1	1.6	6	9.5			54
40–50	9												9
41 GV 6													
Disturbed site	180	10.6	60	3.5			33*	1.9	1,257	74.0	167	9.8	1,697

Harris County

Level	n	%	n	%	n	%	n	%	n	%	n	%	Total
41 HR 50 (Compiled from Ambler 1967)													
"B" 10–20	12	78.0	24	1.3	9	0.5			51	19.2	2	1.4	65
"B" 20–30	1,405								299		23		1,760
"A" 30–40	841	98.0	3	0.9	1	0.1			7	0.8			852
"A" 40–50	46		5										51
41 HR 56 (Compiled from Ambler 1967)													
"C" 0–10	1	54.2	1	9.6									2
"C" 10–20	44		7						30	36.1			81
"B" 20–30	51	78.0			3	3.0			13	16.0	3	3.0	70
"B" 30–40	27								3				30
"A" 40–50	10	100.0											10
41 HR 59 (Compiled from Ambler 1967)													
0–10	1	1.9							2	92.3			2
10–20									46		3	5.8	50
20–30	15	18.8							60	75.0	5	6.3	80
41 HR 80 (from Aten et al. 1976:Table 3)													
Cemetery fill	1,451	95.7	8	0.5	7	0.5			3	0.2	1	0.1	

*Includes 5 incised

*Includes 3 incised and 1 engraved

(continued)

229

TABLE 12.2 (Continued)

Provenience (site; level or stratigraphic zone)[a]	Goose Creek Plain (no.)	(%)	Incised (no.)	(%)	Red-filmed (no.)	(%)	Bone-tempered plain (no.)	(%)	Baytown Plain (no.)	(%)	San Jacinto Incised (no.)	(%)	Miscellaneous types (no.)	(%)	Total sherds[d]	Remarks
	(Tchefuncte Plain)[c]						(Tchefuncte Interior Inc.)[c]		(Tchefuncte Stamped)[c]		(Mandeville Plain)[c] (Tchefuncte Plain)[c]		(Conway Variety)[c] (Mandeville Plain)[c]			
(41 HR 80 cemetery fill continued)																
41 HR 161					20	1.3	2	0.1	1	0.1	6	0.4	9	0.6	1,516	
A	80		1								3				84	
B	221	} 96.4		} 0.2							4	} 2.8	2	} 0.5	227	
C and D	88										6				94	
Miscellaneous	168								1	} 0.2	3		1		173	
Liberty County																
41 LB 2 (from Aten 1967)																
Analysis Unit III	835	83.0	30	3.0	17	1.7	10	1.0	91	9.0	11	1.1	12	1.2	1,006	
Analysis Unit II	320	96.5	2	0.6	7	2.1	3	0.9	2	0.6					331	
41 LB 4																
Single zone	215	67.8	18	5.7	1*	0.3	3	0.9	73	23.0	6	1.9	1	0.3	317	*Incised

[a] All depth measurements are in centimeters unless otherwise noted.

[b] For the purposes of simplifying the organization of Table 12.2, Goose Creek Plain in the heading always refers only to the "unspecified" variety of the type: Baytown Plain may include both the San Jacinto and Phoenix Lake varieties, except in the Brazos Delta-West Bay Area sites in which the Phoenix Lake variety never occurred; likewise San Jacinto Incised may include both the Jamison and the Spindletop varieties, except in the Brazos area in which the latter variety never occurred.

[c] Single lens is an unstratified refuse layer usually not more than 5 cm thick.

[d] All percentages and totals reflect multiple sherds from same vessels counted as only 1 item; thus, 19 San Jacinto Incised sherds excavated, with 13 from the same vessel, are counted in analysis as 7 sherds.

[e] Midden deposit into which the cemetery was placed; therefore this assemblage predates the cemetery.

[f] The total number of Goose Creek Plain sherds was inadvertantly omitted from the original source.

[g] Parenthetical headings apply only to the site for which they are used.

In taking this approach, two factors are pertinent. As Phillips (1970:33–34) has observed, type descriptions are not an effective vehicle for conveying ceramic technological data, especially if the types are defined to be historical classes. A ceramic vessel, first and foremost, is a structure. It is the resultant of the interaction of materials, form, function, and style. While correlations exist between partial sets of vessel attributes, as represented by sherd collections (e.g., on upper coast ceramics there clearly is a correlation between wall thickness and paste category, between rim–base form and vessel stability, and possibly between wall thickness and orifice diameter), there are not now problems being researched which will be usefully served by continuing to describe, with varying degrees of precision, individual attributes as if they were discrete entities. A more holistic approach is needed, even though the preponderance of sherd material may require the use of a probabilistic method.

A large body of data has been accumulated on vessel attributes from the Brazos, Sabine, and Galveston areas. However, on the basis of preliminary examination, very little of this material seems readily susceptible to patterning on an individual attribute basis. If these data are to be used productively, it will be as the result of proposing new hypotheses extending beyond this study. Consequently, the references that have been cited with each pottery class provide an adequate qualitative representation of vessel form attributes.

Untempered Ceramics

Goose Creek Plain

References These are listed under each variety.

Distinguishing characteristics Sandy paste; sediment is a natural association and rarely is well sorted; grain sizes grade from the largest present (usually fine grained, but medium or very fine also are common maximum sizes) down to the clay matrix. A major discontinuity in size distribution between the clay and sand is unlikely to occur naturally on the upper coast and probably indicates a tempered ware (cf. O'Neal Plain, variety Conway).

Firing characteristics vary widely, resulting in varying cohesiveness and colors; insufficient amounts of clay in proportion to sand often result in extremely friable sherds (especially in the Brazos Delta–West Bay Area) and spalling of floated exterior surfaces; firing clouds are common and a minority of sherds display well-developed cores; most have light colored exteriors which grade to darker interior surfaces; in the Brazos Delta–West Bay Area especially, sherds frequently are a uniform light color throughout.

Color varies widely from black to orange and reddish hues, depending on firing conditions and sediment source. For example, Trinity–San Jacinto floodplain and delta clays usually fire brown to black, often with organic inclusions (rootlets, grass, leaf fragments); most upland clays of the Beaumont Formation fire to a light brown or orange color, often with red streaks or small red balls from iron concretions; these upland clays also may contain small white amorphous specks of burned caliche or, rarely, small fragments which appear to be kaolinite. Sabine Lake Area sherds are quite similar to those of the Galveston Bay Area. Brazos floodplain sediments are more uniform and usually fire a homogeneous brown to light tan or light reddish-brown color with very few inclusions. Sherds from the Jamaica Beach Site on Galveston Island may contain sand-sized shell fragments or microscopic gastropod shells (cf. Story 1968:15 ff.).

These characteristics are common to the type; below are described the distinguishing features of the varieties.

Goose Creek Plain, Variety Anahuac

References None, although sherds of this class may have been included by Ambler (1973) in his type, Lost River Plain.

Distinguishing characteristics This category may be recognized by virtue of sharing paste characteristics of both the Goose Creek variety and the Mandeville variety, thus not being either one. Sherds with thick walls and irregular surface treatment characteristic of Mandeville may also have homogeneous and well-wedged paste texture; other sherds may be thin walled and well smoothed but have contorted and poorly wedged paste texture; additional combinations may occur.

Distribution on the upper coast This variety has been recognized only in the earliest ceramics seriated from the Galveston Bay Area and are from sites in the Trinity delta. It has not yet been sought in collections from the Sabine Lake Area. The principal reason for separating it out is precisely because the variety seemed intermediate in character between typical Goose Creek plainware and the sandy paste plainwares (Mandeville Plain) associated with the Tchefuncte culture of south Louisiana. As can be seen on Figure 14.1, the distribution of this variety is closely related to the rise of Goose Creek Plain, variety unspecified, and may reflect a stage in the origin of the other Goose Creek Plain varieties. This will be discussed later.

Goose Creek Plain, Variety Unspecified (Excludes Anahuac Variety)

References Ambler 1967, 1970, 1973; Aten 1967, 1971; Aten and Bollich 1969; Aten *et al.* 1976; McClurkan 1968; Shafer 1968.

Distinguishing characteristics   Paste as described above for Goose Creek Plain; generally this is a thin walled and homogeneous textured ceramic when compared to Mandeville Plain; its color and cohesiveness vary widely, as do source materials and certain vessel form elements such as rims and bases; this residual category can be subdivided readily into additional varieties should the solution of specific problems require it. For example, Ambler's "type," Wallisville Plain, is contained wholly within the unspecified variety and tends to describe early Goose Creek sherds in the Trinity delta dating to the Clear Lake and the Mayes Island periods; unfortunately, it also describes sandy paste plainware of the late Old River Period in the Trinity delta, which is part of the problem described earlier about considering Wallisville Plain a separate type. Most subdivision of the unspecified variety will result in classes of very limited spatial and temporal distribution and in many sherds which will be unassignable.

Distribution on the upper coast   This variety is pervasive on the upper coast and extends at least as far to the southwest as Matagorda Bay, inland at least as far as the Conroe–Livingston areas to the north, and to the McGee Bend reservoir area to the northeast. No essential difference was observed between sherds of Goose Creek Plain and the type Bear Creek Plain proposed by Jelks for east Texas (1965:109–117).

Goose Creek Incised, Variety Unspecified

References   Ambler 1967:13–19; Aten 1967:11; Aten 1971:25–26; Aten *et al.* 1976:20–21; O'Brien 1974:55; Wheat 1953:189.

Distinguishing characteristics   Paste characters are the same as described for Goose Creek Plain. The type is decorated primarily by incision and occasionally by excision (or engraving) and punctations; decoration is confined to the upper part of the vessel wall around the rim. Sherds illustrating the many design motifs of this type have been amply illustrated in the references cited previously. If one places the full range of design motifs from the Galveston Bay Area in a chronological arrangement, a series of design assemblages are recognizable (Figure 12.2) Sets of horizontal lines tend to predominate in all periods. Beyond this, in the Clear Lake Period, wavy lines have been found. A similarly restricted set of motifs occurs in the Mayes Island Period and most of the Turtle Bay Period with the major distinguishing feature of these sherds being their scarcity.

Beginning in late Turtle Bay Period and extending through the Round Lake Period, a large and varied assemblage of motifs is present, consisting of punctations, grid patterns, pendant triangles, and others. This variety of design is absent in the early Old River Period and the only known incised sherds at this time are San Jacinto Incised (grog-tempered). In the remainder of the Old River Period, possibly extending into the Orcoquisac Period, a highly varied assemblage again is present consisting of excised or engraved panels, punctations, zoned designs, pendant triangles, grid patterns, diagonal lines, cross-hatching, and so on. This assemblage, as well as its counterpart San Jacinto Incised, has the distinct appearance of being an imitation of Coles Creek and Plaquemine Period design styles.

At the present time, it would be difficult to sort more than about 30% of the Goose Creek Incised sherds into these motif assemblages on a sherd-by-sherd basis. Ultimately, however, they could form a basis for definition of varieties of the type. For example, the motifs illustrated for Addicks (Wheat 1953) and for the Jamison Site (Aten 1967) most closely resemble the Turtle Bay–Round Lake assemblage, which is consistent with the age of the site levels as estimated by the ceramic seriation. Selected examples are shown in Figure 12.4.

Distribution on the upper coast   Goose Creek Incised sherds in the Sabine occur throughout the ceramic sequence but have not been analyzed on a motif basis as in the Galveston Bay Area; however, the design styles are abundant and one may anticipate the emergence of design assemblages. In the Brazos Delta–West Bay Area, Goose Creek Incised is quite rare and thus far is confined to the equivalent of the Round Lake Period and the Orcoquisac Period. The design styles are extremely limited (horizontal lines and pendant triangles) which would be consistent with most of the design assemblages in the Galveston Bay Area. Only a single occurrence of this type is represented in the Conroe–Livingston seriation, apparently in the Round Lake Period. It is a grid motif which is more characteristic of the Turtle Bay–Round Lake Period assemblage in the Galveston Bay Area than of other assemblages.

Goose Creek Stamped, Variety Unspecified

References   Ambler 1973:87; Aten *et al.* 1976:27; Wheat 1953:190.

Distinguishing characteristics   Sandy paste and thin-walled vessel form typical of Goose Creek Plain, variety unspecified; bears rocker stamping below the rims and, judging from some sherds, well down on the vessel wall; rocker stamping is in the technique of Tchefuncte Stamped (i.e., with both narrow and wide curved instruments, or with a narrow forked instrument).

Distribution on the upper coast   Neither Goose Creek Stamped nor the similar Tchefuncte Stamped have been found in the Sabine Lake Area, although it is difficult to understand how this could be anything other than a fortuitous sample bias. Its presence in the Galveston Bay Area evidently is confined to the Clear Lake Period; altogether it has been found in small quantities in at least seven sites. No specimens have been found in either the Brazos Delta–West Bay Area or at Conroe–Livingston. Selected examples are shown in Figure 12.5.

FIGURE 12.4   Upper Texas coast ceramics—Goose Creek Incised, variety unspecified.

FIGURE 12.5 Upper Texas coast ceramics: a,b,d, Goose Creek Stamped; c,g, Tchefuncte Stamped; e, O'Neal Plain, variety Conway (holes show where nodes have broken off); f, sandy paste cord-marked.

Goose Creek Red-Filmed, Variety Unspecified

References Ambler 1967:38; Aten 1967:11–13; Aten and Bollich 1969; Aten *et al.* 1976:26.

Distinguishing characteristics The paste, form and surface treatment of this type are identical to those described for Goose Creek Plain, variety unspecified. Occasionally, sherds are found which have been incised. A finely powdered red mineral pigment has been applied to the exterior (and occasionally to the interior) vessel surface; this film easily can be worn or washed off the sherd. As a result, sherds of this type may either be overlooked or be identified only during microscopic inspection from traces of pigment in cracks on the sherd surface. Care should be taken not to confuse this red mineral film with red surfaces on highly oxidized sherds. The difference can be determined by observing whether the red color of the surface grades into the browns or black of the interior or, alternatively, whether the film is a sharply defined surface zone about 0.1 mm thick with no color continuity or gradation into the interior.

Distribution on the upper coast   This type occurs frequently in both the Sabine Lake Area and the Galveston Bay Area and extends, in varying proportions, throughout the chronological sequence. It has not been found in the Brazos Delta–West Bay Area; some evidently was present at Addicks (Wheat 1953:185); and only one sherd is known from the Conroe–Livingston Area (Shafer 1968: 49).

"Goose Creek Cord-marked"

Extremely rare sherds with cord-marked design (Figure 12.5) have been encountered on Goose Creek paste in the Clear Lake Period levels of 41 CH 46, both in the 1969 test and by Dillehay (1975:124), as well as 41 HR 82 (O'Brien 1974:53), in what also seems to have been a Clear Lake Period occupation. Other sherds were recovered at the Clear Lake Period Galena Midden (41 HR 61) by E. R. Ring (Texas Archeological Research Laboratory collections).

Mandeville Plain, Variety Unspecified

References   Aten *et al.* 1976:27; Ford and Quimby 1945:62; Phillips 1970:109–110.

Distinguishing characteristics   Paste as described previously for the type Goose Creek Plain; principal additional characteristics are contorted paste texture, poor coil wedging, and irregular surfaces, often with the diagonal ridge and furrow treatment described for Tchefuncte Plain, which it closely resembles, except for the sandy paste. There is no significant difficulty in distinguishing this type from Goose Creek Plain, provided one adheres to the criterion of Tchefuncte-like paste treatment and surface modeling. This may, at times, result in an intermediate category sharing some Tchefuncte-like and some Goose Creek features. These are separated as the Anahuac variety of Goose Creek. Also see the previous discussion of the relationship among Tchefuncte, Goose Creek, and Mandeville types.

Distribution on the upper coast   Although more abundant in the Sabine Lake Area than in the Galveston Bay Area, Mandeville Plain is common in the Tchefuncte Period and Clear Lake Period assemblages, respectively, of both areas. Stratigraphic test data from the Galveston and Sabine areas indicate that the type attains its greatest frequency subsequent to that of Tchefuncte Plain, a situation paralleled in the Tchefuncte Site (Ford and Quimby 1945). Mandeville Plain has not yet been recognized in the Brazos or Conroe–Livingston areas.

Tchefuncte Plain, Variety Unspecified

References   Aten *et al.* 1976:17–18; Ford and Quimby 1945:52–54; Phillips 1970:162–164; Weaver 1963.

Distinguishing characteristics   Soft untempered paste made of fine clay or silty clay; usually brown to gray in color; may be pockmarked where the surface has spalled; vessel walls are thick, coils are poorly wedged, and texture is contorted; surface frequently has a slick, powdery feel; surface is usually uneven and the exterior of the upper vessel wall often has a "ridge and furrow" appearance extending diagonally downward from the rim. Contrary to the original type description, this pottery is not sherd or "clay" tempered, although random vegetal fibers and small red iron concretions may occur. See references for vessel form characteristics; these do not assist in sorting sherds, however.

Distribution on upper coast   This type is abundant in early ceramic contexts of the Sabine Lake Area although its technological characteristics there have not been intensively studied; it frequently occurs in small quantities in Clear Lake Period sites of the Galveston Bay Area; it has not been recovered from sites beyond the immediate northern and western periphery of Galveston Bay.

Tchefuncte Stamped, Variety Unspecified

References   Same as for Tchefuncte Plain.

Distinguishing characteristics   Paste characteristics are the same as described for Tchefuncte Plain; vertical columns of rocker stamping, executed with a forked tool, extend downward from the rim on the vessel exterior (Figure 12.5).

Distribution on upper coast   The only known occurrence is several sherds from a single vessel found in a Clear Lake Period context at Harris County Boys School. Sherds have been reported previously as Tchefuncte Stamped from Addicks (Wheat 1953:190) and Trinity delta sites (Ambler 1973:87; Shafer 1966:22), but these are now recognized as Goose Creek Stamped.

Tempered Ceramics

O'Neal Plain, Variety Conway

References   Aten *et al.* 1976:16–17; Ford and Quimby 1945:65; Phillips 1970:148.

Distinguishing characteristics Abundant and relatively large sand (medium to coarse-grained) embedded in a silty or clayey matrix with no intermediate grain sizes; may have nodes or bosses around the rim made by punching through the vessel wall while the clay was wet; sometimes the rim will have a row of large perforations if the bosses have been broken off the exterior (Figure 12.5); plain sherds may be mistaken for any of the varieties of Goose Creek Plain described here unless sorting criteria are carefully applied.

Distribution on upper coast This variety is relatively abundant in the Sabine Lake Area; it first appears in the earliest ceramics periods and has some attributes which resemble Tchefuncte pottery (e.g., poor wedging, thick walled, irregular surface treatment) but these ultimately disappear; the variety persists in the Sabine until quite late in prehistory. Small quantities have been recovered in the Galveston Bay Area but temporally are confined to the Clear Lake Period; it has not been reported elsewhere on the upper coast. A more complete description of this variety is being prepared by C. N. Bollich, based on Sabine Lake specimens.

Baytown Plain, Variety San Jacinto (Formerly San Jacinto Plain)

References Ambler 1967:39–42; Aten 1967:13–14; Aten 1971:27; Aten and Bollich 1969; Phillips 1970:47–48; Shafer 1968:47.

Distinguishing characteristics The paste consists of a sandy or silty clay (identical to that of Goose Creek Plain) plus the addition of a quantity of fired clay fragments (grogs) which frequently are recognizable as sherd fragments. Sherd surfaces range widely in color from black to light yellowish browns in the Galveston Bay and Sabine Lake areas, and from browns to reds and orange in the Brazos Delta–West Bay Area. Surfaces are commonly bumpy or fractured around grog fragments and, in the Brazos Delta–West Bay Area, tend to spall off.

Grog-tempering in the San Jacinto variety causes difficulty in identification for two principal reasons. First, the grogs often are sherd fragments made from materials identical to that of the new sherd. When the sherds are heavily smudged, as is often the case in the Galveston Bay Area, or are more or less uniformly fired to a light brownish color as in the Brazos Delta–West Bay Area, careful examination is needed to see the grogs. Second, grogs in this variety rarely are as abundant as in LMV grog-tempered plainwares, that is, in other varieties of Baytown Plain. This is especially true for the Old River Period sherds.

For these reasons, identification of grog-tempering in this variety requires considerable familiarity with the variation of its forms in the study area. This variation has misled many analysts into identifying all sorts of natural inclusions (e.g., concretions, clay "galls," organic material, color "ghosts") as grog and, simultaneously, to overlook many of the actual instances of its occurrence. To begin, these sherds must be studied with the aid of magnification—preferably a binocular microscope set at 10 power magnification. Greater magnification should be avoided because then the paste constituents are viewed at a different order of magnitude and scale from that being searched for in the typological analysis; in other words, one cannot see the forest for the trees. It is essential to examine a freshly broken cross section of each sherd (no matter what type it may be), but the remainder of the specimen should not be ignored. When trying to identify grog-tempering in the San Jacinto variety, it often is necessary to examine the whole sherd looking for clues to its presence. The entire surface of the sherd should be examined, including the fresh break, for signs of any inclusions which may be lighter in color than the surrounding matrix. If found, these inclusions should be carefully studied to see whether the color boundary is sharp and distinct, or is gradational, the latter indicating something other than grog. When the surface of the sherd has been floated, star-like fractures radiating away from a central point often give away the presence of a grog fragment underneath. Likewise a bumpy surface, with the bumps about a centimeter or so apart, may indicate grogs. The clay covering the top of such bumps frequently spalls off leaving tiny craters (about 1–2 mm in diameter) with the grog fragment exposed in the bottom.

Many times there will be no surface indication of grog-tempering, or the indications may be equivocal. On these occasions one must rely upon careful examination of the freshly broken cross section. If grog fragments are not immediately obvious, look for lineations or surfaces (which sometimes are flat) that show a different orientation than the texture of the clay matrix. Also look for light color against a darker background, and particles with texture substantially different from the clay matrix. Shrinkage of the matrix away from grogs will sometimes create hairline gaps outlining part of the grog fragment; occasionally the suspected grog fragment may be loose and may even fall out of the broken surface. In very rare instances, a grog fragment will be seen with a flat surface which has red-filming or an incised line on it. Considerable experience in identification should first be obtained before attempting to classify sherds of this kind for publication and use by other workers.

Distribution on the upper coast   Although detailed stratigraphic data are not available for the entire Sabine Lake chronology, this variety occurs in almost every collection known from that area. It was abundantly present in the pimple-mound site stratigraphic test (41 JF 31), an early ceramic context which also contained Tchefuncte and Marksville-like sherds (Aten and Bollich 1981). Consequently, it seems safe to assume its presence in the Sabine throughout nearly the entire ceramic chronology.

This is in substantial contrast to the Galveston Bay Area, where the variety is the marker for the beginning of the Round Lake Period. By the end of the Old River Period, the San Jacinto variety is virtually absent. Because of the substantial displacement of this variety at the end of the Round Lake Period by the short-lived intrusion of the Phoenix Lake variety, it may be that the San Jacinto variety ultimately can be reorganized into early and late varieties. Before that can come about, however, reasonable control should be acquired over sorting criteria between the San Jacinto and the Phoenix Lake varieties. This is a major unsolved methodological problem at the present time and is the reason these varieties of Baytown Plain are not distinguished in the ceramic seriation and the artifact frequency tables.

Although not as abundant as in the Galveston Bay Area, the San Jacinto variety is prominent in seriation of the Brazos Delta–West Bay Area and has a pattern similar to that in the Galveston Bay chronology. The variety is even less abundant in the Conroe–Livingston Area but has a roughly similar position in the seriation to that in the Brazos and in Galveston Bay.

Baytown Plain, Variety Phoenix Lake

References Ambler 1970:22–23; Aten and Bollich 1969; Phillips 1970:47–48.

Distinguishing characteristics In its simplest form, this variety has a very fine clay matrix containing abundant, readily observable grog fragments which do not present the identification problems previously described for the San Jacinto variety. Some sherds have a polished surface finish; rim and base forms tend to differ from those normally found on the upper coast. Attempts, up to this time, to sort sherd collections into these two varieties have been frustrated by low replicability and a large undistributed middle class (see Aten and Bollich [1969] for a discussion of this problem in the Sabine Lake Area). Consequently, sherds have not been sorted for this study according to these varieties in any of the upper coast areas. On the other hand, their existence cannot be ignored; they seem to have significant historical implications in at least the Sabine and the Galveston Bay areas.

Distribution on the upper coast This variety is common throughout the Sabine Lake Area ceramic seriation and is especially well represented at the Phoenix Lake Site (16 CU 104) after which it is named. In the Galveston Bay Area, the variety is known only in sites dating from the late Round Lake Period through the early Old River Period. This coincides with the maximum popularity of grog-tempering on the coast. Sherds of this variety have not been recognized in the Brazos or Conroe–Livingston areas.

San Jacinto Incised, Variety Jamison

References Ambler 1967:39–42; Aten 1967:14; Aten 1971:29; Aten and Bollich 1969.

Distinguishing characteristics   This variety classified those sherds which have the grog-tempered sandy paste described for Baytown Plain, variety San Jacinto, and which were formerly known simply as San Jacinto Incised. It is named here after the site from which it was first described in detail.

When one takes a comprehensive view of the design styles which appear on San Jacinto Incised in the Galveston Bay Area, it is possible to recognize three vague but sequential design style assemblages (Figure 12.3). The first is coincident with the Round Lake Period and is characterized by zoned designs in addition to the usual sets of horizontal lines, punctations, and grid motifs—that is to say, designs in which a border of parallel or triangular lines is filled with punctations or hatchuring. The next assemblage occurs during the early Old River Period, coincident with the presence of the Spindletop variety, and consists primarily of sets of horizontal lines. The last design style assemblage coincides with the remainder of the Old River Period; this ceramic type is not clearly known to have been associated with the Orcoquisac Period. The zoned designs are less evident while diagonals, cross-hatching, reed-like punctations, excised or engraved panels, and pendant triangles all seem notably in imitation of Coles Creek and Plaquemine Period design motifs in the Lower Mississippi Valley (LMV). These design assemblages may provide the basis for further subdivision of this type into other varieties. Selected examples are shown in Figure 12.6.

Distribution on the upper coast   This variety is abundant in the Sabine Lake Area throughout the local ceramic sequence; common in the Galveston Bay Area during the Round Lake and Old River periods; rare in the Brazos Delta–West Bay Area; and essentially is absent in the Conroe–Livingston Area.

San Jacinto Incised, Variety Spindletop

References   None.

Distinguishing characteristics   Paste characteristics are the same as for the Phoenix Lake variety of Baytown Plain. Insofar as is now known, the design motifs are the same as many of those described in Figure 12.3 for San Jacinto Incised.

Distribution on the upper coast   This variety is abundant in the Sabine Lake Area throughout the ceramic sequence and is present in the Galveston Bay Area only during the late Round Lake and early Old River period. It is unknown in the Brazos or Conroe–Livingston areas.

Grog-tempered red-filmed

Ambler (1970:23) reported a single red-filmed sherd on a grog-tempered (Baytown Plain, variety San Jacinto) paste from 41 CH 103 in the Trinity delta;

0   3

cm

FIGURE 12.6 Upper Texas coast ceramics—San Jacinto Incised, variety Jamison.

this is the only known occurrence on the upper coast of red-filming on grog-tempered paste, although it is quite common in the Lower Mississippi Valley.

Bone-tempered plain and incised (descriptive category)

References   Ambler 1970:23; Aten 1967:15; Aten 1971:29–30; Tunnell and Ambler 1967.

Distinguishing characteristics   The paste and appearance of bone-tempered sherds are very similar to the Goose Creek paste with the addition of 5–25% bone fragments; sherd color is more uniform than Goose Creek and tends predominantly to be brown to reddish brown. The rare incised sherds have simple straight line geometric design styles similar to Goose Creek and San Jacinto Incised.

Distribution on the upper coast   This category is exceedingly rare in the Sabine Lake Area; it attains a minor frequency in the early Round Lake and post-Round Lake periods of the Galveston Bay Area; and it becomes modestly abundant in both the Brazos Delta–West Bay Area and the Conroe–Livingston Area. In the excavated sequence from site 41 FB 11, located on the Brazos River (Figure 11.1) immediately north and west of the areas being studied here, bone-tempered ceramics are more abundant and proportionately more significant than on the upper coast (also see Fritz 1975). Clearly, this class is associated with technological developments northwest of the upper coast rather than to the east, as are most of the ceramics (cf. Figure 15.1). Ambler (1970:23–24) proposed that bone-tempered plainware in the Trinity delta sites be named Orcoquizac Plain. This may be valid but the old problem of unequivocal sorting criteria reenters the picture. How is Orcoquizac Plain to be differentiated from other bone-tempered plainwares which occur with increasing abundance to the west? If there are none, then the type Leon Plain (Suhm *et al.* 1954:386–388) has priority with Orcoquizac perhaps as a local variety. Bone-tempered pottery classification is a problem to be solved elsewhere than on the upper Texas coast (Aten 1971:30).

Miscellaneous Ceramics

Shell "tempering"

Rarely, sherds have been found which are reported as shell-tempered. In most cases this "temper" appears to be tiny fragments of *Rangia* shell (usually grayish, equant-shaped and sugary-textured fragments); these probably are fortuitous inclusions and they have not been used as a basis for analysis. Also, a number of the Goose Creek Plain, variety unspecified sherds from the Jamaica Beach Site (41 GV 5) contain fragments of small gastropod shells; similar findings were made by Story (1968:15 ff.) at the Ingleside Cove Site.

Riveted Handle

One of these was recovered from 41 CH 110: 20–30 (late Old River Period). This is characteristic of Rockport and Goliad ceramics of the central coast (Campbell 1962:332, 334).

CHAPTER 13

Nonceramic Artifacts

In this chapter, the remainder of the artifacts are described from the test excavations used to develop the upper coast local chronologies. Although these artifacts do not incorporate the full range of technology known from the upper coast, the differences are largely in stylistic characteristics rather than in functional type. The nonceramic technology described in this chapter is a fair cross section of that used in the coastal zone during the Late Archaic and Late Prehistoric–Woodland. Principally missing are some of the bone and shell industries and many items of either personal equipment or ritual–gaming equipment, most of which are known primarily from mortuary contexts which are not included in this volume. Also included at the end of this chapter is a brief discussion about the status of functional classification and analysis of upper coast technology.

LITHIC ARTIFACTS

Arrow Points

Casual inspection of stone tool classifications in the upper coast literature is sufficient to demonstrate that they have been applied in highly idiosyncratic ways, even for well-known, established projectile point types such as Alba, Perdiz, and Catahoula. This may partially account for the increasing occurrence of reports in which each specimen is described on its own without attempting stylistic classification. For this reason, the projectile point styles may not be an especially good unit of analysis for regional culture-historical integration. Alternatively, some studies use stem form as a summarizing device (cf. Johnson 1962; Aten 1967; Aten *et al.* 1976). The classification used here emphasizes this attribute.

Moreover, the common use of small resource cobbles, bipolar flaking, and materials such as silicified wood and quartzite all contributed to a coastal lithic technology in which the boundaries of style were difficult to control and replicate. This is reflected in the irregularly shaped projectile points and other chipped stone tools commonly found in coastal sites. Nevertheless, distinctive styles do occur on the upper coast. The principal defining characteristics of these styles, or types, are listed in the descriptive narrative; specific attributes of each specimen are listed in Table 13.1. The basic source used for descriptions of all established types is Suhm and Jelks (1962); other sources are cited as needed. Perfection is not claimed for the sorting; indeed, separating specimens among such types as Perdiz, Cliffton, and Bassett often involves splitting a fine hair. On the other hand, errors such as classifying contracting stem points with types defined to encompass expanding stem projectile points, as sometimes occurs, are not made.

Of the attributes which have been used, the need to continue reporting length, width, thickness, stem length, and stem width of each specimen is evident. Stem width conveys information about the projectile shaft itself, and all the measurements taken together build a body of data for holistic treatment of the technological implications of the projectile point (cf. Thomas 1978). Because all stone material had to be imported into the coastal area in one manner or another, recording data on kind of material and its color should permit the formulation of some hypotheses about source areas and importation mechanism (also see Appendix B). Unfortunately, some colors were recorded before use of the Munsell color system was adopted, and those specimens are no longer readily available for reexamination. In such cases, the unstandardized verbal color description is given in parentheses. In the following descriptions of projectile points occurring with the local chronology collections, morphology is described by the terminology proposed by Suhm et al (1954:530, Figure 7).

Expanding Stem Forms

Scallorn   Basic reference is Suhm and Jelks (1962:285). Blades are triangular to slightly recurved lateral edges; straight shoulders; stems are expanding with slightly convex bases (Figure 13.1).

Class A-5   Basic reference is Aten (1967:22, Plate 3). Blade is triangular with approximately straight, serrated lateral edges; straight shoulders; stem is either slightly expanding or bulbous (Figure 13.1).

Expanding Stem Fragment   Stem sides are straight with expansion at the base. This is similar to the fairly distinctive stem found on Class A-5, but the blade is badly broken.

Straight Stem Forms

Alba   Basic reference is Suhm and Jelks (1962:263). Blades are triangular with straight to slightly concave lateral edges; wide straight shoulders to slightly

TABLE 13.1

Frequency Distribution and Metric Attributes of Arrow Points from the Galveston Bay and Brazos Delta–West Bay Areas

Provenience	Length	Width	Thickness	Stem length	Max. stem width	Min. stem width[b]	Thin flake[c]	Material	Color no.[d]	Figure
Expanding Stem										
Scallorn										
41 BO 12: 0–10	20.4	12.2	3.8	6.1	9.7[e]	6.2	Yes	Chert	7.5 yr 5/6	13.1 a
41 BO 12: 20–30	17.9	12.3	3.6	6.2	9.8[e]	5.2	Yes	Chert	10 yr 6/3	13.1 b
41 BO 50: Zone 1	23.0[e]	15.5	5.8	6.1	14.0	7.1	Yes	Chert	10 yr 6/3	13.1 c
41 BO 50: Zone 2		12.3	3.1	5.0	9.7	6.9	Yes	Chert	10 yr 7/2	13.1 d
Class A-5										
41 GV 5: 20–30	18.2[e]	13.3[e]	3.0	4.0[e]	6.0[e]	5.5	Yes	Chert	10 yr 7/1	13.1 e
Expanding stem fragment (Class A-5?)										
41 CH 137: 40–50			3.7	7.5	6.6	5.9	No	Chert	10 yr 6/1	13.1 f
Straight Stem										
Alba										
41 CH 46: 0–10	21.0[e]	18.0[e]	5.5	4.5	7.7		No	Silicified wood	10 yr 5/3	13.1 g
41 CH 46: 0–10	27.6[e]	17.8	4.1	4.0	7.3		Yes	Chert	7.5 yr 4/2	13.1 h
41 CH 46: 20–40	19.2	12.8	4.2	6.4	6.8		No	Silicified wood	5 yr 3/3	13.1 i
41 CH 110: 40–50	26.7[e]	22.6	4.8	3.2	5.9		No	Silicified wood	7.5 yr 5/2	13.1 j
Class A-2										
41 CH 31: Zone 1(B)	22.0	20.0[e]	3.0	7.7	7.1		Yes	Chert	10 yr 6/2	13.1 k
41 CH 46: 0–10	50.0[e]	19.5[e]	4.2	4.6	4.8		No	Silicified wood	10 yr 3/2	13.1 m
Straight stem fragment										
41 CH 98: 30–40			2.9	3.5	5.2		No	Quartzite	5 yr 4/3	
Contracting Stem										
Cliffton										
41 CH 31: Zone 1(B)	19.4	18.8	5.4	4.0	6.6		Yes	Silicified wood	10 yr 3/2	13.1 n
41 CH 36: 50–60	18.4	12.8	2.8	2.8	4.9		Yes	Silicified wood	5 yr 3/2	13.1 o
41 CH 36: 100–110	21.4		3.9	4.3	5.5		No	Other[f]	(black)	13.1 p
41 CH 80: 0–10	14.4	11.5	3.5	2.8	5.6		No	Chert	2.5 yr 3/4	13.1 q

41 CH 98: 40–50	14.2	13.2	4.6	2.6	4.4	Yes	Silicified wood	2.5 yr 5/2	13.1 r
41 CH 98: 50–60	15.5	12.3	2.7	2.3	5.3	Yes	Chert	10 yr 5/3	13.1 s
41 CH 106: 0–10	29.0	21.3[c]	4.3	4.1	5.9	No	Chert	10 yr 7/2	13.1 t
Perdiz									
41 CH 31: Zone 3(C)	26.7	16.0	4.6	6.0	6.0	No	Chert	7.5 yr 6/2	13.1 u
41 GV 6	37.4	17.5	4.0	8.1	5.4	No	Chert	(buff)	13.1 v
41 GV 6	34.3	15.9	3.2	9.0	5.2	No	Chert	(buff)	13.1 w
41 GV 6	23.1	14.4	3.2	5.9	5.2	Yes	Chert	(gray brn)	13.1 x
41 GV 6			2.7	7.3	4.3	Yes	Chert	(buff)	13.1 y
41 GV 6	21.4		2.5	5.3	4.7	Yes	Chert	(red brn)	13.1 z
41 LB 4: 0–10	20.5	12.4	4.0	5.3	5.3	Yes	Chert	10 yr 3/3	13.1 aa
Contracting stem fragment									
41 BO 12: 10–20					6.9	Yes	Chert	10 yr 5/2	13.1 bb
41 CH 31: Zone 3(C)			2.3	5.1	6.0		Chert	—[g]	
41 CH 31: Zone 3(C)							Other[h]	2.5 y 6/0	
Blade fragments									
41 BO 12: 30–40						No	Chert	7.5 yr 5/4	
41 CH 24: 0–10							Silicified wood		
41 CH 46: 10–20			2.8			Yes	Silicified wood	10 yr 4/1	
41 CH 98: 0–10						Yes	Silicified wood	10 yr 6/4	
41 CH 98: 30–40			4.4				Silicified wood	(red-brn)	
41 CH 98: 40–50	11.0[e]		2.8		4.2	No	Chert	10 yr 6/1	
41 CH 110: 20–30	16.1		2.7			Yes	Chert	10 yr 5/2	
41 CH 110: 30–40							Chert		
41 GV 6						Yes	Chert	(brn)	
41 GV 6						Yes	Chert	(brn)	
41 LB 4: 0–10			2.4			No	Chert	10 yr 6/2	
41 LB 4: 0–10						Yes	Chert	10 yr 5/3	
41 LB 4: 0–10			2.9			Yes	Chert	—[g]	
Blade fragments (dart points)									
41 GV 6							Chert	(tan)	
41 GV 6							Chert	(tan)	

[a] All measurements are in millimeters.
[b] For expanding stem projectile points only.
[c] Essentially unifacially chipped.
[d] Munsell color number unless color name is given in parentheses.
[e] Measurement is a close estimate.
[f] Ferruginous sandstone.
[g] Thermal alteration precluded determination of original material color.
[h] Milky quartz.

barbed; stems are straight sided with flat bases (Figure 13.1). The specimen illustrated in Figure 13.1(i) may be the most aberrant, but is within the range of variation classified as Alba at the Jamison Site (Aten 1967).

Class A-2   Basic reference is Aten (1967:21, Plate 3). Blades are triangular with straight, concave or convex lateral edges; prominent broad barbs usually with squared tips, but may be rounded; stems are straight sided with flat bases (Figure 13.1). This style and a closely related one with small contracting stem (classed as A-1 in the Jamison Site report) are commonly found on the upper coast and usually have been misclassified as either Alba (cf. Wheat 1953:Plate 35) or Catahoula (cf. McClurkan 1968:Figure 40). The former, however, has more diminutive barbs, and the latter has an expanding stem. The frequency with which this class (and Class A-1) has been found in upper coast sites and the consistency in its form indicate that it likely will be useful as a formal type.

Straight Stem Fragment   This specimen has a short, straight sided stem like many of the straight stemmed types. The blade is so broken, however, that it is recorded here merely to expand data on the distribution of this stem form.

Contracting stem forms

Cliffton   Basic reference is Suhm and Jelks (1962:269). Blades are triangular with straight to convex lateral edges; blades may be irregular and asymmetrical; lateral edges may be serrated; stems are short and contracting to a rounded or pointed base (Figure 13.1).

Perdiz   Basic reference is Suhm and Jelks (1962:283). Blades are triangular and usually have straight, often serrated lateral edges; some lateral edges may be slightly concave or slightly convex; prominent barbs; usually stems are relatively long and contract to a pointed base; occasionally the base is more rounded (Figure 13.1).

Contracting Stem Fragment   The specimen shown in Figure 13.1 (bb) actually is only the beginning stages of a contracting stemmed point which was never completed beyond finishing the stem and one barb. It and the other fragments are included on Table 13.1 to expand the data on the distribution of this stem form.

Blade Fragments   These fragments are unidentifiable and are included in Table 13.1 to expand the data on the occurrence of arrow points and on kinds of stone materials.

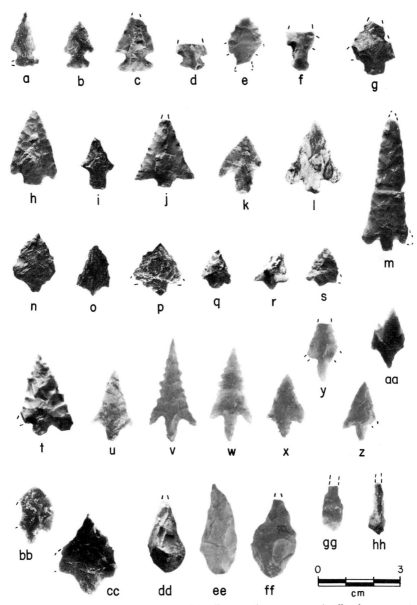

FIGURE 13.1 Chipped stone artifacts. a–d, Scallorn; e–f, type A-5; g–j, Alba; k–m, type A-2; n–t, Cliffton; u–aa, Perdiz; bb, miscellaneous contracting stem; cc, Gary; dd–ff, expanded based perforators; gg–hh, small expanded base drills.

Dart Points

Contracting Stem Forms

Gary   Basic reference is Suhm and Jelks (1962:197). Blade is triangular with irregular but slightly convex lateral edges; straight shoulders; broad contracting stem with rounded base (Figure 13.1). One might argue whether this is a dart point or an arrow point. While the overall size commonly occurs on both kinds of points, the broad stem is more characteristic of dart points. As an experiment, the discriminant functions recently developed by Thomas (1978) were calculated with the result strongly indicating the specimen to be a dart point.

Blade Fragments   These fragments are unidentifiable and are only included in Table 13.1 to extend data on the occurrence of dart points and kinds of stone materials.

Drills and/or Perforators

Objects in this category usually are described as "drills," although evidence for this usage is not always present. Some artifacts having a form suitable for a drill function display the rotary abrasion resulting from use as a drill; others have microflaking at the distal tip which evidently attends use as a perforator; very many specimens, however, have not yet been observed to have wear patterns of any kind (cf. Aten 1967:37–38; Ford and Webb 1956). All artifacts that may belong to either functional class are considered together here because of the present difficulty in separating them.

Several different styles occur in the sites of the upper coast area. Of the styles to be described, the only measurement which it has seemed useful to report is that of the maximum diameter of the bit. The other dimensions are often unavailable, partly because of the usual fragmentary condition of these artifacts; but also, these dimensions are not functionally integrated in the manner of projectile points. Consequently, narrative descriptions of the tool styles are given with tabular data (Table 13.2) confined to bit diameter and material type.

Expanded Base Perforators   These artifacts have relatively large, bulbous proximal ends which taper to the narrow bit end. In many cases, the bulbous end is unmodified from the resource cobble or large flake, with chipping confined to preparation of the bit. The bit of the tool usually is either plano-convex or biconvex in cross section (Figure 13.1).

Small Expanded Base Drill   These artifacts are smaller in a gross sense than expanded base perforators and are made on a flake. The expanded base nar-

TABLE 13.2
Frequency Distribution and Metric Attributes of Drills and Perforators from the Galveston Bay and Brazos Delta–West Bay Areas

	Attributes[a]				
Provenience	Maximum bit diameter	Wear[b]	Material	Color no.	Figure
Expanded base perforator					
41 CH 46: 20–40	4.7	Broken tip	Chert	—[c]	13.1 dd
41 GV 5: 20–30	4.8	Broken tip	Chert	7.5 yr 4/2	
41 GV 6	5.8	No	Chert	(brn)	13.1 ee
41 GV 6	4.8	No	Chert	(brn)	13.1 ff
Small expanded base drill					
41 BO 12: 0–10	4.8	Broken tip	Chert	7.5 yr 6/4	13.1 hh
41 GV 5: 40–50	5.3	Broken tip	Chert	10 yr 4/2	13.1 gg
Bipointed drill					
41 CH 31: Zone 1(A)	9.0	Yes	Chert	10 yr 5/3	13.2 a
41 GV 5: 40–50	4.9	Yes	Chert	10 yr 6/2	13.2 b
41 LB 4: 0–10	4.5	No	Silicified wood	5 yr 3/3	13.2 c
Flat base drill					
41 LB 4: 0–10	5.5	Yes	Chert	2.5 yr 5/2	13.2 d
41 LB 4: 0–10	5.1	Broken tip	Chert	10 yr 6/3	13.2 e
Bit fragments					
41 GV 5: 0–10	5.4	Yes	Chert	10 yr 6/2	
41 GV 5: 10–20	4.4	Yes	Chert	10 yr 6/2	
41 GV 5: 10–20	5.3	Yes	Chert	10 yr 6/2	
41 GV 5: 10–20	4.8	No	Chert	10 yr 6/2	
41 GV 5: 10–20	4.6	No	Chert	10 yr 6/2	
41 GV 5: 10–20	4.5	No	Chert	10 yr 6/2	
41 LB 4: 0–10	5.4	Broken tip	Chert	10 yr 4/2	
41 LB 4: 0–10	5.0	Broken tip	Silicified wood	(gray, brn, white)	
41 LB 4: 0–10	6.3	No	Chert	10 yr 5/2	
41 LB 4: 0–10	5.3	Broken tip	Chert	—[c]	
Microflints					
41 GV 6 (7 specimens)			Chert	(brn, pink)	13.2 F–H

[a]All measurements are in millimeters.
[b]Wear = abrasion facets or surfaces on bit.
[c]Thermal alteration precluded determination of original material color.

rows abruptly to the long, slender bit rather than the gradual taper that is more common on the expanded base perforator. The bits on specimens reported here are plano-convex in cross section (Figure 13.1).

Bipointed Drills   This style of drill is biconvex both in longitudinal and lateral cross section. Usually the proximal end will be less well chipped than the bit end and the bits on some specimens show wear (Figure 13.2).

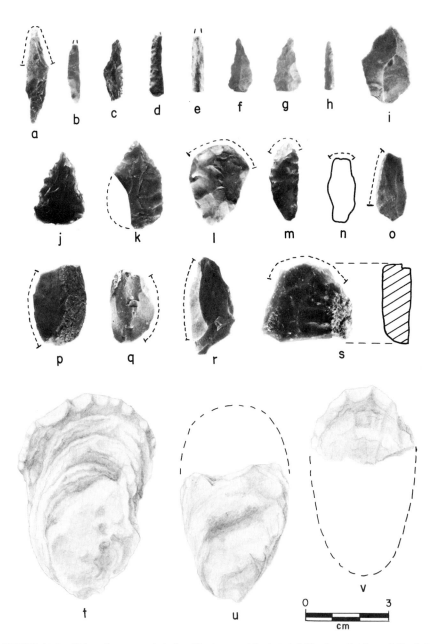

FIGURE 13.2 Chipped stone and shell artifacts. a–c, bipointed drills; d–e, flat base drills; f–h, microflints; i–k, ovoid bifaces; l, ovoid end scraper; m–n, elongate biface endscrapers; o–r, uniface side scrapers; s, uniface end scraper; t, oyster shell scraper; u–v, broken proximal and distal pieces of oyster shell scrapers.

Flat Base Drills These drills are roughly cylindrical in shape with a square or flat base and a rounded distal tip. They are biconvex in cross section and show no variation in dimension as is typical of the other drill and/or perforator styles (Figure 13.2).

Bit Fragments These fragments are indistinguishable as to style and are included here to expand data on bit diameter, wear patterns, and material type.

Microflints Fourteen specimens in the Singing Sands Site collection were described as microflints in much the same technological tradition as those described from the Jamison Site (Aten 1967:37) and from Caplen (Campbell 1957:459–460). Of these, 7 were drill and/or perforator tools and 7 were sidescrapers. Only one of the drills showed abrasion from rotary motion. All were originally made on prismatic chert blades (Figure 13.2). Unfortunately, bit dimensions and material color were not recorded and the collection is not readily accessible.

Other Bifaces

Ovoid Bifaces These artifacts vary from roughly fashioned to well shaped with most effort devoted to making the distal or pointed end. Their shapes range from almost triangular to crudely circular (Figure 13.2), but these specimens and others reported from the upper coast are remarkably consistent in overall dimensions of length, width, and thickness. Although similar in outline to the ovoid end scraper shown in Figure 13.2l, the latter possesses a well-developed bit on the rounded end rather than on the pointed end.

Ovoid End Scraper While similar in outline to the ovoid bifaces described previously, the lengthwise cross section thickens from the pointed end toward the rounded end to form a scraper bit with a bit angle of about 60°. The bit has been resharpened (Figure 13.2).

Elongate End Scrapers These tools tend to be thicker than the previously described bifaces. They vary from lozenge, to lunate, to irregularly rectangular in shape. Both specimens described here show marked abrasion on one end (Figure 13.2).

Biface Fragments These bifacially chipped fragments are unidentifiable as to tool type and are recorded on Table 13.3 to augment the data on distribution of lithic materials.

TABLE 13.3
Frequency Distribution and Metric Attributes of Lithic Unifaces, Bifaces, and Bone Points from the Galveston Bay and Brazos Delta–West Bay Areas

Provenience	Length	Width	Thickness	Material	Color no.	Figure
			Attributes[a]			
Bifaces						
Ovoid bifaces						
41 CH 31: Zone 1(A)	28.3	18.3	5.4	Chert	10 yr 6/2	13.2 i
41 LB 4: 0–10	26.7	19.6	5.2	Chert	5 yr 3/3	13.2 j
41 LB 4: 0–10	31.5	21.4[b]	2.9	Chert	10 yr 4/2	13.2 k
Ovoid end scraper						
41 CH 110: 10–20	29.8	22.1	6.2	Chert	10 yr 6/4	13.2 l
Elongate end scrapers						
41 CH 110: 20–30	28.9	11.0	5.9	Chert	10 yr 3/2	13.2 m
41 LB 4: 0–10	23.2	10.4	6.6	Chert	—[c]	13.2 n
Biface fragments						
41 CH 36: 0–10				Other[d]	10 r 5/4	
41 CH 98: 0–10				Chert	10 yr 3/2	
41 LB 4: 0–10				Chert	10 yr 6/2	
41 LB 4: 0–10				Chert	10 yr 6/2	
Unifaces						
Side scrapers						
41 CH 31: Zone 1(B)	25.4	12.3	3.8	Chert	10 yr 6/3	13.2 o
41 CH 98: 0–10	28.2	20.9		Chert	10 yr 5/2	13.2 p
41 CH 98: 0–10	21.5	17.2		Chert	10 yr 5/2	
41 GV 6 (3 specimens)				Chert	(gray, buff, red-brn)	
41 LB 4: 0–10	27.9	17.7		Chert	10 yr 6/4	13.2 q
41 LB 4: 0–10	37.0	17.2		Chert	10 yr 5/2	13.2 r
End scraper						
41 CH 31: Zone 3	36.7	27.7	11.0	Chert	10 yr 5/2	13.2 s
Ovoid end scraper						
41 BO 4	28.0	18.0	4.9	Chert	10 yr 6/2	13.3 a
Round uniface tools						
41 CH 46: 0–10	18.2	16.4	6.5	Quartzite	—[c]	
41 CH 46: 0–10	18.9	18.2	6.1	Quartzite	—[c]	13.3 b
41 GV 6 (2 specimens)				Chert	(gray brn)	13.3 c
Bone Projectile Points						
41 BO 50: Zone 1	35.3	7.4				13.3 f
41 CH 24: 0–10	32.3	6.8				
41 CH 24: 10–20	55.6	11.2				13.3 e
41 CH 36: 20–30	37.8	6.9				13.3 g
41 CH 36: 180–190	28.5	8.0				13.3 h

[a]All measurements are in millimeters.
[b]Measurement is a close estimate.
[c]Thermal alteration precluded determination of original material color.
[d]Quartz.

Unifaces

Side Scrapers These tools are irregularly elongate flakes. They rarely are shaped more than is necessary to present an approximtely straight side-edge for cutting or scraping (Figure 13.2).

End Scraper This tool is made on a plano-convex secondary cortex flake. The bit end was apparently resharpened several times through removal of marginal retouch flakes; the bit angle is approximately 90°. Although no evidence of wear was seen on the proximal end, this tool must have been hafted to be functional (Figure 13.2).

Ovoid End Scraper Similar in most aspects of form to that previously described as bifacial ovoid end scrapers, this tool is unifacially chipped, a distinction which may not be worth maintaining (Figure 13.3).

Round Uniface and/or Biface Tools Specimens such as these help us to remain humble about the rationale used for artifact classification. The two specimens from 41 CH 46 are both from the same excavation unit, were made from the same resource cobble, and are almost identical in shape. Yet, one is unifacially chipped and the other is bifacially chipped (Figure 13.3). They both are listed here in order to keep them together; they could have been listed under bifaces with equal logic (or illogic). In any event, more or less round to elliptical uniface and biface tools are relatively common in the Galveston Bay Area. It may very well be that the common separation of tools into uniface and biface kinds does not always serve a useful purpose. It certainly is true that many of the gross shapes are duplicated in both groups. Indeed, many of the arrow points on the upper coast are essentially unifaces.

Utilized Flakes These are flakes which are not further modified except for irregular marginal "nibbling" presumably resulting from use.

Other Lithic Material

Chipping Debris As has been pointed out previously, natural outcrops of materials for the manufacture of chipped stone tools do not occur in the coastal zone. However, because the distribution of these tools and chipping debris is so intimately bound up with the activities of the aboriginal inhabitants, all the products and waste of this industry should be considered carefully, meager though they may be in quantity, when compared to many areas of the interior.

A major source of chippage specimens has been the $\frac{1}{16}$-inch (1½-mm) mesh window screens used primarily for collecting small faunal remains. Although

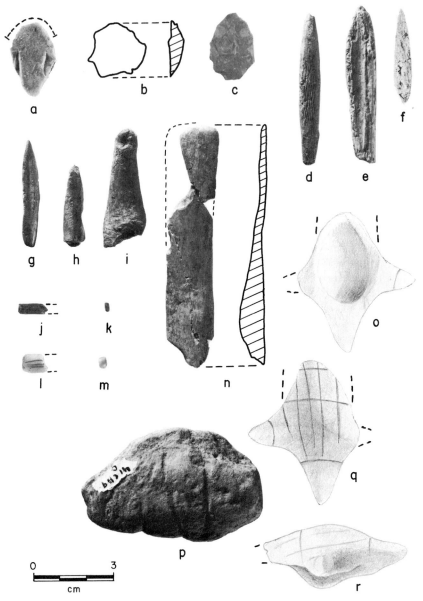

FIGURE 13.3 Other lithic, bone, ceramic, and glass artifacts. a, ovoid unifacial end scraper;
b–c, round uniface/biface tools; d, bone gorge (?); e–h, bone projectile points; i, socketed blunt
point; n, bone spatula; j–m, European glass trade beads; p, sandstone net weight; o, q, r, ceramic
turtle effigy (ventral, dorsal, and lateral views).

TABLE 13.4
Frequency Distribution and Attributes of Lithic Flakes from the Galveston Bay and Brazos Delta–West Bay Areas

Provenience	Initial cortex	Secondary cortex	Single facet	Multiple facet	Other	Flake fragments	Total	Chert	Silicified wood	Quartzite
41 BO 4			5	17	6	23	51	51		
41 BO 12 (1/4-inch screen sample only)										
0–10	1	3	2	5	1	7	19	19		
10–20	1		3	2		6	12	12		
20–30		2	3	3		4	12	12		
30–40		3		2		4	9	9		
41 BO 50										
Zone 1		7	11	16	3	23	60	60		
Zone 2		3	6	17	5	24	55	55		
41 CH 24		1	1	3	1	5	11	6	4	1
41 CH 36										
0–10		1		3	1	6	11	9	1	1
10–20			2			1	3	2	1	
20–30						1	1		1	
30–40		1				3	4	2		2
40–50						1	1	1		
80–90						1	1		1	
90–100						1	1	1		
100–110		1				3	4	3	1	
110–120		1		2		6	9	4	4	1
120–130	1						1	1		
130–140				1		1	2		2	
150–160			1				1	1		
160–170				1			1		1	
180–190		1					1	1		
41 CH 46										
0–10	3	3				4	10	5	2	3
10–20					1	2	3	2	1	
20–40		1					1	1		
41 CH 80										
0–10						2	2	2		
41 CH 87										
80–90		1					1		1	
41 CH 98										
0–10	1	4	5	10	2	19	41	38	3	

(*continued*)

TABLE 13.4   (*Continued*)

Provenience	Initial cortex	Second-ary cortex	Single facet	Multiple facet	Other	Flake fragments	Total	Chert	Silici-fied wood	Quartzite
			Interior							
			Lipped							
						Flake types		**Flake materials**		
10–20		1	1			9	11	2	8	1
20–30						1	1		1	
30–40	3	8	1	1	1	15	29	17	11	1
40–50	3	6	2	5	2	11	29	13	15	1
50–60		4		1		1	6	5	1	
60–80	1	1	1	4	1	7	15	12	3	
80–90					1	3	4	4		
41 CH 106										
0–10	1	2	2	2		14	21	11	9	1
10–20		2	4	2		5	13	7	6	
20–30		1			1	3	5	3	2	
30–40			1				1		1	
41 CH 110										
(1969 test)										
0–10				6[a]	6	4	16	16		
10–20	1	4		3[a]	2	3	13	9	4	
20–30	2	7		16[a]	11	15	51	41	10	
30–40		2		4[a]	1	8	15	15		
40–50		1				1	2	2		
41 CH 137										
20–30		1					1	1		
41 CH 169										
Surface						3	3	2	1	
10–20	1					3	4	2	1	1
41 FB 11										
(1/4-inch screen sample only)										
0–10	10	38		26[a]	17	95	186	186		
10–20	9	73		36[a]	27	144	289	289		
20–30	7	35		18[a]	8	41	109	109		
30–40	1	17		20[a]	4	19	61	61		
41 GV 5										
0–10	1	4	1	14	5	29	54	54		
10–20		5	8	30	3	44	90	90		
20–30		2	10	19		30	61	61		
30–40		2	2	3		7	14	14		
40–50			2	1		7	10	10		
41 GV 6 (types not recorded)								295	6	7
41 LB 4										
0–15	9	48	45	85	33	195	415	295	119	1

[a] Not separated into single and multiple facet types.

260

TABLE 13.5
Material Type of Pebbles (Gastroliths) from the Galveston Bay and Brazos Delta–West Bay Areas

Provenience	Material type			
	Chert	Quartzite	Silicified wood	Quartz
41 CH 24				
0–10			1	
41 CH 36				
20–30			1	
40–50	2		1	
50–60		1	1	
60–70	1			
90–100	1	1		
100–110	3	1	5	
110–120	2		1	
120–130	2	1	2	
130–140	1		1	
140–150	1			1
150–160	4		1	4
160–170	8	1	1	1
170–180	4		2	1
180–190	3		1	1
41 CH 46				
0–10	2		1	
10–20	1			
50–60	1			
41 CH 80				
0–10	1			
41 CH 87				
0–10	1			
41 CH 98				
20–30	3		1	
30–40	1			1
50–60		1		
60–70	1		1	
41 CH 106				
Surface			1	
0–10	1		1	
41 CH 110				
10–20	2			
40–50	1			
41 CH 169				
0–10			1	
41 LB 4				
0–10			1	

these flakes are very tiny, are inconvenient to handle, and require a binocular microscope set at low power (10×) for proper examination, they have provided almost the only data on the local chipped stone industry.

With a little practice and adjustment, it is a simple enough task to identify rock and mineral types and to sort the flakes into their various types. One concession made to the small flake size was not to attempt determination of Munsell color value; this was done only on tools and larger flakes. The flake types occurring in samples of such small flakes proved to be about the same as have been described from collections of larger specimens. Conceivably, the relative frequency of initial cortex flakes might be reduced and that of flake fragments might be increased, but controlled experiment has not been done to determine this. In any event, the fine screen sample was used to augment whatever was recovered (usually very little) in the ¼-inch (6-mm) mesh screen.

The flake classification used was the same used in previous upper coast studies (Aten 1971; Aten *et al.* 1976). Frequency distributions of all flakes recovered are listed in Table 13.4. Further discussion of the significance of this chipping debris is included in Chapter 15 on Technological History.

BONE ARTIFACTS

Bone Gorge(?) This is a bipointed tool made from a smoothed catfish spine from 41 CH 36, level 3. It is estimated to have been about 57 mm long and has a maximum width of 8 mm (Figure 13.3d).

Bone Projectile Points These are all points made from thick-walled, large mammal bone. They have solid bases for hafting and are not socketed (Figure 13.3e–h).

Socketed Blunt Points These particular specimens are both made from deer phalanges by cutting a socket at the proximal end and by grinding flat the distal articular facets. Both specimens have asphalt adhering to the interior of the socket portion. The 41 CH 87: 40–50-cm specimen (Figure 13.3i) is 43.6 mm long and the minimum diameter of the socket is 6.2 mm. The 41 CH 98: 80–90-cm specimen is broken so that its maximum length cannot be measured, although it probably was comparable to the 41 CH 87 specimen. The minimum diameter of the socket is estimated to have been between 6 and 6.5 mm. These specimens are quite blunt and probably are incapable of penetrating anything in normal usage. The 41 CH 87 specimen dates to the early Turtle Bay Period; the 41 CH 98 specimen is from the Mayes Island Period. The only comparable specimens known that are from dated contexts are a similarly proportioned point made of antler found at 41 HR 85 in late preceramic deposits of Analysis Unit 5 (Aten *et al.* 1976:40), and another from Tchefuncte Period refuse at 41 JF 31 in the Sabine Lake Area (Aten and Bollich, unpublished data 1971).

Dyer (1917:5) reported that the early nineteenth-century Lake Charles Atakapa used small, blunt arrows to kill birds to prevent blood from staining the feathers, which were in demand as an exchange item. The upper coast specimens all data to the first millennium A.D. Elsewhere many such points are made of wood (Mason 1893:Plate LIV), which may account for the absence of later-occurring specimens on the upper coast. It also may be significant, from the standpoint of whether feathers were included in coastal exchange with inland groups, that no such points have been recovered west of the Galveston Bay Area.

Bone Spatula   This unique tool, unlike any other from the upper coast, is made on a splinter of thick-walled large mammal bone. Except for the extreme proximal end, the tool has been well formed and smoothed. It is from 41 CH 36, Level 4, is 85.8 mm long, and has a maximum width of 17.7 mm (Figure 13.3n).

Incised Bone Fragments   These are two very small fragments of incised bone artifacts made on a narrow diameter, thin-walled (bird?) bone which was relatively fragile. Both are from 41 BO 50 with one each from Zones 1 and 2.

Blunt Antler Tines   These may or may not be tools; they show no recognizable modification in the form of cuts, scrapes, abrasion, etc. The blunt ends are suggestive of having been used as flaking tools. One specimen comes from level 9 of 41 CH 46, and one each from Levels 3 and 8 of 41 CH 98.

Deer Ulna Tool   While more or less similar to ulna awls, this specimen from 41 BO 12: 10–20 cm has been splintered and worn on the tip and does not have the well-formed point or spatula of those described from Harris County Boys School (Aten *et al.* 1976:40).

Grooved and Snapped Deer Metapodial Articulation   This is an adult deer distal metapodial articulation that has been cut or ground through the cortex around the epiphyseal region and then snapped off from the shaft of the bone. One specimen from 41 CH 98: 80–90 cm is identical to that illustrated in Aten (1971).

Grooved and Snapped Turkey Humerus   This turkey (*Meleagris gallopavo*) distal humerus section was cut and ground through the shaft, about 7 cm from distal end, and then snapped off the remainder of the bone. One specimen from 41 BO 50, Zone 2, is very similar in character to the metapodial described in the preceding paragraph.

These articulations are probably residue from the manufacture of bone tools.

Considering the types of bone artifacts known from the upper Texas coast, the most likely implement represented by the deer metapodials is the "socketed bone point." The turkey humerus also may represent such an implement but none have yet been found, whereas a number made from deer bone are known. The 41 CH 98 specimen dates to a Mayes Island Period zone; the 41 BO 50 specimen dates to a ceramic period equivalent to a pre-Round Lake time period. Other deer metapodials have been found at 41 BO 35 in the preceramic zone (Aten 1971:43–44), 41 HR 85 in Mayes Island Period refuse of Analysis Unit 2 (Aten *et al.* 1976:41), and 41 CH 46 (Dillehay 1975:131) in either a Mayes Island or Clear Lake Period zone. In addition, socketed bone (metapodial) points have been found at 41 HR 50 (Ambler 1967:54) in probable Mayes Island Period refuse, 41 HR 80 and 85 in Mayes Island and Clear Lake Period refuse (Aten *et al.* 1976:39), 41 CH 13 from preceramic levels (Ambler 1973:102), and 41 BO 35 from the early ceramic Zone 3 (Aten 1971:41–43). All occurrences indicate that use of socketed bone points (both the piercement and the blunt types) ended more or less with the introduction of the bow and arrow at the end of the Mayes Island Period.

Tool-Making Residue   This specimen is a splinter from a thick-walled bone of a large mammal. It had been scraped and smoothed, grooved, and the implement snapped off much like the bone point from 41 CH 36, level 19 (Figure 13.3h). It is mentioned here to aid documentation of this type of bone tool technology. This specimen is from 41 CH 98, Level 2.

Bone Tool Fragments   These are unidentifiable worked bone fragments recorded to document the occurrence of this technology. One specimen was found in each of the following proveniences: 41 CH 24, Level 2; 41 CH 31, Zone 1(B); 41 CH 36, Levels 5, 15, and 17; 41 CH 98, Level 5; 41 CH 110, Level 5; and 41 CH 137, Level 13.

SHELL ARTIFACTS

Oyster Shell Cutting Implements   These are oyster shells of widely ranging size which show considerable wear around the ventral margin of the upper (or right) valve. They apparently were used as cutting and scraping tools. Most evidence of use is confined to the edge and outer surface of the ventral edge of the shell. The irregular exterior surface of the shell usually has been smoothed either as a step in preparing it for use as a tool, or as a consequence of such use. Larger specimens may have heavily battered and splintered margins as if they had been used for heavy-duty chopping. Naturally abraded shells usually show intensive smoothing over their entire surface and cannot be confused with the wear which occurs on these tools.

Several of the oyster shell tools have been broken either diagonally to the long axis of the valve or perpendicular to the long axis, apparently as a normally occurring result of their use. Because of this, specimens may be recovered either whole, with ventral edges broken off, or as the broken ventral edges; these are illustrated in Figure 13.2t–v. Many of the broken valves were continued in use as their broken edges show additional wear.

There have been 27 specimens recovered from 41 BO 4; 5 specimens from Level 2, and 3 specimens from Level 3 of 41 BO 12; and 1 specimen from 41 BO 50, Zone 2. In addition, a single specimen was reported from Zone 3B of 41 BO 35 (Aten 1971:44). J. O. Dyer reported that he had several oyster shells used as knives by the Karankawa in lieu of flint (Dyer 1920). These tools are presently the only known kind of shell cutting implements on the upper Texas coast, or on the entire coast save for the shell adzes of the central coast (e.g., Campbell 1947:52–53). Recent excavations at Palmetto Bend Reservoir, near the confluence of the Lavaca and Navidad rivers, have produced additional examples of this kind of shell tool (McGuff 1978).

Among other things, this suggests that the oyster-shell cutting tools may have been one of the coastal items carried into the interior in trade by Cabeza de Vaca (see Part I). Recognition of tools such as this is, of course, dependent to some extent upon the conditions of preservation. Oyster shell is not a material that endures as well as many other kinds of shell and this factor will inhibit their identification in interior sites. On the other hand, the fact that this tool has not yet been recovered from coastal sites east of the Brazos Delta Area probably is notable.

Busycon Fragments The two most complete archaeological *Busycon* species specimens come from 41 GV 6 and consist of columella, spire, and a portion of the whorls. One is partially burned; both were apparently utilized as tools, as the whorl nodes are extensively eroded. In addition, two small specimens were recovered from this site; the columella of one of these is battered from use as a pick-like tool.

Three whorl fragments were also recovered from 41 GV 5 (2 from Level 1 and 1 from Level 2) and another three from 41 GV 6; none of these show any indication of utilization.

Columellas or columella fragments were found more widely. A single fragment (from 41 CH 31, Zone 3) showing much grinding either was functional as is or was to be made into some other object. Two fragments showing no signs of utilization were found at 41 GV 5 (one each in Levels 1 and 2). From 41 GV 6, eight more columellas were collected, five of which show wear at the top from some form of use.

Perforated Rangia Valve This is a large *Rangia cuneata* valve from 41 CH 31, Zone 1(B). It has a hole about 15 mm in diameter punched through from the inside. The edges of the hole are worn; consequently this is not an artifact of the excavation process, as is sometimes the case when picks are used as an excavating tool.

Dinocardium Fragments   These are fragments found inland precluding their occurrence as a residue of food collecting: 41 BO 12, Level 1 (1 specimen); and 41 CH 24, Level 1 (1 specimen).

MISCELLANEOUS ARTIFACTS

Sandstone Fragments   Small fragments of a friable, white, gray, or light tan medium-grained to very fine-grained sandstone occur commonly at sites throughout the upper coast. Often these will have smooth, flat facets indicating some use as a grinding or abrading tool. In the 41 BO 12 collections, one specimen was found in level 1 and four specimens in Level 2; one specimen each in Levels 1 and 7 of 41 CH 46; Levels 2, 6, and 7 of 41 CH 98; level 1 of 41 CH 169; four specimens in Level 1 of 41 LB 4; and four fragments in the collection from 41 GV 6. Also from 41 GV 6, there is a flat, more or less circular (about 33 mm in diameter) specimen with a hole about 10 mm in diameter drilled near the center.

There are some more complete specimens from the area which indicate what these artifacts once may have been. Ambler (1973:98) illustrated one from 41 CH 16 which had been bifacially chipped and had the form of a large chopping tool. Also, in an as yet unreported collection (housed at the Texas Archeological Research Laboratory) made after site 41 CH 9 was damaged by shell removal operations, a small metate-like specimen only 1.5 cm thick and about 10 cm in diameter was collected. An ovoid-shaped piece was found at the same site bearing narrow grooves around the middle as if they had been worn in the sandstone by cordage wrapped and tied around the midsection (see sandstone net weight, Figure 13.3p). Other pieces were even smaller but had smooth, convex surfaces suggestive of small manos.

Pumice Abrader   Fragments of a pumice abrader were recovered from Levels 1 and 2 of 41 GV 5. This artifact is a pale brown pumice with quartz phenocrysts that was shaped into a more or less plano-convex shape with a large concavity in the middle of the planar surface.

An irregular fragment of a dark gray pumice without phenocrysts was recovered from Level 2 of 41 GV 5. There is no indication of shape on this specimen. There also were four large (30 to 50 mm diameter) irregular pumice fragments collected at 41 GV 6.

Mudstone Abrader   One fragment of mudstone (26 by 17 by 14 mm) that has a very flat surface on one side was recovered from level 2 of 41 GV 5; this appears to have been made flat for a purpose or to have become flat through use. Its original size is unknown. The mudstone is pink (5YR 7/3) and is of the type that occurs commonly in the Galveston Bay Area as it forms the substrate for oyster reefs. In this manner, it was frequently collected by Indians incidental to collecting oysters for food; see Aten *et al.* (1976).

Slate   Two fragments of a dark gray slate about 30 mm long by 20 mm wide were recovered from levels 3 and 4 at 41 GV 5. There are no signs of form or function.

Vein Quartz Cobble Fragment   A fragment of a stream-worn cobble of vein quartz measuring about 17 by 16 by 9 mm was recovered from Level 3 of 41 GV 5; there is no indication of use.

Quartzite Cobble Fragments   Nine fragments of a quartzite cobble were recovered from 41 LB 4. The quartzite consists of very large, clear quartz grains that are not well joined together. Consequently the cobble comes apart easily and it is not now possible to determine the original size or form.

Pigment Stone   This is a fragment of a more or less cigar-shaped iron concretion recovered from Level 5 of 41 GV 5. It consists of sand cemented by an earthy brownish yellow (10YR 6/8) limonite and may have been used to prepare yellow pigment. The specimen now is 33 by 25 by 46 mm in size. Similar specimens were recovered from the Caplen Site (Campbell 1956).

Red Ochre   Several fragments of red ochre were found in Trinity delta sites. Small fragments were recovered from 41 CH 98, Levels 5 and 7, and from 41 LB 4, Level 1. A large piece (26 by 13 mm) was recovered from 41 CH 137, Level 3.

Asphalt   Lumps of asphalt, usually not larger than about 4 cm in diameter, are occasionally found on sites throughout the upper coast. Among those sites reported here, it was found at 41 CH 36, 41 GV 5, 41 GV 6, and 41 LB 4. It occurs so frequently both in lump form and as adhesive residue on lithic and bone projectile points, broken sandstone weights, compound bone fishhooks, and ceramics that specific citations are unnecessary.

Pointed Wood Stake Fragment   The end of a pointed stick was recovered from Level 7 of 41 CH 98 well below the permanent water table. The original diameter of the stick is estimated to have been about 24 mm. The species of wood has not been identified.

Cordage, Netting   Although there are several artifact types known which imply some form of cordage (e.g., the bow, compound fishhooks, net weights) these do not, by themselves, imply woven cordage made of plant fibers. However, there is direct evidence for plant fiber cordage in the form of rare sherds of cord-impressed pottery (Figure 12.5g) all dating from the Clear Lake Period, namely, the Hunting Bayou Sites collection made by E. R. Ring and now in the Texas Archeological Research Laboratory; 41 HR 82 (O'Brien 1974:53); and 41 CH 46 (Dillehay 1975:124). Also, there is the net-like impression etched on the large *Busycon* shell pendant from Burial 4 at Harris County Boys School Cemetery (Aten *et al.* 1976:43–44). In this case, the pendant was either inside or situated next to a wallet or pouch made from an open, net-like weave. Although no similar materials are reported ethnohistorically, there is evidence from the Galveston Bay Area for a potentially wide range of woven materials.

Ceramic Turtle Effigy   This specimen was collected from site 41 CH 40 by H. H. Hartman of Baytown, Texas who loaned it for study. It appears to be about two-thirds intact and, although the head is missing, it unmistakably is a representation of a turtle (Figure 13.3o,q,r). It is made from a medium-grained sandy clay (similar to that of the uplands Beaumont Formation) that has been fired to a light brown exterior color with a black core. In its fragmentary condition, the specimen is 47 mm long, 39 mm wide, and 19 mm high. It has been modeled into a stylized turtle shape. The back has been incised in imitation of the tail and limb apertures and of sculpturing on the carapace. The significance of this unique specimen, whether as a toy or a fetish, is unclear. However, turtles figure prominently in mythic stories, tradition, mortuary ritual, and subsistence throughout the southeastern United States. In the Galveston Bay Area, they are well documented in mortuary ritual and subsistence. Consequently, this specimen is of interest with respect to the local cognitive framework.

European Glass Trade Beads   A fragment of a dark blue, tube-shaped bead was recovered from 41 CH 110: 0-10 cm (Figure 13.3j). It is 3.7 mm in diameter and is similar to Type 61 of Harris and Harris (1967:145).

A small, white, donut-shaped glass bead was recovered from 41 CH 110: 20-30 cm (Figure 13.3m). It is 3.8 mm in diameter, 3.1 mm in length, and is similar to Type 44 of Harris and Harris (1967:144).

A fragment of a barrel-shaped white glass bead with three longitudinal blue stripes was found in Level 1 of 41 LB 4 (Figure 13.3l). It is 6.8 mm in diameter and is similar to Type 23 of Harris and Harris (1967:141).

A small blue, translucent, donut-shaped glass bead was recovered from Level 1 of 41 LB 4 (Figure 13.3k). It is similar to either Type 48 or Type 80 of Harris and Harris (1967:144 or 147).

FUNCTIONAL CLASSIFICATION

Archaeological investigations on the upper coast may have reached the stage at which a useful functional synthesis of the technology is possible. The physical characteristics of most artifacts now seem to fall into relatively few categories instead of the proliferation of artifact classes which appears upon inspection of the literature. Even the difficult-to-organize lithic knives and scrapers display limits to their stylistic variation.

A model of the local technology and definition of criteria for functional categories are needed (cf. Winters 1969:30 ff.). These categories, when measured against attributes such as site age, location, and season of occupation should yield a patterned differentiation in their distribution. To continue to make hypotheses operational in terms of individual artifact types or styles, while useful for some purposes, often results in poorly structured spatial distributions. This is analogous to subsistence studies in which use of individual species as the basic analytical unit often results in unmanageably "noisy" distributions. This noise, in the case of both subsistence and technology, can be controlled successfully by use of summarizing classes based upon cross-cutting characteristics.

Functional categories are not merely another exercise in classification. They are an essential middle level of technological synthesis necessary to make the transition from focusing on discrete elements of technology (whether as individual artifacts or stylistic classes) to considering native technology as it was integrated with other cultural subsystems. An analysis of upper coast small sites (Aten 1982) shows that individual habitation episodes occurred with identical structure, but very different artifact (ergo, functional) content. The settlement pattern, the annual schedule, and the long-term geographic and cultural development will structure implementation of different activities at the same site, depending upon the location and time of year. It is likely that functional differentiation of the use of space also occurred at various scales. For example, sandstone abraders are likely to be associated with bone tool-making; in the coastal zone, resharpening was likely to have predominated over other stone tool reduction steps; brush weirs were used in the tidal zone of the coast and were impractical in the interior; and dart points generally were absent on the coast but present in the interior.

There is a need now to experiment with and to refine functional categories, and to use them in mapping the occurrence of various kinds of activities, as opposed to mapping artifact occurrences. Just as there has always been a need perceived for typology, there also is a need for a typology of typologies. This is the only way formulation and validation of hierarchically arrayed models of cultural subsystems can evolve. If nothing else, this might force technological studies directed at correlating the dynamics of an activity with physical attributes of the artifacts. For the upper coast, the following archaeologically detectable functional categories are present and would seem to be a useful initial proposal for future organization of evidence of the region's technology.

1. *Fabricating equipment and residues:* Knives, scrapers, drills, perforators, abraders, hammerstones, anvils, flakers, gravers, asphalt, and tool-making residues, principally made of shell, stone, and bone.

2. *Hunting and butchering tools:* Dart and arrow points, socketed bone points, knives, and scrapers made of stone, bone, and shell.
3. *Fishing equipment:* Dart and arrow points, socketed bone points, gorges, fishhooks, nets, and net weights made of stone, bone, shell, and fiber.
4. *Domestic equipment:* Containers, knives, cordage, and spatulae made of ceramics, stone, shell, bone, and fiber.
5. *Personal equipment:* Pendants, beads, bags, pins, and feathers made of glass, shells, teeth, bone, and feathers.
6. *Ritual–game equipment:* Flutes, pendants, dice, rattles, pipes, and effigies made of stone, bone, ceramics, gourds(?), gravel, shell, and ochre. This also would include symbols or surrogates used in mortuary ritual (possibly from medicine bundles) such as stacked *Dinocardium* shells, ground Scotch Bonnet shell filled with hackberry seeds, red ochre, and broken ground stone objects.

CHAPTER 14

Local Chronologies

As was described in the Introduction to Part III, the chronological framework is based on seriation of ceramic types which have been defined primarily for this purpose. For convenience in using this framework to organize and facilitate communication about the local archaeological record, the ceramic ontogenies (Figures 14.1, 14.3, and 14.5) have been divided when possible into series of ceramic chronological periods for each of the areas discussed. These periods are not intended to describe anything more than an assemblage of ceramic types, varieties, or attributes. With them, however, it is possible to map the temporal and spatial distribution of elements of technology, subsistence, settlement, and ritual.

SERIATION

Graphic seriation, augmented by independent methods of verification, has been the principal technique used. Before describing the upper Texas coast local chronologies, it is worth reviewing the application of this technique on the upper coast in relation to the following basic criteria for its effective use (Dunnell 1970:309–311).

All collections being seriated must represent comparable periods of time. This criterion can be difficult to control. The greatest variability can occur in surface collections, but nearly all of these have been eliminated from seriations for the Galveston Bay, Brazos Delta–West Bay, and Conroe–Livingston areas. The seriation of ceramics from the Sabine Lake Area that is used here (from Aten and Bollich 1969) consists entirely of surface collections.

The nature of the excavated sites is more or less similar within each of the other three areas, although it varies between areas. The Conroe–Livingston data come from deeply stratified earth middens; the Brazos Delta–West Bay data are primarily from thin shell middens representing occupations of short duration. The Galveston Bay data have the greatest variety in site type, although the majority of the seriated collections come from the marshlands of the upper

Galveston Bay estuary. Because of the availability and great reliance on shellfish in the marshes, the vertical rate of midden accumulation per unit of time seems to have been more rapid[1] than at upland bluff sites such as Harris County Boys School and the Cedar Bayou sites (Ambler 1967). Temporal comparability in these collections is reasonably well under control because most seriation pattern discontinuities seem to be confined to those classes with few specimens.

All collections being seriated must represent the same cultural tradition. This is another reason for having maintained the separation of data by the four geographic areas. It is also why data was not included on aboriginal ceramics from the excavations at the Presidio San Agustín de Ahumada (Tunnell and Ambler 1967). The essential conformance of the stratigraphically ordered ceramic class ontogenies to a lenticular model confirms the absence of historical discontinuities within the sequence of data.

All collections being seriated must come from the same local area. The localization of the sites in each of the four geographic areas minimizes spatial variations about as much as is practical. Use of generalized, unequivocally sortable ceramic types provides the amount of redundancy between local typological schemes that is necessary for correlation between local chronologies to be possible.

SABINE LAKE AREA

The historical framework for this area remains one of the less well known. Initial formulation of a ceramic chronology was presented by Aten and Bollich (1969). Since that time, Bollich and I have excavated two stratigraphic tests in pimple mound sites (Aten and Bollich 1981) containing early ceramics; analyzed data from the Texas Archeological Society's 1967 field school excavation at the Gaulding Site; and continued to expand surface collections from numerous sites in the area. Also, a large series of *Rangia cuneata* shell seasonality samples has been made. Analysis of these data is incomplete, however.

Despite this, Sabine Lake Area data on ceramic assemblage development still are based on testing and on surface collections which are too generalized at this time to define a time sequence of assemblages, as will be done shortly for the Galveston Bay Area. Because of the relatively frequent occurrence of Lower Mississippi Valley (LMV) ceramics in these collections, the major periods in the

---

[1]Fine-grained variation in rate of Trinity delta shell midden accumulation also seems to be reflected in the three basic site habitats: beachfronts, distributaries, and round lakes. Because of the different character of these habitats, the size of their associated clam beds differs by quantum levels: beachfronts have the highest density; round lakes have the lowest. This difference is reflected in the number and size of sites associated with these habitats and also, presumably, in their rate of accumulation.

TABLE 14.1
Upper Texas Coast Archaeological Radiocarbon Dates

Laboratory number[a]	Site identification	Source[b]	Sample material	Apparent age B.P.[c]	Radiocarbon date[d]	Remarks
Orcoquisac Period						
		Galveston–Trinity Bay Area, Dates Used in Preparation of Figure 14.2				
Tx-458	41 CH 53	Valastro and Davis 1970a; Tunnell and Ambler 1967	*Rangia cuneata*	290 ± 80	A.D. 1887 ± 103	This sample is from a European site of known date (approximately A.D. 1760, Tunnell and Ambler 1967). Tx-458 and the radiocarbon year equivalent of the known date were used in compiling Figure A-1.
Tx-2022	41 CH 110	Gilmore 1974	*Rangia cuneata*	500 ± 60	A.D. 1678 ± 103	
Tx-2023	41 CH 110	Gilmore 1974	*Rangia cuneata*	390 ± 50	A.D. 1787 ± 103	
Tx-2026	41 CH 110	Gilmore 1974	*Rangia cuneata*	410 ± 60	A.D. 1767 ± 103	
Old River Period						
Tx-2024	41 CH 110	Gilmore 1974	*Rangia cuneata*	800 ± 80	A.D. 1379 ± 103	
Tx-2025	41 CH 110	Gilmore 1974	*Rangia cuneata*	760 ± 60	A.D. 1419 ± 103	
Tx-2027	41 CH 110	Gilmore 1974	*Rangia cuneata*	740 ± 70	A.D. 1439 ± 103	
Tx-2029	41 CH 110	Gilmore 1974	*Rangia cuneata*	880 ± 60	A.D. 1300 ± 103	
Tx-2030	41 CH 110	Gilmore 1974	*Rangia cuneata*	560 ± 50	A.D. 1618 ± 103	
Tx-2031	41 CH 110	Gilmore 1974	*Rangia cuneata*	620 ± 60	A.D. 1558 ± 103	
Round Lake Period						
Tx-527	41 CH 20/4	Valastro and Davis 1970a; Aten 1979	*Rangia cuneata*	840 ± 60	A.D. 1339 ± 103	
Tx-528	41 CH 20/5	Valastro and Davis 1970a; Aten 1979	*Rangia cuneata*	820 ± 60	A.D. 1359 ± 103	
Tx-530	41 HR 50/1	Valastro and Davis 1970a; Ambler 1967	*Rangia cuneata*	850 ± 60	A.D. 1328 ± 103	

(continued)

TABLE 14.1 (Continued)

Laboratory number[a]	Site identification	Source[b]	Sample material	Apparent age B.P.[c]	Radiocarbon date[d]	Remarks
Tx-533	41 HR 56/1	Valastro and Davis 1970a; Ambler 1967	*Rangia cuneata*	950 ± 50	A.D. 1230 ± 103	
Tx-534	41 HR 56/2	Valastro and Davis 1970a; Ambler 1967	*Rangia cuneata*	1190 ± 50	A.D. 991 ± 103	
Tx-946A	41 CH 36/3	Valastro et al. 1975; Aten 1979	*Rangia cuneata*	1100 ± 70	A.D. 1081 ± 103[e]	
Tx-946B	41 CH 36/3	Valastro et al. 1975; Aten 1979	Charcoal	720 ± 90	A.D. 1230 ± 90[e]	
Tx-949B	41 CH 46/1	Valastro et al. 1975; Aten 1979	Charcoal	1120 ± 70	A.D. 830 ± 70	
Tx-1051	41 CH 24/3	Valastro et al. 1975; Aten 1979	*Rangia cuneata*	1560 ± 80	A.D. 623 ± 103	This date is from midden overlying channel Stage 3 deposits and agrees with similarly positioned Tx-529, 948, and 1057. There appears to have been Mayes Island Period occupation at this site that was undetected in the ceramics.
Turtle Bay Period						
Tx-529	41 CH 20/6	Valastro and Davis 1970a; Aten 1979	*Rangia cuneata*	1550 ± 60	A.D. 633 ± 103	
Tx-532	41 HR 50/3b	Valastro and Davis 1970a; Ambler 1967	*Rangia cuneata*	1510 ± 60	A.D. 673 ± 103	Ambler associated this sample with preceramic occupation; however, sherds were found at this level.
Tx-947A	41 CH 36/4	Valastro et al. 1975; Aten 1979	*Rangia cuneata*	1300 ± 70	A.D. 882 ± 103[e]	
Tx-947B	41 CH 36/4	Valastro et al. 1975; Aten 1979	Charcoal	1120 ± 110	A.D. 830 ± 110[e]	
Tx-948	41 CH 36/5	Valastro et al. 1975; Aten 1979	*Rangia cuneata*	1470 ± 70	A.D. 713 ± 103	

Sample	Site	Material	Date (B.P.)	Calendar date	Reference	Comments
Tx-968B	41 HR 85/1	*Rangia cuneata*	1500 ± 70	A.D. 683 ± 103	Valastro et al. 1975; Aten et al. 1976	
Tx-1059	41 HR 80/B-1	Human bone	640 ± 130	A.D. 1310 ± 130	Valastro et al. 1975; Aten et al. 1976	Demonstration of association with Turtle Bay Period is only circumstantial; see Aten et al. 1976.
Tx-1060	41 HR 80/B-2	Human bone	2140 ± 380	B.C. 190 ± 380	Valastro et al. 1975; Aten et al. 1976	
Mayes Island Period						
Tx-394	41 CH 16/23	*Rangia cuneata*	1810 ± 90	A.D. 374 ± 103[e]	Valastro and Davis 1970a; Ambler 1973	Ceramic period assignment is based on reevaluation of the associated ceramics.
Tx-402	41 CH 16/23	Charcoal	1400 ± 110	A.D. 550 ± 103[e]	Valastro and Davis 1970a; Ambler 1973	
Tx-535	41 HR 56/3	*Rangia cuneata*	1840 ± 50	A.D. 344 ± 103	Valastro and Davis 1970a; Ambler 1967	Ambler (Valastro and Davis 1970a) considered the cultural context of this date to be preceramic; however, the presence of a few Goose Creek Plain sherds is more consistent with the date.
Tx-949A	41 CH 46/1	*Rangia cuneata*	1740 ± 70	A.D. 444 ± 103	Valastro et al. 1975; Aten 1979	
Tx-951A	41 CH 98/5	Charcoal	1060 ± 90	A.D. 890 ± 90[e]	Valastro et al. 1975; Aten 1979	This shell-charcoal pair agrees internally and was used in compilation of Figure A-1; despite the clear stratigraphic association of dates and ceramics, the ceramics indicate the earlier Mayes Island Period; see Aten (1979) for discussion.
Tx-951B	41 CH 98/5	*Rangia cuneata*	1310 ± 60	A.D. 872 ± 103[e]	Valastro et al. 1975; Aten 1979	
Clear Lake Period						
0-911	41 HR 61/ upper	*Rangia cuneata*	1900 ± 105	A.D. 285 ± 103	Brannon et al. 1957:147–150; King 1961	*Rangia* shells that have been in physical contact with the Beaumont Formation yield abnormally old dates; see Appendix A for discussion.
0-912	41 HR 61/ lower	*Rangia cuneata*	3350 ± 115	—	Brannon et al. 1957:147–150; King 1961	

275

(continued)

TABLE 14.1 (Continued)

Laboratory number[a]	Site identification	Source[b]	Sample material	Apparent age B.P.[c]	Radiocarbon date[d]	Remarks
Tx-342	41 CH 13/10	Valastro and Davis 1970a; Ambler 1973	*Rangia cuneata*	1840 ± 90	A.D. 344 ± 103[e]	
Tx-344	41 CH 13/10	Valastro and Davis 1970a; Ambler 1973	Charcoal	1560 ± 100	A.D. 390 ± 100[e]	
Tx-392	41 CH 16/12	Valastro and Davis 1970a; Ambler 1973	*Rangia cuneata*	2040 ± 90	A.D. 145 ± 103[e]	
Tx-400	41 CH 16/12	Valastro and Davis 1970a; Ambler 1973	Charcoal	1880 ± 90	A.D. 70 ± 90[e]	
Tx-313	41 CH 16/10	Valastro and Davis 1970a; Ambler 1973	*Rangia cuneata*	1890 ± 90	A.D. 295 ± 103[e]	
Tx-401	41 CH 16/10	Valastro and Davis 1970a; Ambler 1973	Charcoal	1780 ± 100	A.D. 170 ± 100[e]	
Preceramic Shell Midden						
Tx-341	41 CH 13/6	Valastro and Davis 1970a; Ambler 1973	*Rangia cuneata*	1990 ± 100	A.D. 195 ± 103[e]	
Tx-343	41 CH 13/6	Valastro and Davis 1970a; Ambler 1973	Charcoal	1890 ± 100	A.D. 60 ± 100[e]	
Tx-345	41 CH 13/8	Valastro and Davis 1970a; Ambler 1973	*Rangia cuneata*	2280 ± 90	B.C. 93 ± 103[e]	
Tx-346	41 CH 13/8	Valastro and Davis 1970a; Ambler 1973	Charcoal	2070 ± 110	B.C. 120 ± 110[e]	
Tx-395	41 CH 16/19	Valastro and Davis 1970a; Ambler 1973	Charcoal	2260 ± 110	B.C. 310 ± 110	
Tx-396	41 CH 16/25	Valastro and Davis 1970a; Ambler 1973	Charcoal	1900 ± 90	A.D. 50 ± 90[e]	
Tx-389	41 CH 16/25	Valastro and Davis 1970a; Ambler 1973	*Rangia cuneata*	2240 ± 90	B.C. 54 ± 90[e]	

Lab no.	Site	Source	Material	Age (B.P.)	Date	Notes
Tx-397	41 CH 16/8	Valastro and Davis 1970a; Ambler 1973	Charcoal	2540 ± 100	B.C. 590 ± 100	This shell-charcoal pair was not used in Figure A-1 because of inversion of age relationship; see Appendix A.
Tx-388	41 CH 16/8	Valastro and Davis 1970a; Ambler 1973	Rangia cuneata	2150 ± 60	A.D. 36 ± 103[e]	
Tx-398	41 CH 16/5	Valastro and Davis 1970a; Ambler 1973	Charcoal	1890 ± 150	A.D. 60 ± 150	
Tx-399	41 CH 16/1	Valastro and Davis 1970a; Ambler 1973	Charcoal	1740 ± 100	A.D. 210 ± 100[e]	
Tx-390	41 CH 16/1	Valastro and Davis 1970a; Ambler 1973	Rangia cuneata	2010 ± 90	A.D. 175 ± 103[e]	
Tx-449	41 CH 16/3	Valastro and Davis 1970a; Ambler 1973	Charcoal	1950 ± 80	A.D. 1 ± 80[e]	
Tx-457	41 CH 16/3	Valastro and Davis 1970a; Ambler 1973	Rangia cuneata	2180 ± 90	A.D. 6 ± 103[e]	
Tx-450	41 CH 16/26	Valastro and Davis 1970a; Ambler 1973	Charcoal	2020 ± 80	B.C. 70 ± 80[e]	
Tx-460	41 CH 16/26	Valastro and Davis 1970a; Ambler 1973	Rangia cuneata	2220 ± 80	B.C. 34 ± 103[e]	
Tx-455	41 CH 16/6	Valastro and Davis 1970a; Ambler 1973	Rangia cuneata	1950 ± 70	A.D. 235 ± 103	This shell-charcoal pair not used in Figure A-1 because of inversion of age relationship; see Appendix A.
Tx-456	41 CH 16/6	Valastro and Davis 1970a; Ambler 1973	Charcoal	2010 ± 90	B.C. 60 ± 90	
Tx-968A	41 HR 85/1	Valastro et al. 1975; Aten et al. 1976	Charcoal	2170 ± 180	B.C. 220 ± 180	See sources for discussion; association is probably preceramic rather than Clear Lake Period
Tx-969	41 HR 85/2	Valastro et al. 1975; Aten et al. 1976	Rangia cuneata	3670 ± 80	B.C. 1476 ± 103	
Tx-1058	41 CH 172/2	Valastro et al. 1975	Rangia cuneata	3270 ± 80	B.C. 1078 ± 103	This sample came from near the base of a totally buried shell midden probed with a shovel test. No ceramics were recovered.

(*continued*)

TABLE 14.1 (Continued)

Laboratory number[a]	Site identification	Source[b]	Sample material	Apparent age B.P.[c]	Radiocarbon date[d]	Remarks
Tx-1113	41 CH 57/1	Valastro et al. 1975	Rangia cuneata	3670 ± 90	B.C. 1476 ± 103	This sample was obtained from testing conducted by W. L. Fullen.
Tx-1892	41 CH 32	Dillehay 1975	Rangia cuneata	2615 ± 110	B.C. 427 ± 103	From top of lower midden.
			Dates not used in preparation of Figure 14.2			
Tx-690	41 GV 10/ upper	Valastro and Davis 1970b	Rangia cuneata	740 ± 70	A.D. 1439 ± 103	Ceramic period association unclear although presence of grog-tempered ceramics indicates occupation in Round Lake Period or later.
Tx-691	41 GV 10/ lower	Valastro and Davis 1970b	Rangia cuneata	2450 ± 70	B.C. 263 ± 103	Association evidently was sometime between Clear Lake and Round Lake Periods, but abnormally old date may relate to contact of shells with Beaumont Formation; see Appendix A.
Tx-887	41 LB 3/29-30	Valastro and Davis 1970b	Human bone	4080 ± 430	B.C. 2130 ± 430 }	The cultural association of this material is unclear, but apparently is more or less coeval with ceramics and arrow points. These dates along with Tx-1059 and 1060 indicate erratic results from dating human bone. The nature of the problem is not clear. Artifacts are few but indicate possible pre-Round Lake Period occupation.
Tx-896	41 LB 3/2	Valastro and Davis 1970b	Human bone	4500 ± 160	B.C. 2550 ± 160 }	
Tx-953	41 CH 170/1	Valastro et al. 1975; Aten 1979	Rangia cuneata	1110 ± 50	A.D. 1071 ± 103	Dates natural clam bed underlying beach facies underlying 41 CH 9; dated primarily for geologic
Tx-1050	41 CH 9/1	Valastro et al. 1975	Rangia cuneata	1650 ± 70	A.D. 533 ± 103	

Lab No.	Site	Reference	Material	Age	Corrected date	Comments
						association, but sets maximum age for overlying sites.
Tx-1057	41 CH 165/1	Valastro et al. 1975	Rangia cuneata	1510 ± 80	A.D. 673 ± 103	Dates bottom of CH 165 (ceramic period undetermined) and sets minimum age for underlying back swamp facies associated with Channel Stage 3.
Tx-1114	41 CH 57/2	Valastro et al. 1975	Rangia cuneata	5570 ± 100	—	These shells were taken from the floor pad (?) of a presumed French or Spanish structure excavated by W. L. Fullen. These shells were in contact with the Beaumont Formation and thus yield an abnormally old date; see Appendix A.
Tx-1891	41 CH 46	Dillehay 1975	Rangia cuneata	814 ± 70	A.D. 1365 ± 103	Ceramic period association unclear.
Tx-1893	41 CH 32	Dillehay 1975	Rangia cuneata	1599 ± 80	A.D. 584 ± 103	Ceramic period association unclear.
Tx-1894	41 CH 47	Dillehay 1975	Rangia cuneata	1221 ± 80	A.D. 960 ± 103	Ceramic period association unclear.
Tx-1895	41 CH 47	Dillehay 1975	Rangia cuneata	1970 ± 110	A.D. 215 ± 103	Ceramic period association unclear.
Dates from Other Upper Texas Coast Archaeological Sites						
Sabine Lake Area						
Tx-1230	16 CU 108/1	Valastro et al. 1975	Rangia cuneata	2020 ± 110	B.C. 70 ± 110	No correction needed; see Appendix A.
E. I. DuPont[f]	41 OR 49/1	Eddleman and Akersten 1966	Rangia cuneata?	4400 ± 300	—	Abnormally old, in contact with Beaumont Formation; see Appendix A.
E. I. DuPont[f]	41 OR 49/2	Eddleman and Akersten 1966	Rangia cuneata?	500 ± 150	A.D. 1450 ± 150	No correction; see Appendix A.
Brazos Delta–West Bay Area						
Tx-1116A	41 BO 15/1	Valastro et al. 1975	Rangia cuneata	860 ± 50	—	Can not seriate ceramics, but appears to be relatively recent.
Tx-1116B	41 BO 15/1	Valastro et al. 1975	Charcoal	180 ± 60	A.D. 1770 ± 60	

(continued)

TABLE 14.1 (Continued)

Laboratory number[a]	Site identification	Source[b]	Sample material	Apparent age B.P.[c]	Radiocarbon date[d]	Remarks
Tx-1066	41 BO 35/1	Valastro et al. 1975; Aten 1971	Rangia cuneata	2360 ± 60	A.D. 490 ± 60	
Tx-1067	41 BO 35/2	Valastro et al. 1975; Aten 1971	Rangia cuneata	2370 ± 80	A.D. 480 ± 80	The basis for "correction" of all 41 BO 35 samples is different than for other Rangia samples. See Aten (1971: 47–50) for detailed discussion.
Tx-1117	41 BO 35/3	Valastro et al. 1975; Aten 1971	Rangia cuneata	1830 ± 80	A.D. 1320 ± 80	
Tx-1115	41 BO 35/4	Valastro et al. 1975; Aten 1971	Rangia cuneata	1250 ± 70	—	
Tx-1167	41 BO 35/5	Valastro et al. 1975; Aten 1971	Rangia cuneata	1680 ± 70	—	
Tx-1205	41 BO 35/6	Valastro et al. 1975; Aten 1971	Rangia cuneata	1330 ± 50	A.D. 1820 ± 50	
Tx-1259A	41 BO 50/1A	Valastro et al. 1975; Aten 1979	Charcoal	1650 ± 90	A.D. 300 ± 90	Paired sample; see Appendix A.
Tx-1259B	41 BO 50/1B	Valastro et al. 1975; Aten 1979	Rangia cuneata	1870 ± 70	—	
Shell Development Co.[g]	41 GV 5/ Burial K	Aten et al. 1976; Aten 1979; Ring 1963	Dosinia sp.	490 ± 100	A.D. 1460 ± 100	Dosinia sample materials were grave goods.
Shell Development Co.[g]	41 GV 5/NA 103	Aten et al. 1976; Aten 1979; Ring 1963	Littorina sp.	430 ± 150	A.D. 1520 ± 150	Apparently from midden fill between burials N and O according to notes on file at TARL.
Shell Development Co.[g]	41 GV 5/SB 108	Aten et al. 1976; Aten 1979; Ring 1963	Littorina sp.	450 ± 110	A.D. 1500 ± 110	All three SB108 samples came from same location in midden at depth of about 35 cm according to notes on file at TARL.

Site/Provenience	Sample no.	Reference[b]	Material	Radiocarbon years B.P.[c]	Corrected date[d]	Comments
Shell Development Co.[g]	41 GV 5/SB 108	Aten et al. 1976; Aten 1979; Ring 1963	Crassostrea virginica	830 ± 120	A.D. 1120 ± 120	Same as above.
Shell Development Co.[g]	41 GV 5/SB 108	Aten et al. 1976; Aten, 1979; Ring 1963	Crassostrea virginica	670 ± 120	A.D. 1280 ± 120	Same as above.
Anaqua Site, Lower Lavaca River						
Tx-2783	41 BO 126	Dering and Ayres 1977	Rangia cuneata	1450 ± 60	—	See Appendix A for discussion of Anaqua site dates.
Tx-2784	41 BO 126	Dering and Ayres 1977	Rangia cuneata	1800 ± 60	—	
Tx-2785	41 BO 126	Dering and Ayres 1977	Rangia cuneata	1440 ± 60	—	
Tx-641	41 JK 7/23	Valastro and Davis 1970a	Rangia cuneata	2690 ± 80	—	
Tx-642	41 JK 7/25	Valastro and Davis 1970a	Rangia cuneata	5160 ± 90	—	
Tx-643	41 JK 7/39	Valastro and Davis 1970a	Rangia cuneata	5200 ± 90	—	
Tx-644	41 JK 7/40	Valastro and Davis 1970a	Rangia cuneata	5130 ± 70	—	
Tx-654	41 JK 7/24	Valastro and Davis 1970a	Rangia cuneata	3240 ± 80	—	
Tx-655	41 JK 7/38	Valastro and Davis 1970a	Rangia cuneata	2100 ± 80	—	
Jones Hill Site, Livingston Reservoir, Polk Co.						
Tx-325	41 PK 8/A	Valastro et al. 1967	Charcoal	970 ± 120	A.D. 980 ± 120	Zone II, upper (levels 7–9)
Tx-330	41 PK 8/021	Valastro et al. 1967	Charcoal	390 ± 100	A.D. 1560 ± 100	Zone IV, upper (levels 1–3)
Tx-335	41 PK 8/017	Valastro et al. 1967	Charcoal	810 ± 80	A.D. 1140 ± 80	Zone IV, lower (levels 4–6)
Tx-336	41 PK 8/022	Valastro et al. 1967	Charcoal	1410 ± 190	A.D. 540 ± 190	Zone II, lower (levels 10–14)

[a] Tx refers to Radiocarbon Laboratory, The University of Texas at Austin; O refers to Humble Oil and Refining Company, Radiocarbon Laboratory

[b] Where possible, both the radiocarbon laboratory listing and the primary site report are cited

[c] Apparent years before present based on measured C-14 activity.

[d] That is, date in radiocarbon years (not to be confused with sidereal years which may differ significantly). All Rangia cuneata dates shown are corrected to a "charcoal scale" by means of the regression equation given in Figure A-1; the range of error shown (± 103 years) is the standard error of prediction.

[e] Paired shell-charcoal samples used in compilation of Figure A-1.

[f] Samples from the Eddleman Site (41 OR 49) were run by E. I. DuPont de Nemours Sabine River Works at Orange, Texas.

[g] All samples reported by Ring (1963) were run by Shell Development Company, Houston, Texas; no laboratory sample numbers have ever been reported.

Sabine Lake local chronology temporarily are being identified by cross-dating to corresponding periods in the LMV chronology (Phillips 1970). The approximate contemporaneity of the earliest of these ceramic periods in both areas is suggested by the single radiocarbon date of 70 B.C. ± 110 (Tx-1230; Table 14.1) from a site (16 CU 108) containing substantial quantities of Tchefuncte Plain sherds.

A stratigraphic test excavated in a pimple mound midden (Aten and Bollich 1981) yielded, among other things, a sequence of Tchefuncte Plain, Goose Creek Plain (variety unspecified), Mandeville Plain, and O'Neal Plain (variety Conway). The cultural deposits penetrated by this test are datable to the Sabine Lake equivalent of the Tchefuncte Period. Of particular significance for later correlation of this chronology with others to the west is that in the upper levels, Baytown Plain (varieties San Jacinto and Phoenix Lake) are present in proportions greater than 20% of the assemblage. This confirms the conclusion reported in the 1969 paper of grog-tempered ceramic technology appearing circa 1900 years ago. It also constitutes a major point of contrast with the upper Galveston Bay Area, where grog-tempered ceramics do not appear until much later.

Based on what is now known about the Sabine Lake chronology, small-scale stratigraphic tests in three or four deeply stratified sites probably would establish a detailed chronological outline for the area. The most suitable sites for this purpose would include the shell middens at Trapper Shack (16 CM 101), the Demahy Site (41 JF 41), and Conway D (16 CU 108).

GALVESTON BAY AREA

The ceramic seriation for the Galveston Bay Area is shown in Figure 14.1. It represents 72 excavation levels or collections, either singly, as excavated, or grouped to enhance sample sizes for each seriated unit. The data used are given in Table 12.2. This seriation represents an attempt to produce a pattern of lenticular time–frequency distributions for each type or variety which at the same time to not violate the order of stratigraphic successions in the excavations. Because of the latter constraint, the resulting patterns often are less well shaped than if pattern development had been the only consideration.[2]

Before proceeding with analysis and discussion of these patterns, it is necessary to verify whether this particular seriation is in fact chronological. Numerous lines of evidence suggest this is so—the occurrence of historic trade artifacts at one end of the sequence; fragmentary trends of ceramic change seen in

---

[2]It has been pointed out by others that a well-shaped lenticular pattern need not be a chronology (e.g., see Dunnell 1970).

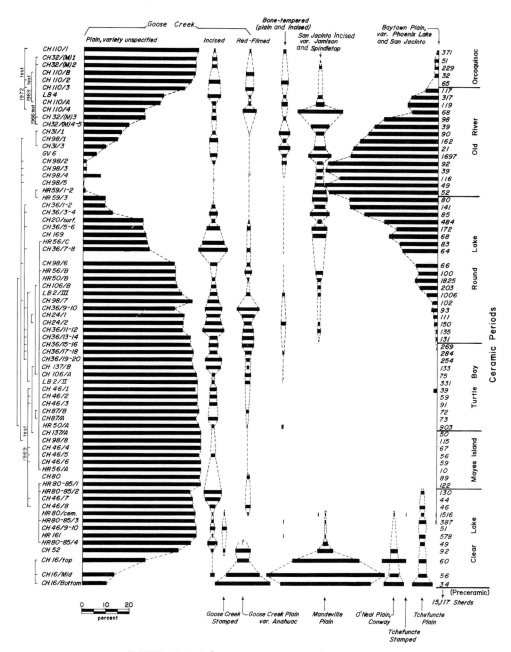

FIGURE 14.1 Galveston Bay Area ceramic seriation.

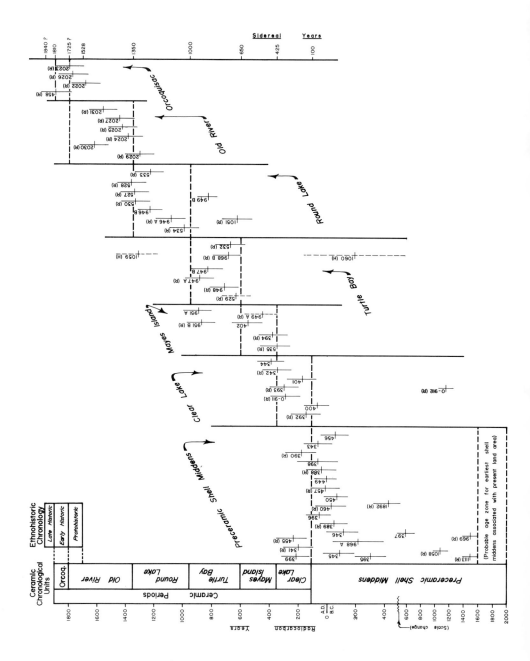

TABLE 14.2
Culture–chronological Period Intervals for the Galveston Bay Area.

Chronological periods		Period limits			
		Estimated initial dates[a]		Estimated terminal dates[a]	
Ethnohistoric	Archaeological	Radiocarbon	Sidereal[b]	Radiocarbon	Sidereal[b]
Late Historic	(Unrecognized)	—	1810	—	1840(?)
Early Historic	Orcoquisac	1800	1725(?)	1900	1810
Protohistoric	Old River				
	(protohist.)	1700	1528	1800	1725(?)
	Old River				
	(prehist.)	1350	1350	1700	1528
	Round Lake	950	1000	1350	1350
	Turtle Bay	500	650	950	1000
	Mayes Island	350	425	600	650
	Clear Lake	100	100	350	425
	Preceramic shell				
	middens	—	—	100	100

[a]All dates are A.D..
[b]Sidereal estimates (Suess 1970:Plate I) are to nearest 25 years.

individual test excavations; the correlation of declining proportion of sandy paste sherds in surface collections with the relative chronology of channel stages in the Trinity River delta (Table 12.1).

The best line of verification, however, is in radiocarbon dating. A series of more than 60 radiocarbon dating estimates (Table 14.1)[3] is available from many of the contexts for which sherds were seriated. Once the ceramic seriation was finished, each radiocarbon date was plotted graphically in the same sequential order as the position of its associated ceramic assemblage in the seriation. The results, presented in Figure 14.2 represent a forceful confirmation of the chronological validity of the ceramic ordering. Once the ceramic seriation had been subdivided into a sequence of ceramic periods, the distribution of radiocarbon dates for that period was then used to estimate the time range for the period (Table 14.2). Before returning to discuss the seriation pattern, com-

[3]Most of these dating estimates were made on *Rangia cuneata* shell and have been corrected for the effect of nonradioactive carbon dilution in estuarine waters. The studies performed to develop correction factors for the upper coast are described in Appendix A.

FIGURE 14.2   Galveston Bay Area radiocarbon dates associated with ceramic periods. Note—all dates are shown as a mean (horizontal bar) and a range of 1 standard deviation (vertical bar). All dates are assayed on charcoal, unless indicated otherwise; (R) indicates *Rangia cuneata* and (H) indicates human bone. Samples plotted as dashed lines are questionably associated with the given ceramic periods. See Table 14.1 for details.

ment should be given on those few radiocarbon dates which appear to depart from the main trend of the seriation (cf. Figure 14.2). First, the very early date (0-912) from a Clear Lake Period assemblage evidently has been diagenetically altered as discussed in Appendix A. Next, there are two samples of human bone from the Harris County Boys School Cemetery which are associated with a Turtle Bay Period context but date far from the expected age range for reasons probably associated with problems in obtaining dates on bone material (see discussion in Aten *et al.* 1976:14).

There also are several dates associated with preceramic middens which overlap with dates for the Clear Lake Period. The Clear Lake Period marks the first appearance of ceramics in the Galveston Bay Area and they occur in very low densities. This poses a difficulty for differentiating ceramic from preceramic midden. Under these low ceramic density conditions, dates for the positive occurrence of ceramics have been emphasized as the basis for estimating the initial appearance of pottery in the Galveston Bay Area. Thus, samples Tx-341, 390 to 399, and 455 easily could be early ceramic midden rather than preceramic. This leaves a remainder of four radiocarbon dates (Tx-951A, 951B, 949B, and 1051) for which there is no plausible explanation, at present, of all the available dates.

Having verified that the ceramic seriation is indeed a chronology, its properties may be reviewed. One of the most striking features of this seriation is that its major category, Goose Creek Plain, variety unspecified, violates one of the conventions of frequency seriation which is that the artifact classes should have unimodal time–frequency distributions. Goose Creek Plain clearly has a bimodal distribution; a similar situation would occur with Baytown Plain, variety San Jacinto, if the Phoenix Lake variety actually had been separated out, the latter being restricted in its distribution to the center of the peak of the Baytown Plain unimodal distribution. Goose Creek Red-Filmed, Goose Creek Incised and possibly San Jacinto Incised also show potentially significant polymodality. The occurrence of polymodal classes, however, is not a fatal methodological defect; it merely points the way to definition of more refined artifact historical classes. When frequency polymodality occurs, the usual prescription for reduction of these to unimodal classes is to identify new criteria and reformulate the class (Dunnell 1970:309). This is not so simple a matter in the upper Texas coast area because most redefinition would need to be done at the variety level rather than at a typological level. This is not undertaken in the present study but a number of associated considerations can be discussed.

As was discussed in the section on ceramic descriptions, the Goose Creek Plain type is a fertile field for definition of new varieties, but many of these will be extremely difficult to sort at the level of the individual sherd. Similarly, in the artifact descriptions, comments have been offered on the varieties of Baytown Plain. It will be difficult to develop a replicable subdivision of Baytown Plain, variety San Jacinto, into separate classes reflecting distributional differences during the Round Lake and the Old River Periods which now are embodied within the present variety.

Of special interest is the possibility for subdividing the types Goose Creek

Incised and San Jacinto Incised. In describing these types, the rather vague tendencies toward chronologically sequential incised design assemblages (also see Figure 12.2) were noted. The suggestion was made that these might ultimately be developed into varieties, but that their discrimination at the sherd level would be possible only with certain specialized design motifs. It is significant to note here that there is a correspondence between the design assemblages and the modes in the time–frequency distributions of the types. Specifically, for Goose Creek Incised, there is a potential for a variety in the Clear Lake Period, another from Turtle Bay through early Round Lake Periods, possibly another in late Round Lake, and another in the middle Old River through the Orcoquisac Periods. For San Jacinto Incised, there is a vague suggestion of one class extending through the Round Lake Period, and another extending through the Old River Period.

The suggestion also has been noted of three modes in the Goose Creek Red-Filmed ontogeny and two for the bone-tempered ceramics. In any event, many of these pattern "bulges" may be insignificant. For those that are of significance, it presently seems highly unlikely that they can be defined with the unequivocal sorting criteria which characterize types. However, such a directed and parsimonious approach to the problem of recognizing new taxonomic classes is one of the applications to be made of the chronological ceramic seriation. It also allows a clearer focus on the definition of research problems which may be associated with these artifact patterns.[4]

It remains now to describe the basis for the sequence of ceramic chronological periods in the Galveston Bay Area. These begin with the Clear Lake Period.[5] It is marked by the initial appearance of ceramics about A.D. 100, and continues until about A.D. 425. This interval is characterized by a greater variety of ceramic classes than at any other time. These include the several types and varieties characteristic of the Tchefuncte culture of southern Louisiana as well as early phases of the Goose Creek types. The presence of any rocker stamping or Tchefuncte-associated ceramics is a definite marker for the Clear Lake Period.

From inspection of the ceramic seriation in Figure 14.1, it is obvious that the Clear Lake Period can be differentiated into an early and a late portion. The early part is dominated by Mandeville Plain; secondary classes are the Anahuac variety and the unspecified varieties of Goose Creek Plain, Tchefuncte Plain and the Conway variety of O'Neal Plain. The late part is dominated by the unspec-

---

[4]For example, was the appearance of the Phoenix Lake variety of Baytown Plain associated with the westward expansion of LMV exchange and/or belief systems as a result of a decline of Caddoan hegemony (if this existed) in southeast Texas? Was the marked expansion of Goose Creek Red-Filmed beginning in the Turtle Bay Period related to the appearance of cemeteries, as discussed in Aten et al. (1976)? What was the functional and/or social context of the apparent high negative correlation between Goose Creek Red-Filmed and the Baytown Plain varieties?

[5]All of these periods were named after geographic features associated with sites producing major data pertinent to recognition of the ceramic assemblages of that period. The time intervals are described in sidereal years, rather than radiocarbon years, to make it less confusing when incorporating the protohistoric and historic periods. Both sidereal and radiocarbon ages may be found in Table 14.2.

ified variety of Goose Creek Plain; secondary classes are Goose Creek Incised, Goose Creek Stamped, and Tchefuncte Plain. Based on the ceramic patterns of this period, the possibility should be considered that Mandeville Plain and the varieties of Goose Creek were specialized technological variants derived from the more generalized (in terms of paste characteristics) Anahuac variety of Goose Creek Plain.

The Mayes Island Period extended from the end of the Clear Lake Period to about A.D. 650. In terms of ceramic technology, this is by far the most austere period in the entire history of the Galveston Bay Area. Indeed, it stretches a point to refer to these ceramics as an assemblage. Rather, the ceramics consist almost entirely of Goose Creek Plain (variety unspecified) with an occasional sherd of Goose Creek Incised and of Goose Creek Red-Filmed. Because the character of this period is built almost entirely on negative criteria, it can easily go unrecognized in stratigraphic tests; for example, recall the problems for interpretation of radiocarbon dates at 41 CH 24 related earlier in Chapter 11.

The Turtle Bay Period extended from the end of the Mayes Island Period to about A.D. 1000. Although Goose Creek Plain is still the dominant pottery type, the period is notable for a resurgence of Goose Creek Red-Filmed and especially for the elaboration of design motifs on Goose Creek Incised. An ambiguous early occurrence of bone-tempered ware may have begun in this period.

The Round Lake Period extended from the end of the Turtle Bay Period to about A.D. 1350. It is marked by the initial appearance of grog-tempered ceramics and by the relatively rapid decline nearly to extinction of the sandy paste wares. At the very end of this period the Phoenix Lake variety of Baytown Plain dominates the entire ceramic assemblage.

The Old River Period extended from the end of the Round Lake Period to about A.D. 1700. For a short period of time, the Phoenix Lake variety continued to dominate the assemblage. Overall, the period is marked by major decline of grog-tempered wares, and by resurgence once again of Goose Creek Plain, Goose Creek Incised, and Goose Creek Red-Filmed. Bone-tempered ceramics become clearly established as part of the Galveston Bay Area ceramics. This period overlaps both prehistoric and the entire protohistoric time intervals. Consequently, European trade goods someday may be found, especially from the last half-century of this period.

The Orcoquisac Period extended from the end of the Old River Period to about the first decade of the nineteenth century. It is characterized by the near disappearance of grog-tempered ceramics from aboriginal sites (and their absence at the contemporaneous Presidio Ahumada; see Tunnell and Ambler 1967:90) and a decline in all other classes except Goose Creek Plain. This, of course, is the period of active European colonization in the area, and the presence of European trade wares most often will be an indicator.

At this point, it is appropriate to take up the question of the historic and ethnohistoric record for the Galveston Bay Area. The protohistoric has been defined as the transitional period between the initial receipt of European goods by the aboriginal inhabitants of a region which signals the end of the prehistoric, and the arrival of Europeans in the area which marks the beginning of the historic period. (Ray 1978:26)

This is more or less the way in which I have viewed the situation on the upper Texas coast. It means, however, that a judgment must be made about which arrivals of Europeans are of importance for changing the cultural pattern. Drawing on the narrative presented in Part I, it may be agreed that the arrival of Cabeza de Vaca (rather than European goods) in 1528 marked the end of prehistoric times. However, it is unlikely that Cabeza de Vaca, La Salle, de Leon, or De Bellisle (cf. Part I) had any lasting impact on native society (except possibly for the transmission of disease) because there were no significant functional linkages established between the native and European cultural systems. La Salle and de Leon kept the natives at arms length; and Cabeza de Vaca and De Bellisle were functioning essentially as natives rather than as Europeans. A more logical time from which to mark the beginning of the historic period on the coast would be in the second quarter of the eighteenth century, but not later than 1740, by which time fur trading had been established between the Galveston Bay natives and the Louisiana French.

Once the historic period had begun, the dynamics of European–Indian relations varied from time to time, and from place to place. Broadly speaking, relations in the earliest periods of contact were dominated by a world view in which European objectives were thought to be achievable while the Indian simultaneously became assimilated to European civilization (Pearce 1957). Later, Pearce notes "the cruelty and rigor of events, White impatience, and Indian stubbornness" caused European attitudes to change direction such that there was resignation by them to the belief that the "gap" between cultures was too broad to be closed. On the upper Texas coast, this change in attitude occurred with the appearance of colonists from the United States, if not earlier. From this time (ca. 1820) on, Indian-hating was a pervasive feature of the nineteenth century settlement of Texas. To be sure, specific examples of attitudes contrary to those described here can be identified. From a normative viewpoint though, these appear to be valid generalizations.

Given these considerations, it is reasonable to envision three European-related periods: (a) the Protohistoric, when little may have happened to the Indians, but a period in which important ethnohistoric records were made; (b) the early Historic, when relations between the European and the Indian tended to be economically symbiotic, although the major destruction of native populations occurred at this time; and (c) the late Historic period when the European was resigned to, or deliberately sought, extermination or removal of the vestigial Indian populations.

In the Galveston Bay Area, the Protohistoric can be aligned with the latter half of the Old River Period; and the early Historic essentially aligns with the Orcoquisac Period. The late Historic is comparable to no known aboriginal archaeological remains in the Galveston Bay Area. These alignments are shown

in Figure 14.1 and Table 14.2, and will be of value later when connecting the
ethnohistoric data from Part I with the archaeological record.

BRAZOS DELTA–WEST BAY AREA

The chronology for this area is still at an early phase of development and three
problems must be overcome.

1.   There are few deeply stratified sites; most are thin middens, although
sometimes a series of these thin lenses accumulated at a single location with
stratigraphic separation provided by sterile floodbasin deposits (as at the
Dow–Cleaver Site, 41 BO 35).

2.   There is limited diversity of ceramics; the major class by far is Goose
Creek Plain, variety unspecified, with very few sherds of any other class. The
late Raymond Walley and others have shown me thousands of sherds from
dozens of sites in the area, and incised sherds, for example, were exceedingly
rare.

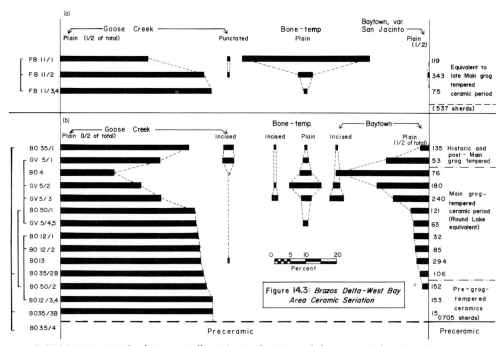

FIGURE 14.3   (a) **Inland Brazos Valley (Big Creek) Area and** (b) **Brazos Delta–West Bay Area
ceramic seriation.**

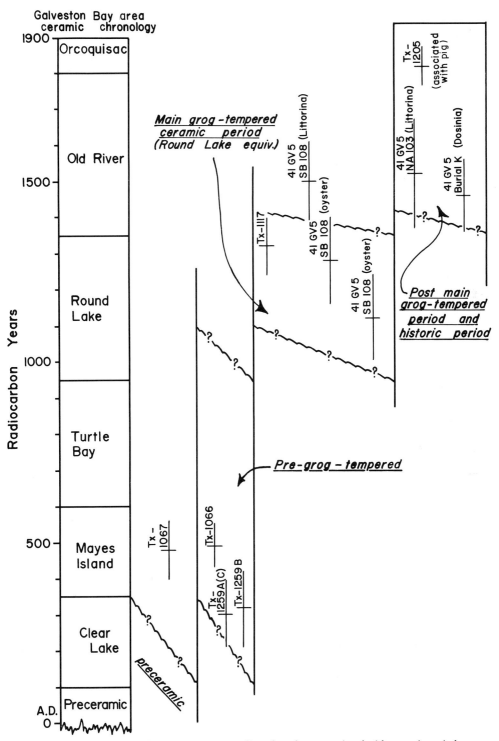

FIGURE 14.4   Brazos Delta–West Bay Area radiocarbon dates associated with ceramic periods.

3. Sequence verification is difficult because of more than the usual problems in the use of *Rangia cuneata* as a radiocarbon dating medium; for a discussion of this problem, see Appendix A.

Nearly all of the sites excavated in the Brazos Delta–West Bay Area are of the thin lens (unstratified or limited stratification) type and it is a reasonable assumption that most assemblages to be seriated accumulated over comparably short times. They also are all from a reasonably limited area, although the inclusion of the Jamaica Beach Site (41 GV 5) is based partly on proximity, and partly on an overall physical similarity of ceramics to those of Brazos delta sites. It is assumed that these sites all represent the same cultural tradition, one which continued on into the protohistoric and historic periods with the native groups later identified as the Karankawa (and locally as the Cocos).

If these assumptions are not true, at least insofar as the ceramic technological tradition is concerned, this probably will be reflected in the existence of discontinuous class distributions in the ceramic seriation. The seriation prepared for this area is shown in Figure 14.3 as it currently stands. Although some alternative aligning could be done (e.g., one could invert the order of BO 4 and GV 5, level 2), these would not significantly alter the basic patterning. The rather equivocal set of radiocarbon dates for this seriation is given in Figure 14.4, along with correlation of the Brazos Delta–West Bay ordering with that of the Galveston Bay Area.

The principal noteworthy features of this seriation are great similarity in basic patterns to the Galveston Bay chronology while, at the same time, the variety of classes is diminished. The patterns in the Brazos delta seriation which are consistent with those in the Galveston Bay seriation provide a rudimentary basis for chronological ordering of archaeological data. There is little else to say about the Brazos Delta–West Bay chronology except that it needs a great deal more work.

CONROE–LIVINGSTON AREA

Throughout this study, an attempt has been made to broaden understanding of the regional context within which the aboriginal societies of the upper Texas coast once functioned. In Part I, it was of great value to review the ethnohistoric data for the Bidai and to include this into the examination of the processes and events affecting the other native groups of the upper coast during the historic period. It is in this sense that a consideration now of ceramic chronological data from the Conroe–Livingston Area is important. As much as anything else, this provides points of contrast for the Galveston Bay data.

What follows is a trial formulation designed to explore some of the formal features of a ceramic chronology for Conroe–Livingston. The only data used

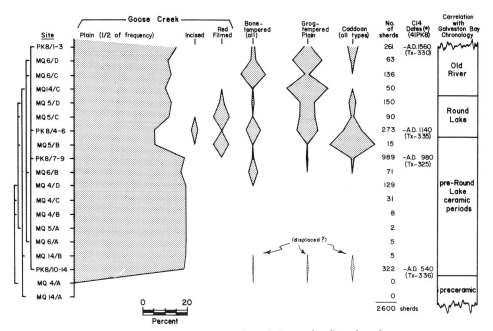

FIGURE 14.5   Conroe–Livingston Area ceramic seriation and radiocarbon dates.

have been from stratigraphic tests excavated by others, primarily in the Conroe Reservoir (Shafer 1968; C. K. Chandler, unpublished data 1979). Data also has been included from the Jones Hill Site (41 PK 8) in the Livingston Reservoir (McClurkan 1968). Jones Hill is located about 55 km northeast of Conroe Reservoir (Figure 11.1) and is well within the historically known territory of the Bidai.[6] Jones Hill is of particular interest because it is the only one of the several prehistoric sites tested in this immediate area from which radiocarbon dates have been obtained. For this reason, the ceramic frequency data were compiled from this site and included with the data from Conroe.

The resulting ceramic seriation is presented in Figure 14.5; the manner in which published data were consolidated is given in Table 14.3. Applying seriation to data from these sites poses problems different from those encountered with shell midden data. These particular inland earth middens are incorporated in loose, sandy deposits which must be heaven on earth to the gopher population judging from the vigor with which they burrow. This surely has had some effect on the distribution of artifacts within the middens but just how much is hard to estimate. Because studies have shown that other disturbances,

[6]Although one might not be able to assume continuity between these prehistoric ceramics and the historical Bidai, neither should the basis for making such a linkage be obscured by discussing the archaeological data according to spatial parameters different from the known Bidai territory.

TABLE 14.3
Proveniences of data for Conroe–Livingston ceramic seriation

	Livingston Reservoir
Jones Hill Site (41 PK 8)[a]	
PK 8/1-3	Levels 1, 2, and 3
PK 8/4-6	Levels 4, 5, and 6
PK 8/7-9	Levels 7, 8, and 9
PK 8/10-14	Levels 10, 11, 12, 13, and 14
	Conroe Reservoir
Site 41 MQ 4[b]	
MQ 4/D	Levels 1 and 2
MQ 4/C	Levels 3 and 4
MQ 4/B	Levels 5 and 6
MQ 4/A	Levels 7 and 8
Site 41 MQ 5[b]	
MQ 5/D	Levels 1 and 2
MQ 5/C	Levels 3 and 4
MQ 5/B	Levels 5 and 6
MQ 5/A	Levels 7 and 8
Site 41 MQ 6[b]	
MQ 6/D	Levels 1 and 2
MQ 6/C	Levels 3 and 4
MQ 6/B	Levels 5 and 6
MQ 6/A	Level 7
Site 41 MQ 14[c]	
MQ 14/C	Levels 1 and 2: Goose Creek Plain = 41
	Baytown Plain = 9
MQ 14/B	Levels 3 and 4: Goose Creek Plain = 5
MQ 14/A	Levels 5 and 6: Goose Creek Plain = 3

[a]From McClurkan 1968.
[b]From Shafer 1968.
[c]From C. K. Chandler, unpublished data.

such as repeated plowing, often do not erase larger distributional patterns within a site (cf. Talmage and Chesler 1977), it seemed worth making the effort to see if time seriation patterns could be recognized.

There is no basis for determining if the collections to be seriated all represent similar time duration and this lack of control may account for some of the apparently erratic bulges in the patterns; no doubt the gophers also have contributed to this by displacing some materials. This seriation was performed before completion of the version of the Galveston Bay Area seriation described earlier. Consequently, there was limited possibility for gerrymandering the data to reproduce or reflect the Galveston Bay patterns. Control imposed by the stratigraphic order of test excavations also placed constraints on the discretion which could be exercised in developing patterning in ceramic ontogenies.

At the time this seriation originally was made, it also included data on arrow and dart point stem forms. Consequently, some of the ordering results from concurrent best fit among the lithics rather than simply the ceramic patterning.[7] This, in particular, is the reason for the attenuated series of proveniences with very small sherd samples consisting entirely of Goose Creek Plain in the early portion of the seriation.

The results of this seriation are encouraging. Patterns have resulted which generally are similar to those in the Galveston Bay Area. Also, the ordering of the radiocarbon dates from the Jones Hill Site (41 PK 8) is extremely helpful in confirming the basic sequence. The most likely correlation of the Conroe–Livingston seriation with the Galveston Bay Area chronology is shown on Figure 14.5. The Round Lake–pre-Round Lake boundary placed at the beginning of the grog-tempered plainware in the Conroe–Livingston seriation is bracketed by radiocarbon dates in nearly the same time range as occurs in the Galveston Bay Area. The Old River–Round Lake boundary is placed to coincide with the maximum occurrence of grog-tempered plainware, as in the Galveston Bay Area. This boundary is bracketed by radiocarbon dates into an interval of time which likewise is consistent with the Galveston Bay chronology.

The tiny representation of Goose Creek Incised coincides with the period of this type's maximum representation in the Galveston Bay chronology, and the same occurs for the larger proportions of Goose Creek Red-Filmed. The distribution of bone-tempered sherds is suggestive of bimodality, as in the Galveston Bay seriation, with these modes occurring at similar chronological positions.

The grog-tempered sherds have been identified by the excavators as San Jacinto Plain. I have not examined the sherds and have been more noncommittal by simply categorizing them Baytown Plain, variety unspecified. This class is irregular in its distribution, but occurs in a similar stratigraphic position and has a vaguely similar frequency pattern to that in the Galveston Bay Area.

Caddoan ceramics are rare in the Galveston Bay, Brazos, and Sabine areas, and so their prominent frequency in the Conroe–Livingston seriation is a new feature in this synthesis. The bimodal distribution is quite plausible, however, in terms of a hypothesis that some process or activity from the LMV expanded westward around A.D. 1000, briefly displacing certain indigenous ceramic technologies, and perhaps their associated institutions. Evidence for this occurs more strongly in the Galveston Bay Area. However, the distribution in the Conroe–Livingston Area is further indication that the presence of Caddoan ceramics was interrupted for a time, during which the absolute and relative abundance of grog-tempered ceramics markedly increased.

Overall, the ceramics of the Conroe–Livingston Area appear reduced in variety and, perhaps, in absolute abundance when compared to Galveston Bay and the Sabine. Furthermore, it must be significant that all patterns evident in the seriation are recognizable and accountable in terms of patterns within the Galveston Bay Area seriation. This absence of unaccounted patterns and the

---

[7]Because there are no comparable lithic data for the coastal zone to afford a contrast, the Conroe–Livingston lithic seriation is not included here.

consistency between the four radiocarbon dates, their associated ceramic assemblages, and similar dates and assemblages in the Galveston Bay Area lead to
the conclusion that the Conroe–Livingston seriation is valid and does permit
correlation with certain regional historical trends, albeit with less precision
than is possible for the Galveston Bay Area at the present time.

CHAPTER 15

Technological History

The historical patterns of occurrence of material culture found in the four major areas of the upper coast are described in this chapter. Discussion of sociological and/or ecological implications of these patterns will be reserved mainly for the concluding chapter, when they may be integrated with the results of Parts I and II.

CERAMICS

Ceramics appeared in the Sabine Lake Area by at least 70 B.C.; in the Galveston Bay Area by A.D. 100; in the Brazos Delta–West Bay Area by at least A.D. 300; and in the Conroe–Livingston Area by A.D. 500. This east to west time transgressive character in the appearance of ceramics is further supported by their dated occurrence progressively earlier as one goes eastward, and their later appearance around A.D. 1100 in the Corpus Christi vicinity (Story 1968; Valastro and Davis 1970a). Broadly speaking, the history of ceramic technology in the central Gulf Coast begins with the appearance of temperless wares (Tchefuncte, Mandeville, Goose Creek) succeeded by tempered wares. The latter are differentiable (in order of their advent) into sand-tempered (e.g., Alexander, O'Neal), grog-tempered (e.g., Baytown), bone-tempered (e.g., Leon), and shell-tempered (e.g., Mississippian wares which are not known to occur on the upper Texas coast); the few sherds reported to be shell-tempered in the literature for the upper coast appear to be fortuitously so.

That the early ceramics of the upper coast are derived from or share a common origin with those of the Lower Mississippi Valley (LMV) and the Louisiana coast is amply attested either by the common occurrence of LMV ceramic types or by the aboriginal use of LMV ceramic attributes in both the Sabine Lake and Galveston Bay Area. Although stratigraphic test data from the Sabine Lake Area are still rather sparse, it is clear that many LMV types were present throughout the entire ceramics-using period (Aten and Bollich 1969). In the Galveston Bay Area, ceramics identical or similar to those of the LMV are present only in the Clear Lake Period and briefly in the early Old River Period. None of these eastern ceramic features has yet been found in either the Brazos delta or at Conroe–Livingston. Indeed, all indications are that ceramics came into regular use in these areas possibly as much as 400 years later than in the Galveston Bay Area.

The presence in the Galveston Bay sequence of Tchefuncte, Mandeville, Goose Creek Plain (variety Anahuac), and the more commonly recognized variations of Goose Creek (here called Goose Creek Plain, variety unspecified), taken together with their patterns of relative abundance in the Clear Lake Period, suggest the differentiation of these four ceramic taxa from a common, more generalized technology. Because of the paucity of data from the Sabine it is not yet possible to suggest to what extent the inhabitants of the Galveston Bay Area participated in the elaboration and modification of the early LMV ceramics into a distinctive new form, as opposed to being receivers of technology and styles developed elsewhere. However, the type Goose Creek Stamped currently is known only from sites in the Galveston Bay Area and may have been used only in that locality. Certainly the abundance and variety of the early ceramics in the Galveston Bay Area, especially when contrasted to the limited abundance and variety in the Brazos and Conroe–Livingston areas, argues for active participation in the developmental processes associated with these early ceramics.

Except for prominent LMV relationships during the Clear Lake Period, the basic pattern of the ceramic chronologies for Galveston, Brazos, and Conroe–Livingston is quite similar. The substantially greater elaboration evident in the Galveston sequence probably is not a function solely of more extensive sampling in the latter area. Examination of the numerous surface collections available for the Brazos and Conroe–Livingston show that Goose Creek Incised and Red-Filmed, Baytown Plain, and San Jacinto Incised simply are not present in the quantities evident in the Galveston Bay Area. Likewise, the prominent occurrence of Caddoan ceramics in the Conroe–Livingston Area as well as the greater abundance there of bone-tempered sherds is not duplicated in the coastal Brazos, Galveston and Sabine areas. Incised ceramics occur principally in the Sabine and in the Galveston Bay areas. The former area has not been well studied, but in the latter, a sizable range of design styles occurs principally subsequent to the middle Turtle Bay Period (Figure 12.3).

The existence of a common pattern and structure to the history of ceramics in each of these three areas (compare Figures 14.1, 14.3, and 14.5) gives confidence that each has validity. As a result, they are useful for guiding the selection of sites for additional testing to fill out this framework, and, in the interim, for formulation of regional and interregional historical and processual hypotheses. A summary of the interregional patterns of the major elements of this ceramic technology is given in Figure 15.1.

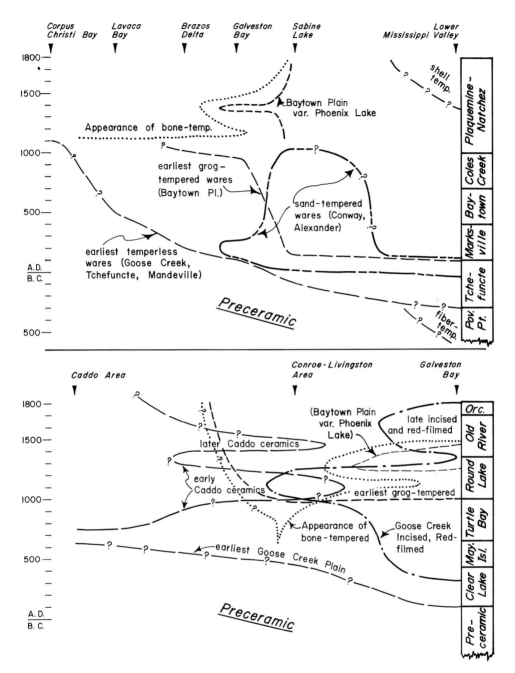

FIGURE 15.1 Preliminary historical interpretation of ceramic technology of the upper Texas coast.

CHIPPED STONE TECHNOLOGY

The lithic materials from the three major coastal drainage basins examined in this study also seem to have distinctive character. In the Brazos delta area, the only archaeological lithic material encountered has been chert. The description presented in the report on the Dow–Cleaver Site (Aten 1971) has proved to be typical in characterizing this chert as dense, earthy, yellowish brown to dark brown in color, and having few imperfections in grain.

In Galveston Bay Area sites, chert, quartzite, and silicified wood are all fairly common. The cherts range widely in color, tend to be more translucent than in the Brazos, and often have imperfections in the form of open or filled vugs. The quartzites generally are medium to fine grained, probably are metaquartzites, and usually are red to purplish in color. The silicified wood varies widely in color and structure because of its origin.

In the Sabine Lake Area sites, chert, quartzite, and silicified wood also are found. Although insufficient comparison has been done to determine whether these can be distinguished from Galveston Bay Area specimens, this may some-day be feasible at least on an assemblage basis.

On Table 15.1 are shown several features of the chipped stone technology, mainly as they occur in the three coastal areas.[1] These data are structured for presentation in terms of (a) geographic area; (b) major time period; and (c) dart or arrow manufacture, on the assumption that by noting where these occur, gross differences in resource cobble size, sources, and chipping technique can be suggested.

In the Galveston Bay Area, flake densities associated with dart point chipping are moderate and the predominant material used was chert with modest increases through time in the amount of quartzite being used. Arrow point manufacture begins in the Mayes Island Period, accompanied by a sharp drop in flake density. This slowly increases in the Old River Period, and then undergoes a major decline in the Orcoquisac Period. With the advent of arrow points, much greater use initially is made of silicified wood and quartzite, although this declines significantly by the historic period.

In the Brazos Delta–West Bay Area, flake densities are uniformly low and the material exclusively chert. The flake densities for the two Sabine Lake Area sites also are low. All three major stone material types are used in the Sabine sites, as in the Galveston Bay Area, although the proportions are different. Against this background, it is striking to see that the flake density recorded for 41 FB 11, a site in the inland Brazos Valley (Figure 11.1), is seven times greater than the

---

[1]The Galveston Bay and Brazos delta data were compiled from Table 13.1; the Sabine Lake and 41 FB 11 data are unpublished but are included here to provide added contrast. Data from other upper coast habitats may yield different quantities, but their structural relationships should remain the same.

TABLE 15.1
Summary of chipping debris type, density, and material

Geographic area and chronological period	Focus of Projectile point manufacture	Flake type percentages[a]		Interior Lipped				Flake Density per 1/10 cu. m.	Material type percentages	Silicified wood	Quartzite
		Primary cortex	Secondary cortex	Single facet	Multiple facet	Other	Frags		Chert		
Sabine Lake Area											
Troyville-Coles Creek equiv. (JF26)	Arrow	—	12.5	17.2	26.6	1.2	42.2	6.9	86.2	7.7	6.2
Tchefuncte equivalent (JF31)	Dart	5.4	12.5	21.4	30.4	—	30.4	2.9	55.2	27.6	17.2
Galveston Bay Area											
Orcoquisac	Arrow	2.9	14.7	(29.4)		17.6	35.3	17.0	87.1	12.9	—
Old River	Arrow	2.6	10.9	10.2	20.5	8.5	47.4	40.8	74.6	25.2	0.2
Round Lake	Arrow	4.1	12.2	6.1	16.3	3.1	58.2	2.5	61.8	31.4	6.9
Turtle Bay	Arrow	7.9	26.3	15.8	7.9	5.3	36.8	.8	51.1	38.3	10.6
Mayes Island	Arrow (?)	—	—	—	—	12.5	87.5	.3	100.0	—	—
Clear Lake	Dart	1.4	18.5	8.6	25.7	7.7	38.3	15.9	96.6	1.3	2.1
Preceramic (B)	Dart	3.2	12.7	11.0	30.4	2.8	39.9	27.2	95.5	1.7	2.7
Preceramic (A)	Dart	2.4	5.9	5.3	45.9	5.3	35.3	10.1	97.2	2.2	.6
Brazos Delta-West Bay Area											
Historic-post Round Lake	Arrow	3.7	12.3	9.5	49.2	7.4	28.4	7.4	100.0	—	—
Round Lake equivalent	Arrow	1.1	7.1	14.2	28.3	1.5	47.8	5.8	100.0	—	—
Pre-Round Lake Ceramic	Arrow	—	10.5	11.8	28.9	6.6	42.1	3.6	100.0	—	—
Interior Brazos Valley											
Round Lake equivalent (FB11)	Arrow & Dart	4.3	26.0	(13.1)		8.9	47.7	78.4	(not available)		

[a] Percentages are calculated synchronically for each assemblage. Data are from Table 13.1.

average flake density in the coastal sites. Chronologically, 41 FB 11 probably is equivalent to a Round Lake Period occupation (Figure 14.3).

The sequences of flake types for the Brazos and Galveston areas both contain several trends which may have significance for understanding the evolution and adaptation of the lithic technology. It undoubtedly is significant that each arrow versus dart chronological segment within each geographic area has a distinctive character. These probably are the resultant of several forces: materials, skill levels, type of artifact being made, as well as its intended use, group motor habit patterns, and so on. Chipping debris is much more common on the upper coast than completed stone artifacts. Consequently, the chipping debris should be looked to as a practical data base for measuring such things as technological evolution and adaptation, and functional identification of activities in individual occupation episode sites.

OTHER TECHNOLOGY

Because the most extensive and detailed stratigraphic testing is available for the Galveston Bay Area, the history of the nonceramic aboriginal technology is clearest for this locality. These data are examined first on the expectation that patterns for the other areas should be more readily interpretable by reference to those for Galveston. The data for all four areas are summarized in Figure 15.2.

Galveston Bay Area

Lithic knives–scrapers occur throughout the sequence since 1500 B.C., although their specific styles do change to some extent. Dart points are not found on the coast subsequent to the end of the Clear Lake Period, although they do continue until much later at sites in the interior (e.g., the Jamison Site [Aten 1967] and the Addicks Basin sites [Wheat 1953]).

Socketed bone projectile points appear in coastal sites in the late preceramic and last until the early Turtle Bay Period. All known socketed bone points for the upper coast, as well as all known grooved and snapped metapodial articulations (which are assumed to be produced during the manufacture of these points), date to this same time period. This is a curious fact because, in the LMV, socketed bone points are known to be significantly earlier as well as later in occurrence than is the case on the Texas coast (e.g., Ford 1951:123; Gagliano 1970:11).[2] Socketed bone points in both the Galveston Bay Area and in the

---

[2]Because of the relative paucity of nonceramic artifacts in coastal sites, it still is difficult to discuss their technology in terms of relative proportions rather than presence and absence as is being done here. Probably very few of the distributional arguments made previously would be materially

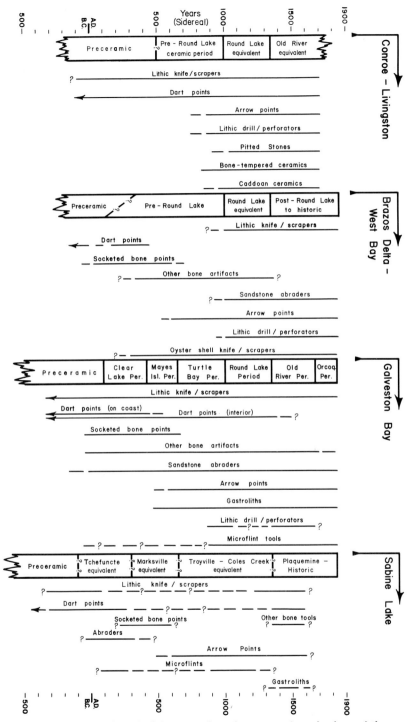

FIGURE 15.2 Preliminary historical interpretation of non-ceramic technology of the upper Texas coast. Sources are the same localities and literature citations used for Chapter 14.

Sabine include blunt points presumably used for stunning or killing prey without mutilating the body. This may mark the initial use of bird feathers in ceremonies and in trade. Other bone artifacts have not been discovered in refuse earlier than late preceramic, but once introduced, these continued in use into the Orcoquisac Period. Sandstone abraders have the same distribution (although their greatest abundance is in the Clear Lake Period) and may be associated with bone artifacts as a fabricating tool.

The earliest occurrence of arrow points is at 41 CH 137 in deposits dating to the Mayes Island Period (probably during the latter part of this period). The frequency of arrow points increases sharply during the Old River Period, although it still is unclear if this occurs generally throughout the period or is confined to the protohistoric portion. This is an especially important matter pertaining to the nature of native response to the potential alternative stimuli of bison returning to southern ranges after A.D. 1200 and/or to the initiation of the fur trade by European traders. The occurrence of gastroliths in Galveston Bay Area sites is concurrent with the appearance and duration of arrow points and may be the source material for their manufacture using the bipolar technique. The evidence for use of gastroliths is discussed in Appendix B. For reasons that are not at all clear, the temporal distribution of lithic drill/perforator tools begins in the late Turtle Bay Period and continues into the Orcoquisac Period. Microflint tools, on the other hand, evidently appear in the late preceramic and probably are present from then on to the historic period. These tiny tools are quite diversified in shape, and presumably in their use as well, and may be the reason that larger lithic drill/perforating tools do not appear until much later. Because artifacts of very similar shape to many of the large lithic drill/perforators have been discovered lodged in human bones and obviously were projectile points (Wilson 1901:517–518), an alternative possibility is that some of the Texas coastal specimens also were used as projectile points.

Brazos Delta–West Bay Area

Lithic knives/scrapers are known only from and subsequent to the local equivalent of the Round Lake Period. Because of the ubiquity of these tools elsewhere, it is difficult to consider the lateness of this distribution anything other than a sampling problem. Dart points are known only from the late preceramic to the early ceramic period. Although the lateness of their initial appearance may be a sampling problem, the terminal age is consistent with that documented from shell middens in the Galveston Bay Area. Socketed bone projectile points have a short period of use similar to that in the Galveston Bay Area. Other bone artifacts presently are documented from the beginning of the ceramic period

---

affected by the discovery of, say, a socketed bone point at a historic site. The issue is that the major (if not the exclusive) occurrence of these items seems to be as described on Figure 15.2.

through the local equivalent of the Round Lake Period. This is nearly the same distribution as in Galveston. Sandstone abraders are documented from the beginning of the Round Lake equivalent through the historic period.

Arrow points are first documented from about the middle of the pre-Round Lake equivalent ceramic period and continue through the historic period; this is about the same distribution as in the Galveston Bay Area. Lithic drill/perforators are known from the beginning of the Round Lake equivalent and continue through the historic period; this, too, is nearly the same distribution as in the Galveston Bay Area.

A major new tool type, thus far documented only from the coastal territory of the historic Karankawa, is the oyster shell knife/scraper. These are documented from the late preceramic through the historic period and may partially account for the minimal occurrence of the lithic knife/scrapers.

Another significant technological innovation first becomes evident about the middle of the pre-Round Lake ceramic period; this is the tidal brush weir. The evidence for weirs, aside from their mention in ethnohistoric accounts (Bandelier 1905:65; Dyer 1917:3) is faunal data.[3] This is mentioned here only because it is mentioned later (Chapter 17). Whether weirs were used in the other areas remains unknown because the subsistence data have not been analyzed, but it is a reasonable assumption.

Sabine Lake Area

Testing in this area has been very sparse and the data are extremely sketchy. Use of the LMV chronology is continued until better data are available. The temporal correlation between this chronology and that for the Galveston Bay Area is shown on Figure 15.2.

Lithic knife/scrapers appear to occur from the late preceramic through to the local equivalent of the Plaquemine-Historic period. Dart points are documented from the late preceramic into the Tchefuncte Period equivalent; and again in the Plaquemine-Historic Period. Socketed bone projectile points are documented in the equivalent of late Tchefuncte and Marksville periods, about the same time range as elsewhere on the upper coast. Other bone tools presently are known only from the Plaquemine-Historic Period; undoubtedly this range is skewed by the limited sample. Abraders on the other hand are known only from the Tchefuncte Period equivalent; this, too, is likely a skewed distribution.

Arrow points are documented from the local equivalent of the Troyville–Coles Creek Period (and perhaps a little earlier) through the remainder of the sequence; this is approximately the same distribution as in the other areas of

---

[3]At this time in the Brazos sequence, and in contrast to faunal assemblages from earlier sites, the content of the midden faunal refuse includes a broad range of aquatic and amphibious taxa of much smaller average size than were previously caught.

the upper coast. Gastroliths, however, are presently known only from the Plaquemine-Historic Period. Microflints are documented from the local Tchefuncte Period on into the local equivalent of the Troyville–Coles Creek Period. No lithic drill/perforators have yet been identified.

Conroe–Livingston Area

Lithic knife/scrapers are documented from the late preceramic through to the Old River Period equivalent, which is the latest period presently recognizable in the Conroe–Livingston data. Dart points also occur over this same time range. No bone tools of any kind have been documented, evidently because of poor soil conditions for their preservation. Arrow points have been documented from near the beginning of the pre-Round Lake ceramic period which, temporally, is about the same as the time of their appearance in the Galveston Bay Area. Lithic drill/perforators have about the same distribution as arrow points, which may be an earlier appearance than in the three other areas; see the previous discussion of this class. Pitted stones, an artifact class unique to Conroe–Livingston among the four areas, are confined in their distribution to the Round Lake equivalent and later. This distribution reinforces the argument that they functioned as anvil stones for bipolar toolmaking.

In spite of the vagaries associated with the detection and dating of what amount to rare specimens, there are basic trends in the occurrence of various elements of the nonceramic technology which are evident in these data from the four areas of the upper coast. Among those to which attention should be drawn are

1. The disappearance of dart points in the coastal zone by about A.D. 400–500, although they continued in use at sites in the interior.

2. Arrow points first appear around A.D. 600 throughout the upper coast. Their proportions remain more or less constant in the Brazos and Conroe–Livingston; in Galveston, however, they increase dramatically during the Old River Period, probably as a consequence either of renewed bison hunting, of the fur trade, or of both.

3. Arrow points, lithic tools, gastroliths, and flake density all decline almost to the vanishing point in the Galveston Bay Area during the Orcoquisac Period. This may be explained by the fact that only two Indian sites dating to this period have been excavated. On the other hand, it may also be an effect of coming more fully within the ambit of the European colonial and trading networks resulting in native use of metal knives and projectile points, although none of these has yet been identified.

4. Socketed bone projectile points appear to have been experimented with, at least on the coast if not the interior, and evidently helped technologically to bridge the transition from darts and spears to the bow and arrow.

5. Other bone tools appear about the same time but continue in use after the socketed bone points cease to be manufactured. The sandstone and pumice, often found in sites throughout the area, appear in midden refuse at this time possibly because of their use in fashioning bone artifacts.

6. Chipped stone drill/perforators consistently do not appear in sites in this area until the latter part of the first millennium A.D. Microflint tools, however, may have been in use from the late preceramic times.

CHAPTER 16

Archaeological Evidence for Group Territories

In Part I, ethnohistoric evidence was described for the existence of tribal groups and their territories. This evidence indicates the basis for the alignments of the inhabitants of the upper Texas coast and their manners of distinguishing themselves from other people. Available records of the spatial distributions of members of these tribal groups indicate more or less mutually exclusive occurrences, thereby implying the spatial dimension of the local concept of group. At the same time, at least during the Historic Period, it is evident that personnel and materials moved with varying degrees of ease across these boundaries.

At the present data level of the upper Texas coast archaeological record, there is very little tangible evidence for these boundaries. However, Barth (1969:9) makes the case that communication, rather than isolation, is essential for the drawing of distinctions and formation of boundaries, and that ethnic distinctions depend more on "social processes of exclusion and incorporation" than on an "absence of mobility, contact, and information." If there is no one to be distinguished from, the notion of a local group would remain implicit at best.

This latter point is not academic if a longer historical view is taken than is the focus of Part III. Although neither Paleo-Indian nor Transitional Archaic sites are known from the upper coast, projectile points typical of these times have been found quite frequently; Early and Middle Archaic artifacts and sites have not been found at all (except for very late Middle Archaic). The absence of Early and Middle Archaic remains is of interest because it corresponds in time to the hydrologic and geologic evidence for the Altithermal as discussed in Part II. Therefore, it is necessary to consider that, during the period from roughly 8000 to 5000 B.C., the upper Texas coastal plain either was depopulated or, as I think more likely, inhabited by a significantly smaller population than either before or since.

This reduced population presumably lived through a specialized settlement system suited to the arid climate; this implies a strong ecological tether to estuaries, coast, and stream courses, probably in that order. Consequently, the possibility should be considered of a demographic history in which the Early and Middle Archaic upper Texas coast population consisted of only a few rela-

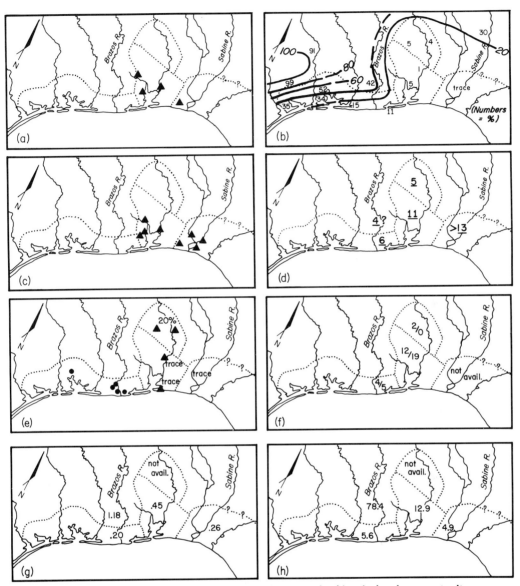

FIGURE 16.1 Spatial distribution of artifacts in relation to ethnohistoric data for group territories: (a) blunt socketed bone point (▲) circa A.D. 1–700 (Aten present volume; Aten and Bollich, unpublished stratigraphic test data 1971; Aten et al. 1976; Wheat 1953); (b) percentage of bone-tempered ceramics, circa A.D. 1400 (Ambler 1967; Aten present volume; Aten and Bollich 1969; Fox et al. 1974; Fritz 1975; McClurkan et al. 1966); (c) Tchefuncte ceramics, circa 100 B.C.–A.D. 100 (Aten present volume; Aten and Bollich 1969, unpublished stratigraphic test data 1971); (d) number of indigenous ceramic types, circa 100 B.C.–A.D. 1800 (Aten present volume); (e) oyster shell knives/scrapers, ●, and Caddoan ceramics, ▲, (Aten present volume, 1967, 1971; Aten and Bollich, unpublished stratigraphic test data 1971; Campbell 1957; McGuff 1978); (f) maximum percentage of Goose Creek Incised (above solidus) and San Jacinto Incised (below solidus) (Aten present volume); (g) secondary cortex to interior flake ratios for the ceramic period.(Aten present volume); and (h) approximate average lithic flake densities for the ceramic period (see Table 15.1).

tively isolated bands. Under these circumstances presumably there was little stimulus for the development of boundary markers for group territories. Beginning about 4000 years ago, the local population apparently began to expand its range and size with the advent of semihumid and humid environments. As the frequency of group contact increased, the initiation of boundary marking mechanisms must have proceeded. This led continuously, so far as can be determined, through a host of adaptive developments to the native cultures of the Historic Period. Further elaboration of a model for this development is included in Chapter 17.

Increase in population and the resulting increase in frequency of contact with other groups and individuals carry with them the consequent formation of boundary concepts by the native populations. At the present time, my assumption is that these boundaries on the upper coast first and foremost marked territoriality and entitlement to natural resources. Presumably they also marked some discontinuities in belief or value systems, as reflected in the distribution of different mortuary practices seen over the upper coast (Aten *et al.* 1976; Hall 1981).

The archaeological distribution of various items in the local technology may or may not indicate upper coast group boundaries; this cannot be determined or predicted at present. However, Barth (1969:15) concluded that the critcal focus in ethnic distinctions becomes the boundary itself rather than what is enclosed. A similar conclusion was reached by Hodder (1979). Assuming for the moment that this conclusion is valid, it implies that the distribution of various items of material technology over the upper coast region forms polythetic sets and that these sets will reflect group territories to a significant extent.

In an effort to see whether territories might be suggested in prehistory on the basis of the available archaeological data, the occurrence of several artifact categories was mapped, whose distributions are presumed to represent cultural factors rather than ecological factors, at least in certain geographic directions. Thus, oyster shell cutting tools may be less likely to be found in the interior than on the coast (Figure 16.1e). However, there is no such limitation in source for oyster shell tools laterally along the coast. These artifact distributions are shown in Figure 16.1. They generally confirm the assumption of polythetic sets and each is substantially consistent with some portion of the ethnohistoric territorial pattern. At the same time, they do not appear to reflect simple attrition or distance decay functions.

The nature of the processes is unknown which result in such patterned associations between native groups and specific items of technology, although there are a number of possibilities (cf. Hodder 1977). In any event, new research can be designed to focus on these processes and to collect specific evidence for boundary development and maintenance in the upper coast region. In the interim, it is assumed here that group territories similar to those of the Historic Period either already were in existence or were in the process of coming into existence by roughly 2000 years ago.

PART IV

Conclusions

CHAPTER 17

Regional Implications

INTRODUCTION

The upper Texas coast is an area in which the relationship between the dynamic coastal environment and the evolution of American Indian cultures has been so intimate that an ideal setting exists for examining this evolution from an ecological perspective. However, very little investigation has taken place and none at a regional scale. As a result, what is known about the area constitutes a loose collection of odds and ends which have limited meaning because of the absence of integrative frameworks. If we agree that the basic elements of a sociocultural system are its population, a social structure to relate the components of the population to each other, a technology to cope with the environmental setting, and a mechaism for transmitting information throughout the system (cf. Plog 1974:55–73; Segraves 1974:531), then these elements must be woven together in a conceptual structure reflecting the dimensions of the whole system. Achieving this will set a foundation for more advanced studies.

This is not to advocate or to attempt description and/or analysis of every conceivable aspect of upper coast cultural systems. On the other hand, as Plog (1974:76) has noted, analysis too often focuses on a single dimension or variable of culture, such as ceramics or lithic technology, settlement patterns, subsistence, and so on. If it is accepted that a culture system as an entity has characteristics wholly beyond that of its parts, it should be obvious that the system cannot be understood in terms of its parts, but rather quite the reverse.

The present study brings together, for these purposes, most of the ethnohistorical and archaeological information currently available. It is not too helpful to simply accumulate this information in the expectation that it will appear isomorphic when "enough" has been accumulated. A more direct approach making immediate use of existing data is to redefine them according to common denominators. The two most obvious dimensions common to the ethnohistoric and archaeological information classes are their temporal dimensions and their spatial patterns of population interaction.

Three empirically oriented research questions were posed in Chapter 1 as tasks to be addressed. These questions were directed at an initial formulation of

313

regional integrative frameworks based on both classes of data. They pertained to (a) describing, largely from ethnohistoric sources, the cultural characteristics of upper coast native populations; (b) devising bases for differentiating and organizing the archaeological materials found in the region; and (c) organizing both the ethnohistoric and archaeological data into a system of models constituting broad sociocultural frames of reference about the indigenous peoples of the upper Texas coast.

Characterization of Native Groups

The first step in this direction was taken with the study of the evolution of prehistoric mortuary practices in the Galveston Bay Area and describing their implications primarily for reconstructing population and information flow data (Aten *et al.* 1976). In this volume, further efforts are made to draw together a coherent description of the nature and history of upper coast populations and their social structure, their organization, their material technology, and their social information subsystems (i.e., ritual and cognition), as well as a description of regional environmental reconstructions. Studies still in progress are synthesizing data on the spatial dimensions of settlement and site, and on subsistence exploitation and energy budgets.

In Part I, the documentary evidence available for the existence of native tribal entities on the upper coast was described. Certainly, there are many untidy elements in this documentation but it can hardly be doubted that Indian and European alike recognized the existence of separate native groups. It has often been noted that "terminology is generally the best index to behavior [Schusky 1972:11; also see Buchler and Selby 1968; Sturtevant 1968:494]." A review of the commonly understood characteristics of an ethnic group concluded that the most critical attribute is that of self-ascription and ascription to the group by others (Barth 1969:10–14). Ethnic groups tend to be marked by overt signs, and by basic value orientations. In this framework, the critical focus of attention becomes the ethnic boundary, not the cultural attributes that are enclosed. Indeed, Barth (1969:11) concluded that a common culture within an ethnic group is more likely to be a result of ethnic group formation than to be a defining character.[1]

Operation of these principles is not difficult to recognize among the historic upper coast tribes. For example, the Atakapa, Akokisa, Bidai, and Karankawa were all known to employ distinctive and exclusive patterns of tattooing as a technique for signaling their affiliation (Dyer 1916:3, 1917:4; Gatschet 1891:62; Oliver 1891:19). The recognition of group distinctiveness at the village or max-

---

[1]This may operationalize the broadly held generalization that cultural processes are fundamentally geared toward generating both diversity and homogeneity (Ribeiro 1968) or, as stated by Wallace (1961:26–28), toward organizing diversity and replicating uniformity.

imum band level is reflected in the willingness of the several Akokisa and Bidai villages to enter a mission provided they could have one in their own territories, rather than enter the consolidated mission at Orcoquisac (Bolton 1913:372). In contrast to this evidence for unifying elements, other basic features such as language were not distinctive at the level of the tribe, and, in the case of technology, were heavily influenced by ecological determinants.

Although ethnic groups basically are social constructs they ordinarily have spatial correlates. The boundaries of these group territories usually are permeable to the passage of personnel and materials into or through adjacent territories. As a result of the data on group territories presented in Part I, a scaling in the permeability of some upper coast boundaries is intuitively perceived in the following order (from most permeable to least permeable; also see Figure 3.1) for the Late Prehistoric and Historic periods: (a) between Akokisa and Western Atakapa; (b) between Bidai and Akokisa; (c) between Coco and Akokisa; (d) between Coco and inland groups to the north; and (e) between Akokisa and inland groups to their west.

In Part I, a hierarchy of human population aggregates was identified, which apparently operated on the upper coast at various spatial, ecological, and social scales. These were the tribe, the village, the band, the family, and other special purpose groups consisting of only a few individuals. The significance of the named tribal groups and their territorial limits probably is in marking diminished interaction frequency rather than absolute limitations in regional exchange systems. The concept of tribal distinctions on the upper coast may set apart those villages (or maximum bands) related to each other in the exchange of women, goods, services, and intervillage coordination for special purposes such as raiding or winter hunting. The permeability scaling of boundaries just described (and in Figure 5.1) should reflect differences in the intensity of these forms of exchange between the adjacent groups.

In Part III, evidence suggestive of archaeological correlates of the tribal level of organization was presented. Other studies are in progress to report data on archaeological correlates of the band and smaller populations (e.g., Aten 1982) as well as the archaeological correlates of the ecological scales of population interaction, that is, the settlement system. The village scale is as yet unknown archaeologically, although the requirements for research needed to deal with this issue can be derived from ethnohistoric documents. Given this, the present study focuses primarily on the tribal scale of population organization. Further characteristics of the populations, their organization, world view, and interaction at this scale are furnished in Part I.

Differentiating Archaeological Materials

By employing both geological and archaeological techniques of historical reconstruction it has been possible, in Parts II and III, to construct a chronological framework for the upper coast. Broadly speaking, this framework consists of three parts which essentially follow the major periods of late glacial to interglacial history on the Gulf coast:

1. The Paleo-Indian Period extended from about 12,000 to 9,000 B.P. and embraced all of the regional contemporaneous cultures that adapted to the late full glacial environments, regardless of the technology used.

2. The Early to Middle Archaic Period extended from the end of the Paleo-Indian Period to about 3,000 B.P. This period spanned the major post-Pleistocene environmental changes and the concomitant cultural shifts in adaptive poses.

3. The Late Archaic to Late Prehistoric/Woodland Period extended from the final phases of the Archaic through the Historic Period and consisted of cultures adapted to a sharply differentiated annual environmental cycle through a primary orientation to hunting and gathering. As shown in Part III, the chronological succession of the ethnohistoric record significantly overlaps that of the archaeological record, thereby establishing a controlled temporal framework for relating one to the other.

In Part III, it was argued that the distribution of Late Prehistoric/Woodland archaeological features, which of themselves might be responding to cultural and/or ecological determinants, collectively described polythetic sets. If it is correct that a common culture is likely to be a result of ethnic group formation rather than to be their defining characteristic, the archaeological sets should approximate the spatial distribution of ethnic groups, probably as described for the Historic Period. A further implication of this thesis is that the polythetic sets reflecting ethnic groups in the archaeological record should display increasing distinctiveness through time. The archaeological items whose distributional data are used to develop the polythetic sets date to the period after about A.D. 100. This implies support for the conclusion of increasing cultural distinctiveness arising from the Late Archaic. Subject to further verification and refinement, it is assumed that identity and continuity exist at the level of the tribe between the ethnohistoric groups and groups inferred from the archaeological record.

Because of the apparent continuities between history and prehistory in various classes of environmental and cultural data, the ethnohistoric record for the upper coast is a source of descriptive and organizational hypotheses for ethnographic interpretation about native groups subsequent to circa 3000 years ago. Prior to that time is another matter. The geography, the biota and climate, and the technology all were significantly different. At these earlier periods, group identity probably existed. But the manner of signifying this must have been quite different because of much lower population densities. The situation must commonly have existed of a band with few neighbors or competitors to be distinguished. In any event, there is no known basis for applying uniformitarian principles to interpreting the region's late Wisconsin to Middle Holocene cultures.

A System of Models

The idea of a process framework based on a system of models also was introduced in Chapter 1. Its basic components are:

1. Specification of the parameters of scale, resolution, and degree of abstraction,[2] and a commitment to hold these specifications constant throughout the description of a particular system of models.
2. Synchronic culture system models dealing with the 4 dimensions of population, organization, technology, and information.
3. An array of a series of synchronic system models according to either their actual spatial or temporal sequence so that system dynamics become evident.

Such a system in its synchronic and diachronic variety is too complex to represent graphically or verbally beyond the two dimensional representations of interactions so often employed in the literature. Suffice it to say, however, that it is premature for quantitative estimates of the flow of either information or energy along the paths connecting our 4 dimensions of population, technology, organization, and information in the case of the prehistoric upper Texas coast.

Nevertheless, the connections or linkages between these models will be obvious to most users. Because of the substantial redundancy in linkages, the system of models has greater methodological robusticity than is the case when dealing only with a single set of point to point relationships. A particular hypothesis about the behavior of a particular cultural variable must satisfy the predictions of effect resulting from the several models which may describe the variable, albeit from the perspective of different sets of linkages.

Models are presented in Parts I, II, and III which may be classified according to which basic element of a sociocultural system they pertain—population, organization, technology, or information. Organization of these models according to the chronological frameworks provided in Chapters 9 and 14—for exam-

[2]Scale: the units of measure are similarly proportioned and are at the maximum size to be represented in the model. For example, one could not readily integrate models of tribal organization and band subsistence.

Resolution: the smallest constituent parts needed to be distinguished to provide adequate definition to the entities comprising the level at which scale is set. For example, if the scale of models is to be the tribal level of organization, the resolution probably does not need to be set below the next lower organizational level.

Degree of abstraction: Determination of the extent to which behavioral variability needs to be stated. For example, models scaled to higher organizational levels may consist of normative formulations to a greater extent than models scaled to lower organizational levels.

ple, late glacial, altithermal, or contemporary—begins to provide the dynamic dimension needed for an evolutionary process framework. Finally, organization of the models according to the tribal (spatial) framework provided in Chapters 3 and 16 provides the dynamic dimension needed for creating an interactive process framework.

An index to these models is provided in Table 17.1. Their scale is to the tribe or tribal group level; their resolution generally is the next lower organizational level—the tribe or sometimes the village (maximum band); the degree of abstraction was not rigorously held constant. In addition, there are numerous auxiliary models here which do not directly describe native cultural phe-

TABLE 17.1
Index to Models of Cultural Phenomena on the Upper Texas Coast

Cultural Dimensions	Time/Environments				Space/Organization				
	Lg[a]	Alt[b]	Con[c]	Und[d]	Ata[e]	Ako[f]	Bid[g]	Kar[h]	Und[d]
POPULATION									
Size	9[i]	9	4 ,17	—	4	4 ,17	4	4	—
Density	—	—	4	—	—	4	4	4	—
Structure	—	—	A[j]	—	—	A	—	A	—
ORGANIZATION									
Ethnic groups	—	—	3	—	3	3	3	3	—
Group territories	—	—	3,16	—	3,16	3,16	3,16	3,16	—
Social org/structure	—	—	5	—	—	—	—	—	5
Village formation	—	—	17	—	—	17	—	—	—
Statuses	—	—	5	—	5,A	5,A	5	5	—
Reciprocity	—	—	5	—	—	5	—	—	5
TECHNOLOGY									
Functional artifact classification	—	—	—	13	—	—	—	—	13,15
Ceramic typology	—	—	12	—	14	14	14	14	12,15
Lithic sources	9	9	—	App.B	—	—	—	—	App.B
Trade	—	—	5	—	—	—	—	—	5
INFORMATION									
"World view"	—	—	6	—	—	—	—	—	6
Mortuary ritual	—	—	—	A,6	—	A	—	A	6
Domestic ritual	—	—	6	—	—	—	—	—	6
UNDIFFERENTIATED									
Early Cultures	9	9	—	—	—	—	—	—	9

[a] Late glacial
[b] Altithermal
[c] Contemporary
[d] Undifferentiated
[e] Atakapa
[f] Akokisa
[g] Bidai
[h] Karankawa
[i] Chapter numbers.
[j] Aten *et al.* (1976).

nomena, but which aid in understanding them. These include such matters as paleoenvironmental reconstruction, and how to evaluate radiocarbon dating performed on *Rangia cuneata* shells. It is clear from Table 17.1 that some of these models are extremely elementary, and that other important issues have not yet been synthesized at all. If nothing else then, Table 17.1 gives a graphic sense of the extent of progress toward comprehensive synthesis of cultural information on the upper Texas coast. Conversely, it summarizes the dimensions of the foundation available for future research.

THE AKOKISA MODEL

Because of the relative abundance of data from the Galveston Bay Area Akokisa, a hypothesis of tribal population growth and village formation from the Late Archaic into the Historic Period can be proposed. Although similar hypotheses are not attempted for the other coastal archaeological areas and ethnohistoric tribes, the Akokisa model illustrates most of the basic principles pertinent to these other groups. Indeed, with slight modifications, it can serve as a basic post-Altithermal culture-historical hypothesis applicable to the upper Texas coast region. Because of the very generalized nature of the information currently available pertaining to earlier periods, a synthesis probably cannot be prepared for them that is more specific than that given in Chapter 9.

Construction of the Akokisa model (Figure 17.1) begins with plotting the Historic Period population reconstruction given in Part I. Because of the likelihood of very small population size during the Early–Middle Archaic (Part II), it also may be assumed that a population trend declined back through prehistory to a very small number around 4000 years ago. The first problem is to suggest how these two population extremes may be linked together.

Ethnohistoric and archaeological data not included in this study both establish that the Akokisa populations were dispersed in small, band-sized or less groups during warm seasons and were aggregated into villages during cold seasons. By the advent of the Historic Period, there appear to have been five of these cold season villages with maximum populations reaching the range of 400–500 persons. The minimum functional size of these villages may be indicated by the population size at which composite bands, evidently, were formed, or around 200 persons (cf. Figures 4.1, 17.1).[3] These minimum and maximum

[3]Ewers (1973:109) suggested that among the Caddo, it was rare for a group's population to fall below 150 persons before they would merge with another group to insure survival. The interpretation of minimum Akokisa village size (and perhaps the Caddo example as well) may be explained by considering the implications of incest rules. As noted in Part I, in the Atakapa language, aunts and female cousins are terminologically merged as sisters. The prohibition on marriage with sisters, also described in Part I, thereby implies a prohibition on marriage with first and, perhaps, second

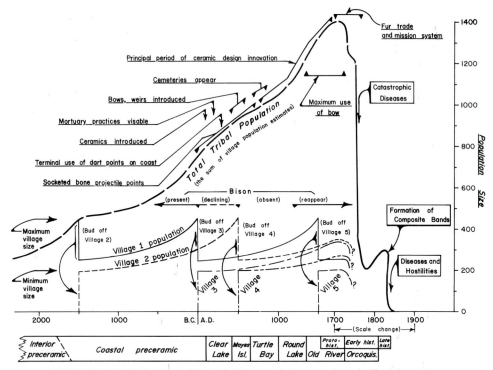

FIGURE 17.1   Preliminary model of Akokisa population growth and village formation.

group size limits (200–450) are assumed to form the demographic constraints or consequences of the social organization present in the several Akokisa villages. That is, populations below about 200 individuals could not function and group sizes above approximately 450 individuals necessitated a fissioning process in which a group sufficiently large to function independently as a village budded off. In this manner, the Akokisa social organization could have replicated itself when the need arose.

In Figure 17.1, this history of budding off is hypothesized in such a way that the time interval between the Altithermal and the Historic Period can be

---

cousins. Hammel *et al.* (1979) have shown that in order for groups below about 150 persons in size to maintain a stable population level, a variety of fertility techniques is needed to sidestep the demographic cost of an incest prohibition. Therefore, strongly enforced incest rules constitute an incentive not to let group size fall below about 150 persons. Consequently, the empirically-based estimate of a minimum village size of about 200 persons also has a functional and theoretical basis. This raises the possibility that the ultimate decline to extinction of the Akokisa population as shown in Figure 17.1 could have been less exclusively a matter of disease and hostilities in the nineteenth century. It could have been as much a natural consequence of incest taboo enforcement necessitating individuals to move away and to join with other tribes forming composite bands once population dropped below 150–200.

bridged. The frequency of budding is entirely hypothetical; the remainder of the data, has some factual basis. This model also provides for a substantially stable population,[4] the assumption used in developing demographic information in the Galveston Bay Area mortuary study (Aten *et al.* 1976). This is a framework for considering the evolution of indigenous cultures on the upper Texas coast through the gradual expansion of a sociologically more generalized small population experiencing infrequent interaction with other groups. As demographic expansion of this population took place, the social processes of boundary formation accelerated. As population increased, the relationships among population size, technology, and available resources must have been adjusted. This may be the basis for understanding the reconstructed average family size of 6.4 persons at Harris County Boys School Cemetery (ca. A.D. 700–900) declining to 4 persons at the Jamaica Beach Cemetery (ca. A.D. 1500) (Aten *et al.* 1976). The decline in birth rate may have been one of the essential adaptive mechanisms late in the prehistory of the Akokisa territory.

Having suggested a model of Akokisa population growth and village formation, it is useful to go on to examine the relationship of this model to other cultural and environmental elements. On Figure 17.1 is shown the time of occurrence of the major technological and cultural features identified in Parts I and III. On this basis, the model can be partitioned into at least five sequential parts.

Late Archaic (ca. 3000 B.C. to A.D. 100)   After the initial documentation of Late Archaic technology, as represented at sites such as Harris County Boys School, Jamison, and Addicks, no major technological innovations are recognizable in this time range.

A.D. *100 to A.D. 800*   This period contains major changes in technology and mortuary practices which imply significant changes in subsistence, cognition and possibly social organization. It is in this period that artifact distributions first form recognizable polythetic sets paralleling the organization of Historic Period tribal territories. Therefore, it is the earliest time in which boundaries, as they are known later, first existed. It also is in this period that important energy harnessing technology enters the Akokisa system: (*a*) the initial use of ceramic containers; (*b*) the initial use of the bow and arrow as a replacement for the dart; and (*c*) the probable appearance of tidal fish weirs.[5] The latter two innovations probably mark an important shift in emphasis for subsistence from exclusively larger animals to a wider range of species and smaller individual

[4]If a generation is assumed to be approximately 20 years for the native populations, then the budding model would incorporate an average population increase per village per generation of 2.7 individuals.

[5]Fish weirs made of brush or other materials used to block tidal streams are known ethnohistorically and probably have been identified in the unpublished subsistence data from the Brazos Delta Area; I assume this will be identifiable in the Galveston Bay Area as well.

body sizes. This adaptation of the subsistence technology to a more specialized mode may signify (*a*) growing competition for resources, (*b*) increased length of stay at a given location, (*c*) reduction in procurement range about a given location, (*d*) shift in division of labor, (*e*) change in absolute availability of other food sources (e.g., the bison), or may have been due to several of these causes acting in concert.

This period also is marked by the first visible mortuary practices and by the first cemeteries.[6] Although the content of mortuary ritual likely served the spiritual purposes described on the preliminary cognitive model (Figure 6.1) in Part I, cemetery location in or near habitation sites also may constitute a symbol or sign of entitlement to or use of the resources of an area by village groups (maximum bands) or by their subunits such as minimum bands. Because this is the period in which the number of villages may have doubled, it is difficult not to see the growing formalization of ritual as another evolving element needed in a period when the subdivision and exploitation of space and of contained resources by the area's inhabitants was becoming more competitive and much more highly organized.

A.D. 800 to A.D. 1700   The third period in the model is characterized archaeologically by innovation in ceramic design styles, although demographic changes have been inferred from mortuary data. Late in this time range, during the Old River Period, the use of the bow and arrow expands significantly. This may reflect an altered hunting pattern, for by this time the bison had returned to southern ranges (Dillehay 1974). It also is possible that most or all of this increased use of the bow occurred very late in the Old River Period reflecting the inception of the fur trade during the early Historic Period.

First Half of the Eighteenth Century   This was the period in which the fur trade and mission system, as well as the first effects of epidemic diseases, began to seriously disrupt and stress the native cultural and social systems.

Late Eighteenth to Early Nineteenth Century   Although not marked by archaeological data as clearly as earlier periods, a final segment of this history is recognizable during the time in which the Akokisa tribe was becoming extinct. Because of the brief period of time involved, archaeological research cannot explore this period very effectively without significant assistance from ethnohistorical sources. However, testable models exist (e.g., Gould *et al.* 1972) to guide the considerable archival research that is needed.

Effects of environmental changes are difficult to assess during the period encompassed by the Akokisa model. The broad shift from arid Altithermal conditions to the seasonally moist conditions of the present day are obvious.

---

[6]Aside from any other significance, this association of cemeteries and energy harnessing tools is a correlation suggested earlier by Binford (1968:272–273).

Finer grained changes undoubtedly occurred, however. For this reason, Dillehay's (1974) sequence of bison appearances on the southern range (including the coastal plain) is shown on Figure 17.1. Although bison, even when present, formed a very modest portion of coastal subsistence, they are an indicator for other less obvious conditions (also cf. Bryson *et al.* 1970).

In this light, significant increase of population, major reorientation of the technology and important changes which probably occurred in the relationships among groups (both within and between tribal areas) all are attributable to the period in which bison were at first declining in numbers and then were absent entirely. Bison *per se* probably figure very slightly in this interpretation; the environmental modifications to which the bison were responding, however, must have been causing significant impact upon upper Texas coast cultural patterns. Identification of these modifications and of their impact must be the subject of new research.

SYSTEMIC ADJUSTMENTS

To recapitulate, the Akokisa model describes a generalized cultural system expanding into unoccupied spaces in the Late Archaic following the formation or expansion of more favorable habitats in the Middle Holocene. These generalized cultures subsequently diversified into more specialized systems. The model describes a sequence of alternating phases of culture growth (i.e., when the available culture elements expanded into the social and/or geographic space available; see Adams 1975:285 after Carneiro), and culture development (i.e., when new cultural elements were coming into being; see same source).

The two developmental phases were from roughly A.D. 100–900 and from A.D. 1700–1770. The earlier of these periods was quite extended and incorporated the following systemic changes:

1. A major rise in energy demand resulting from population increases;
2. Adoption of a technology which permitted focusing food and other raw materials acquisition on previously inaccessible quantitative and qualitative segments of the area's biotic resources;
3. Improvements in the efficiency of energy-harnessing technology;
4. Use of cemeteries to signify or assert entitlement to resources thereby controlling or attempting to control the absolute size of the potential energy reservoir;
5. Use of mortuary symbolism to gain support, seek intervention, or to neutralize any negative impact of the supernatural upon secular affairs, per the cognitive model given in Part I, and to guarantee the renewability of resources;
6. Improvements in "social efficiency" by introduction of coordinating mechanisms (cf. Adams 1975:210) including the establishment or for-

malization of ethnic boundaries, and increases in organizational and demographic complexity.

The later developmental period probably was qualitatively different from the earlier period in several respects. For one thing, its duration was very brief, such that major changes must have been evident within the span of a single generation. For another, as new cultural elements appeared (e.g., linkage with the European economic system through the fur trade and missions), destruction of the native cultures also was proceeding through the media of severe population losses to diseases, rapid cognitive disruption probably including significant levels of mental illness, and possibly, through severe depletion of available subsistence resources as a consequence of removal of fur-bearing animals.[7]

Because of the rapidity with which the latter changes occurred, it is very difficult to identify adaptive processes at work during these final years of Akokisa existence. More than likely, however, their cultural system dissipated into small-scale producing units, probably at or near the level of the family.

What factors in the larger ecological setting of the Akokisa culture system stimulated these developmental phases is unclear. At a minimum, the bison data make clear that there were alterations occurring in the natural environment. Whether these were sufficient to stimulate cultural systemic reactions is not known. The functional nature of the changes also may be considered in another way.

The purpose of information feedback in a system is to make its performance less dependent upon the input load (Wiener 1961:107–108); in other words, to insulate a system's performance from stress. Moreover, a complex system (such as a cultural system) cannot be stabilized by a single feedback mechanism. This leads to the recognition that, in the face of the significant environmental load on the Akokisa cultural system, the importance of changes in technology, social efficiency, and mortuary symbolism in the A.D. 100–900 period of cultural development was to introduce additional feedback channels between information flow and energy flow. These would have stabilized the new stresses on population levels and organizational structures.

During the cultural developments of the Historic Period, the Akokisa system was subjected to such severe stresses from its external social environment as to overload the system's feedback mechanisms, causing the system to be destroyed. Identification of the actual behavioral correlates of these systemic events awaits future investigation, especially in archival sources.

Data available for the other three tribal areas on the upper Texas coast are not as detailed as for the Akokisa, but all indications are that a similarly structured model ultimately can be prepared for each of them, even though the precise timing and behavioral manifestations within each area may differ to some extent.

---

[7]Recall that when arrested at Orcoquisac, the French trader Blancpain had 2300 deer skins in his possession (Nixon 1946:50)!

In this study, a host of descriptive and explanatory models have been advanced about historical, developmental, and sociocultural features of the now-extinct cultures of indigenous Indian peoples on the upper Texas coast. In most cases these models should not be taken at face value. These are hypothetical (i.e., reflect my imagination) and provide what seems to be a best interpretation of the meaning of the analyzed data while interpolating for certain missing elements. They provide guidance and a tangible framework for the design of critical experiments in testing these models and for the development of new ones.

Further, the historical interpretation of these models may be articulated as a hypothesis demonstrating the applicability of systems theory to understanding processes of culture change. Thus, a cultural system may be subjected to natural or social environmental load (i.e., inputs) only to a limit which is defined by the system's capacity to generate new feedback mechanisms. Load beyond this limit causes disintegration of the system, possibly into its component subsystemic elements, but certainly into less extensive and less complex elements. A corollary hypothesis is that with increasing system complexity, the potential capacity for inputs to be made probably increases exponentially. Thus it may also be proposed that the disintegration of a system into component subsystems is itself an adaptive mechanism to partition a population into organizational systems of reduced complexity capable of bearing their environmental input load.

Looking over the longest range of possibilities for testing these proposals, several periods of stress and recovery from stress in upper coast culture history are readily identifiable: (a) the end of glacial period environments and the onset of the Altithermal; (b) recovery from the Altithermal; (c) environmental and social stresses in the early Late Prehistoric; and (d) the social stresses of the Historic Period. These hypotheses can be tested through the means of integrated and quantitative analysis of societal energetics, that is, through a joint consideration of population, subsistence, subsistence technology and settlement patterns, and, where feasible, through inferences on ideological systems. This becomes possible by building on the ethnohistoric and archaeological frameworks presented here.

Appendixes

APPENDIX A

Rangia Cuneata as a Carbon-14 Dating Medium on the Upper Texas Coast

INTRODUCTION

One of the immediate problems for archaeological research on the upper Texas coast is the need for absolute dating of archaeological contexts. The most heavily inhabited areas of this region during the Holocene were covered predominantly with grasses and shrubs; woodlands have been very limited in their extent. The consequence of using these fuel resources was that fires usually were made with insubstantial woody materials, leaving small quantities of charcoal to be preserved in archaeological sites. While wood charcoal is not encountered often enough for the dating of many excavated contexts, shell is almost always available.

It is reasonable to estimate that at least 90% of the archaeological shell middens on the upper Texas coast are composed entirely, or in their majority, of the brackish water clam, *Rangia cuneata*. To develop understanding of *Rangia cuneata* as a practical radiocarbon dating tool would constitute an important technical improvement supporting archaeological research in this area. But the practical use of any medium for radiocarbon age determinations depends on an understanding of carbon isotope behavior in that medium and the field conditions in which these materials occur.

Discrepancies in the radiocarbon behavior of some carbonaceous materials often has led to a premature conclusion that a given material is unsuitable for absolute date measurement. Even Libby (1955:11) reacted negatively to the initial findings of subnormal radiocarbon levels in certain natural habitats (Deevey *et al.* 1954). However, the phenomena responsible for such variations often can be observed, and their effects compensated. In fact, natural and anthropogenic variations from the behavior described by Libby's basic theory are now known to be so widespread that the development of correction tech-

329

niques may be almost a *sine qua non* of the radiocarbon method (Arundale 1981).

Shell carbonate has been widely regarded as one of the problem materials (cf. Keith and Anderson 1963; and Ralph 1971 for a brief review) and attempts have been made either to devise correction factors (e.g., Berger *et al.* 1966; Bullen and Bryant 1965; Pearson 1965; Tamers 1970), or alternative methods (Berger *et al.* 1964). In this Appendix is described the approach to development of a correction process for radiocarbon assays made on the shell of *Rangia cuneata*.

TRINITY DELTA AREA INVESTIGATIONS

The results reported here build on the initial steps taken on lower Trinity River shell midden samples by J. Richard Ambler of Northern Arizona University and Sam Valastro, Jr. of The University of Texas at Austin Radiocarbon Laboratory. Ambler was aware of the problems experienced in other regions with radiocarbon assays performed on various types of shell carbonate and was dubious of the uncritical use of *R. cuneata* shell for this purpose. In an attempt to evaluate the reliability of *R. cuneata*, a field procedure was adopted whereby shells associated with any charcoal sample were collected along with the charcoal. Radiocarbon assays were made on both materials and a sequence of paired dates was obtained ranging in apparent age from about 500 B.C. to about A.D. 500. These indicated that *R. cuneata* shells were diluted with 1–3% "dead" carbon and measured older than charcoal by 100 to 400 years (Valastro and Davis 1970a:265–266). Ambler (1973:138–143) described a range of conceivable depositional factors which might have caused this deviation. Because of the consistent results observed from these initial paired samples, additional work seemed justified (Valastro and Davis 1970a:265).

PHYSICAL BASIS FOR SHELL–CHARCOAL DEVIATION

There are several carbon reservoirs in nature which vary in their impact on the composition of organic matter according to local, or even microenvironmental, conditions (Broecker 1964). It has long been known that mollusk shell carbonate materials are susceptible to exchange with carbon mobilized by water and by weathering, soil-forming, erosion and other processes. This results in alteration of the amount of radioactive carbon remaining in the shell (Bathurst 1964; Broecker and Walton 1959; Deevey *et al.* 1954). Most approaches to this problem have focused on eliminating "contaminated" shell by leaching the outer layers with hydrochloric acid and then dating the inner shell material in the usual manner. Other methods have been developed to avoid using the inorganic carbonate and instead to extract the 1–3% organic component, conchiolin (Berger *et al.* 1964; Turekian and Armstrong 1961).

While acid-leaching sample preparation deals with certain postdepositional alteration of the shell surface, neither of the methods described directly copes with the problem of the water chemistry of the original mollusk habitat. The impact of carbonate-rich water upon the original carbon-14 content of aquatic organisms has been noted at least as far back as 1954 (Deevey *et al.* 1954). The proportion of carbon-14 in water which has passed through ancient limestones and taken up nonradioactive carbonate ions in solution could be as low as half that in atmospheric carbon dioxide and, as a result, dates could be anomalously old by thousands of years (Deevey *et al.* 1954; Olsson 1968; Rubin and Taylor 1963). Indeed, this process has been asserted to be the major cause of radiocarbon deficiency in surface waters (Broecker and Walton 1959).

Restricted circulation of surface waters likewise limits the process of carbon dioxide exchange with the atmosphere and the mixture of the products of this exchange throughout the aqueous system. It has been predicted that this process alone would cause shellfish from Gulf coast estuaries such as Galveston Bay in Texas and Lake Ponchartrain in Louisiana to have subnormal radioactive carbon content (Berger *et al.* 1966:866).

However, it can be seen from any geologic map of Texas that most major streams traversing the upper coast from the Louisiana border westward to near the coastal bend region drain the Cretaceous carbonate terrain of central Texas to a significant degree. It seems fairly obvious that there is a high likelihood for estuarine waters to be significantly enriched with nonradioactive carbon derived from the abundant outcrops of ancient carbonates in the interior of the state. In view of this, the assumption was made that the dominant source of apparent age deviation in Ambler's shell–charcoal sample pairs was due to this dilution factor.

SAMPLING CONSIDERATIONS

The solution usually employed in such a situation is to collect and measure the radiocarbon activity in modern carbonaceous materials of like kind. The observed radiocarbon activity deviation of these modern materials from that of the present (i.e., A.D. 1950) atmospheric levels is then taken to be a correction factor to be subtracted from age measurements made on older samples (Ogden 1967:177). This is a weak solution because of the progressive enrichment of atmospheric carbon dioxide with nonradioactive carbon derived from the combustion of fossil fuels. Radioactive carbon enrichment derived from nuclear testing in the atmosphere probably also has had an effect. The paired sample approach begun by Ambler was suited to overcoming this problem because it aimed at developing a correction factor solely in terms of the archaeological materials. As a result, the paired sampling approach was continued in my own research whenever possible.[1]

In the process of this more recent work, certain caveats about paired samples have become apparent. Current information indicates that fire hearths were frequently situated on top of preexisting shell midden surfaces. This means the shell and charcoal samples would only coincidentally represent the same event and/or age. Thus, as a fire was built on a shell pile, probably for its refractory qualities, and as clams were steamed or roasted, it is possible that a few contemporary shells remained in the hearth to be included in the shell radiocarbon sample. More likely, though, most shells being heated were tossed aside onto a new pile (Aten 1982). This reveals the assumption of shell–charcoal sample contemporaneity instead to be one of penecontemporaneity. The time between shell pile deposition and its subsequent use as a refractory base for a fire hearth might be either days, or centuries.

On the other hand, shell midden surfaces may remain exposed for a very long period of time without accumulating a superficial layer of sediment. Subsequent reoccupation of the site results in an unconformity of uncertain duration. Major unconformities extending throughout a site are evident in the stratigraphic sections recorded at 41 CH 13 and 41 CH 16 (Ambler 1973). Paired samples from a hearth placed directly on such an old surface undergoing reoccupation can obviously produce shell dates substantially older than the charcoal dates. This evidently is the case with samples Tx-949A and Tx-949B from 41 CH 46 (Table 14.1). At this site, the fire hearth rests directly on an unconformity in the stratigraphic section (see Figure 11.12), the significance of which was not immediately appreciated at the time of excavation. The shell and charcoal samples were dated as a pair with the results indicating the unusually long (for the Trinity delta) chronological separation of 620 radiocarbon years. After analysis of the associated ceramics, it was realized that the unconformity separated ceramic assemblages of the Mayes Island Period (below) and the Turtle Bay Period (above). These ceramic assemblage periods jointly span a period of about 600 radiocarbon years, easily accounting for the measured radiocarbon age discrepancy between the two samples.

A few other samples exist for which the association between them is in doubt. In the next section, two sample pairs from 41 CH 16 will be discussed; and another pair from 41 HR 85 was discussed in Aten *et al.* (1976:12). These simply constitute reminders of the need for careful documentation of field relations and for continuous effort to gain better understanding of the cultural and natural processes which generate these relations.

---

[1]Brief reports on the results of this later work have been presented in Valastro *et al.* (1975:76–77) and in Aten (1976:2–5).

RESULTS

Out of a total of 15 sample pairs dated, 13 proved to have sufficiently sound stratigraphic and cultural associations to be used for this analysis. The two excluded pairs (Tx-388/397 and Tx-455/456 from site 41 CH 16) reversed the normal relationship of shell being apparently older than contemporaneous charcoal (Ambler 1973:Figure 21). The reason for this appears to be that the abundant charcoal found at the base of the midden was thought to be contemporaneous with the immediately overlying shell. Clearly this was not the case.

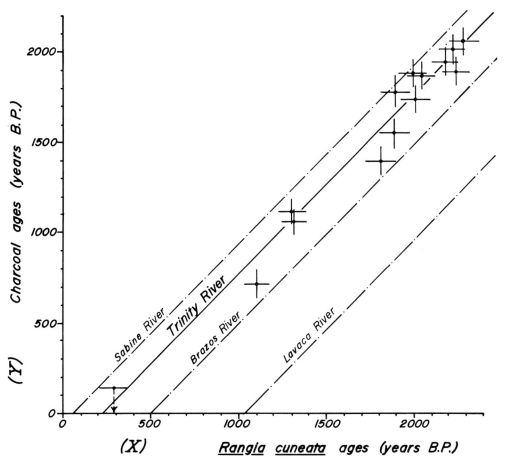

FIGURE A.1 Scattergram of paired radiocarbon samples for the Trinity delta, in which the correlation coefficient (r) equals 0.985, y equals 0.995x − 225.241, and SEEy equals 103 years. The predicted regression of shell on charcoal, based on Figure A.2, for the Sabine, Brazos, and Lavaca river mouth areas are depicted here by — · —.

In addition, a date was determined for a shell sample from the Presidio San Agustín de Ahumada (41 CH 53) occupied from 1756–1766, for which a comparable charcoal radiocarbon age was predicted from the published graphs of Suess (1970). A scattergram of these paired samples is presented in Figure A.1. As can be seen, the correlation between *Rangia cuneata* shell and charcoal apparent ages is very high (Pearson's R = .985). From these data, the following regression equation has been derived for predicting charcoal ages corresponding to those of contemporaneous *Rangia cuneata*.[2]

$$y = 0.995x - 225.241,$$

$$\text{SEE}_y = 103 \text{ years,}$$

where

> y = the predicted shell radiocarbon age after transformation to a charcoal scale, in radiocarbon years B.P.;
>
> x = the apparent or assayed age of *Rangia cuneata* shell, in radiocarbon years B.P.;
>
> SEE_y = standard error of the estimate of this regression equation, in radiocarbon years. This estimate of error is based on the sampling distribution of the individual radiocarbon sample means and replaced the use of sample standard deviations for corrected age estimates plotted on Figure 14.2.

With this regression equation and its standard error, Trinity delta *Rangia cuneata* shell dates may be transformed into a charcoal radiocarbon scale. This is the primary basis for all absolute dating of upper Galveston Bay Area cultural contexts done for this study. When necessary, the derived wood charcoal scale may be corrected further for radiocarbon variations in the atmosphere (cf. Damon *et al.* 1974; Ralph *et al.* 1973; and Suess 1970).[3]

BEYOND THE TRINITY DELTA

At the present time, very scant paired sample data exist for other upper Texas coast estuaries. Given this, an attempt has been made to develop a general

---

[2]No significant error is anticipated to have been introduced into this equation as a result of long-lived shellfish. All archaeological *Rangia cuneata* collected on the upper Texas coast which have been examined for age at death have ranged between 1 and 8 years; most valves used for radiocarbon dating purposes have fallen in the 2 to 4 years age grades.

[3]For information purposes only, there is a sidereal chronological scale shown on Figure 11.2. In compiling this, the Suess correction was used.

hypothesis covering the use of *Rangia cuneata* as a dating medium for the upper coast as a region. This would serve the purposes of providing a plausible framework for tentative interpretations of the meager culture-chronological evidence from elsewhere in the region, as well as to suggest specific data collection activities which, if they were undertaken, would provide more refined chronological control.

Southwest Louisiana

Rangia cuneata shells and charcoal from a fire pit at the Pierre Clement Site (16 CM 47) were dated with the following results: Charcoal, 585±60 B.P.; *R. cuneata*, 665±65 B.P. (Springer 1973:147). Although the shell date is older than the charcoal date, which we would expect, comparison of the dates by the method of Spaulding (1958:309) indicates nearly 20 chances in 100 that these results may have been obtained from materials of the same radioactive carbon content. An additional consideration is the location of the site on Little Chenier where it is intersected by the Mermentau River. The Mermentau drains only the Quaternary formations of the coastal plain rather than any ancient limestone terrain. Given this hydrologic setting, a shell radiocarbon date should be only modestly older than contemporaneous charcoal. Springer's results are consistent with this expectation.

Sabine Lake Area

No paired radiocarbon dates exist which enable an evaluation of the relationship of *Rangia cuneata* to charcoal dates. The fact that only a very small portion of the Sabine–Neches drainage basin includes Cretaceous outcrops suggests that any subnormal radiocarbon in this estuary will be slight in magnitude and be due primarily to the normal exchange processes in coastal estuaries which were described earlier.

Trinity Delta Area

As previously described in this Appendix, the measured deviation of *R. cuneata* from charcoal dates in this area is about 225 radiocarbon years ± 103 years. This deviation occurred, at least, within the time interval of about 150 to 2100 radiocarbon years B.P.

Brazos Delta Area

Two sample pairs are available from sites 41 BO 15 and 41 BO 50 (Table 14.1). In both cases the shell dates are older than the charcoal dates. The 41 BO 15 dates are separated by 680 years; the 41 BO 50 dates are separated by 220 years. The former sample pair may or may not be affected by the problem of hearth fires being built on much earlier shell surfaces. Although the ceramics from 41 BO 15 are too few to seriate, they do include bone-tempered sherds which would be compatible with a recent age. We simply cannot be sure at this point and have accepted this pair at face value.

A third sample exists which might have been used, but was not. Shell sample Tx-1205 from 41 BO 35 (Table 14.1) came from the upper zone of the site in association with a mandible fragment of pig (*Sus scrofa*). This shell sample could have been treated in the same manner as was the shell from Presidio San Agustín de Ahumada, yielding an estimated corresponding charcoal date. However, the radiocarbon properties of shell from this site appear to be substantially altered by chemical residues and effluents from a nearby chemical manufacturing plant (see Aten 1971:47–50 for discussion). For this reason, the sample has not been used.

The present indications are that *Rangia cuneata* shell in the Brazos Delta Area may date older than contemporaneous charcoal by 220 to 680 radiocarbon years. Although the deviation in the Brazos Delta Area cannot now be estimated any more precisely than this, it is worth noting that there is reason to suspect samples from this area may not show the consistency evident in the Trinity delta. The Trinity–Galveston Bay system, and most other estuaries on the upper Texas coast as well, form a largely connected aquatic system in which most clam resource areas are linked together. A gradual transition from fresh to brackish to saline water occurs with the attendant bicarbonate conditions and dilution effects of rainfall being more uniformly dispersed through the system.

The aquatic habitats of the Brazos–Colorado deltaic plain, however, are more disconnected. Many of the major clam resource areas are isolated lakes on the floodplain which are, or were, nourished periodically by overbank flooding. In intervening periods, however, these would be greatly affected in their water quality either by evaporation, precipitation, or respiration. Lake Jackson, Shy Pond, intermittent lakes near 41 BO 35, and numerous other water-filled floodplain depressions and cutoff meanders which do not have continuous exchange of water with main streams like the Brazos and Oyster Creek dot the Brazos Delta Area. One consequence of this could have been substantial local differences in bicarbonate conditions leading to a great deal of variation in radiocarbon determinations for contemporaneous samples. This may mean that radiocarbon dating in the Brazos delta should be accompanied by mass spectrometric determinations of carbon isotope ratios (Rubin and Taylor 1963) provided the carbon isotope composition of *Rangia cuneata* is uniform for the species (cf. Weber and LaRocque 1963).

Lower Lavaca River Area

Even though not part of the immediate archaeological problem, it is worth extending consideration to the Lavaca River area as this is about the westernmost limit of *Rangia cuneata* middens on the Texas coast. The only radiocarbon data available are those obtained on *R. cuneata* from excavation of the Anaqua Site (Story 1968; Valastro and Davis 1970a:275). These dates have always been puzzling because of their extreme age. The cultural deposit is rarely more than 30 cm thick and the artifact assemblage in the dated excavation units consists of plain sandy paste ceramics and arrow points. In the Brazos Delta Area, such a combination, based on extrapolation from the Galveston Bay chronology, would roughly occur in the period between A.D. 500–1100. The Anaqua dates should not be older than this, but, in fact, were measured as much older. Since a very substantial body of data exists indicating that the introduction of ceramics was time-transgressive to the southwest along the coast, it is exceedingly unlikely that the misalignment of radiocarbon dates and cultural assemblages at the Anaqua Site is only apparent and that ceramics may indeed be as old as 5000 years in this area. A far more likely possibility is that factors of isotope chemistry in the dating medium have again entered the picture.

The Anaqua dates (Table 14.1), when viewed in terms of their stratigraphic position, form two groups. Tx-642, 643, and 644 all originated from the base of the midden in contact with the underlying Beaumont Formation. These dates are all in close agreement and are, by far, the oldest dates from the site. The second group consists of Tx-641 and Tx-655. These are from a position in the midden and above the basal contact with the Pleistocene deposit. They are also the youngest of the dates from the site. A sixth sample, Tx-654, is a composite midden sample which includes material from the basal portion. This sample dates between the two groups mentioned previously.

At the end of this Appendix are described several dates obtained on samples taken from positions in proximity to the Pleistocene Beaumont Formation. All of these are abnormally old, apparently as a result of isotopic exchange with the highly calcareous Beaumont. Since this is the simplest explanation for the three oldest dates, and since the middle date, Tx-654, apparently is affected to some extent by this problem as well, use is made only of the information to be had from Tx-641 and 655. As nearly as can be determined by extrapolation from the Galveston Bay Area, these should be dating cultural assemblages which are not likely to be more than 1450 radiocarbon years old. Therefore, these two Anaqua dates suggest a *Rangia cuneata* age deviation from comparable charcoal samples of about 650 to 1240 years in the lower Lavaca River area.

These data on *R. cuneata* charcoal radiocarbon deviations, or predicted deviations, are all consistent with the theoretical expectations of increasing deviation as one moves westward along the Texas coast.

WATER CHEMISTRY

If data on water chemistry will correlate sufficiently well with estimates of shell–charcoal deviations, a basis may be indicated for prediction of correction factors for *Rangia* shell dates. Specifically, it must be determined if the relative differences in concentration of bicarbonate ions in the rivers described above can be significantly correlated with the estimates previously made of shell–charcoal deviations in apparent age. Data on bicarbonate concentrations were obtained from publications of the Texas Water Quality Board. Only those data obtained from samples collected shallower than 10 feet (or about 3 m) were used, on the assumption that samples from greater depths probably would not reflect the water chemistry in the clam habitats ordinarily exploited by natives (cf. Part I).

Sabine River

The average of four measurements made in 1968 (Station 8, TWDB 144),[4] 1969 (Station 15, TWDB 171), 1972, and 1973 (Station 15, TWDB 208) is 37.5 milligrams per liter. This extremely low value confirms the earlier stated expectation of little or no carbonate derived from ancient limestone deposits.

Trinity Delta Area

The average of measurements made over the 15-year period from 1950 to 1964 at Cove on the Old River channel of the Trinity delta (TWDB 67) is 113.6 milligrams per liter.

Brazos Delta Area

Averaging measurements made during 5 years yielded a mean of 139 milligrams of bicarbonate per liter. These years were: 1962, 1963, 1964 (at Brazoria, TWDB 55), 1972, and 1973 (Station 10 above West Columbia, TWDB 208).

---

[4]The data used here are averages compiled from several Texas Water Development Board (TWDB) Reports. Because these reports are readily available, and because the data as given here do not constitute a definitive presentation of bicarbonate values, only the TWDB report number and sample station are cited.

Lower Lavaca River Area

The average of 12 measurements on samples taken from just above the mouth of the Navidad was 269 milligrams of bicarbonate per liter. The years were 1969 (Station 1, TWDB 144), 1970 (Station 17, TWDB 171), 1971 (Station 17, TWDB 191), 1972 and 1973 (Station 17, TWDB 208).

These data from the lower Lavaca, the Brazos delta, and the Trinity delta were paired with the measured or estimated deviations between shell and charcoal radiocarbon dates from the respective locations, along with a hypothetical data pair of no bicarbonate and no deviation. This latter situation is approximated by the Sabine River data, but does not actually exist in nature. When plotted in a scattergram on logarithmic scales, a regression approximating linearity resulted (Figure A.2). At a gross scale, this regression provides some idea of the impact of nonradioactive carbon dissolved from central and north Texas carbonate rocks upon the *Rangia cuneata* carbon isotope ratios for clam populations growing in major river mouth areas.

In fact, five aquatic environments may be distinguished on the upper Texas coast which should have naturally differing radiocarbon characteristics (as opposed to man-induced characteristics). These are as follows: (*a*) major rivers draining the interior, which would contain bicarbonate ions enriched with nonradioactive carbon isotopes; (*b*) minor rivers and streams draining the Tertiary and Quaternary formations of the coastal plain, which would receive much less nonradioactive carbon enrichment; (*c*) the Gulf of Mexico, which would display carbon isotope ratios most nearly in equilibrium with the atmosphere; (*d*) the coastal estuaries, reflecting a composite of the water chemistry of the previous three environments; and (*e*) isolated floodplain lakes, which would be highly variable in their water chemistry.

The correlation described here is primarily for application to the first environment listed—that is, major rivers draining the interior. Even so, the results are preliminary. Although the bicarbonate, radiocarbon and geographic information is consistent, a conclusion is not quite this simple. In the case of most streams, bicarbonate measurements have been recorded only in very recent years. Moreover, there is a need to screen the date and location of sampling station use against the inception of industrial discharges into streams which affect their bicarbonate concentrations.

Water chemistry data are just beginning to be collected from the minor rivers and streams draining only the Beaumont Formation and perhaps the Montgomery Formation surfaces on the coastal plain. Some of these local drainages are of substantial size but they have different bicarbonate sources than the large rivers and estuaries, which could significantly affect the resulting carbon isotope ratios. Because of the magnitude of this problem and the improbability of obtaining paired shell–charcoal samples for all drainages, it probably is timely and justifiable to make more substantial use of mass spectrometric determina-

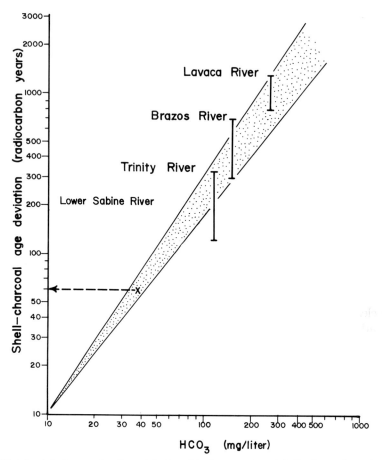

FIGURE A.2   A first approximation of the logarithmic regression of shell–charcoal age deviation on bicarbonate concentrations. The stippled area indicates the zone within which regression of age deviation on HCO_3 is expected to occur. In the lower Sabine River, the predicted maximum age deviation of *Rangia cuneata* from charcoal is indicated by the broken arrow.

tions of carbon isotope ratios. With this approach, relatively refined chronological frameworks will be possible on the upper Texas coast using *Rangia cuneata* as the prime medium.

ERRATIC *RANGIA CUNEATA* RADIOCARBON DATES

There is one category of upper coast *Rangia cuneata* radiocarbon sample which is not correctable by the method of paired samples, or by relationships derived from this method. All *R. cuneata* samples known to have been taken from or near the stratigraphic contact between archaeological midden and the Pleistocene Beaumont Formation are too old by amounts far exceeding that predicted by the model described above. These are Tx-642, 643, 644, 961, 1114, 0-912 and sample no. 1 from 41 OR 49 (Sabine Lake Area); all are described in Table 14.1. Because it is well known that marine shells are susceptible to exchange with carbon mobilized by groundwater (Ralph 1971:6), it seems probable that the explanation for this problem relates to diagenesis (i.e., mineral solution and redeposition).

Diagenetic alteration of shell carbonate has been known as a process for some time (Bathurst 1964; Turekian and Armstrong 1961). Diagenesis may occur with elements and isotopes expected to move along density or concentration gradients. Thus, carbon-14 would be expected to move out of the younger *Rangia* shell and into the older Pleistocene Beaumont Formation. Other carbon isotopes would do the opposite because of their relative differences in concentration. The extent of such exchanges probably can be determined by mass spectrometer.

Since every one of the *Rangia* samples which does not fit the clam habitat model comes from this Beaumont–midden contact position, the implication is fairly clear that, unless one is prepared to control for the large magnitude in radiocarbon alterations which have occurred, *Rangia cuneata* samples physically contacting the Beaumont Formation should not be used for archaeological dating purposes. Samples taken 10 centimeters or more from such stratigraphic contacts do not appear to be measurably affected. Because the cases where this precise contact needs to be dated are relatively few, it may not be worth the effort to develop a correction process for this particular problem.

Finally, it should be noted that, although the approach taken here is crude, it has been effective in demonstrating the controllability of *Rangia cuneata* as a dating medium. The reliability of *Rangia cuneata* samples can be improved and similar control can be developed over other species of mollusk encountered in Texas coastal sites, especially *Crassostrea virginica* and the surf zone species common in some sites on barrier islands and around coastal lagoons.

APPENDIX B

The Case for Alligator Gastroliths as Lithic Material Source

Based on analysis of diachronic changes in archaeological lithic materials at the Jamison Site (Aten 1967) and the Harris County Boys School (Aten *et al.* 1976), there is reason to suspect that the assemblages of stone types in use (i.e., basically chert, quartzite, and silicified wood) are characteristic of any given period in time on the upper coast. Similarly, a comparison of the differences in types of lithic materials in use at the Jamison Site with those at the Dow–Cleaver Site (Aten 1971) suggests that these assemblages reflect stone sources from drainage basins immediately inland from the coastal locality rather than significant lateral dispersion of materials along the coast. These observations establish a set of explanatory implications ranging from undiscovered local gravel sources to various types of exchange relations. The data and analysis described in this Appendix, however, reflect a rather different approach to consideration of lithic material sources.

The nearest gravel deposits to the upper Texas coast occur in a band roughly 140 km or so inland from the Gulf (Garner 1967). Because no alternative sources of stone have been identified in the coastal zone, it has been assumed previously that all stone materials occurring in coastal sites were imported by Indians either as unmodified pebbles and cobbles, or as artifacts. Given this, it becomes a matter of some interest to explain the occurrence of numerous pebbles incorporated into Galveston Bay Area shell midden deposits (especially those in the Trinity River delta) attributable primarily to the post-Clear Lake periods.

Pebbles and larger-sized sediments are not carried by streams through the upper coast area today[1] and do not form part of the normal point-bar or levee

[1]Sherwood Gagliano (personal communication) has suggested that this is not strictly true. He believes it likely that very small amounts of coarse sediments are transported as part of the bed load of major coastal rivers during peak flow periods. Although this material would rarely, if ever, occur in deposits other than those of the channel thalweg, it could be found and concentrated by a mechanism such as alligators searching for gastroliths.

deposits in which many of the coastal shell middens are incorporated (e.g., see McEwen 1969 for description of sediment assemblages of the Trinity River delta). It is possible, though not yet demonstrated, that pebble-sized material occurs locally in the fluvial deposits of the late Pleistocene Deweyville terraces which, after subaqueous erosion, may release this material to become part of the bed load in the bottom of the main channel of the Trinity. In any event, there is no reasonable basis for speculating that these pebbles were deposited directly on Trinity delta shell middens as a result of fluvial processes.

When considering whether the human inhabitants of these sites may have introduced the pebbles, it is necessary to account for several conditions in the sample. First, the range of pebble sizes (from 7 to 35 mm) contains many small specimens for which chipping was out of the question; indeed, over 50% of the sample would have been unsuitable. Second, if one had traded or traveled inland far enough to obtain material in the 35 mm size range, then even larger pebbles and cobbles more suited to stone chipping techniques also would have been available. These sizes, however, generally do not occur in the coastal sites. Third, many of the pebbles in the sample, regardless of their size, are unsuitable for chipping because of their irregular shape and/or vuggy texture. Many of these archaeological pebbles had been examined as potential resource materials for chipped stone tools because 25% of the pebble sample has had one or more cortex flakes removed to expose the unweathered interior. Since these flake scars are not eroded, polished, or in any way worn, the flakes presumably were removed by Indians to inspect the stone for its suitability for tool manufacture shortly before discard and incorporation in the midden.

To explain the presence of these pebbles solely by means of some form of human importation would require contrived explanations. On the other hand, the relatively frequent occurrence of the skeletal remains of large birds and alligators as food remains in these sites directly accounts for the origin of the stones as gastroliths. In fact, if these pebbles are not gastroliths, then it must be asked what did happen to gastroliths from the numerous birds and alligators which were consumed at these sites.

As might be expected, the archaeological literature on gastroliths is not large, but a very useful paper has been published by Bottema (1975). Gastroliths are usually thought to be recognizable by their high polish. Bottema points out, however, that polish is a function of the stone's duration of stay in the animal stomach. High polish usually comes about only when replacement stones are not available. This would occur in birds, for example, when there was an extended period of snow cover on the ground. Recognition of gastroliths, especially when not highly polished, is difficult and has been successful only when they can be distinguished from the normal constituents of the natural or cultural strata (Bottema 1975:405). This condition has been established for the Galveston Bay Area sites in the preceding discussion.

Test excavations at the mouth of the Trinity, in sites essentially postdating the Clear Lake Period, have produced a sample of 87 pebbles ranging in size from 7

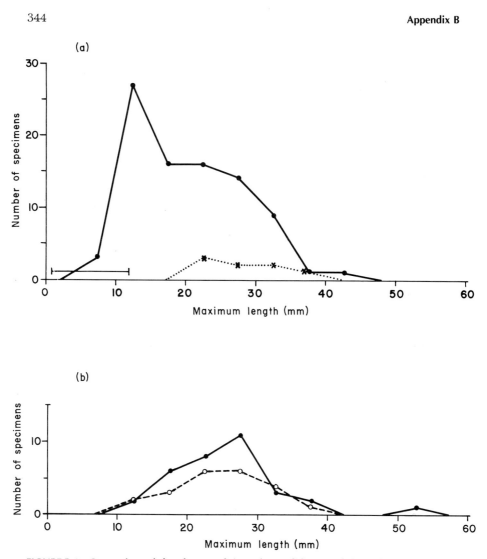

FIGURE B.1   Comparison of abundance and sizes of gastroliths (*a*) and chipped stone tools (*b*) in the Trinity delta area. In the top figure (*a*), ·——· indicates pebbles recovered from excavation in the Wallisville Reservoir (*N* = 87), x·····x indicates gastroliths from modern alligator (*N* = 8), and |——| indicates bird gastrolith size range from Bottema (1975). In the bottom figure, (*b*) ·——· indicates chipped stone artifacts from Wallisville (*N* = 33), and ○----○ indicates pebbles with inspection flake removed (*N* = 22).

to 35 mm (Table 13.1); the size and frequency of these specimens is shown in Figure B.1. In this figure also are plotted the size range of gastroliths for birds (Bottema 1975) and the size–frequency distribution of a small sample of gastroliths taken directly from the stomach of a modern alligator, about 2 m in length, which expired at the Houston Zoo. The shape of the size–frequency distribution of the archaeological pebbles is very suggestive of two overlapping distributions. This impression is reinforced by the congruence of the two major parts of that distribution with the size ranges of the bird and alligator gastroliths. This compatibility of the archaeological pebble distribution with those of bird and alligator gastroliths, the highly-polished to dull and heavily-worn surface appearance of the pebbles, and the absence of any plausible physical or direct anthropogenic explanation leads to the conclusion that these pebbles are gastroliths.

Given this interpretation and the evidence that the interior of at least some of these pebbles was examined by native toolmakers, it remains to consider whether gastroliths actually were transformed into chipped stone artifacts. The outer limits of this argument can be defined by a comparison of the maximum sizes of the pebbles against the maximum sizes of chipped stone tools in the Wallisville sites. If the latter are consistently larger than the population of gastroliths, there may not be much connection between the two. In Figure B.1 also is plotted a size–frequency distribution of the maximum length of local chipped stone artifacts.

The distribution that results is almost completely enclosed within the size limits of the pebble (gastrolith) distribution shown in Figure B.1. Moreover, plotting the size–frequency distribution of these pebbles from which inspection flakes have been removed results in a distribution which is almost identical to that of the chipped stone artifacts. Finally, it is noted that not only are the sizes compatible, but also the quantity of gastroliths occurring in the sites is large enough to account for the quantity of chipped stone tools. That is to say, if there had been 100 tools and 20 gastroliths we might have to consider whether there could have been enough gastroliths to support such a chipped stone industry. On the other hand, these data include 87 gastroliths and 59 chipped stone tools (only 33 were measurable as to maximum length), probably indicating that an adequate gastrolith supply existed to support this "industry."

As a result of these data, it must be concluded that a large part of the lower Trinity River area and, by extension, of the Galveston Bay Area chipped stone (bipolar?) industry in the post-Clear Lake periods could have existed with gastroliths as the source of raw material. Of course, this hypothesis does not preclude the use of other sources, no matter what size material was involved. It does, however, mean that artifacts larger than about 40 mm usually should be accounted for on the basis of importation, either through trade or through direct procurement. Artifacts smaller than this size could have been manufactured with locally occurring materials.

Gastrolith pebbles rarely are present in quantity in any given site. In the Trinity River delta and at Harris County Boys School, where the fine-mesh screening techniques would have resulted in the recovery of any pebbles which were present, most sites produced only three or four; 41 CH 36 was a significant exception (see Table 13.1). Pebbles also were recovered primarily from post-Clear Lake Period levels of the Jamison Site (Aten 1967:Figure 4) and from the

Plaquemine level of the Gaulding Site near Beaumont (Aten and Bollich, unpublished information 1971). Pebbles did not occur in testing at the Pipkin Ranch sites south of Beaumont. Similarly, fine-mesh screening in the Brazos delta produced no specimens of gastroliths, although lithic artifacts of any kind are relatively more rare in the Brazos delta than in sites to the east.

The occurrence of alligator and bird bones far more frequently than gastroliths in Galveston Bay Area shell middens suggests that gastroliths were frequently used for lithic toolmaking and/or that butchering of these animals took place away from the habitation site, a conclusion previously suggested by faunal analysis (Aten 1967:42) and by analogy with numerous ethnographically recorded situations. Consequently, the presence of gastroliths in archaeological sites also may reflect the joint occurrence of an alligator kill and a need for lithic raw materials.[2]

Finally, if this explanation for the occurrence of pebbles in coastal middens is valid, it provides a noncultural explanation for the strong tendency for similarity in the assemblage of pebble materials from a coastal archaeological locality with gravel source areas perpendicular to the coast (the trend of the major stream drainages) rather than for there to be similarities between sites in adjacent drainages along the coast. However, within each major coastal drainage or estuary system, diachronic changes in the proportion of material types which have been selected for use in toolmaking may reflect long-term cultural shifts in material preferences, which can be correlated across drainages.

---

[2]The only known description of alligator hunting on the upper coast comes from Nicolas De Lafora who observed this at Orcoquisac in 1767: "They [i.e., the Indians] depend, for their final recourse, upon the lagoon, where there are many fish which they harpoon. Alligators also abound there. The Indians play with them, catching them by the snout and dragging them to shore where they kill them [Kinnaird 1958:172]."

References

Ackerknecht, Erwin H.
    1971   The shaman and primitive psychopathology in general. In *Medicine and ethnology: select essays*, edited by H. H. Walker and H. M. Koelbing. Pp. 57–90. Baltimore: Johns Hopkins Press.

Adams, Richard N.
    1975   *Energy and structure: a theory of social power.* Austin: University of Texas Press.

Ambler, J. Richard
    1967   Three prehistoric sites near Cedar Bayou, Galveston Bay Area. *Texas State Building Commission, Archeology Program, Report* **8.** Austin, Texas.

    1970   Additional archeological survey of the Wallisville Reservoir area, southeast Texas. *Texas Archeological Salvage Project Survey Report* **6.** Austin, Texas.

    1973   Excavation in the Trinity River Delta: the Lost River phase. *Texas Archeological Survey*, (unnumbered report). Austin, Texas.

Anonymous
    1887   Gatschet's ethnological maps of the Gulf States. *Science* **9**(221):404–406.

Aronow, Saul
    1971   Quaternary geology. In *Ground-water resources of Chambers and Jefferson Counties, Texas*, by J. B. Wesselman. *Texas Water Development Board Report* **133:**34–53. Austin, Texas.

Arundale, W. H.
    1981   Radiocarbon dating in eastern Arctic archaeology: a flexible approach. *American Antiquity* **46**(2):244–271.

Aten, Lawrence E.
    1965   Five crania from the Jamaica Beach site (41 GV 5), Galveston County, Texas. *Bulletin of the Texas Archeological Society* **36:**153–162.

    1966a   Late Quaternary alluvial history of the lower Trinity River, Texas: a preliminary report. Appendix in *An archeological survey of Wallisville Reservoir, Chambers County Texas*, by Harry J. Shafer. *Texas Archeological Salvage Project Survey Reports* **2:**Appendix I. Austin, Texas.

    1966b   *Late Quaternary surface geology of the lower Trinity River area, southeastern Texas.* Ms. on file, Department of Geology, University of Houston.

    1967   *Excavations at the Jamison Site (41 LB 2), Liberty County, Texas. Houston Archeological Society, Report* **1.** Houston, Texas.

    1970   Coastal southeast Texas archeology—1970. Paper presented at the 12th Caddo Conference, Magnolia, Arkansas.

    1971   *Archeological excavations at the Dow-Cleaver site, Brazoria County, Texas. Texas Archeological Salvage Project, Technical Bulletin* **1.** Austin, Texas.

    1972   *An assessment of the archeological resources to be affected by the Taylors Bayou drainage and flood control project, Texas. Texas Archeological Salvage Project, Research Report* **7.** Austin, Texas.

347

1976 Three notes on *Rangia cuneata* as a source of archeological data. Paper presented at 33rd Southeastern Archeological Conference, Tuscaloosa, Alabama.

1979 Indians of the upper Texas coast: ethnohistoric and archeological frameworks. Unpublished Ph.D. dissertation, Department of Anthropology, The University of Texas at Austin.

1981 Determining seasonality of *Rangia cuneata* from Gulf Coast shell middens. *Bulletin of the Texas Archeological Society* **52:**179–200.

1982 *Analysis of discrete habitation units in the Trinity River Delta, upper Texas coast.* Ms. on file at the Texas Archeological Survey, The University of Texas at Austin.

Aten, Lawrence E., and Charles N. Bollich

1969 A preliminary report on the development of a ceramic chronology for the Sabine Lake area of Texas and Louisiana. *Bulletin of the Texas Archeological Society* **40:**241–258.

1981 Archeological evidence for pimple (prairie) mound genesis. *Science* **213:**1375–1376.

Aten, Lawrence E., and Charles K. Chandler

1971 *Archeological investigations at the Harris County Boys School Cemetery.* Ms. on file at the Texas Antiquities Committee, Austin.

Aten, Lawrence E., Charles K. Chandler, Al B. Wesolowsky, and Robert M. Malina

1976 *Excavations at the Harris County Boys School Cemetery: analysis of Galveston Bay area mortuary practices. Texas Archeological Society, Special Publication* **3.**

Austin, S. F.

1904 Journal of Stephen F. Austin on his first trip to Texas, 1821. *The Quarterly of the Texas State Historical Association* **7:**286–301.

Baker, V. R., and M. M. Penteado-Orellana

1977 Adjustment to Quaternary climatic change by the Colorado River in central Texas. *Journal of Geology* **85:**395–422.

Bandelier, Fanny (translator)

1905 *The journey of Álvar Núñez Cabeza de Vaca and his companions from Florida to the Pacific, 1528–1536.* New York: Barnes.

Barth, Fredrik (editor)

1969 Introduction. In *Ethnic groups and boundaries: the social organization of culture difference.* Boston: Little, Brown. Pp. 9–38.

Barton, Donald C.

1930 Deltaic coastal plain of southeastern Texas. *Bulletin of the Geological Society of America* **41**(3):359–382.

Baskett, James Newton

1907 A study of the route of Cabeza de Vaca. *Southwestern Historical Quarterly* **10:**246–279.

Bateson, Gregory

1979 *Mind and nature: a necessary unity.* New York: E. P. Dutton.

Bathurst, R. G. C.

1964 The replacement of aragonite by calcite in the Molluscan shell wall. In *Approaches to paleoecology,* edited by John Imbrie and Norman Newell. New York: Wiley. Pp. 357–376.

Beard, John H.

1973 Pleistocene–Holocene boundary and Wisconsinan substages, Gulf of Mexico. *Geological Society of America Memoir* **136:**277–316.

Beers, Henry Putney

1979 *Spanish and Mexican records of the American southwest.* Tucson: University of Arizona Press.

Benedict, James B.
  1979   Getting away from it all: a study of man, mountains, and the two-drought Altithermal. *Southwest Lore* **45**(3):1–12.
Berger, R., A. G. Horney, and W. F. Libby
  1964   Radiocarbon dating of bone and shell from their organic components. *Science* **144**:999–1001.
Berger, Rainer, R. E. Taylor, and W. F. Libby
  1966   Radiocarbon content of marine shells from the California and Mexican west coast. *Science* **153**:864–866.
Berlandier, Jean Louis
  1969   *The Indians of Texas in 1830*, edited by John C. Ewers. Washington, D.C.: Smithsonian.
Bernard, H. A.
  1950   Quaternary geology of southeast Texas. Unpublished Ph.D. dissertation, Department of Geology, Louisiana State University, Baton Rouge.
Bernard, H. A., and R. J. LeBlanc
  1965   Resume of the Quaternary geology of the northwestern Gulf of Mexico Province. In *The Quaternary of the United States*, edited by H. E. Wright and D. G. Frey. Princeton University Press. Pp. 137–185.
Bernard, H. A., R. J. LeBlanc, and C. F. Major
  1962   Recent and Pleistocene geology of southeast Texas. In *Geology of the Gulf Coast and central Texas and guidebook of excursions*, edited by E. H. Rainwater and R. P. Zingula. Houston: Houston Geological Society. Pp. 175–224.
Bernard, H. A., C. F. Major, and B. S. Parrott
  1959   The Galveston barrier island and environs: a model for predicting reservoir occurrence and trend. *Gulf Coast Association of Geological Societies Transactions* **9**:221–224.
Bernard, H. A., C. F. Major, Jr., B. S. Parrott, and R. J. LeBlanc, Sr.
  1970   Recent sediments of southeast Texas. *Bureau of Economic Geology Guidebook* **11**. University of Texas, Austin.
Binford, Lewis R.
  1962   Archaeology as anthropology. *American Antiquity* **28**:217–225.
  1968   *Methodological considerations of the archeological use of ethnographic data.* In *Man the hunter*, edited by R. B. Lee and Irven DeVore, Chicago: Aldine. Pp. 268–273.
Birmingham, W. W. and T. R. Hester
  1976   Late Pleistocene archaeological remains from the Johnston-Heller site, Texas coastal plain. *Special Report of the Center for Archaeological Research* **3**:15–33. The University of Texas at San Antonio.
Bloom, Arthur L. (compiler)
  1977   Atlas of sea-level curves: IGCP Project **61.** Cornell University, Ithaca, New York.
Bollaert, William
  1850   Observations on the Indian tribes in Texas. *Journal, Ethnological Society of London* **2**:262–283.
Bolton, Herbert E.
  1906   The founding of Mission Rosario: a chapter in the history of the Gulf Coast. *The Quarterly of the Texas State Historical Association* **10**(2):113–139.
  1908   The native tribes about the east Texas Missions. *The Quarterly of the Texas State Historical Association* **11**:249–276.
  1913   Spanish activities on the lower Trinity River, 1746–1771. *Southwestern Historical Quarterly* **15**:339–347.

1914   *Athanase de Mézières and the Louisiana–Texas Frontier, 1768–1780.* Cleveland: Arthur H. Clarke Co.

1915   *Texas in the middle eighteenth century. University of California Publications in History* **3.** Berkeley: University of California Press.

1916   (editor) *Spanish exploration in the Southwest, 1542–1706.* New York: C. Scribner's Sons.

1924   The location of La Salle's colony on the Gulf of Mexico. *Southwestern Historical Quarterly* **27**(3):171–189.

Bonnell, George W.

1840   *Topographical description of Texas: to which is added an account of the Indian tribes.* Austin: Clark, Wing, and Brown.

Bottema, S.

1975   The use of gastroliths in archaeology. In *Archeozoological studies*, edited by A. T. Clason. Amsterdam: North-Holland. Pp. 397–406.

Bradford, A. L., and T. N. Campbell (editors)

1949   Journal of Lincecum's travels in Texas, 1835. *Southwestern Historical Quarterly* **53**(2):1–22.

Brannon, H. R., Jr., L. H. Simons, D. Perry, A. C. Dougherty, and E. McFarland, Jr.

1957   Humble Oil Company radiocarbon dates II. *Science* **125:**919–923.

Braun, David P.

1974   Explanatory models for the evolution of coastal adaptation in prehistoric eastern New England. *American Antiquity* **39**(4):582–596.

Broecker, W. S.

1964   Radiocarbon dating: a case against the proposed link between river mollusks and soil humus. *Science* **143:**596–597.

Broecker, W. S., and A. Walton

1959   The geochemistry of C-14 in fresh-water systems. *Geochemica et Cosmochimica, Acta* **16:**15–38.

Bryant, Vaughn M., Jr., and Harry J. Shafer

1977   The Late Quaternary paleoenvironment of Texas: a model for the archeologist. *Bulletin of the Texas Archeological Society* **48:**1–25.

Bryson, R. A., D. A. Baerreis, and W. M. Wendland

1970   The character of late glacial and post-glacial climatic changes. In *Pleistocene and Recent environments of the central Great Plains*, edited by W. Dort and J. K. Jones. *University of Kansas Special Publication* **3:**53–73. Lawrence, Kansas: University of Kansas Press.

Brune, Gunnar

1975   *Major and historical springs of Texas. Texas Water Development Board, Report* **189.** Austin, Texas.

Buchler, Ira R., and Henry A. Selby

1968   *Kinship and social organization: an introduction to theory and method.* New York: Macmillan.

Bullen, Ripley P., and William J. Bryant

1965   *Three archaic sites in the Ocala National Forest, Florida. The William L. Bryant Foundation, Report* **6.** Orlando, Florida.

Bureau of Economic Geology

1968a   *Geologic Atlas of Texas, Houston sheet.* University of Texas, Bureau of Economic Geology, Austin.

Bureau of Economic Geology

1968b   *Geologic Atlas of Texas, Beaumont sheet.* University of Texas, Bureau of Economic Geology, Austin.

Butzer, K. W.
    1964   *Environment and archeology.* Chicago: Aldine.

Castañeda, Carlos E.
    1939   *Our Catholic heritage in Texas, 1519–1936.* Austin: Von Boeckman-Jones.

Campbell, Thomas N.
    1947   The Johnson site: type site of the Aransas focus of the Texas Coast. *Bulletin of the Texas Archeological and Paleontological Society* **18:**40–75.

    1952   *A bibliographic guide to the archaeology of Texas. Archaeology Series* **1.** Austin: Department of Anthropology, The University of Texas at Austin.

    1956   Archeological materials from five islands in the Laguna Madre, Texas coast. *Bulletin of the Texas Archeological Society* **27:**7–46.

    1957   Archeological investigations at the Caplen site, Galveston County, Texas. *Texas Journal of Science* **9:**448–471.

    1958   Archeological remains from the Live Oak Point site, Aransas County, Texas. *The Texas Journal of Science* **10:**423–442.

    1962   Origins of pottery types from the coastal bend region of Texas. *Bulletin of the Texas Archeological Society* **32:**331–336.

    1972   Systematized ethnohistory and prehistoric culture sequences in Texas. *Bulletin of the Texas Archeological Society* **43:**1–11.

    1977   *Ethnic identities of extinct Coahuiltecan populations: case of the Juanca Indians. Pearce-Sellards Series* **26.** Austin: Texas Memorial Museum.

Campbell, Thomas N.
    1976   Archaeological investigations at the Morhiss site, Victoria County, Texas, 1932–1940. In Fox, Anne A., and T. R. Hester, An Archaeological Survey of Coleto Creek, Victoria and Goliad Counties, Texas. *Archaeological Survey Report, No. 18, Center for Archaeological Research. The University of Texas at San Antonio.* Pp. 81–85.

Casteel, Richard W.
    1972   Two static maximum population-density models for hunter–gatherers: a first approximation. *World Archaeology* **4**(1):19–40.

Celiz, Fray Francisco
    1935   *Diary of the Alarcon expedition into Texas, 1718–1719,* translated by Fritz Leo Hoffman. Los Angeles: Quivira Society.

Chang, K. C.
    1967   *Rethinking archaeology.* New York: Random House.

Clarke, David L.
    1968   *Analytical archaeology.* London: Methuen.

Cook, Sherburne F.
    1973   The significance of disease in the extinction of the New England Indians. *Human Biology* **45:**485–508.

Corbin, James E.
    1976   The archaic of the Texas coast. In *The Texas archaic: a symposium,* edited by T. R. Hester. *Center for Archaeological Research Special Report* **2:**91–97. San Antonio: The University of Texas at San Antonio.

Covey, Cyclone (editor and translator)
    1961   *Cabeza de Vaca's adventures in the unknown interior of America, 1528–1534.* New York: Collier.

Cowgill, G. L.
    1972   Models, methods and techniques for seriation. In *Models in archaeology,* edited by D. L. Clarke. London: Methuen. Pp. 381–424.

Cox, Isaac Joslin (editor)
  1905   LaSalle's last journey in search of the Mississippi—his assassination. In *The jour-
            neys of Rene Robert Cavelier, Sieur de La Salle* (2 volumes). New York: Barnes.
Damon, P. E., C. W. Ferguson, A. Long, and E. I. Wallick
  1974   Dendrochronologic calibration of the radiocarbon time scale. *American Antiquity*
            39:350–366.
Davenport, Herbert, and Joseph K. Wells
  1918   The route of Cabeza de Vaca. *Southwestern Historical Quarterly* **22:**111–142.
Deevey, E. S., Jr., M. S. Gross, G. E. Hutchinson, and H. L. Kraybill
  1954   The natural C-14 content of materials from hard-water lakes. *Proceedings: Na-
            tional Academy of Science* **40:**285–288.
Dering, Phil, and David Ayers
  1977   *Archeological investigations in the village of Oyster Creek, Brazoria County, Texas: a
            reassessment of economic archeology on the Texas coast.* College Station: Texas
            A&M Research Foundation.
DeSolís, Fray Gaspar José
  1931   Diary of a visit of inspection of the Texas missions made by Fray Gaspar José de
            Solís in the year 1767–1768, translated by Margaret K. Kress. *Southwestern Histor-
            ical Quarterly* **35:**28–76.
Dillehay, Tom D.
  1974   Late Quaternary Bison population changes on the southern plains. *Plains An-
            thropologist* **19**(65):180–196.
  1975   *Prehistoric subsistence exploitation in the lower Trinity River Delta, Texas. Texas
            Archeological Survey, Research Report* **51.** Austin, Texas.
Dobyns, Henry F.
  1966   Estimating aboriginal American population: an appraisal of techniques with a
            new hemispheric estimate. *Current Anthropology* **7:**395–416.
Doering, John A.
  1956   Review of Quaternary surface formations of Gulf Coast region. *Bulletin of American
            Association of Petroleum Geologists* **40**(8):1816–1862.
Duke, A. R.
  1962   *Preliminary report on the Damek site, Liberty County, Texas. Houston Archeological
            Society Newsletter* **8:**4.
Dunnell, Robert C.
  1970   Seriation method and its evaluation. *American Antiquity* **35:**305–319.
Dyer, J. O.
  1916   *Historical sketch: comparisons of customs of wild tribes near Galveston a century
            ago with ancient Semitic customs.* Galveston: Privately printed.
  1917   *The Lake Charles Atakapas (cannibals): period of 1817–1820.* Galveston: privately
            printed.
  1920   Secret brotherhood of Texas Indians. *Galveston Daily News,* April 26, 1920.
Eddleman, Charles D., and W. A. Akersten
  1966   Margay from the post-Wisconsin of southeastern Texas. *Texas Journal of Science*
            18:378–385.
Emery, K. O.
  1967   Estuaries and lagoons in relation to continental shelves. In *Estuaries,* edited by G.
            H. Lauff. *American Association for the Advancement of Science Publication* **83:**9–11.
            Washington, D.C.
Ewers, John C.
  1973   The influence of epidemics on the Indian populations and cultures of Texas. *Plains
            Anthropologist* **18**(60):104–115.

Faulk, Odie B.
  1964   *The last years of Spanish Texas, 1778–1821.* The Hague: Mouton.
Fisher, W. L., J. H. McGowen, L. F. Brown, Jr., and C. G. Groat
  1972   *Environmental Geologic Atlas of the Texas Coastal Zone: Galveston–Houston Area.*
           Bureau of Economic Geology, University of Texas, Austin.
Fisher, W. L., L. F. Brown, Jr., J. H. McGowen, and C. G. Groat
  1973   *Environmental Geologic Atlas of the Texas Coastal Zone: Beaumont–Port Arthur
           Area.* Bureau of Economic Geology, University of Texas, Austin.
Flannery, Kent V. (editor)
  1976   *The Early Mesoamerican Village.* New York: Academic Press.
Flannery, Kent V., and Joyce Marcus
  1976   Formative Oaxaca and the Zapotec cosmos. *American Scientist* **64:**374–383.
Flint, R. F.
  1959   Pleistocene climates in eastern and southern Africa. *Geological Society of America
           Bulletin* **70:**343–374.
  1971   *Glacial and Quaternary geology.* New York: Wiley.
Folmer, Henri
  1940   De Bellisle on the Texas Coast. *Southwestern Historical Quarterly* **44:**204–231.
Ford, James A.
  1951   *Greenhouse: a Troyville–Coles Creek period site in Avoyelles Parish, Louisiana.*
           American Museum of Natural History, Ahthropological Papers **44.** New York.
  1962   *A quantitative method for deriving cultural chronology.* Washington, D.C.: Pan
           American Union.
Ford, James A., and George I. Quimby
  1945   *The Tchefuncte culture, an early occupation of the lower Mississippi Valley.* Society
           for American Archaeology, Memoir **2.** Menasha, Wisconsin.
Ford, James A., and Clarence H. Webb
  1956   Poverty Point, a Late Archaic site in Louisiana. *American Museum of Natural
           History, Anthropological Papers* **46**(1). New York.
Fox, Anne A., D. William Day, and Lynn Highley
  1980   Archaeological and historical investigations at Wallisville Lake, Chambers and
           Liberty Counties, Texas. *Archaeological Survey Report* No. 90, Center for Archae-
           ological Research, The University of Texas at San Antonio.
Fox, Daniel E., Robert J. Mallouf, Nancy O'Malley and William M. Sorrow
  1974   *Archaeological resources of the proposed Cuero I Reservoir, Dewitt and Gonzales
           Counties, Texas.* Texas Historical Commission and Texas Water Development
           Board, Archeological Survey Report **12.** Austin, Texas.
Fried, Morton H.
  1967   *The evolution of political society: an essay in political anthropology.* New York:
           Random House.
Fritz, Gayle
  1975   *Matagorda Bay area, Texas: a survey of the archeological and historical resources.*
           Texas General Land Office and Texas Archeological Survey, Research Report **45.**
           Austin, Texas.
Gagliano, S. M.
  1963   A survey of preceramic occupations in portions of south Louisiana and south
           Mississippi. *FLorida Anthropologist* **16**(4):105–132.
Gagliano, S. M.
  1967   Occupation sequence at Avery Island. *Coastal Studies Institute Report* **22.** Loui-
           siana State University, Baton Rouge.
  1970   *Progress report on archeological and geological studies at Avery Island, 1968–1970.*
           Baton Rouge: Coastal Studies Institute, Louisiana State University Press.

1977   *Cultural resources evaluation of the northern Gulf of Mexico continental shelf.*
        Cultural Resource Management Studies. Washington, D.C.: National Park Service.

Gagliano, S. M., and B. G. Thom
1967   Deweyville Terrace, Gulf and Atlantic coasts. *Coastal Studies Institute Bulletin*
        1:23–41. Louisiana State University, Baton Rouge.

Gagliano, S. M., C. E. Pearson, R. A. Weinstein, D. E. Wiseman, and C. M. McClendon
1982   *Sedimentary studies of prehistoric archaeological sites: criteria for the identification*
        of submerged archaeological sites of the northern Gulf of Mexico continental shelf.
        Baton Rouge: Coastal Environments.

Galloway, W. E.
1975   Process framework for describing the morphologic and stratigraphic evolution of
        deltaic depositional systems. In *Deltas: models for exploration*, edited by M. L.
        Broussard. Houston: Houston Geological Society. Pp. 87–98.

Garner, L. E.
1967   *Sand resources of the Texas Gulf coast. The University of Texas at Austin Bureau of*
        Economic Geology, Report of Investigations **60**. Austin, Texas.

Garrett, Julia Kathryn
1944   Dr. John Sibley and the Louisiana-Texas frontier, 1803–1814. *Southwestern Histor-*
        ical Quarterly **47**:319–324.

Gatschet, Albert S.
1887   Two ethnographic maps. *Science* **9**(221):413–414.

1891   *The Karankawa Indians, the coast people of Texas. Archaeological and Ethnological*
        Papers of the Peabody Museum **1**(2). Cambridge, Massachusetts.

Gatschet, Albert S., and John R. Swanton
1932   A dictionary of the Atakapa language: accompanied by text material. *Bureau of*
        American Ethnology, Bulletin **108.**

Geertz, Clifford
1963   *Agricultural involution: the processes of ecological change in Indonesia.* Berkeley:
        University of California Press.

1966   Religion as a cultural system. In *Anthropological approaches to the study of re-*
        ligion, edited by M. Banton. *ASA Monographs* **3**. London: Tavistock Publications.

Gibson, Jon L., R. B. Gramling, C. R. Brassieur, S. J. Brazda, and S. G. Lark
1978   *An archaeological reconnaissance of the lower Sabine River valley, Toledo Bend*
        Dam to Gulf Intracoastal Waterway, Louisiana and Texas. Center for Archaeologi-
        cal Studies, Report **4.** Lafayette, Louisiana: The University of Southwestern
        Louisiana.

Gilmore, Kathleen
1974   *Cultural variation on the Texas coast: analysis of an aboriginal shell midden,*
        Wallisville Reservoir, Texas. Texas Archeological Survey, Research Report **44.** Austin,
        Texas.

Gould, H. R., and Edward McFarlan, Jr.
1959   Geologic history of the chenier plain, southwestern Louisiana. *Gulf Coast Associa-*
        tion of Geological Societies Transactions **9**:261–270.

Gould, Richard A., Don D. Fowler, and Catherine S. Fowler
1972   Diggers and doggers: parallel failures in economic acculturation. *Southwestern*
        Journal of Anthropology **28**:265–281.

Gracy, David B., II
1964   Jean Lafitte and the Karankawa Indians. *East Texas Historical Journal* **2**(1):40–44.

Graf, Claus H.
1966   The Late Pleistocene Ingleside Barrier Trend, Texas and Lousiana. Unpublished
        M.A. thesis, Department of Geology, William Marsh Rice University, Houston,
        Texas.

Hackett, Charles Wilson (editor)
    1931–1932   *Pichardo's Treatise on the Limits of Louisiana and Texas*. Austin: The University of Texas Press.

Hall, Grant D.
    1981   Allens Creek: a study in the cultural prehistory of the lower Brazos River Valley, Texas. *Texas Archeological Survey Research Report* **61.** The University of Texas at Austin.

Hamilton, Don
    1970   *Archeological investigations at Shy Pond, Brazoria County, Texas*. Ms. on file, Archeological Research Laboratory, Austin, Texas.

Hammel, E. A., C. K. McDaniel, and K. W. Wachter
    1979   Demographic consequences of incest tabus: a microsimulation analysis. *Science* **205:**972–977.

Hardesty, Donald L.
    1977   *Ecological anthropology*. New York: Wiley and Sons.

Harris, R. K., and Inus Marie Harris
    1967   Trade beads, projectile points, and knives. In *A pilot study of Wichita Indian archeology and ethnohistory*, assembled by R. E. Bell, E. B. Jelks, and W. W. Newcomb. Dallas: Southern Methodist University, Anthropology Research Center. Pp. 129–158.

Hartman, Daniel
    1963   *A boatstone and plumb bob from Lake Stevenson. Houston Archeological Society Newsletter* **10:**8.

Hatcher, Mattie Austin (translator)
    1927   Descriptions of the Tejas or Asinai Indians, 1691–1722. *Southwestern Historical Quarterly* **30:**206–218; 283–304.

Hawley, Amos H.
    1973   Ecology and population. *Science* **179:**1196–1201.

Haynes, C. Vance
    1970   Geochronology of Man–Mammoth sites and their bearing on the origin of the Llano Complex. In *Pleistocene and recent environments of the central Great Plains*, edited by W. Dort and J. K. Jones. *University of Kansas Special Publication* **3:**77–92. Lawrence, Kansas: University of Kansas Press.

Helm, Mary S.
    1884   *Scraps of Early Texas History*. Austin: privately printed.

Henderson, Mary Virginia
    1928   *Minor Empresario contracts for the colonization of Texas, 1825–1834. Southwestern Historical Quarterly* **31.**

Henry, Vernon J.
    1956   *Investigations of shoreline-like features in the Galveston Bay region, Texas. Texas A&M College Department of Oceanography Technical Report, Project* **24.** College Station, Texas.

Hester, Thomas R.
    1976a   *The Texas Archaic: a symposium. Center for Archaeological Research, Special Report* **2.** (editor). University of Texas, San Antonio.
    1976b   Late Pleistocene aboriginal adaptations in Texas. *Center for Archaeological Research, Special Report* **3:**2–14. University of Texas, San Antonio.
    1977   The current status of Paleoindian studies in southern Texas and northeastern Mexico. In *Paleoindian lifeways*, edited by Eileen Johnson. *The Museum Journal* **17:**169–186. Lubbock: Texas Tech University.
    1980   A survey of Paleo-Indian archaeological remains along the Texas coast. *Center for*

Archaeological Research, Special Report **11**:1–12. The University of Texas, San Antonio.

Hickerson, Harold
    1965   The Virginia deer and intertribal buffer zones in the upper Mississippi Valley. In *Man, culture, and animals*, edited by Anthony Leeds and Andrew P. Vayda. *American Association for the Advancement of Science, Publication* **78**:43–65. Washington, D.C.

Hodder, Ian
    1977   Some new directions in the spatial analysis of archaeological data at the regional scale (macro). In *Spatial archaeology*, edited by D. L. Clarke. New York/London: Academic Press. Pp. 223–351.
    1979   Economic and social stress and material culture patterning. *American Antiquity* **44**:446–454.

Hodge, Frederick Webb (editor)
    1907a   *Handbook of American Indians north of Mexico. Bureau of American Ethnology, Bulletin* **30.** Washington, D.C.
    1907b   The narrative of Álvar Núñez Cabeza De Vaca. *Spanish Explorers in the Southern United States, 1528–1543.* New York: Charles Scribner's Sons.

Hole, Frank (editor)
    1974   *Archeological investigations along Armand Bayou, Harris County, Texas. Houston Archeological Society, Report* **2.** Houston, Texas.

Hole, Frank, and Richard G. Wilkinson
    1973   Shell Point: a coastal camp and burial site in Brazoria County. *Bulletin of the Texas Archeological Society* **44**:5–50.

Holley, Mary Austin
    1973   *Texas: observations, historical, geographical and descriptive.* New York: Arno Press. (Reprint of 1833 ed.)

Hopkins, S. H., J. W. Anderson, and K. Horvath
    1973   *The brackish water clam Rangia Cuneata as indicator of ecological effects of salinity changes in coastal waters.* U.S. Army Engineer Waterways Experiment Station, Vicksburg.

Hunter, Robert Hancock
    1966   *The Narrative of Robert Hancock Hunter.* Austin: The Encino Press.

Jelks, Edward B.
    1965   The archeology of the McGee Bend Reservoir, Texas. Unpublished Ph.D. dissertation, The Department of Anthropology, University of Texas at Austin.
    1978   Diablo range. In *Chronologies in New World archaeology*, edited by R. E. Taylor and Clement W. Meigham. New York: Academic Press. Pp. 71–111.

Jennings, Francis
    1976   *The invasion of America: Indians, colonialism, and the cant of conquest.* New York: W. W. Norton.

Johnson, Eileen
    1977   Animal food resources of Paleoindians. In *Paleoindian lifeways*, edited by Eileen Johnson. *The Museum Journal* **17**:65–77. Lubbock: Texas Tech University.

Johnson, LeRoy, Jr.
    1962   The Yarbrough and Miller sites of northeastern Texas, with a preliminary definition of the LaHarpe aspect. *Bulletin of the Texas Archeological Society* **32**:141–284.

Joutel, Henri
    1962   *A journal of La Salle's last voyage.* New York: Corinth Books.
    1966   *A journal of the last voyage perform'd by Monsr. de La Sale, to the Gulph of Mexico, to find out the mouth of the Mississippi River.* Ann Arbor: University Microfilms. (Facsimile of the 1714 ed.)

Keith, M. L., and G. M. Anderson
    1963   Radiocarbon dating: fictitious results with mollusk shells. *Science* **141:**634–637.
Kelley, J. Charles
    1955   Juan Sabeata and diffusion in aboriginal Texas. *American Anthropologist* **57:**981–995.
Kennedy, William
    1841   *Texas: the rise, progress, and prospects of the Republic of Texas.* London: Hastings.
Kennett, J. P., and N. J. Shackleton
    1975   Laurentide ice sheet meltwater recorded in Gulf of Mexico deep-sea cores. *Science* **188:**147–150.
Kenney, M. M.
    1897   Tribal society among Texas Indians. *Texas State Historical Association, Quarterly* **1:**26–33.
Ker, Henry
    1816   *Travels through the western interior of the United States, from the year 1808 up to the year 1816.* New Jersey: Elizabethtown.
Kinnaird, Lawrence (editor)
    1958   *The frontiers of New Spain. Nicholas de LaFora's description, 1766–1768. Quivera Society Publication* **13.** Berkeley, California.
Kirchoff, Paul
    1954   Gatherers and farmers in the greater Southwest: a problem in classification. *American Anthropologist* **56:**529–550.
Koestler, Arthur
    1967   *The ghost in the machine.* New York: Macmillan.
Krieger, Alex D.
    1944   The typological concept. *American Antiquity* **9:**271–288.
    1946   Culture complexes and chronology in northern Texas. *University of Texas Publication* **4640.** Austin: University of Texas Press.
    1948   Importance of the "Gilmore Corridor" in culture contacts between Middle America and the eastern United States. *Bulletin of the Texas Archeological and Paleontological Society* **19:**155–178.
    1956   Food habits of the Texas coastal Indians in the early sixteenth century. *Bulletin of the Texas Archeological Society* **27:**47–58.
Kroeber, A. L.
    1939   *Cultural and natural areas of native North America. University of California Publications in American Archaeology and Ethnology* **38.** Berkeley: University of California Press.
Kuykendall, J. H.
    1903   Reminiscences of early Texans. *Texas State Historical Association, Quarterly* **6:**236–253.
Kwon, H. J.
    1969   *Barrier Islands on the northern Gulf of Mexico Coast: sediment source and development. Coastal Studies Series* **25.** Baton Rouge: Louisiana State University Press.
Landar, Herbert
    1968   The Karankawa invasion of Texas. *International Journal of American Linguistics* **34:**242–258.
Langbein, Walter B., and Luna B. Leopold
    1966   River meanders and the theory of minimum variance. *U.S. Geological Survey Professional Paper* **422-H:**1–15.
Langway, C. C., Jr., W. Dansgaard, S. J. Johnsen, and H. Clausen
    1973   Climatic fluctuations during the Late Pleistocene. *Geological Society of America Memoir* **136:**317–321.

Leopold, Luna B., and W. B. Langbein
    1966   River meanders. *Scientific American* **214**(6):60–70.
Leopold, L. B., M. G. Wolman, and J. P. Miller
    1964   *Fluvial processes in geomorphology.* San Francisco: W. H. Freeman.
Levins, Richard
    1966   The strategy of model building in population biology. *American Scientist*
                54:421–431.
    1968   *Evolution in changing environments: some theoretical explorations.* Princeton:
                Princeton University Press.
Libby, Willard F.
    1955   *Radiocarbon dating* (second ed.). Chicago: The University of Chicago Press.
Long, Russell J.
    1977   *McFaddin Beach. Spindletop Museum* **1.** Lamar University, Beaumont, Texas.
Lundelius, Ernest L., Jr.
    1967   Late-Pleistocene and Holocene faunal history of central Texas. In *Pleistocene extinc-
                tions: the search for a cause,* edited by P. S. Martin and H. E. Wright, Jr. New
                Haven, Connecticut: Yale University Press. Pp. 287–319.
McClurkan, Burney B.
    1968   *Livingston Reservoir, 1965–1966: Late Archaic and Neo-American occupations. Pa-
                pers of the Texas Archeological Salvage Project* **12.** Austin, Texas.
McClurkan, Burney B., W. T. Field, and J. Ned Woodall
    1966   *Excavations in Toledo Bend Reservoir, 1964–65. Papers of the Texas Archeological
                Salvage Project* **8.** Austin, Texas.
McEwen, Michael C.
    1963   Sedimentary Framework of the Trinity River Delta. Unpublished Ph.D. thesis, De-
                partment of Geology, Rice University, Houston, Texas.
    1969   Sedimentary facies of the modern Trinity Delta. In *Holocene geology of the Gal-
                veston Bay area,* compiled by R. R. Lankford and J. J. W. Rogers. Houston: Houston
                Geological Society.
McGuff, Paul R.
    1978   *Prehistoric archeological investigations at Palmetto Bend Reservoir: phase 1, Jack-
                son County, Texas. Texas Archeological Survey, Research Report* **58.** Austin, Texas.
McGuff, Paul R., and Wayne N. Cox
    1973   *A survey of the archeological and historical resources of areas to be affected by the
                Clear Creek flood control project, Texas. Texas Archeological Survey, Research Report*
                28. Austin, Texas.
McIntire, William G.
    1958   *Prehistoric Indian settlements of the changing Mississippi River Delta. Louisiana
                State University, Coastal Studies Series* **1.** Baton Rouge: Louisiana State University
                Press.
MacNeish, R. S.
    1964   Ancient Mesoamerican civilization. *Science* **143**:531–537.
    1976   Early man in the New World. *American Scientist* **64**(3):316–327.
Mason, O. T.
    1893   North American bows, arrows, and quivers. *Annual Report, Smithsonian Institu-
                tion, 1893:* pp. 631–679. Washington, D.C.
Mayhall, Mildred P.
    1939   The Indians of Texas: the Atakapa, the Karankawa, the Tonkawa. Unpublished
                Ph.D. dissertation, Department of Anthropology, University of Texas, Austin.
Mooney, James
    1928   *The Aboriginal population of America north of Mexico. Smithsonian Miscellaneous
                Collections* **80**(7). Washington, D.C., Smithsonian Institution.

Morfi, Fray Juan Agustín de
    1932   *Excerpts from the "Memorias" for "The History of the Province of Texas,"* Prologue, appendix, and notes by Frederick C. Chabot. San Antonio, Texas: privately printed. (Revised by C. E. Castañeda.)
    1967   *History of Texas, 1673–1779*, translated by C. E. Castañeda. *Quivira Society Publications* **6.** New York: Arno Press. (Originally published in 1935.)

Morse, Jedidiah
    1822   *A report to the Secretary of War of the United States, on Indian Affairs, comprising a narrative of a tour performed in the summer of 1820.* New Haven: privately printed.

Muckleroy, Anna
    1922   The Indian policy of the Republic of Texas. *Southwestern Historical Quarterly* **25:**229–260.

Murphy, Robert F., and J. H. Steward
    1955   Tappers and trappers: parallel process in acculturation. *Economic Development and Cultural Change* **4:**335–355.

Nelson, H. T., and E. T. Bray
    1970   Stratigraphy and history of the Holocene sediments in the Sabine–High Island area, Gulf of Mexico. In *Deltaic sedimentation, modern and ancient*, edited by J. P. Morgan and R. H. Shaver. *Society of Economic Paleontologists and Mineralogists Special Publication* **11:**48–77. Tulsa, Oklahoma.

Newcomb, W. W., Jr.
    1956   A reappraisal of the "cultural sink" of Texas. *Southwestern Journal of Anthropology* **12:**145–153.
    1961   *The Indians of Texas from prehistoric to modern times.* Austin: The University of Texas Press.

Newell, H. Perry, and Alex D. Krieger
    1949   *The George C. Davis site, Cherokee County, Texas. Society for American Archaeology, Memoir* **5.** Menasha, Wisconsin.

Neyland, Wayne B.
    1970   Pond sites investigated. *Houston Archeological Society Newsletter* **33:**5–6.

Neyland, W. B., and L. E. Aten
    1971   Interior incising in coastal southeast Texas: its presence and significance. *Houston Archeological Society Newsletter* **35:**6–9.

Nixon, Pat I.
    1946   *The Medical Story of Early Texas, 1528–1853.* Lancaster.

Nunley, John P.
    1963   *Appraisal of the archeological resources of Livingston Reservoir, Polk, San Jacinto, Trinity, and Walker Counties, Texas.* Texas Archeological Salvage Project, Austin.

O'Brien, M. J.
    1971   The Fullen Site, 41 HR 82. *Bulletin of the Texas Archeological Society* **42:**335–361.
    1974   The Armand Bayou survey and excavations. In *Archeological investigations along Armand Bayou, Harris County, Texas*, edited by Frank Hole. *Houston Archeological Society Report* **2.**

Ogden, J. Gordon, III
    1967   Radiocarbon determinations of sedimentation rates from hard and soft-water lakes in northeastern North America. In *Quaternary Paleoecology*, edited by E. J. Cushing and H. E. Wright, Jr. New Haven, Connecticut: Yale University Press. Pp. 175–183.

Oliver, Alice Williams
    1891   Notes on the Carancahua Indians. In *The Karankawa Indians, the coast people of Texas*, by Albert S. Gatschet. *Archaeological and Ethnological Papers of the Peabody Museum* **1**(2). Cambridge, Massachusetts. Pp. 15–20.

Olsson, I. U.
  1968   C-14/C-12 ratio during the last several thousand years and the reliability of C-14 dates. In *Means of correlation of Quaternary successions*, edited by Roger B. Morrison and H. E. Wright, Jr. *Proceedings, 7th Congress, International Association for Quaternary Research* **8**:241–252. Salt Lake City, Utah: University of Utah Press.

Otvos, Ervin G., Jr.
  1980   Age of Tunica Hills (Louisiana–Mississippi) Quaternary fossiliferous creek deposits: problems of radiocarbon dates and intermediate valley terraces in coastal plains. *Quaternary Research* **13**(1):80–92.

Oviedo y Valdez, Gonzalo Fernandez
  1923–1924   The expedition of Panfilo de Narvaez, edited by Harbert Davenport. *Southwestern Historical Quarterly* **27**:120–139, 217–241.

Padilla, Juan Antonio
  1919   Texas in 1820, report of the barbarous Indians of the Province of Texas, translated by Mattie Austin Hatcher. *Southwestern Historical Quarterly* **23**:47–68.

Patterson, L. W.
  1979   *Bibliography of the prehistory of the upper Texas coast, Number 4.* Houston Archaeological Society Special Publication.
  1980   *The Owen site, 41 HR 315: a long occupation sequence in Harris County, Texas.* Houston Archeological Society Report **3.**

Pearce, J. E.
  1932   The present status of Texas archeology. *Bulletin of the Texas Archeological and Paleontological Society* **4**:44–54.

Pearce, Roy Harvey
  1957   The metaphysics of Indian-hating. *Ethnohistory* **4**:27–40.

Pearson, F. J., Jr.
  1965   Use of C13/C12 ratios to correct radiocarbon ages of materials initially diluted by limestone. In *Proceedings, Sixth International Conference, Radiocarbon and Tritium Dating*, compiled by Roy M. Chatters and E. A. Olson. Pullman, Washington.

Phelps, David S.
  1964   The final phases of the eastern archaic. Unpublished Ph.D. dissertation, Department of Anthropology, Tulane University, New Orleans. Ann Arbor: University Microfilms.

Phillips, Philip
  1970   *Archaeological survey in the lower Yazoo Basin, Mississippi, 1949–1955. Papers of the Peabody Museum of Archaeology and Ethnology* **60.** Cambridge, Massachusetts.

Pires-Ferreira, Jane W., and Kent V. Flannery
  1976   Ethnographic models for formative exchange. In *The early Mesoamerican village*, edited by Kent V. Flannery. New York: Academic Press. Pp. 286–292.

Plog, Fred T.
  1974   *The study of prehistoric change.* New York: Academic Press.

Polzer, Charles William, Thomas C. Barnes, and Thomas H. Naylor
  1977   *The Documentary Relations of the Southwest Project manual.* Tucson: Arizona State Museum.

Pratt, Willis W. (editor)
  1954   *Galveston Island: the journal of Francis C. Sheridan, 1839–1840.* Austin: University of Texas Press.

Ralph, Elizabeth K.
  1971   Carbon-14 dating. In *Dating techniques for the archaeologist*, edited by Henry N. Michael and Elizabeth K. Ralph. Cambridge: MIT Press.

Ralph, Elizabeth K., H. N. Michael, and M. C. Han
  1973   Radiocarbon dates and reality. *MASCA Newsletter* **9**(1):1–20.

Rappaport, Roy A.
  1968   *Pigs for the ancestors: ritual in the ecology of a New Guinea people.* New Haven, Connecticut: Yale University Press.
  1971   Ritual, sanctity, and cybernetics. *American Anthropologist* **73**:59–76.
Ray, Arthur J.
  1978   History and archaeology of the northern fur trade. *American Antiquity* **43**:26–34.
Read, Dwight W.
  1974   Some comments on typologies in archaeology and an outline of a methodology. *American Antiquity* **39**:216–242.
Rehkemper, L. J.
  1969   Sedimentology of Holocene estuarine deposits, Galveston Bay. In *Holocene geology of the Galveston Bay Area*, edited by R. R. Lankford and J. J. W. Rogers. Pp. 12–52. Houston Geological Society.
Ribeiro, Darcy
  1968   *The civilizational process*, translated by Betty J. Meggars. Washington, D.C.: Smithsonian Press.
Ring, E. Raymond, Jr.
  1961   An evaluation of radiocarbon dates from the Galena site, southeastern Texas. *Bulletin of the Texas Archeological Society* **31**:317–325.
  1963   Opened by accident. *Houston Archeological Society Newsletter* **10**:2–7.
Ritchie, William A.
  1969   *The archaeology of Martha's Vineyard.* Garden City: The Natural History Press.
Roberts, O. M.
  1898   Prehistoric races in Texas. *Texas State Historical Association, Quarterly* **1**:145–150.
Roessler, A. R.
  1883   Antiquities and aborigines of Texas. *Smithsonian Institution Annual Report for 1881. Pp. 613–616.*
Ross, Herbert H.
  1970   The ecological history of the Great Plains: evidence from grassland insects. In *Pleistocene and recent environments of the central Great Plains*, edited by W. Dort and J. K. Jones. *University of Kansas Special Publication* **3**:225–240. Lawrence, Kansas: University of Kansas Press.
Rubin, M., and D. W. Taylor
  1963   Radiocarbon activity of shells from living clams and snails. *Science* **141**:637.
Ruddiman, W. F., and A. McIntyre
  1981   The mode and mechanism of the last deglaciation: oceanic evidence. *Quaternary Research* **16**(2):125–134.
Sahlins, Marshall D.
  1965   On the sociology of primitive exchange. In *The relevance of models for social anthropology*, edited by Michael Banton. *ASA Monograph* **1**. London: Tavistock Publications.
Sanchez, Jose Maria
  1926   *A trip to Texas in 1828*, translated by Carlos E. Castañeda. *Southwestern Historical Quarterly* **29**:249–288.
Saucier, Roger T.
  1981   Current Thinking on Riverine Processes and Geologic History as Related to Human Settlement in the Southeast. *Geoscience and Man*, Vol. 22:7–18. Louisiana State University, Baton Rouge, Louisiana.
Sayles, E. B.
  1935   *An archaeological survey of Texas. Medallion Papers* **17.**
Schaedel, Richard P.
  1949   The Karankawa of the Texas Gulf coast. *Southwestern Journal of Anthropology* **5**:117–137.

Schusky, Ernest L.
    1972   *Manual for Kinship Analysis*. New York: Holt, Rinehart & Winston.

Segraves, B. Abbott
    1974   Ecological generalization and structural transformation of sociocultural systems. *American Anthropologist* **76**:530–552.

Sellards, E. H.
    1940   Pleistocene artifacts and associated fossils from Bee County, Texas. *Geological Society of America Bulletin* **51**:1627–1658.

Service, Elman R.
    1971   *Primitive social organization: an evolutionary perspective* (second ed.). New York: Random House.
    1975   *Origins of the state and civilization: the process of cultural evolution*. New York: Norton.

Shafer, Harry J.
    1966   *An archeological survey of Wallisville Reservoir, Chambers County, Texas. Texas Archeological Salvage Project, Survey Reports* **2.** Austin, Texas.
    1968   *Archeological investigations in the San Jacinto River Basin, Montgomery County, Texas. Texas Archeological Salvage Project, Papers* **13.** Austin, Texas.
    1977   Early lithic assemblages in eastern Texas. In *Paleoindian lifeways*, edited by Eileen Johnson. *The Museum Journal* **17**:187–197. Lubbock: Texas Tech University Press.

Shepard, Anna O.
    1963   *Ceramics for the archaeologist. Carnegie Institution of Washington, Publication* **609.** Washington, D.C.

Sibley, John
    1807   Historical sketches of the several Indian tribes in Louisiana south of the Arkansa River and between the Mississippi and River Grand. In *Travels in the interior parts of America: communicating discoveries made in exploring the Missouri, Red River and Washita by Captains Lewis and Clark, Doctor Sibley, and Mr. Dunbar.* London: Richard Phillips.

Simmons, H. J.
    1903   Human bones found near Galveston (a letter communicated by Mr. James Douglas). *American Geographical Society Bulletin* **35**:548–549.

Sjoberg, Andree F.
    1951a   The Bidai Indians of southeastern Texas. Unpublished M.A. thesis, Department of Anthropology, The University of Texas at Austin.
    1951b   The Bidai Indians of southeastern Texas. *Southwestern Journal of Anthropology* **7**:391–400.

Skeels, Lydia L. M.
    1972   *An ethnohistorical survey of Texas Indians. Texas Historical Survey Committee, Archeological Report* **22.** Austin Texas: Texas Historical Commission.

Slaughter, Bob H.
    1967   Animal ranges as a clue to Late-Pleistocene extinction. In *Pleistocene extinctions: the search for a cause*, edited by P. S. Martin and H. E. Wright, Jr. New Haven, Connecticut: Yale University Press. Pp. 155–167.

Slaughter, B. H., and B. R. Hoover
    1965   An antler artifact from the Late Pleistocene of northeast Texas. *American Antiquity* **30**(3):351–352.

Smithwick, Noah
    1900   *The Evolution of a State, or Recollections of Old Texas Days*. Austin: Gammel.

Sollberger, J. B., and T. R. Hester
    1972   The Strohacker site: a review of pre-Archaic manifestations in Texas. *Plains Anthropologist* **58**(1):326–344.

Spaulding, Albert C.

1958   The significance of differences between radiocarbon dates. *American Antiquity* **23**:309–311.

1973   The concept of artifact type in archaeology. *Plateau* **45**(4):149–164.

Spiro, Melford E.

1966   Religion: problems of definition and explanation. In *Anthropological approaches to the study of religion*, edited by M. Banton. *ASA Monographs* **3.** London: Tavistock Publications.

Springer, James W.

1973   The prehistory and cultural geography of coastal Louisiana. Unpublished Ph.D. dissertation, Department of Anthropology, Yale University, New Haven, Connecticut.

Stearn, E. Wagner, and Allen E. Stearn

1945   *The effect of smallpox on the destiny of the Amerindian.* Boston: Humphries.

Stephenson, Robert L.

1950   Culture chronology in Texas. *American Antiquity* **16**:151–157.

Steward, J. H.

1955   *Theory of culture change: the methodology of multilinear evolution.* Urbana: University of Illinois Press.

1969   Postscript to bands: on taxonomy, processes, and causes. In *Contributions to anthropology: band societies*, edited by D. Damas. *National Museums of Canada Bulletin* **228**:288–295. Ottawa.

Story, Dee Ann

1968   *Archeological investigations at two central Texas Gulf coast sites. Texas State Building Commission, Archeology Program Report* **13.** Austin, Texas.

1976   The east Texas Archaic. In *The Texas Archaic: a symposium* edited by T. R. Hester. *Center for Archaeological Research Special Report* **2**:46–59. The University of Texas at San Antonio.

1980   Adaptive strategies of Archaic cultures of the west Gulf Coastal Plain. Paper presented at School of American Research Advanced Seminar on "The Origins of Plant Husbandry in North America," March 28, 1980. Santa Fe, New Mexico.

Sturtevant, William C.

1968   Studies in ethnoscience. In *Theory in anthropology: a sourcebook*, edited by R. A. Manners and D. Kaplan. Chicago: Aldine–Atherton.

Suess, H. E.

1970   Bristlecone-pine calibration of the radiocarbon time-scale, 5200 B.C. to the present. In *Radiocarbon variations and absolute chronology*, edited by I. U. Olsson. *Proceedings; Twelfth Nobel Symposium, Uppsala.* New York: Wiley.

Suhm, Dee Ann, and Edward B. Jelks

1962   *Handbook of Texas archaeology: type descriptions. Texas Archeological Society Special Publication* **1** and *Texas Memorial Museum Bulletin* **4.** Austin, Texas.

Suhm, Dee Ann, Alex D. Krieger, and Edward B. Jelks

1954   *An introductory handbook of Texas archeology. Bulletin of the Texas Archeological Society* **25.**

Suhm, Raymond W.

1980   The La Paloma mammoth site, Kenedy County, Texas. *Center for Archaeological Research Special Report* **11**:79–103. The University of Texas at San Antonio.

Swanton, John R.

1907   Mythology of the Indians of Louisiana and the Texas coast. *Journal of American Folklore* **20**:285–289.

1911   *Indian tribes of the lower Mississippi valley and adjacent coast of the Gulf of Mexico. Bureau of American Ethnology Bulletin* **43.** Washington D.C. Smithsonian Institution.

1924   Southern contacts of the Indians north of the Gulf of Mexico. *Annaes do XX Congresso. Internacional de Americanistas, Rio de Janeiro.* Pp. 53–59.

1946   *Indians of the southeastern United States. Bureau of American Ethnology Bulletin* **137.** Washington, D.C.: Smithsonian Institution.

1952   *The Indian tribes of North America. Bureau of American Ethnology Bulletin* **145.** Washington, D.C.: Smithsonian Institution.

Talmage Valerie, and Olga Chesler

1977   The importance of small, surface, and disturbed sites as sources of significant archaeological data. *Cultural Resource Management Studies.* Washington, D.C.: National Park Service.

Tamers, M. A.

1970   Validity of radiocarbon dates on terrestrial snail shells. *American Antiquity* **35:**95–100.

Taylor, Herbert C., Jr.

1961   Archeological notes on the route of Cabeza de Vaca. *Bulletin of the Texas Archeological Society* **41:**273–290.

Taylor, Walter W.

1948   *A study of archeology. American Anthropological Association Memoir* **69.** Menasha, Wisconsin.

Thomas, David Hurst

1978   Arrowheads and atlatl darts: how the stones got the shaft. *American Antiquity* **43:**461–472.

Trigger, Bruce G.

1968   *Beyond history: the methods of prehistory.* New York: Holt, Rinehart and Winston.

Tunnell, Curtis D., and J. Richard Ambler

1967   *Archeological excavations at Presidio San Agustín de Ahumada. Texas State Building Commission, Archeological Program Report* **6.** Austin, Texas.

Turekian, K. K., and R. L. Armstrong

1961   Chemical and mineralogical composition of fossil molluscan shells from the Fox Hills formation, South Dakota. *Geological Society of America Bulletin* **72:**1817–1828.

Turner, V.

1966   Colour classification in Ndembu ritual. In *Anthropological approaches to the study of religion,* edited by M. Banton. *ASA Monographs* **3.** London: Tavistock Publications.

Ubelaker, Douglas H.

1974   *Reconstruction of demographic profile from ossuary skeletal samples. Smithsonian Contributions to Anthropology* **18.** Washington, D.C.: Smithsonian Institution.

1976   The sources and methodology for Mooney's estimates of North American Indian populations. In *The Native Population of the Americas in 1492,* edited by William M. Deneven. Madison: The University of Wisconsin Press. Pp. 243–288.

Valastro, S., Jr., and E. Mott Davis

1970a   University of Texas at Austin radiocarbon dates VII. *Radiocarbon* **12:**249–280.

1970b   University of Texas at Austin radiocarbon dates VIII. *Radiocarbon* **12:**617–639.

Valastro, S., Jr., E. Mott Davis, and Alejandra G. Varela

1975   University of Texas at Austin radiocarbon dates X. *Radiocarbon* **17:**52–98.

Valastro, S., F. J. Pearson, Jr., and E. Mott Davis

1967   University of Texas radiocarbon dates V. *Radiocarbon* **9:**439–453.

Vayda, A. P., and R. Rappaport

1968   Ecology, cultural and non-cultural. In *Introduction to cultural anthropology,* edited by J. Clifton. Boston: Houghton Mifflin. Pp. 477–497.

Wallace, Anthony F. C.

1961   *Culture and personality.* New York: Random House.

Walley, Raymond
  1955   A preliminary report on the Albert George site in Fort Bend County. *Bulletin of the Texas Archeological Society* **26:**218–234.

Weaver, Elizabeth C.
  1963   Technological analysis of prehistoric lower Mississippi ceramic materials: a preliminary report. *American Antiquity* **29:**49–56.

Weber, J. N., and A. LaRocque
  1963   Isotope ratios in marine mollusk shells after prolonged contact with flowing fresh water. *Science* **142:**1666.

Weir, Frank A.
  1976   The central Texas Archaic reconsidered. In *The Texas Archaic: a symposium*, edited by T. R. Hester. *Center for Archaeological Research Special Report* **2:**60–66. The University of Texas at San Antonio.

Weissner, Polly
  1974   A functional estimator of population from floor area. *American Antiquity* **39:**343–350.

Wendland, Wayne M.
  1978   Holocene man in North America: the ecological setting and climatic background. *Plains Anthropologist* **23**(82):273–287.

Wheat, Joe Ben
  1947   Archaeological survey of the Addicks Basin: a preliminary report. *Bulletin of the Texas Archeological and Paleontological Society* **18:**143–145.

  1953   An archeological survey of the Addicks Dam Basin, southeast Texas. *Bureau of American Ethnology Bulletin* **154:**143–252. Washington, D.C.: Smithsonian Institution.

White, Leslie A.
  1975   *The concept of cultural systems.* New York: Columbia University Press.

Wiener, Norbert
  1961   *Cybernetics: or control and communication in the animal and the machine.* Cambridge, Massachusetts: MIT Press.

Wilbarger, J. W.
  1889   *Indian depredations in Texas.* Austin: privately printed.

Wilkinson, B. H., J. G. McGowen, and C. R. Lewis
  1975   Ingleside strandplain sands of central Texas coast. *American Association of Petroleum Geologists Bulletin* **59:**347–352.

Willey, Gordon R.
  1968   *An introduction to American archaeology: volume 1, North and Middle America.* Englewood Cliffs, N.J.: Prentice-Hall.

Williams, B. J.
  1974   *A model of band society. Society for American Archaeology Memoir* **29.** Washington, D.C.

Williams, Stephen and James B. Stoltman
  1965   An outline of southeastern United States prehistory with particular emphasis on the Paleo-Indian era. In *The Quaternary of the United States*, edited by N. E. Wright and D. G. Frey. Princeton: Princeton University Press. Pp. 669–683.

Wilson, Thomas
  1901   Arrow wounds. *American Anthropologist* **3:**513–531.

Winchester, P. D.
  1971   Geology of the Freeport Rocks, offshore Texas. *Gulf Coast Association of Geological Societies Transactions* **21:**211–222.

Winters, Howard D.
  1969   *The Riverton culture: a second millenium occupation in the central Wabash Valley. Illinois State Museum, Report of Investigations* **13.** Springfield, Illinois.

Wobst, H. Martin
    1974   Boundary conditions for Paleolithic social systems: a simulation approach. *American Antiquity* **39**(2):147–178.
Worthington, R. B.
    1959   San Jacinto wares, a proposed pottery type. Paper presented at the Houston Archeological Society Pottery Symposium, December 6, 1959, Houston, Texas.
    1961   Some immediate problems on the upper Texas Gulf coast. *Houston Archeological Society Newsletter* **6:**1–3.
Yellen, John E.
    1977   *Archaeological approaches to the present: models for reconstructing the past.* New York: Academic Press.

Index